Yale Broadway Masters

ALSO IN THE SERIES

Richard Rodgers, BY GEOFFREY BLOCK
Andrew Lloyd Webber, BY JOHN SNELSON
Jerome Kern, BY STEPHEN BANFIELD

FORTHCOMING

Irving Berlin, BY JEFFREY MAGEE
Leonard Bernstein, BY CAROL OJA
George M. Cohan, BY CHARLES JOSEPH
George Gershwin, BY LARRY STARR
John Kander and Fred Ebb, BY JAMES LEVE
Frank Loesser, BY THOMAS L. RIIS
Stephen Sondheim, BY KIM KOWALKE
Kurt Weill, BY JOEL GALAND

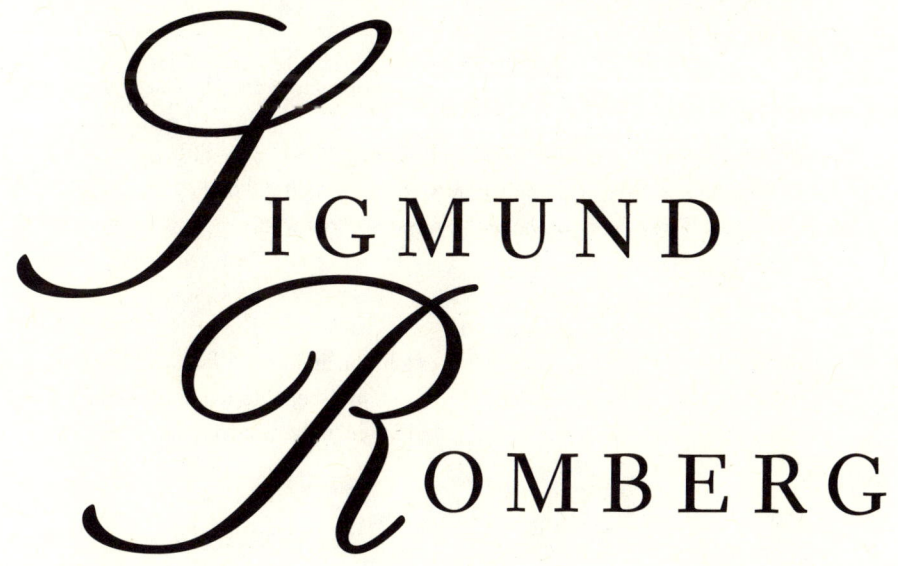

SIGMUND ROMBERG

WILLIAM A. EVERETT

With a Foreword by
GEOFFREY BLOCK, *General Editor*

YALE UNIVERSITY PRESS   NEW HAVEN & LONDON

Copyright © 2007 by Yale University.
All rights reserved.
This book may not be reproduced, in whole or in part, including illustrations, in any form (beyond that copying permitted by Sections 107 and 108 of the U.S. Copyright Law and except by reviewers for the public press), without written permission from the publishers.

Designed by James Johnson and set in Electra Roman types by Tseng Information Systems, Inc.
Printed in the United States of America.

Library of Congress Cataloging-in-Publication Data
Everett, William A., 1962–
Sigmund Romberg / William A. Everett ; with a foreword by Geoffrey Block.
p. cm. — (Yale Broadway masters)
Includes bibliographical references (p.   ), discography (p.   ), and index.
ISBN 978-0-300-11183-5 (hard cover : alk. paper)
1. Romberg, Sigmund, 1887–1951. 2. Operetta — United States — 20th century. I. Title.
ML410.R66E94 2007
782.1′2092 — dc22
[B]
2006102531

Frontispiece: Sigmund Romberg at the Great American Restaurant, Kansas City, Missouri, May 3, 1950. Used by permission of the University of Missouri–Kansas City Libraries, Special Collections Department.

A catalogue record for this book is available from the British Library.
The paper in this book meets the guidelines for permanence and durability of the Committee on Production Guidelines for Book Longevity of the Council on Library Resources.

10 9 8 7 6 5 4 3 2 1

To Lynda

Contents

List of Tables ix

Foreword, by Geoffrey Block xi

Acknowledgments xv

Prologue 1

CHAPTER 1. Sigmund Romberg: The Man and His Music 6

CHAPTER 2. Finding a Voice: Operetta, Revue, and Musical Comedy 37

CHAPTER 3. Staging Nostalgia: The Road to *Maytime* 77

CHAPTER 4. Continued Success: *The Magic Melody* and *Blossom Time* 104

CHAPTER 5. Young Love in Old Heidelberg: *The Student Prince* 124

CHAPTER 6. Romance and Exoticism in North Africa: *The Desert Song* 155

CHAPTER 7. Exploring New Possibilities: From *Cherry Blossoms* to *The New Moon* 181

CHAPTER 8. Emulating the Past: Later Stage Works   210

CHAPTER 9. Romberg in Hollywood   245

CHAPTER 10. Building a Legacy   275

Epilogue: Romberg's Influence on the American Musical Theater   290

Appendix A: Work List   297

Appendix B: Broadcasts of *The Railroad Hour* Featuring Operettas by Romberg   300

Appendix C: Selected Discography   302

Notes   311

Selected Bibliography   337

Index   343

Credits   359

Tables

1.1 Musical program of *Deep in My Heart* (MGM, 1954) 12
2.1 Locations and music in "A Musical Trip Through Old Vienna" 40
3.1 Adaptations by Romberg, 1915–1917 84
4.1 *Blossom Time* numbers and their parallels in *Das Dreimäderlhaus* 116
4.2 Principal *Blossom Time* numbers and their sources in the works of Franz Schubert 116
5.1 Musical program for *The Student Prince* (according to the opening night playbill) 133
5.2 Waltzes in *The Student Prince* 134
5.3 Sectional construction of "Deep in My Heart, Dear," from *The Student Prince* 139
5.4 Marches in *The Student Prince* 141
5.5 Sectional construction of the act 1 finale of *The Student Prince* 145
6.1 Musical program for *The Desert Song* (according to the opening night playbill) 170
7.1 Musical numbers in *The New Moon* retained from the original Philadelphia production 194
7.2 Musical program for *The New Moon* (according to the opening night playbill) 202
8.1 Musical program for *Up in Central Park* (according to the opening night playbill) 234
9.1 Songs in the 1943 and 1953 film versions of *The Desert Song* 264

Foreword

Sigmund Romberg, who famously reworked melodies by Schubert in the 1920s *Blossom Time*, was once reputedly asked at a party whether he had composed Offenbach's hummable Barcarolle from *Les Contes d'Hoffmann*, which at that moment was playing in the background. Romberg's alleged witty response, "Not yet," depicts a man not overly worried about accusations regarding his lack of originality. Romberg could afford to joke about his indebtedness to a famous tune. From the late 1910s to the end of the 1920s, this master of operetta enjoyed five of the greatest hits of the era: *Maytime* (1917), *Blossom Time* (1921), *The Student Prince* (1924), *The Desert Song* (1926), and *The New Moon* (1928). The songs in these shows are saturated with unforgettable waltzes, marches, and other gorgeous (and original) melodies: "Will You Remember?" (a.k.a. "Sweetheart, Sweetheart") from *Maytime*; "Serenade" and "Deep in My Heart, Dear" from *The Student Prince*; "One Alone" from *The Desert Song*; "Stouthearted Men," "Softly, As in a Morning Sunrise," and "Lover, Come Back to Me" from *The New Moon* (the latter two songs, as William A. Everett documents, have, surprisingly, achieved a secure place in the jazz canon).

At 608 performances, *The Student Prince* was the most successful show of the 1920s. The other shows from Romberg's Ruritanian reign were among the eleven longest running shows of the decade. The great Jerome Kern himself wrote no more than three major hit shows in the 1920s; Rudolf Friml, the composer to whom Romberg is often compared, only two. We may think of the 1920s as the jazz age dominated by the musical comedies of George and

Ira Gershwin, Rodgers and Hart, Vincent Youmans, and Henderson, Brown, and De Sylva, the respective principal creators of *Lady, Be Good!*, *A Connecticut Yankee*, *No, No, Nanette*, and *Good News!* But operetta, while less prevalent, not only held its own, it actually could boast most of the decade's greatest popular successes. In the cases of *Blossom Time* and *The Student Prince*, long runs were followed by an endless series of tours that would last at least another generation.

After the string of blockbuster hits in the twenties, Romberg would continue to compose musicals for another two decades, albeit with only one additional hit with Dorothy Fields, *Up in Central Park* (1945). Beginning in the 1930s, the Romberg shows from the glory days (1917–28) were adapted and readapted, often with greatly altered plots and varying musical completeness, into popular films. Highlights include the second version of *The New Moon* (1940), with Jeanette MacDonald and Nelson Eddy, the second of the three film versions of *The Desert Song* (1943), and the second filming of *The Student Prince* (1954), which featured the beautiful dubbed voice of Mario Lanza, whose portly appearance was replaced on screen by the more visually appealing Edmund Purdom. Among Romberg's nearly sixty musicals, even the popular successes of the 1920s would gradually fade from Broadway, at the same time finding new homes in "light" and other opera houses, such as the British revivals with John Hanson in the 1950s and the New York City Opera productions of the great 1920s trilogy (*The Student Prince*, *The Desert Song*, and *The New Moon*) in the 1980s. In 2003, the latter show also enjoyed a visible return when it appeared in New York's City Center Encores! Series.

Until the publication of this volume by Everett, who among his credits is the co-editor of *The Cambridge Companion to the Musical*, those who wanted to learn about Romberg were forced to rely on Elliott Arnold's often unreliable *Deep in My Heart* (1949) and the still more fictional biopic starring José Ferrer, which retained Arnold's title in 1954, three years after the real death of its fictionalized subject. In the present volume, for the first time, Everett sets the biographical as well as the artistic record straight, no easy task. He fills us in on what we need to know about Romberg and many of his shows, especially the productive and memorable collaborations with the Shubert Brothers (including the Shubert's Schubert), Oscar Hammerstein, and Dorothy Fields. By focusing not only on analytical and critical issues but also on the rich cultural meanings behind the nostalgia of *The

FOREWORD   xiii

Student Prince and the exoticism in *The Desert Song,* Everett sheds much-needed light on Romberg's important but often unacknowledged place in Broadway history.

GEOFFREY BLOCK
General Editor

Acknowledgments

Producing an operetta is a collaborative process, and so is producing a book. Without the time, talents, and efforts of many people, this volume would not exist. I am deeply grateful to all of them.

Special thanks go to Geoffrey Block, series editor for Yale Broadway Masters, for his unfaltering support of this project from initial conception through completion. His advice, suggestions, and encouragement were always welcomed and deeply appreciated. His encyclopedic knowledge of the musical theater came to the fore many times—his watchful eye caught many discrepancies and found many connections between Romberg's work and that of other Broadway composers. Thanks also are due to Keith Condon at Yale University Press for his assistance in bringing this book to fruition, and to the editors at Yale University Press, especially Jeffrey Schier, for their copyediting and formatting expertise.

I am also extremely grateful to the librarians and archivists at the various places I conducted research, especially the Shubert Archive (Maryann Chach, Reagan Fletcher, Mark Swartz, and Sylvia Wang), for their continued graciousness, assistance, and interest in my work since I first visited the Archive in 1990 to begin research on Romberg, his music, and his legacy. Teresa Gipson in the Special Collections Department at the Miller Nichols Library at University of Missouri–Kansas City enthusiastically shared with me the Romberg materials she found among the papers and other memorabilia of L. P. Cookingham, former city manager of Kansas City, Missouri. Two photos from the Cookingham Collection appear in this book, and I am extremely grateful to Ms. Gipson and to Robert Ray, Special Collections

Librarian, for their assistance with my research. Romberg, I must add, is well represented in the Popular American Sheet Music Collection in UMKC's Special Collections.

Other librarians and archivists were also extremely helpful, including those at New York Public Library, Museum of the City of New York, Library of Congress, University of Missouri–Kansas City Music/Media Library (Laura Gayle Green, Debbie Keeton), Marr Sound Archive, University of Missouri–Kansas City (Chuck Haddix), University of California, Berkeley Music Library, University of California, Los Angeles Music Library, UCLA Film and Television Archive, University of Southern California Film and Television Library, Harvard Theatre Collection, Free Library of Philadelphia, British Library, and Theatre Museum (London). Thanks also to the Performing Arts Museum in Melbourne, Australia, for providing information on Australian productions of Romberg operetta, and especially to the interlibrary loan divisions at Mabee Library at Washburn University and Miller Nichols Library at the University of Missouri–Kansas City for their assistance in obtaining hard-to-find books and obscure articles.

Heaps of gratitude go to the following people who provided me with various bits of "Rombergiana" that helped make this project a true joy on which to work: Brenda Allen, Sylvia Boyd, J. Bunker Clark, Anna Wheeler Gentry, John Koegel, Paul Laird, Daniel T. Politoske, Margaret Tritch, and Anna Mary Weller. It is always extremely gratifying when someone thinks of you when they spot a piece of Romberg-related material—sheet music, a recording, a concert program, a copy of Elliott Arnold's *Deep in My Heart*—and then makes sure that you receive it. Thanks are also in order to the Small Research Grant Fund and the Sweet Summer Sabbatical program at Washburn University for grants that made much of the research possible. The opportunity I had to present part of this book at an Interdisciplinary Faculty Workshop at UMKC, coordinated by Andrew Bergerson, and the feedback I received, helped strengthen the arguments of not only the section I presented but also the book as a whole.

Other people helped in a variety of ways. Valerie Langfield, Lynda Payne, Kathy Rode, and Katie Schuermann read early drafts of the book and made extremely helpful comments. I am deeply indebted to Sarah Jacobs and John Koegel for their careful reading of the manuscript as it neared completion, and for their probing questions and keen insights into the material and its presentation. Thanks also go to Sarah Jacobs for preparing the musical examples on Sibelius software. I hope the "Romberg withdrawal" has

ACKNOWLEDGMENTS xvii

subsided. I deeply appreciate the many individuals whose remarks and assistance with various aspects of the book at different phases of its development helped tremendously and made it a reality: Stephen Banfield, John Blair, Victoria Botero, Rodney Boyd, Sylvia Boyd (who once described a melody from Prokofiev's *Romeo and Juliet* as being "so beautiful it could have been written by Romberg"), David Brodsky, Patricia Brodsky, J. Bunker Clark, Olga Dolskaya-Ackerly, Hali Fieldman, Elizabeth Hille-Cribbs, Dr. Paul Koontz, Miles Kreuger, Jonathan Krinke, Paul Laird, Felicia Londré, Jay Martin, Kay Norton, Basil and Lorna Payne, Daniel T. Politoske, Dr. David Robinson, Michael Rubinoff, Katie Schuermann, Ann Sears, John Snelson, Fran Vogt, Harry White, Jack B. Wright, and Richard Wright. Thanks to all those who provided hospitality while I was doing the research for this book, especially David Juritz and Jane Davies, Bob and Kitty Keller, John Koegel, Orly Krasner, and Valerie Langfield. I greatly appreciate the friends who have invited me to speak about Romberg to their students, including Paul Laird (University of Kansas) and Jane and George Ferencz (University of Wisconsin, Whitewater); their support and the enthusiasm of their students are heartwarming. Thanks also go to my friends in Croatia who provided me with opportunities to share my research with students and colleagues in Zagreb and Osijek—Branka Ban, Vjera Katalinić, and Stanislav Tuksar—and for taking me to the Romberg sites in Osijek and Belišće. Thanks are also due to my colleagues and students at Washburn University and the University of Missouri–Kansas City for their sustained enthusiasm for Romberg and his music, and for their interest in this book. It has been a learning experience for all of us.

To my dear wife, Lynda, many thanks for your unfaltering support during this process and for all the wonderful things you bring to my life. To Bentley the wonder dog, thanks for the company—you've probably heard more of Romberg's music than any other dog on the planet—and for providing ample opportunities for fresh air and exercise on your many walks.

Yale Broadway Masters Advisory Board

STEPHEN BANFIELD,
   Stanley Hugh Badock Professor of Music,
   University of Bristol

ALLEN FORTE,
   Battell Professor of the Theory of Music,
   Yale University

CHARLES HAMM,
   professor of music emeritus,
   Dartmouth University

ROBERT KIMBALL,
   author and adviser in the fields of musical theater
   and popular music

KIM KOWALKE,
   professor of music,
   University of Rochester

PATRICK O'CONNOR,
   author

MAURY YESTON,
   composer

Sigmund Romberg

PROLOGUE

When Sigmund Romberg (1887–1951) arrived in New York in 1909 ready to embark on a musical career, few would have predicted the tremendous impact he would have on the Broadway musical. Born in Hungary in the waning years of the Habsburg Empire, Romberg played piano in restaurants until the legendary impresario and producer J. J. Shubert included his music in the 1914 revue *The Whirl of the World*. From then on, the immigrant composer's career flourished. Over a period lasting more than thirty-five years, Romberg composed more than sixty works for the musical stage (which collectively contain over eight hundred songs), including *Blossom Time* (1921), *The Student Prince* (1924, also known by its longer title, *The Student Prince in Heidelberg*), *The Desert Song* (1926), and *The New Moon* (1928). These four shows were among the top box office draws of the 1920s; in fact, *The Student Prince* had the longest run of any musical during the decade at 608 performances. *Blossom Time* and *The New Moon* also enjoyed extraordinary runs for their era, with 516 and 509 performances, respectively.[1] Falling just short of the 500-performance mark was *The Desert Song*, with an impressive 471 performances. Romberg thus wrote four of the decade's longest-running musicals, a greater number than any of his contemporaries, including George Gershwin, Rudolf Friml, Jerome Kern, Vincent Youmans, and Richard Rodgers.

Romberg's success on Broadway was certainly not limited to the 1920s. In 1917, his first complete operetta, *Maytime*, played 492 performances. Then in 1945, after seventeen years without a commercial success on Broadway,

Romberg returned with *Up in Central Park*, a nostalgia-driven musical that ran for 504 performances.

When it comes to revivals and even new recordings of his classic works, Romberg's legacy is still going strong in the early twenty-first century. New York's City Center Encores! produced *The New Moon* in 2003, and the Ohio Light Opera staged *Maytime* in 2005. Both were recorded and subsequently released on CD. Romberg's music is experiencing a much-deserved renaissance. Even the title character in the television series *House* knows Romberg's music, for its Golden Globe–winning star Hugh Laurie sings the opening of "Serenade" from *The Student Prince* ("Overhead the moon is beaming") in one episode.[2]

Why, then, if Romberg is so important, is this the first serious monograph on the composer and his music? Why has he been ignored, or at least severely marginalized, in the ever-growing body of scholarship on the Broadway musical? Two primary reasons can be given for this omission: 1) the genre in which he excelled—operetta—and 2) the historiography of the Broadway musical. The operetta extolled an old-fashioned maudlin world of disguised royals, mismatched lovers, and faraway locales. Fantasy, not veracity, was the driving force. Its musical style was unashamedly attractive, light, and—dare one say—popular. But at the same time it required trained singers capable of negotiating its technical demands. Operetta found itself possessing neither the prestige of opera nor the accessibility and popular flavor generally associated with the Broadway musical. Instead, it occupied a middle ground between the two. It was too operatic for Broadway and too "Broadway" for opera. But this is exactly what gives operetta its particular charm and appeal.

Operettas reside unashamedly in the sentimental world of nostalgia and nevermore. Although they were extremely popular on stage in the 1920s (and before) and on screen in the 1930s, by the 1940s, the genre itself was the frequent subject of parody and was all too often associated with bad taste, over-the-top acting, and amateur theatrical productions of questionable standards. Operetta certainly did not deserve this negative image, for it was a genre filled with great music, fine stars, and, perhaps surprisingly, a large number of contemporary cultural references.

The passing of time seems to have improved operetta's reputation. Classic works from the 1910s and 1920s are finding new audiences, and their historicity as period pieces is now a factor in their favor, rather than a liability. Time has distanced these works from performers and audiences in the early twenty-first century and is allowing these once-popular pieces to be reconsidered on their own artistic merits.

The second reason for Romberg's neglect concerns the historiography of the Broadway musical. Many narratives focus on the so-called "Golden Age," which generally is said to begin with *Show Boat* in 1927. But Romberg was at his zenith as a Broadway composer when *Show Boat* appeared. He had already written four shows (*Maytime, Blossom Time, The Student Prince*, and *The Desert Song*) with extremely long and lucrative runs and was revered as one of Broadway's top composers. Although Romberg's contemporaries in musical comedy and revue such as George Gershwin, Irving Berlin, Jerome Kern, and Rodgers and Hart have received strong scholarly attention in recent years, the operetta composers, namely Romberg, Victor Herbert, and Rudolf Friml, have not.

What, then, did Romberg accomplish? Why should he be acknowledged? First, he wrote some of the classic Broadway songs of the early twentieth century, including "Will You Remember?" (Sweetheart, Sweetheart) from *Maytime*, "Serenade" and "Deep in My Heart, Dear" from *The Student Prince*, and "Stouthearted Men," "Softly, As in a Morning Sunrise," and "Lover, Come Back to Me" from *The New Moon*. Second, he established not one, but two distinct models for American operetta. The first was characterized by stories with bittersweet, if not outright sad, endings. All of these works, which include *Maytime, Blossom Time*, and *The Student Prince*, have a recurring waltz duet as the centerpiece of the score. The driving force behind these evocative, sentimental, and nostalgic pieces was the legendary theatrical impresario and producer J. J. Shubert. Romberg and Shubert shared the same artistic vision in creating these tales of ill-fated love.

The second model, which grew out of the first, had stories with happy endings: in these works, such as *The Desert Song* and *The New Moon*, the lovers *are* together at the final curtain. Musically, although waltzes are still prominent, a duple-meter love duet coexists with the waltz duet, and in some ways takes over some of its central dramatic function. In *The Desert Song*, for example, the title song is a splendid waltz, while "One Alone," a duple-meter ballad, is the key to the true identity of the operetta's disguised hero and is subsequently the basis for the *finale ultimo*. Oscar Hammerstein 2nd was lyricist for these works, and his influence in the realm of character-defining music and musical-dramatic integrity is clearly evident. These shows are further characterized by their rousing marches, such as "Stouthearted Men" in *The New Moon*, in which the male chorus sings about overcoming tyranny and oppression. Musical exoticism is also a significant component of these shows, whether it is the Orientalist dimensions of *The Desert Song*, especially the use of pentatonicism and the minor mode to evoke the aural image of the Other, or the Latin American evocations in *The New Moon*, most notably the tango "Softly, As in a Morning Sunrise."

This book, while not a comprehensive life-and-works study of Romberg, will illuminate specific aspects of Romberg's Broadway career and legacy. The first chapter provides an overview of his life, professional career, and working methods, while the second considers the various influences on the aspiring composer, including Viennese operetta and, once Romberg arrived in America, his work in revue and musical comedy.

Romberg's first operetta paradigm, the nostalgic waltz-centered one, is the overarching theme of the following three chapters. Each chapter focuses on one of the three defining shows of the archetype—*Maytime*, *Blossom Time*, and *The Student Prince*—and also includes coverage of lesser-known pieces written between 1914 and 1925. Chapters 6 and 7 concern the second model, the one with happy endings and exemplified by *The Desert Song* and *The New Moon*. These five works form the cornerstone of Romberg's legacy, and likewise are the stars of this study.

After the phenomenal success Romberg experienced during the 1910s and 1920s, his career faded. Operetta as a genre lost luster after the 1929 stock market crash—mounting productions became nearly cost-prohibitive and audiences grew to prefer the brash style of musical comedy as opposed to the sentimental one of operetta. Despite these substantial changes and challenges, Romberg continued to compose for Broadway during the 1930s and 1940s. This repertory, of which the nostalgic Americana operetta *Up in Central Park* was the most significant, is surveyed in the chapter 8. Themes of exoticism, modernity, and nostalgia appear in various ways in these works, and Romberg discovered innovative ways in which to incorporate his most characteristic and identifiable song style, the glorious waltz, into his scores that followed *The New Moon*.

Hollywood played a major role in Romberg's career. The chapter devoted to this aspect of the composer's craft begins with a survey of his original film operettas, the most famous of which is the Jeanette MacDonald–Nelson Eddy feature *The Girl of the Golden West* (1938). These works are closely related to his Broadway operettas in terms of overall aesthetic and musical style. The chapter continues with a survey of film adaptations of Romberg's stage operettas, the versions through which these works are best known in the early twenty-first century. The faithfulness to the original stage versions varies greatly; factors such as the studio star system, having to excise nearly half the show in order to make it fit the time requirements of a film, and world events, namely World War II, account in large part for the radical reworkings.

While the screen renditions of Romberg's operettas certainly contributed to his reputation and legacy, many other factors also figured into this formation, including Romberg's own concert tours, revivals, and touring productions of the composer's most popular works, recordings, and cultural references to the repertory, often in the form of parodies. After a discussion of these aspects of Romberg's career in the final chapter, the epilogue focuses on Romberg's lasting impact on the American musical theater.

Sigmund Romberg was a highly gifted composer who created some of the most beautiful and beloved music to be heard on Broadway during the first half of the twentieth century. His music is his greatest legacy, and it still continues to delight performers and audiences.

CHAPTER 1

Sigmund Romberg: The Man and His Music

SIGMUND ROMBERG POSSESSED AN INTRIGUING ARRAY OF CULtural backgrounds. Firmly planted in the European tradition, he made his mark on American soil. The gifted composer integrated the fundamental principles of pre–World War I Viennese operetta with post–World War I American musical styles and tastes. He bridged two musical worlds, providing a direct link between nineteenth-century European musical theater and the twentieth-century Broadway musical.

But what do we know about the man behind the music? The conventional wisdom about Romberg comes largely from his own personal reminiscences given on radio and television interviews and from a handful of articles by or about the composer. Most of this knowledge, whether fact or fiction, was promoted in two places: first, in the pseudo-biographical book *Deep in My Heart: A Story Based on the Life of Sigmund Romberg* by Elliott Arnold, which appeared in 1949, two years before Romberg's death, and second, in the 1954 MGM biopic based on Arnold's book, also called *Deep in My Heart*, but without the subtitle.[1] Because of the nature of its medium and its subsequent broader audience, the film was more influential than the book in creating an enduring image of Sigmund Romberg.

The film, dedicated in the opening credits "To all those who love the music of Sigmund Romberg," is a lavish spectacle with performances of Romberg's music by some of MGM's greatest stars, including Ann Miller, Rosemary Clooney, Cyd Charisse, Gene Kelly, and Howard Keel. Romberg, as played by José Ferrer (1909–1992), is a lovable, slightly exotic, and mildly eccentric composer, pianist, singer, and dancer. He possesses an uncanny ability to delight everyone he encounters, whoever they may be. The film's basic plot is like that of an operetta: a poor yet very talented young man finds fame and fortune along with true love. Of course, in order to make an interesting story line, he must overcome numerous obstacles on his journey to success. A somewhat chronological offering of songs from selected shows is performed throughout the film, and each is preceded by a marquee with the show's name and creators before the theatrically (or at least sound-stage) conceived performance of the song.

Biographical veracity was not the primary concern in MGM's series of popular songwriter biopics from the late 1940s and early 1950s, and *Deep in My Heart* was no exception. As early plans were being made for the film, Romberg expressed his concern about the venture: "I don't like it; look what happened to Jerry (Jerome) Kern," referring to the Kern biopic *Till the Clouds Roll By* (1946).[2] In reality, Romberg fared neither better nor worse than most of his contemporaries in this regard. The studio wanted to capitalize on name recognition of the songwriters and their tunes, and on its own singing and dancing stars. The primary purpose of *Deep in My Heart* was to give audiences who loved the music of Romberg the opportunity to see and hear some stunning performances of the composer's finest songs. Especially since the film appeared only three years after Romberg's death, it functioned not just as a biopic and lavish studio production but also as a tribute to the man and his music.

This is where the film succeeds, almost. All of the songs included in the film were written in the 1910s, '20s, and early '30s. However, the string-rich orchestrations and crooning style of many of the performances are characteristic of the 1950s film musical style, rather than the more legitimate, classically trained singing of the originals.[3] Thus, the film's musical numbers are basically updated "remakes" of the originals, recast and re-envisioned for MGM's legendary star-studded treatment.

What the film does offer, and correctly so, is a picture of Sigmund Romberg as an artist simultaneously poised on three different yet related continua: 1) Old World v. New World; 2) low brow v. high brow; and 3) familiar v. exotic. These dualities form a large part of Romberg's persona, and are appropriately central to the film.

Throughout *Deep in My Heart*, Romberg finds himself at Café Vienna, a fictional restaurant run by the very Viennese Frau Mueller (a character created for the film and played by operatic soprano Helen Traubel [1899–1972]).[4] "Rommy" is "discovered" at this Old World café, and Mueller hosts receptions for him in her garden after each opening night. After living and working in the New World of New York sophisticates, producers, and critics, Romberg consistently returns to the Old World of Vienna through Frau Mueller's café. He can function in the New World as long as he retains a footing in the Old. A nostalgic remembrance of the past gives him the strength and fortitude to live in the present.

In the film, as in real life, Romberg considered himself to be well above the average popular song composer of the day, the purveyors of "low brow" musical culture. His disparaging attitude toward ragtime, for example, is evident in one scene where he tells a publisher, "Baboons play songs like this." His wife, Lillian (played by Doe Avedon), confirms his "high brow" aspirations later in the film when she tells him, "You've graduated from Tin Pan Alley. I want to see you in Carnegie Hall. I want to hear your music at its peak. I want a symphony orchestra to play it." Romberg is not immediately drawn to Lillian's dream. He had significant self-doubts, an understandable result of his lack of formal conservatory training, a prerequisite, at least in Romberg's opinion, for a composer to be heard in Carnegie Hall. Lillian gets her wish, however, and the film's final sequence is a Carnegie Hall concert featuring Romberg, his orchestra, and his music.

During the Carnegie Hall sequence, Romberg speaks to the audience, as he would have done in real life. (This was one way in which Romberg endeared himself to his fans.) In the film Romberg tells his audience something the real Romberg said repeatedly regarding his musical style, namely that his music was "middle brow—too high brow for jazz conductors and too low brow for symphony conductors."

Finally, there is the play between the familiar and the exotic. Romberg loved people, and savored the opportunity to talk about music, whether on radio or television, or to a live audience. He enjoyed telling stories and relished admiration from his fans. He wanted to communicate with people directly, something he accomplished through both music and the spoken (and occasionally written) word. However, he also enjoyed having an air of sophistication about him. Romberg was proud of his European heritage and intentionally maintained his Hungarian accent. He enjoyed being a showman, and used his personal charisma—a blend of the familiar and the exotic—to great effect. Romberg was in many ways an Everyman, but with added élan.

Although the film portrays Romberg as likeable and gregarious, it does not address and even negates several aspects of his life. No mention is made of his Hungarian nationality—he is assumed to be Viennese (which is still

Film still from *Deep in My Heart*, featuring Doe Avedon (as Lillian Romberg), José Ferrer (as Sigmund Romberg), and Helen Traubel (as Frau Mueller). Author's collection.

foreign). Ferrer does not attempt a Hungarian accent, though his speech is certainly affected. In reality, Romberg was proud of his Hungarian birthright, calling himself a Hungarian subject on his World War I registration card and listing his first language as Magyar on census reports. The suppression of his ethnic identity is almost certainly due to Cold War politics of the 1950s: Hungary was communist, and a hero from a communist country in a mainstream Hollywood film was simply intolerable. Neither is Romberg's Jewishness mentioned at all. As film scholar John C. Tibbetts asserts, the film set out to "whiten" Romberg's image.[5] Romberg is made into a Western European. His Jewish identity is suppressed in order to make him less marginalized, and therefore in a position to be accepted more fully by Protestant America.

Furthermore, no mention is made (in either the film or the book) of Romberg's first marriage. He listed himself as married on his World War I registration card in 1917, and Romberg's entry in the 1920 Federal Census includes a wife, Eugenia, age twenty-eight, born in Austria and whose first language is German. The marriage presumably ended in divorce. By neglecting any mention of this marriage, two things happen in the film: first, Romberg becomes morally acceptable to mid-century mainstream America, since divorce was frowned upon; and second, it allows for the love story between Romberg and Lillian Harris to take center stage as the film's romantic tale.

In *Deep in My Heart*, the couple's early courtship appears in a version similar to that told by both Rombergs, but not identical to it. The scene was invented to give José Ferrer an opportunity to display his extraordinary solo talents. In the film, Romberg, along with two fictional associates, is writing a show called *Jazzadoo*. No such score by Romberg exists—Romberg, along with Al Jolson (who does not appear in the film) and Buddy De Sylva and Harold Atteridge (both of whom were also excised) were writing *Bombo* when the supposed events took place. Romberg gives a one-man performance of the entire *Jazzadoo* show, complete with Jolson impersonations (one of which is in blackface), for Lillian, her prim-and-proper mother, and Mr. Townsend, the fictional manager who represents the real Shubert brothers. (J. J. and Lee Shubert, owners of the Shubert Theatrical Corporation, were among the most powerful and influential Broadway producers in the first half of the twentieth century.) Jolson exists in the film only through Ferrer impersonating Romberg impersonating Jolson. Romberg was many things, but not a song-and-dance man. This was Ferrer's moment of glory.

Several characters were invented for the film, while many real-life ones had their roles either minimized or eliminated. Romberg's principal collaborators from his early years, as they appear in the film, were celluloid creations. Manager Bert Townsend (Paul Stewart), librettist Ben Judson (Jim Backus), and lyricist Lazar Berrison Sr. (David Burns) simply did not exist in real life. By inventing them and eliminating their real-life counterparts, people such as Harold Atteridge, Buddy De Sylva, Rida Johnson Young, and even Al Jolson, attention remained on Romberg rather than on his collaborators.

The French dancing sensation Gaby Deslys (1881–1920, played by Tamara Toumanova with the singing voice of Betty Wand), the star of Shubert revues who performs Romberg's music early in the film, was in fact on the Shuberts' artist roster, but Romberg did not write any music for her. He certainly did not create "Softly, As in a Morning Sunrise" for her. "Softly" came from *The New Moon*, which opened on Broadway in 1928. Deslys's role was created for the film; the dancer does not appear in Arnold's book. The frenetic performance by Deslys, complete with cascading falls off most notes, aggressive interjections from the orchestra, and a female chorus overdoing French accents, was intended to show a "poor" interpretation of a Romberg song, while the languidly emotive rendition by Mrs. Mueller (Traubel, the operatic soprano) shortly thereafter demonstrated the "proper" manner of singing the same number.

Dorothy Donnelly (Merle Oberon), who wrote words for *Blossom Time*, *The Student Prince*, *My Maryland*, and *My Princess*, was an important collaborator for Romberg, but their first meeting did not take place as early as implied in the film. She was not responsible for Romberg writing *Maytime*, although another female lyricist and librettist, Rida Johnson Young, was Romberg's collaborator on that project.

Another of Romberg's significant lyricists was Oscar Hammerstein 2nd (1895–1960), who penned words for *The Desert Song* and *The New Moon* on Broadway and *Viennese Nights* and *The Night Is Young* in Hollywood. The role of Hammerstein (Mitchell Kowall) is minimized in the film, likely because the premier wordsmith was actively involved in his legendary partnership with Richard Rodgers when it opened. Any association with a composer other than Rodgers may have confused audiences and taken the spotlight away from "Rodgers and Hammerstein."

Along with these inaccuracies in plot details, songs from one show are billed as being from another (especially in the first part of the film). Moreover, because MGM failed to secure the rights to use music from *Blossom Time*, one of Romberg's biggest commercial and artistic successes is not represented in the film. (See Table 1.1 for a list of music in *Deep in My Heart*.) *Deep in My Heart* focused more on individual songs than on the shows from which they came.

The film provided a rosy public picture of Romberg for his fans. Like the characters in his operettas, Romberg finds personal happiness and professional success amid glorious music. He lives in a world that is real enough to be grasped yet imaginary enough to offer an inviting opportunity for escapism.

The book on which the film was based and whose title it shares is essentially a novel in the guise of a popular biography. It makes no pretense about this fact: on the title page the author, Elliott Arnold, even calls *Deep in My*

Table 1.1 Musical program of *Deep in My Heart* (MGM, 1954)

Song	Performer	Source in film	Actual source
"You Will Remember Vienna"	Helen Traubel	Café Vienna	*Viennese Nights* (film)
"Leg of Mutton"	José Ferrer and Helen Traubel	Café Vienna	piano piece, lyrics added for film by Roger Edens
"I Love to Say Hello to the Boys (Girls)" (fragments)	Betty Wand (singing voice for Tamara Toumanova)	Revue of Revues	*Poor Little Ritz Girl*
"Softly, As in a Morning Sunrise"	Betty Wand (singing voice for Tamara Toumanova) and chorus	Revue of Revues	*The New Moon*
"Softly, As in a Morning Sunrise"	Helen Traubel	Café Vienna	
"Mr. and Mrs."	José Ferrer and Rosemary Clooney	Midnight Girl	*The Blushing Bride*
"I Love to Go Swimmin' with Wimmin"	Gene and Fred Kelly	Dancing Around	*Love Birds*
"Road to Paradise"	Vic Damone	*Maytime*	*Maytime*
"Will You Remember"	Vic Damone and Jane Powell	*Maytime*	*Maytime*
"Girls Goodbye"	José Ferrer	*Jazzadoo*	*The Blushing Bride*
"The Very Next Girl I See"	José Ferrer	*Jazzadoo*	*Bombo*
"Fat Fat Fatima"	José Ferrer	*Jazzadoo*	*Love Birds*
"Jazza-Dada-Doo"	José Ferrer	*Jazzadoo*	*Bombo* (as "Jazza-Da-Dada")
"It"	Ann Miller and chorus	Artists and Models	*The Desert Song*
"Serenade"	William Olvis and chorus	*The Student Prince*	*The Student Prince*
"One Alone"	Carol Richards (singing voice for Cyd Charisse)	*The Desert Song*	*The Desert Song*

Table 1.1 Continued

Song	Performer	Source in film	Actual source
"The Desert Song Ballet" (One Flower Grows Alone in Your Garden, One Alone)	Cyd Charisse and James Mitchell	*The Desert Song*	*The Desert Song*
"Your Land and My Land"	Howard Keel and chorus	*My Maryland*	*My Maryland*
"Auf Wiedersehn"	Helen Traubel	Dorothy Donnelly's apartment	*The Blue Paradise*
"Lover, Come Back to Me"	Tony Martin and Joan Weldon	*The New Moon*	*The New Moon*
"Stouthearted Men"	Helen Traubel	Café Vienna, changes to Carnegie Hall concert	*The New Moon*
"When I Grow Too Old to Dream"	José Ferrer and chorus	Carnegie Hall concert	*The Night Is Young* (film)

Heart "a story based on the life of Sigmund Romberg." Arnold interviewed Romberg for the book in 1947, but exactly what Romberg told Arnold and what made it into the book and in what form is unknown. Like any good novel, many historical aspects are embellished or even invented in order to add to the book's readability and general interest level. Rather than telling of the hardships of a young Hungarian Jew in the final years of the Habsburg Empire, for example, we are treated to a rags-to-almost-riches story as fresh and heartwarming as an operetta plot.

The main narrative's creative license aside, the book's work list (though incomplete, since the book appeared two years before Romberg's death) and chronology provide limited documentary evidence for the composer's life. The work list is problematic, however, for the catalog of musical numbers that appeared under each individual show is often inaccurate. Where entries are correct, many songs appear under alternate titles, that is, ones that differ from what appeared either in the playbill or on the published sheet music. Fortunately, these variants are usually close enough to be recognizable. Titles are further complicated by the fact that what appears on the covers of popular sheet music from the first part of the twentieth century sometimes differs from what is given on the first page of the music itself. This is certainly the case for a significant amount of Romberg's music, especially his earlier works.

A Personification of *Gemütlichkeit*

So, who was Sigmund Romberg, the subject of *Deep in My Heart?* To begin with, Sigmund Romberg was not really Sigmund Romberg. He was born Siegmund Rosenberg on July 29, 1887, in Nagykanizska, Hungary, a town in the southwest part of the country. He spent his youth in the nearby village of Belišće and its closest city, Osijek, both of which were then part of the Hungarian part of the Dual Monarchy and today are in Croatia. After working as a coach-accompanist in Vienna and gaining practical experience regarding the methods and mechanics of operetta, he moved to New York to become a professional musician. References to his adopted name begin when he arrived on American shores. He became a naturalized American citizen in 1919.

Romberg's American career divides conveniently by decade, according to his areas of primary focus: 1910s—revues, musical comedies, and adaptations of Central European operettas (mostly for the Shuberts); 1920s—original operettas; 1930s—film scores; and 1940s—conductor of a traveling orchestra. Throughout his life, Romberg remained active as a Broadway composer and was acutely aware of the changes and transformations that were taking place in the American musical theater.

By all accounts, Sigmund Romberg was a jovial, fun-loving person who was the very embodiment of traditional Viennese *Gemütlichkeit*. He was a genuine "nice guy." Lillian described him as "a fine man, a perfect husband."[6] Romberg enjoyed many hobbies, with dining at fine restaurants at the top of his list. He also liked deep-sea fishing and driving at high speeds, the latter an activity that terrified his staff. Romberg took great pleasure in smoking, and kept a supply of dozens of cigarette boxes readily available.

One of Romberg's favorite eating establishments was Lüchow's Restaurant, at 110 E. 14th Street in the Union Square area. This was a popular gathering place whose regulars included, in addition to Romberg, Victor Herbert, Lillian Russell, O. Henry, and the Vienna Arts Quartet. Employees and patrons of Steinway Hall congregated in the Steinway room, just down the hall from the room reserved for Heinrich Conried and his German actors and musicians from the nearby Irving Place Theatre. The theatrical ambiance, cuisine, and beer all contributed to the restaurant's reputation as a "gastronomic cathedral." The elegant upstairs rooms and the downstairs rooms, with their heavy Teutonic décor, exuded a nostalgic spirit of Old Vienna.[7] With its outstanding food and drink, German spirit, and musical clientele, it is obvious why this was one of Romberg's favorite places. Lüchow's possessed the same friendly spirit—fundamentally hospitable but with added stylishness—that characterized Romberg's personality and his music.

In addition to Lüchow's, Romberg was a regular at other high-class venues in New York, including the Plaza Hotel, with its Oak Room, and the Majestic Hotel, an eleven-story structure known for its popular roof garden and red-and-gold Pompeian Room.[8]

Romberg was famous for his humorous malapropisms, or "Rommyisms," as his friends called them. These were the so-called slips that Romberg claimed he made because Hungarian, not English, was his first language. Their intellectual level, however, was too high for them to be accidental or unintentional; Romberg knew exactly what he was saying and was simply unwilling to admit that his witticisms were the product of a very quick mind and an extremely sharp intellect. Among the legendary quips is the one he made to Jerome Kern at Belmont Park, who was wearing a yachting cap at the time. Romberg remarked, "You look like a race trout."[9] Another time, after he and Kern had crushingly defeated their bridge opponents, Romberg remarked to his partner, "We won our shirts."[10]

Aside from his Rommyisms, the composer was known for his keen sense of humor. At a meeting of the American Society of Composers and Publishers, he once said, "If anyone here has an opinion, this is a democracy, they can express it." When Irving Caesar started to speak, Romberg quipped, "Irving, one word from you and you're out the window!"[11]

Romberg treasured good company and solid conversation. As he wrote to his friend Lt. Cdr. C. B. Cranford in 1944: "But that, dear Commander, is one of the subjects upon which we could drink innumerable highballs or beers in the Oak Room of the Plaza Hotel about eleven o'clock at night, and have one of those interesting discussions that we used to have."[12]

Romberg enjoyed people, and they enjoyed him. He had good working relationships with all of his collaborators, but maintained especially strong professional and personal respect for Hammerstein, with whom he worked closely during the late 1920s and early 1930s. Even after the period of their intense activity ended, Romberg continued to offer support, encouragement, and praise to the wordsmith. For example, in 1939, when Hammerstein was suffering terrible depression after the failure of *Very Warm for May* and its horrible reviews, Romberg wrote:

> I am not trying to throw bouquets or compliments at you[,] Oscar, but I do have a very soft spot in my heart for you, and somehow or other have the feeling that not only do we understand each other thoroughly, but you have a knack for bringing out my best qualities, and I am vain enough to feel that perhaps I have the same influence on you. . . .
>
> I'll close now, and just want to tell you that I still love you, and as a parting shot, I'll just tell you one thing more. Out of one hundred outstanding authors, writing dramatic plays, I don't think you'll find three who have the knowledge, the feeling and the sentiment to know how to write a book to which music is supposed to be interwoven with the action. You are one of the few, and that's where the "rub" comes in.[13]

Twelve years later, in 1951, after the opening of *The King and I*, Romberg rearticulated his strong opinion about Hammerstein's talent: "[A] monumental piece of work. I think to be in a position to write what you want to write, when you want to write it, is reaching the highest pinnacle of one's ambition and just puts you, in my estimation, in a unique class, leading all other men in your field bar none."[14]

Romberg's best friend and closest confidant was his second wife, Lillian. The story of how Sigmund Romberg and Lillian Harris met and fell in love may well be a fabrication, but it is what both Romberg and Lillian told and therefore was their reality. The account involved negative first impressions and parental concerns, all overridden by sincere devotion, with a bit of artistic inspiration thrown in for good measure.[15]

In 1924, Romberg was working on the score for *Bombo* with Al Jolson, Buddy De Sylva, and Harold Atteridge. In order to complete the musical, the men sequestered themselves in a cabin in the Adirondack Mountains and made a pact that none of them would shave until the show was completed.

Meanwhile, Lillian Harris, then living in Washington, D.C., was on vacation with her parents in the Adirondacks, and by chance met the bristly bearded Sigmund. When she spoke to her future husband for the first time, she told him, "You write music," disclosing that she knew who he was. Romberg complained about the work he was doing at the time, thinking it too down-market. Lillian encouraged him by reminding him of his beautiful sentimental music for *Maytime* and *Blossom Time*. Already strongly attracted to each other, the couple arranged to meet the next day.

Romberg wanted to make a good impression, and, in a romantic gesture, ordered violets to be delivered to Lillian at the inn where she was staying. Jolson, however, intervened and told the florist to distribute the flowers to every girl in the hotel, telling each recipient that the flowers were courtesy of the famous Broadway composer Sigmund Romberg. As a result of Jolson's ruse, Lillian, who was understandably feeling hurt, somewhat betrayed, and certainly upset, quickly left the inn. When the composer arrived, he was hoping to find Lillian smiling and eager to see him, but instead was surprised that she simply was not there. After he assessed the situation and realized that Jolson had played an ill-conceived joke, he became livid, despite the attention of all the young women in the hotel.

The couple did not see other again until another chance meeting, this time in the lobby of the Plaza Hotel in New York. They ventured into nearby Central Park, where they sat and talked. Romberg told Lillian about a love theme he was writing for *The Student Prince* and that he needed her inspiration. (This scenario followed that of Franz Schubert in *Blossom Time*.) The resulting song was "Deep in My Heart, Dear," the principal waltz duet of *The Student Prince*. For the couple, the tune became "Lillian's theme song."

Hoping to impress Lillian's well-to-do parents, Romberg sent them tickets to his latest show, *Artists and Models of 1924*. The revue included nude females on stage, and the Harrises, who deemed public nudity immoral, were shocked and appalled at what they saw. But when *The Student Prince* appeared shortly thereafter, the Harrises attended and forgave Romberg for *Artists and Models*. Finally, Sigmund Romberg and Lillian Harris married on March 28, 1925, in Paterson, New Jersey. They remained together until Romberg's death in 1951 and never had children.

Romberg was undoubtedly one of America's most beloved musical personalities during the second quarter of the twentieth century. He reached audiences not only as a composer but also as a radio host, television guest star, and conductor. He was a true charmer, and his gregarious personality endeared him to many. Romberg's Hungarian accent and Central European mannerisms gave him a certain kind of sophistication, but he was neither stuffy nor arrogant. Instead, he seemed to be an old family friend to everyone he encountered, whether in the theater, on the radio, or in the concert hall. According to an unnamed writer for *Click: The National Picture*

Monthly, Romberg was: "[A]n artist who doesn't act like an artist, a composer who doesn't act like a composer, a famous person who would be deeply chagrined if he ever found himself acting the part of a famous person. In his contacts with non-musical people he reflects an almost antique old-world courtesy which has the same Johann Strauss flavor as his music. But though he carries on the Viennese tradition, Romberg and his music are thoroughly American."[16]

In essence, Romberg was an amalgamated personification of the best qualities of his operettas. To make an operetta succeed, there had to be an expertly conceived mixture of sentiment, nostalgia, realism, and humor: Romberg the operetta creator embodied all these traits.

The Theatrical Advocate

Romberg also had another, practical side. He was a Broadway professional and used his position to assist others at the beginning of their careers. Among the people he helped were George Gershwin (1898–1937), Cole Porter (1891–1964), the team of Richard Rodgers (1902–1979) and Lorenz Hart (1895–1943), Vivienne Segal (1897–1992), and Fred (1899–1987) and Adele (1896–1981) Astaire.

In 1916, the neophyte Gershwin took his song "The Runaway Girl," with lyrics by Murray Roth, to the Winter Garden, where Gershwin and Roth performed it for "Ma" Simmons, J. J. Shubert's musical casting director. Simmons liked the music he heard (but not the words), and arranged for Gershwin to meet the Shuberts' staff composer, Romberg. The Winter Garden composer was impressed with the young man's talent, chose one of his tunes, and gave it to Harold Atteridge, the staff lyricist. The result was "The Making of a Girl," which appeared in *The Passing Show of 1916*.[17] As was the practice of the time, Romberg's name appeared on the song as co-composer. Gershwin apparently did not mind—he was thrilled to have his name appear on a song in a staged theatrical production.

Romberg continued to provide opportunities for Gershwin on Broadway. "Swanee," one of Gershwin's early hits, was interpolated into the musical comedy *Sinbad* (1918), an Al Jolson vehicle with a mostly Romberg score and one over which Romberg presided. Although Romberg wrote most of the music for *The Dancing Girl* (January 24, 1923, Winter Garden), the Gershwin–Irving Caesar song "That American Boy of Mine" also appeared in the show.[18] Later, the two composers co-wrote *Rosalie* (January 10, 1928,

New Amsterdam), which was produced by Florenz Ziegfeld. (For a discussion of *Rosalie*, see chapter 7.)

Romberg and E. Ray Goetz also introduced composer-lyricist Cole Porter's work to Broadway audiences in their revue *Hands Up* (July 22, 1915, 44th Street). At the request of Elizabeth "Bessie" Marbury, a literary agent turned producer, the creators inserted Porter's song "Esmerelda" into their show. Marbury's influence on Broadway was substantial, for she is credited with conceiving the idea behind the Princess Theatre shows of Guy Bolton, Jerome Kern, and P. G. Wodehouse and subsequently financing them. She certainly had the clout to promote her favorite young composers and lyricists, a group that included Porter.[19]

Porter's music also appeared in the aforementioned *The Dancing Girl*. His song "The American Punch," originally in *Hitchy-Koo of 1922* (a show that closed during its tryout in Philadelphia), was recycled and interpolated into the first-act finale.[20] *The Dancing Girl*, therefore, included music by Romberg, Gershwin, and Porter, three of the decade's leading Broadway composers.

Romberg was also involved with the professional Broadway debut of the team of Richard Rodgers and Lorenz Hart, but in a very different way. The novice team, whose musical comedy *Poor Little Ritz Girl* (July 28, 1920, Central) was about to have its Broadway opening, was immensely disappointed to learn that their producer, Lew Fields (half of the famous vaudeville team of Weber and Fields), not only set aside the show's original storyline and rewrote it during its Boston tryout but also cut many of their songs, replacing them with new numbers by Romberg and Alex Gerber. Rodgers and Hart were understandably disappointed and hurt at the events that transpired without their knowledge. (See chapter 2 for a discussion of *Poor Little Ritz Girl*.)

In addition to composers, Romberg also was involved with the Broadway debuts of some of the American musical theater's greatest performers. Broadway audiences first saw and heard Vivienne Segal in Romberg's *The Blue Paradise* (August 5, 1915, Casino). Segal later starred in *The Desert Song* (November 30, 1926, Casino) and the film *Viennese Nights* (1930). The brother and sister dance team of Fred and Adele Astaire first appeared on Broadway in *Over the Top* (November 28, 1917, 44th Street Roof), a revue with a Romberg score. They subsequently were featured in the *Passing Show of 1918*, again singing and dancing to Romberg's music.

As a composer who knew the practical issues involved with writing for

Broadway, Romberg was justifiably concerned about the business side of musical theater. He was a founding member of three associations concerned with composers' and writers' rights: American Society of Composers, Authors, and Publishers (ASCAP), Dramatists' Guild, and Song Writers' Protective Association (SPA). Each organization was slightly different in its purpose, but they all protected those who earned their livings writing for the theater.

ASCAP began in 1914 (the same year Romberg started his professional career) as a royalty collecting agency for performances of musical works. Originally, it was a voluntary unincorporated nonprofit association. During the 1920s, however, with the introduction of radio broadcasting, ASCAP was forced to establish its position as a representative of composers' rights through court action.[21] Romberg was a lifelong supporter of the society and its activities.

The Dramatists' Guild, established in 1925, was an organization of composers, authors, and playwrights that protected creators from unfair treatment by producers. Producers were to abide by the Guild's regulations, and Guild members could not work with producers who refused to cooperate with the Guild. Romberg, along with Jerome Kern, Irving Berlin, George Gershwin, Richard Rodgers, and Oscar Hammerstein 2nd, were among the Guild's first members.[22]

The Song Writers' Protective Association was formed in 1931 to create a unified front for composers when dealing with publishers. Its chief purpose was "to obtain and make secure for the song writer an equitable share in the profits realized from his efforts, talents and genius." Billy Rose was the organization's first president, and Romberg its first vice president. In March 1932, Romberg became the Association's second president. During Romberg's presidency, Ira Gershwin served as treasurer, and Irving Berlin headed what was called the "council," whose members included, among others, Irving Caesar, Ray Henderson, Howard Dietz, Billy Rose, and Richard Rodgers.[23]

Romberg also had a brief career as a producer. In 1919, Romberg and Max Wilner formed their own company, Wilner-Romberg Productions. Only three works appeared during the enterprise's short existence: *The Magic Melody* (November 11, 1919, Winter Garden), a "romantic musical play" (a synonym for operetta at the time) with a score by Romberg, *Pagans* (January 4, 1921, Princess), an original play by Charles Anthony, and *Love Birds* (March 15, 1921, Apollo), a musical comedy again with a score by Romberg. Wilner-Romberg Productions went out of business in 1921. An actor's strike was the impetus for the company's rapid decline into bankruptcy.[24]

The Collector

When not composing or involved with the business side of music, one of Romberg's greatest passions was collecting musical scores.[25] His personal music library (today at the University of California, Berkeley, although some items are in other University of California libraries) contained some 4,500 scores representing virtually the entire history of music for the stage. Opera formed the cornerstone of the collection, with a strong representation of works by twentieth-century composers such as Albéniz, Hindemith, Janáček, Korngold, Milhaud, Prokofiev, Ravel, Richard Strauss, Stravinsky, Siegfried Wagner, Weingartner, and Wolf-Ferrari. Romberg's collection was incredibly comprehensive and included both European and American works. The shelf list includes important American operas such as John Knowles Paine's *Azara* (1898) and Horatio Parker's *Mona* (1910) and *Fairyland* (1914), demonstrating the collector's eclecticism.

In addition to the late nineteenth- and twentieth-century imprints, there are many rare scores, which are indicated by red underlining in Romberg's own shelf list. Especially significant among these 283 items are 145 scores of English comic operas from the late eighteenth and early nineteenth centuries, including works by Arne, Bishop, Boyce, and Shield.

Manuscript copies of all of Romberg's works, including full orchestral scores for many of his operettas, appear in the collection as well, most of which are in the hands of copyists. Romberg had them bound in identical covers (like a set of complete works) and incorporated them into his library.

Romberg was justifiably proud of his collection. His knowledge of its contents was impressive, as a writer for *International Musician* observed: "This spacious room [Romberg's Beverly Hills studio], occupying the sunken first story, has its walls lined with Romberg's library of musical plays, one of the most comprehensive in existence. He will challenge you to name any vocal score, from revue up to grand opera. We tried him once with what we thought a relatively obscure work: Vaughan Williams' folk opera, *Hugh the Drover*. A quick glance at the catalogue, and Romberg pulled the volume out of a nearby shelf."[26]

Romberg's music library remains one of the most extensive collections of opera scores in the United States. Searches for obscure operettas on World-

Romberg composing at the organ with his music library in the background. Licensed by Corbis.

Cat (an electronic database that lists library holdings worldwide) sometimes yield only one or two results for libraries that own the rare titles, and one location that appears again and again is the University of California, Berkeley.

The Composer

Romberg was first and foremost a composer. He preferred to write at the keyboard and had an exceptional ability to play by ear. After all, he began his New York musical career playing piano in restaurants. Romberg played in a popular vein with an "unlearned" technique, as opposed to that of a classical performer with formal training. In this respect he was like Jerome Kern, who, along with Romberg, sometimes attended dinner parties where George Gershwin was also a guest. Gershwin, rather than Kern or Romberg, was consistently asked to play piano, often leaving Kern to wonder if people no longer liked his songs or if they simply thought he didn't play well.[27] The truth was that neither Kern nor Romberg was the virtuoso pianist that Gershwin was, though all three were accomplished players.

From the 1930s onward, Romberg maintained a residence in southern California. His grand pianos, organ, and portable desk resembling a draftsman's table occupied the sunken first floor studio of his Beverly Hills home. The instruments were arranged so that Romberg could comfortably play the organ and the piano simultaneously. He liked to compose at the organ, stating, "Somehow melody flows from an organ, and is not forced from it."[28] Each console was connected to a secretaries' office, where tape, wire, and transcription recorders were located, in the event that the composer wanted his improvisations recorded. Later, an assistant could transcribe these home recordings.

Romberg's Beverly Hills studio was also equipped with a recording system with which Romberg made acetate disc recordings of selections from his operettas. These historic discs are now housed at the Library of Congress. Romberg prepared a catalog of these recordings, divided into three parts: an alphabetical index of songs, an alphabetical index of shows, and a shelf list.[29] None of the recordings have been issued commercially.

Romberg had a similar arrangement in his New York residence. The organ and piano were connected, and he could play the piano from the organ keyboard. After he conceived a song on the organ, he would complete it on the piano.[30]

Romberg had a very strong command of the musical theater and operatic repertory. This came largely from his massive music library. His knowledge of existing music was so extensive that it often led to accusations of musical thievery. As Gershwin is said to have quipped about Romberg's work, "It's the kind of music you go into the theatre whistling."[31] A critic once stated that Romberg "never overlooks a melody that has done good service before. He has the most infallible memory of any of our popular composers."[32]

One story concerning Romberg's "creative borrowing" comes from the composer's early days in Hollywood. When Oscar Hammerstein 2nd, with whom Romberg was writing the score for the Warner Brothers' film operetta *Children of Dreams* (1931), was away, Romberg decided to work on his piano skills, diligently practicing passages of Tchaikovsky's Piano Concerto No. 1. Someone who heard him playing is said to have remarked, "There goes Rommy. He must be writing a Russian show."[33] He wasn't writing a Russian show at the time, but his reputation for borrowing tunes was so strong that it was an understandable conclusion.

The good-humored composer himself participated in these accusations. One classic anecdote concerns a party at which a piano version of Offenbach's "Barcarolle" from *Les contes d'Hoffman* was being played in the background. When Romberg was asked if it was his music, he dryly replied, "Not yet."[34]

Even in the early years of his career, specific references to the similarity between Romberg's music and that of other composers appeared in print. Several reviewers of the 1921 musical comedy *Love Birds* noted the closeness of the title song to Carl Sinding's piano piece "Frühlingsrauschen," or "Rustle of Spring."[35] The two numbers have the same fundamental contour in their opening eight measures; both begin on the sixth scale degree over a tonic chord (a non-harmonic tone), and they share the same intervallic configuration for the first six measures. (See examples 1.1 and 1.2.)

The melodies, however similar, are not identical. For example, the rhythm of the second half of the first and second measures (and also the fifth and sixth) is double dotted in the Sinding piece while Romberg employs notes of equal duration. Sinding's melody is conceived for the piano, hence its double dotting against a treble arpeggiated accompaniment, while Romberg set his melody for voice with pit orchestra accompaniment and likewise gave it a more straightforward rhythmic aspect.

One of the most famous instances of a Romberg tune sounding suspiciously like a preexistent melody is "One Kiss" from *The New Moon* (1928). The waltz refrain bears an uncanny resemblance to the title song of *No, No, Nanette!*, Vincent Youmans's hit show from 1924. (See examples 1.3. and 1.4.) The meter is altered, as is the overall aesthetic of the song. Romberg's version is a luxurious waltz, as opposed to Youmans's fast-paced duple-meter dance number. The opening melodic shape of both songs, with its minor second descent and return, followed by a descending perfect fourth and upward arpeggiation, is identical. Even the choice of arpeggiation, a major seventh chord built on the tonic, is the same.

There are indeed certainly similarities between Romberg's melodies and those of other composers. But this does not necessarily constitute a lack of originality or imagination. Romberg was a product of his time, a craftsman who knew how to synthesize various musical styles to achieve his musical ends. One reviewer of *Love Birds* elaborated upon the idea of melodic adaptation: "[B]ut nowadays composers are rather fond of adapting popularities

Example 1.1. Carl Sinding. "Rustle of Spring," mm. 1–8

Example 1.2. Sigmund Romberg. "Love Birds" (*Love Birds*), refrain, mm. 1–8 (piano version by George J. Trinkaus)

Example 1.3. Vincent Youmans, "No, No, Nanette" *(No, No, Nanette)*, refrain, mm. 1–4

Example 1.4. Sigmund Romberg, "One Kiss" *(The New Moon)*, refrain, mm. 1–4

from Chopin downwards. It is a sort of mania, and as nobody protests, why let the good work go on. Then to one the old airs are better than the new ones, and if furbished up, renovated and cleaned, they make a good 'showing.' Then people have bad memories for airs and they are hard to place."[36]

For *Blossom Time*, Romberg based several songs on actual melodies by Franz Schubert. Since the operetta was a fictionalized tale concerning the Viennese composer, this made perfect sense. But Romberg did not just arrange Schubert's tunes so that librettist Dorothy Donnelly could create new words for them, but rather made them his own. (See chapter 4 for a more detailed discussion of this procedure in *Blossom Time*.)

Hammerstein once remarked that Romberg's music was just like its creator: romantic, exuberant, and positive.[37] Romberg knew what it took to construct a good melody—one that had direction and focal points. Melody was undoubtedly the driving force behind Romberg's creative energies, and its importance cannot be overstated. A well-supported and carefully focused melodic direction and unexpected shifts and twists that made perfect sense after they occurred were some of the features of his musical style. He internalized the craft of assembling a well-constructed tune.

Sometimes that extra spark of inspiration that made a tune great was present; other times it was not, as Brooks Atkinson observed in his review of *May Wine* (1935): "Although Mr. Romberg is not an inspired composer, plucking arias out of the still night air, it is common knowledge that he is a workmanlike musician. For 'May Wine' he has put together a sheaf of well-bred tunes that have pleasant melodies and manners[.]"[38]

Part of Romberg's craftsmanship was the knowledge of how to create specific emotional responses through musical means. He was aware of historical precedents for the association of certain motives with particular affects. If he thought, for example, that a descending minor second could create a symbolic meaning of remorse or regret, as often occurs in the music of J. S. Bach, he used it accordingly, for instance in the opening of "One Kiss" from *The New Moon*. Likewise, the ecstasy represented by an ascending octave (Richard Strauss's *Don Juan*, for example) found its way into Margot's expression of elation when she sings the title word of "Romance" in *The Desert Song*.

Romberg worked at an incredibly fast pace, as was necessary for a musical theater composer of his generation. Accusations of unoriginality could stem in part from the speed at which he was required to work. During the tryout of *My Princess* in 1927 (when it was still called *My Golden Girl*), for example, Romberg reportedly wrote one of the duets in twenty minutes. He then passed it on to lyricist Dorothy Donnelly, who completed her part two hours later.[39]

Romberg's style was unquestionably based on melody. This is evident from his sketches, many of which consist of a single melodic line. His best tunes possess a strong direction that often reaches an apex near the end. (Consider "Will You Remember" from *Maytime*.) When it comes to rhythm and meter, Romberg is relatively conservative: gentle syncopation may appear in his duple-meter songs, but nothing extravagant or pervasive. Likewise, his harmonic language, which is rooted in nineteenth-century diatonic-chromatic ("common practice") usage, is reserved. Romberg employs a consistent tonal language with a conventional approach to non-harmonic tones and key relationships. In Romberg's work, salient aspects of rhythm, meter, and harmony are all generated from the all-important melodic line.

Romberg considered himself to be above the average musical play composer of the 1920s, as mentioned earlier regarding the film *Deep in My Heart*. In real life, producer J. J. Shubert conveyed the composer's attitude in two letters to publisher J. Witmark. In the first, dated August 9, 1922, he wrote: "Of course, Mr. Romberg has been very reluctant to write anything along the lines of the plays you mention, as he wants to be a Lehar or a Richard Strauss. He thinks all of these things are beneath his dignity as a musician."[40] The second, from April 17, 1923, concerned the musical *Bal Tabarin*: "I want to assure you that the matter was not my fault at all. Romberg said he could not do the play as it was not the kind of play he cared to do. He is getting rather classical. It seems ragtime is a little beneath his dignity."[41] These letters appeared after the success of *Blossom Time* and before the appearance of *The Student Prince*, during the time when Romberg was achieving enough professional clout to assert his own voice and choose his own projects.

Romberg often strove for a high-brow operatic style in his Broadway work, and frequently succeeded. As a Boston reviewer wrote regarding *My Golden Girl* (which became *My Princess* when it reached Broadway): "In the third act, where Mr. Romberg has proved that he can write operatic music about as good as Giordano's, one forgot that the Shubert Theatre was not an Italian opera house."[42]

When it came to creating musical atmosphere, Romberg employed a relatively straightforward approach. He articulated his method in a 1928 article titled "A Peep into the Workshop of a Composer": "Music is in two keys, major and minor. Hungarian, Russian, and Balkan States, Persia, and India take music in the minor key; Anglo-Saxon and Latin countries are written in major."[43]

By self-definition, as a Hungarian, Romberg's native tongue was the minor mode. However, he spent his career in the United States, a major-mode domain. This dichotomy resonated strongly for Romberg. What appears to be a rather simplistic statement influenced much of his thinking about music. When he wanted to communicate immediately and directly with his audience, he usually employed the major mode. But when the mission was to create an aural locale far from the present time and place, he chose the minor mode, as was the case for North Africa in *The Desert Song*, Japan in *Cherry Blossoms*, and Saigon in *East Wind*. Romberg embellished this rather simplistic musical Orientalism in various ways, but the minor mode was at its root. Additionally, Romberg's gypsy music, another aural Other, in *Forbidden Melody* favors the minor mode.

Romberg equated the minor mode with various sorts of exoticism and, based upon his own statement, probably considered himself to be exotic.[44] His sentimentality, Old World mannerisms, and Hungarian accent did not endorse modernity, especially in America. On the other hand, he was a thoroughly modern composer in his incorporation of popular elements, his work in Hollywood in the relatively new film industry, and his adoption of technology (recording equipment, radio broadcasts) to further his career. He was in essence a man caught between two modes.

Music and Words

It is not just melody that immortalizes Romberg's songs—they are remembered equally well for their lyrics. Romberg worked with some of the century's most talented wordsmiths, including Harold Atteridge Jr., Rida Johnson Young, Dorothy Donnelly, Otto Harbach, Oscar Hammerstein 2nd, and Dorothy Fields. To create a memorable song, there must be an artful combination of music and words. It is this merging of words and music, the synchronicity described by Stephen Banfield in *Sensibility and English Song*, that underlies and supports Romberg's best work.[45]

Romberg did not completely agree with this assessment, however, for he believed in the supremacy of music in the word-music (or music-word) relationship. Following the process of most composer-lyricist teams of the 1920s and 1930s, Romberg wrote the music first, and then gave it to a lyricist to create expressions that would match the general mood of the music. The oft-quoted (and sometimes revised) anecdote about a bridge game in which Romberg and Jerome Kern were partners bears repeating here. Romberg could not figure out how many trump cards Kern had, so Kern began to whistle "One Alone." Romberg missed the hint, quipping afterward, "Who knows from lyrics?"[46]

During the creation of *The Desert Song*, Romberg let Hammerstein, his lyricist, know in no uncertain terms what he thought of the relationship between music and lyrics. Hammerstein brought a new lyric to Romberg, who put it on the piano, played and sang through it, looked at Hammerstein, and stated simply, "It fits." Hammerstein later remarked: "I have written many plays and pictures with Rommy, and his highest praise has always been the same 'It fits.' Disappointed at first with such limited approval, I learned later that what he meant was not merely that the words fitted the notes, but that they matched the spirit of his music, and that he thought they were fine."[47]

When writing the lyrics for "When I Grow Too Old to Dream" for the film *Viennese Nights*, Hammerstein was concerned about the quality of his lyric and its perhaps elusive nature. (Hammerstein questioned if someone could ever be too old to dream.) He concluded that Romberg's music legitimized his words. Linked to the music, the lyrics became music superimposed upon music. An emphasis on sound was equal to the meaning and clarity of a lyric.[48]

Romberg's Operetta Contemporaries: Victor Herbert, Rudolf Friml, and Emmerich Kálmán

While Romberg was certainly significant in establishing a recognizable style of American operetta in the late 1910s and early 1920s, he was not the only person working in the genre. Neither was he the only operetta composer to incorporate Tin Pan Alley–style syncopated songs, as well as other popular American dance styles, into his work. Many composers on both sides of the Atlantic tried their hand at writing operettas with varying degrees of success, but the three that bear the closest resemblance to Romberg are Victor Herbert and Rudolf Friml in America and Emmerich Kálmán in Europe. (One could certainly add notable figures such as Harry Tierney [1894–1965], Oscar Straus [1870–1954], and Leo Fall [1873–1925], along with many others, to this short list.)

The Irish-born and German-trained cellist and conductor Victor Herbert (1859–1924), whose year of death coincided with that of the premieres of Friml's *Rose Marie* and Romberg's *The Student Prince*, created operettas that entered the standard repertory soon after their appearances. The most famous of these were *Babes in Toyland* (1903), *The Red Mill* (1906), *Naughty Marietta* (1910), and *Sweethearts* (1913), the last two of which were made into films starring Jeanette MacDonald and Nelson Eddy. Herbert's

virtuoso vocal writing along with his gift for creating memorable melodies—
ones that became famous outside of their theatrical contexts—made him
one of the genre's most important figures.

Naughty Marietta is especially important in the Romberg legacy. First,
its librettist and lyricist, Rida Johnson Young, also provided the words for
Maytime. But there were other connections as well. Naughty Marietta's
story involves recognition and fulfillment through a song, "Ah, Sweet Mystery of Life," through which Marietta will know the identity of her true love.
"Once upon a Time" in Romberg's The Magic Melody (1919) has a similar,
though certainly not identical, dramatic function. Furthermore, Naughty
Marietta's American setting, New Orleans, then still exotic for New Yorkers,
proved the viability of an American locale for an operetta, something that
occurs in many Romberg shows, including The New Moon (1928), which
is also set in New Orleans.[49] The musical style of Naughty Marietta is fundamentally operatic, partly because the role of Marietta was created for the
Italian soprano Emma Trentini. The coloratura demands in numbers such as
"Italian Street Song" complement the rugged male march "Tramp, Tramp,
Tramp." This approach to soprano writing occurs again and again in Romberg's work.

Herbert fully embraced Ruritanian ideals, Viennese operetta's traditional
domain, in Sweethearts (1913). With its emulation of Vienna, the score of
course had a waltz as its centerpiece, in this case "Sweethearts," also known
by the curiously fatalistic title "Every Lover Must Meet His Fate."

Herbert's music, when compared to that of Romberg, is more virtuosic
and operatic, and, in general, gives the impression of having faster tempos.
The coloratura in Naughty Marietta's "Italian Street Song" somehow seems
more dazzling than that of The Student Prince's "Students Marching Song."
Both require fine and agile sopranos, but the former, perhaps because of its
solo setting (without a male chorus providing musical support) and slightly
faster tempo, *sounds* more difficult. Herbert, because of his formal training
and experience, was more comfortable in the world of the opera house than
Romberg, and this comes across in his operettas. He knew and understood
the abilities of the trained voice and wrote accordingly. Finally, the impression of faster tempos in Herbert's works gives his marches a lightness that
contrasts with the more Germanic grounding of those by Romberg. Herbert
moves through his scores in a blaze of sure compositional technique while
Romberg lingers in his, savoring every emotive moment.

The careers of Herbert and Romberg intersected in the pivotal year of

1924. Herbert died on May 26, leaving his operetta *The Dream Girl* incomplete. Romberg finished the score, although only two of his contributions were listed in the playbill, "All Year Round" and "I Want to Go Home." Romberg wrote two of the operetta's most memorable songs, "Dream Girl" and "The Broad Highway," neither of which was credited in the playbill. One reviewer cited the title waltz, mentioning the hearsay manner in which he learned of its composer: "By report, Mr. Woolf's [the lead actor] tune in the first act—amorous, ardent, languorous, waltz-like—is handiwork of Mr. Romberg."[50] Herbert's operetta opened posthumously on August 20, 1924, at the Ambassador Theatre.

As he did for Romberg, Herbert also provided a Broadway opportunity for Rudolf Friml (1879–1972). When Herbert refused to write a new operetta for Emma Trentini, the producer, Arthur Hammerstein, immediately needed to find a new composer. He took a chance on a young Czech pianist, Rudolf Friml, who had never written for Broadway, though he had composed a substantial number of songs and solo piano pieces. The resulting work, *The Firefly* (1912), immediately established its composer as a significant Broadway personality. Friml's first appearance on Broadway was thus much more significant than Romberg's, for Friml wrote a complete score for an established star. Furthermore, this happened two years before Romberg wrote his first Broadway songs for the revue *The Whirl of the World*. Friml did not have the same frenzied level of productivity as Romberg, but since he was not a staff composer for the Shuberts, he did not have to. He wrote several successful shows during the 1910s, though, including *High Jinks* (1913) and *Katinka* (1915).

Friml's background was substantially different from that of Romberg. Friml was born and raised in Prague and studied piano at the Prague Conservatory, where he also had composition lessons with Antonín Dvořák. The extent of these lessons is unknown, but Friml gave tremendous credit to Dvořák as a fine and inspiring teacher. Friml was an extremely fine pianist, and accompanied his countryman Jan Kubelík, one of the early twentieth century's great violinists, on his concert tours. Friml wrote extensively for piano, voice and piano, violin and piano, various other chamber music ensembles, and, later in life, orchestra. Although his reputation relies largely upon his work for Broadway, especially *The Firefly*, *Rose Marie* (1924), *The Vagabond King* (1925), and *The Three Musketeers* (1928), he was an extremely versatile composer.

Friml scored a career success with *Rose Marie* (September 2, 1924, Imperial), an operetta that rivaled those by Romberg for popularity in the 1920s. *Rose Marie* includes the oft-parodied "Indian Love Call" as well as the now politically incorrect "Totem Tom Tom." It also contained the glorious waltz "Door of My Dreams" and the rousing march "Song of the Mounties."

Although Friml also wrote stunningly beautiful waltzes, such as "Door of My Dreams" in *Rose Marie,* and "Huguette's Waltz" and "Love Me Tonight" in *The Vagabond King,* the idiom does not have the central position in an operetta by Friml as it does in one by Romberg. Duple meter songs such as "Only a Rose" in *The Vagabond King* are every bit as common as principal love duets in Friml's work. The reason for this difference is, simply put, Vienna. Friml did not have the admiration for Viennese operetta and firsthand experiences with the city and its music that Romberg did.

Friml's music is generally more sophisticated and has a more assured and richer harmonic vocabulary than that of Romberg. This comes from Friml's formal conservatory training and his fascination with nineteenth-century piano virtuosi, neither of which were part of Romberg's background. While Friml had formal training in Prague, Romberg had practical experience in Vienna. Unfortunately, even though they were both active in New York in the 1910s and '20s, and both lived in Los Angeles from the 1930s onward, evidence of their relationship and their opinions about each other's work remains unknown.

In Europe, Romberg's fellow Hungarian Emmerich Kálmán (1882–1953) helped create a new stock version of Viennese operetta in the 1910s, the same time Romberg was establishing himself in New York. Rather than employing a varied cast of characters and quasi-operatic ensembles, Kálmán created a new formula in which romantic numbers for soprano and tenor alternate with comic routines for buffo and soubrette characters. Act finales with prominent choral contributions often included reprises of musical numbers, all of which served the dramatic plot.[51] Romberg adopted this model in his works for Broadway. Kálmán, like Romberg, often incorporated musical styles closer to American musical comedy and revue into his works, bridging the fissure between Central European and American-based musical styles. This is readily apparent in *Czárdásfürstin* (The Czardas Princess, 1915), the romantic tale of an aristocrat and a cabaret dancer, and again in *Die Herzogin von Chicago* (The Duchess of Chicago, 1928), an operetta parody about impoverished European aristocrats. In Romberg's works, syncopated numbers were typically set pieces and independent musical entities, while in operettas by Kálmán, their treatments were more elaborate and expansive and often formed part of larger musical-dramatic scenes. In a way, Kálmán, when adapting American idioms for Central European audiences, reversed what Romberg did when arranging European works for Broadway. Kálmán expanded the musical context for the American-style music, while Romberg pared down the scale of the European models for Broadway.

Nontheatrical Works

While Romberg's greatest significance resides in his music for Broadway, he also composed music for nontheatrical purposes. Among these works are solo piano pieces, songs, and even a mute film score. Although they are not directly related to his Broadway career, they offer glimpses into other dimensions of Romberg's craft.

Piano pieces span Romberg's career. Three early works in an intentionally popular vein, the turkey trot "Leg of Mutton" ("Le gigot"), the rag "Some Smoke" ("De la fumée"), and the waltz "Le poème" ("The Poem"), were published in 1913 with English and French titles. Their bilingual titles may be the result of Romberg being asked to write the pieces in a French manner, but they could also be allusions to the pro-French (and anti-German) sentiment in the United States just before World War I.[52] "American Humoresque," which also exists in versions for small orchestra and piano and orchestra, was commissioned by Meredith Willson (composer of *The Music Man*) and first presented on the *Maxwell House "Good News of 1940"* radio program. Described as "a modern composition for the piano," the work is filled with Gershwinesque sounds reminiscent of *An American in Paris* (1927). A version for voice and piano with lyrics by Charles Tobias, "He Walks with Me," was published in 1951, months before Romberg's death.

Romberg wrote independent songs in a variety of styles. One of the most intriguing is "Baby's Asleep" from the late 1930s, with lyrics by Eddie Heyman.[53] The authors offered the following preface at the beginning of the song: "This song is inspired by the innocent sufferers in the world, and dedicated to those who are endeavoring to ease their pain." Written on the eve of World War II, Romberg was acutely aware of the situation in Europe because of his Jewish-Hungarian upbringing. The song begins as a lullaby and ends as a dirge. In the middle section of the song, an air raid takes place during which a child is killed. The following note appears in the manuscript at this point: "When broadcasting this song, bring sound effect of an airplane attack at this point, gradually increasing so that it climaxes at the word 'crash'—from then on gradually disappearing in the distance." Even without the aid of prerecorded sampling, Romberg effectively portrays the falling bombs through tone clusters, descending scales, and trills in the lower register of the piano.

This song illuminates a very different aspect of Romberg. It was not an endorsement or promotion of the sunny climes of nostalgia and optimism but rather a direct confrontation of world problems. The song does not end happily—a child dies in its parent's arms. "Baby's Asleep" is a late 1930s reincarnation of Schubert's "Die Erlkönig"; however, the horrors of war, not illness, cause the child's death.

By contrast, "Faithfully Yours," with lyrics by Charles Tobias, is a sophisticated waltz. In verse-refrain-verse-refrain form, the musical language is notably more chromatic than most of Romberg's waltzes. Equally evocative are the frequent caesuras that occur after the second beat in several measures. In this song, Romberg melds the more languid chromaticism associated with radio pop singers, with a typical Viennese waltz. ("Faithfully Yours" was also published in a version for solo piano.)

Another of Romberg's most famous songs is "Zing Zing, Zoom Zoom," again with lyrics by Charles Tobias. Perry Como's 1950 recording of the number propelled it into fame, and many other performers, including Percy Faith, offered their own renditions of the pop standard. The fast-paced waltz extols joy and effervescence. Its perfectly matched lyric tells how a simple, catchy tune can improve one's quality of life, and can assist in everything from getting rid of daily troubles to finding love and marriage.

Romberg wrote one mute film score, for the Universal Pictures release *Foolish Wives* (1922).[54] The legendary Erich von Stroheim (1885–1957) directed and starred in the epic two hour and twenty minute feature. The plot centered on the exploits of the deposed and financially bereft Russian Captain Count Wladislaw Sergius Karamzin (Stroheim), who is in Monte Carlo with two of his female cousins. He befriends Helen (Miss Dupont), the wife of American diplomat Andrew J. Hughes, hoping to gain access to her money. She succumbs to his entrancing charms, but Karamzin dies at the hands of the father of another woman he is also trying to seduce, and the diplomat is none the wiser about his wife's secret activities. Throughout the film, Mrs. Hughes is reading the book *Foolish Wives*, by Stroheim, a coy effort at self-reflexivity.

Romberg based his score on recurring themes, a typical practice in film scoring of the time and one that Romberg also used in his operetta scores for the Shuberts. Two lightly swaying waltz themes dominate the score to *Foolish Wives*: the identifiable musical topos matches the sweeping visual depiction of a glamorous European world, which in this case involves a flirtation with danger as well as a romantic fantasy. By contrast, the theme for Mr. and Mrs. Hughes is a calm duple-meter tune in an ordered sixteen-bar structure without any surprises or impulsiveness, just like their relationship. Other instances of recurring music in the film are the ominous motif that is sounded at each of Karamzin's appearances and the hymn-like quality of the priest's music.

Romberg's nontheatrical music follows many of the tenets associated with his stage work: waltzes are prevalent, and other types and styles of music surround this fundamental center. All of these musical devices are means toward the same end: appropriate musical expression and characterization. Whether it is the wishful thinking of Marianne as she sings "One Kiss" in *The New Moon* or the eminent danger associated with Karamzin in *Foolish Wives*, Romberg adds depth and dimension to dramatic characters through music.

Numerous intriguing and sometimes intersecting dimensions lie behind the story of Sigmund Romberg. The enduring popular image of his persona was created through the biopic *Deep in My Heart* and the novelized biography that preceded it. Romberg, like his film incarnation, was a gregarious individual with a good sense of humor. He assisted many Broadway luminaries in the early years of their careers, and advocated strongly for composers' rights. He was an avid collector of musical scores, and had studios equipped with recording technology in both his Los Angeles and New York residences. Melody dominates his musical language, the harmonic and rhythmic aspects of which are relatively conservative. Romberg believed strongly in the synchronicity of words and music, an attitude summed up in the concise phrase "It fits." His approach to operetta was similar to that of his contemporaries, yet it had its own distinguishing features, primarily the prominence of the waltz. While Romberg is best known as a theater—and to a lesser extent film—composer, he also wrote pieces in other genres, mainly piano miniatures and songs.

This, then, is the kaleidoscopic array that runs through the sum of Romberg's life and work. But how did Romberg's distinctive voice emerge? What influences affected the budding composer? What were the early sources of his inspiration? These are some of the questions to be addressed in the next chapter.

CHAPTER 2

Finding a Voice: Operetta, Revue, and Musical Comedy

ROMBERG'S DISTINCTIVE OPERETTA VOICE AND THE MANNER IN which he approached the genre grew out of four roots: 1) his European heritage and musical training; 2) Viennese operetta; 3) the American revue, especially as envisioned by the Shuberts; and 4) the American musical comedy of the 1910s. Each of these sources played a significant role in Romberg's development as a composer. Romberg grew up in provincial Hungary and received his most extensive musical training in Osijek (Esseg in German), which now is part of Croatia. He spent several years in Vienna, where he became enamored with the spirit of the city, especially its operetta tradition. Although Romberg arrived in New York in 1909, it was not until 1914 that his first music was heard on Broadway in a Shubert-produced show, *The Whirl of the World*. While working as a staff composer for the Shuberts, Romberg wrote a large amount of music for their spectacular revues. It was here that he acquired the skill of creating songs based on popular social dances of the era, especially ragtime dances. The Shuberts also engaged Romberg to write for musical comedies, musically similar to revues but dramatically different in that musical comedies typically had narrative plots.

Romberg wrote for revues and musical comedies throughout the 1910s and early 1920s; during the same time, the Shuberts were having him add interpolations to their Broadway adaptations of successful European operettas. Romberg's Viennese background and experience, along with that of writing for Broadway, made him ideal for this sort of work. An investigation of this aspect of his career will have to wait until the following chapter: it is the four dimensions that complement his Broadway operettas that are of concern here. These are the starting places for his particular operetta voice and the strands that consistently intertwine with it.

Romberg's European Roots

Romberg spent his youth in what was essentially an ideal setting for an operetta—rural Hungary. This was the imagined ideal of colorfully dressed peasants who blissfully sing and dance as if they do not have any cares in the world, except for finding true love. It was vastly different from the hardships and reality of agrarian life in the late nineteenth century.

Although much of Romberg's European life story as it appears in Elliott Arnold's *Deep in My Heart* consists of romantic embellishment, several facts can be documented. Soon after Sigmund's birth in the market town of Nagykanizska, Hungary, on July 29, 1887, the family moved to the nearby village of Belišće when Romberg's father took over the management of the village's chemical manufacturing plant. When Romberg lived there, Belišće was in Hungary; today, it is in the eastern part of Croatia. While chemical manufacturing provided the family's income, artistic endeavors were an integral part of life in the Rosenberg household.

Sigmund and his younger brother Hugo (born in 1891 in Belišće) were raised in a cultured environment. Their father, Adam, spoke and wrote in the four languages common to the region—Hungarian, German, Croatian, and Italian—and was also proficient in English and French. He was an avid amateur musician who enjoyed playing the piano. The boys' mother, Clara, was a writer of poetry and short stories who published under the pen name Clara Berg. Her work appeared in Viennese publications such as the *Neue Freie Presse* and the *Wiener Tageblatt*.[1] Their bourgeoisie home was a cultural center of the community, a place where poets, musicians, and painters gathered.

After leaving Belišće, Romberg spent four formative years, 1897–1901, in Osijek, the closest city to his boyhood home, which, according to the 1900 census, had a population of 24,930. Most of Osijek's inhabitants were Hungarians or Croats, but there were also a few Germans and Jews. Romberg went to Osijek to study engineering-related subjects at the Realnaškola (Practical School), but was quickly drawn to the school's music program. He benefited from the tutelage of the zealous and enthusiastic Italian professor Luigi Boggio, who taught art but also loved music.[2] Romberg played violin in the school orchestra, studied piano, and completed a four-year musical course in just three years (1898–1901).

Osijek was a city filled with music. Live musicians frequented restaurants, cafés, and parks. Romberg had numerous opportunities to hear local musical groups, including the military band, gypsy orchestras, and tamburiza ensembles. All of these experiences had a strong influence on the young musician. But it was the discovery of the theater, in particular the musical theater, that had the greatest impact on the future operetta composer.

Romberg lived in several different cities during the ensuing years, spending one and a half years in compulsory military service as a lieutenant in the Hungarian Regular Infantry, and ultimately arriving in Vienna, "the City of Dreams," in 1906. While working as a *corepetitor* (vocal coach) at the Theater an der Wien, a house known for its operetta productions, he studied composition and orchestration with Victor Heuberger (1850–1914), conductor of the Wiener Männergesangverein (Vienna Men's Chorus) and composer of operettas such as *Der Opernball* (The Opera Ball, 1898). Romberg also befriended Franz Lehár (1870–1948), composer of the hugely successful *Die lustige Witwe* (The Merry Widow, 1905).

Romberg adored the fin-de-siècle Vienna of waltzes, operettas, and coffeehouses, the glorious Vienna of legend, the metropolis represented by Mrs. Mueller's Café Vienna in *Deep in My Heart*. In 1935, Romberg appeared on Deems Taylor's radio program *Studio Party*. In "A Musical Trip Through Old Vienna," a group of tourists led by Romberg and an unnamed orchestra are visiting the Austrian capital.[3] At each stop on the itinerary, an appropriate musical selection is played, presumably selected by Romberg, or at least chosen with his input. The program is in effect a musical autobiography, for in it Romberg articulates his principal musical Old-World influences: marches, waltzes, opera, operetta, and Hungarian music. These are the types of music that appear again and again in his operettas. (See Table 2.1.)

Since food and drink were among the composer's favorite pleasures, it is no surprise that two of the featured venues in the tour are dining establishments: Sacher's Restaurant (famous for its namesake torte) and a café. Geographic veracity was challenged in the last two locales, for "Maxim's Café" (of *Merry Widow* fame) is in Paris and "Laguna" refers to Venice. Actual Viennese tourist sites, however, including the Staatsoper, the Prater, and the Theater an der Wien, capture the magic and charm of the city. Importantly, the opera excerpts are sung in English—the language of Romberg's radio

Table 2.1 Locations and music in "A Musical Trip Through Old Vienna"

Location	Music
Soldiers—guard relief	Strauss *Radetsky March*
Sacher's restaurant	Kreisler: "The Old Refrain"
Staatsoper	Leoncavallo: Prologue to *I pagliacci* (sung in English)
Prater—Volksgarten	"Wiener Meiner"
Theater an der Wien	Strauss: *A Night in Venice,* act 1 finale (sung in English)
"Maxim's Café"	Hungarian czardas with cimbalom
"Laguna" ballroom	Strauss: *Blue Danube Waltz,* "Won't You Waltz with Me" (ballroom waltz)

audience. Romberg believed in the importance of words and wanted his listeners to experience the texts in their own tongue.

Viennese operetta—the mainstay of the Theater an der Wien—was the genre that Romberg experienced and embraced in his youth, adapted for American audiences after his arrival in New York, and maintained as his muse during his long and distinguished compositional career. Throughout his lifetime, he longed for a world like those in his operettas. Viennese operetta was the conceptual base for Romberg's finest output, and some background into the genre is necessary for an understanding of his work for Broadway.

Viennese Operetta

During the late nineteenth century, Vienna was the city of not only Johannes Brahms and Anton Bruckner but also Franz von Suppé and Johann Strauss Jr. In the realm of popular musical theater, Vienna developed its own particular brand of operetta that showcased the most Viennese of dances, the waltz. These were operettas conceived by their creators for trained voices; part of the appeal of the Viennese musical theater comes from the vocal pyrotechnics required of the principal singers, especially sopranos. One particular Viennese trait was to have the solo soprano sing a florid obbligato filled with scales and arpeggios while the orchestra played the aria's principal melody a final time.

Romberg endorsed and drew upon several aspects of nineteenth-century Viennese operetta in his works. Waltzes, other dances and musical set pieces (such as marches, polkas, mazurkas, and czardas), references to students and the military, exoticism, and impersonation or disguise all appear regularly in Viennese operetta. While these themes are certainly not unique to operettas created by either nineteenth-century Viennese composers or Romberg, their prominence in Romberg's output reflects the composer's great love for the genre.

During the 1860s, Johann Strauss Jr. (1825–1899) wrote some of his greatest waltzes, including "An der schönen blauen Donau" ("On the Beautiful Blue Danube," 1867), "Künstlerleben" ("Artist's Life," 1867), "Geschichten aus dem Wienerwald" ("Tales from the Vienna Woods," 1868), and "Wein, Weib und Gesang" ("Wine, Women, and Song," 1869). At the end of the decade, the management of the Theater an der Wien summoned "the waltz king" to create operetta in the hope that he would be able to loosen Jacques Offenbach's hold on the Viennese musical theater establishment.[4] They made the right choice, for Strauss created operettas such as *Die Fledermaus* (*The Bat*, 1876) that were unmistakably and definably Viennese.

A large part of this specific Viennese operetta identity stemmed from the central position given to waltzes. In Strauss's first operetta, *Indigo und die vierzig Räuber* (*Indigo and the Forty Thieves*, 1871), one of the waltzes included the words: "Ja, so singt man, ja, so singt man, In die Stadt, wo ich geboren" (Yes, they sing so; yes, they sing so; In the city where I was born).[5] This self-endorsement of Vienna with the waltz was paramount, and the relationship between the two is a major theme in Romberg's output, palpably evident in the waltz "You Will Remember Vienna" from the film *Viennese Nights* (1930).

Although waltzes dominate Viennese operetta, other musical forms are present as well. Karl Millöcker, in *Der Bettelstudent* (*The Beggar Student*, 1882), used marches to portray Saxons and mazurkas to depict Poles. The Countess in *Die Fledermaus* sings a czardas, and, in the same operetta, guests dance a polka near the end of act 2, just before the final waltz sequence. This successful combination, rather than haphazard placement, of various musical forms for dramatic effect is necessary for any integrated musical score, including those by Romberg.

Student and student life are at the heart of some of the most successful nineteenth-century Viennese operettas. Franz von Suppé's *Flotte Bursche* (*Navy Lads*, 1863) is a tale of student escapades with a score filled with student songs, while Millöcker's *Der Bettelstudent* shares a significant title word with Romberg's *The Student Prince*, even though the qualifying class reference is radically different. *The Student Prince* continues the Viennese tradition of operettas that glorify student life and love.

A military backdrop, another Viennese convention, appears in von Suppé's *Leichte Kavallerie* (*Light Cavalry*, 1866); billed as an "operette militaire," the show is about an ingénue looking for her military father. *Der Bettelstudent* also involves military conflict, hence the presence of Saxon marches. In Romberg's work, military themes are central to *The Desert Song* and *My Maryland*, and it is the Saxon Corps who invite Karl Franz to join their ranks in *The Student Prince*.

Musical exoticism is another recurring motive in Romberg's operettas and those of his adopted Vienna. The Arab world is the setting for both Romberg's *The Desert Song* and Strauss's *Indigo und die vierzig Räuber*, the latter a version of the Ali Baba tale from 1,001 *Nights*. Other Europeans (that is, ones who were not Viennese) often are exoticized in Viennese operettas. For example, the title character in von Suppé's *Fatinitza* (1876) is a cross-dressing Russian officer; Poles dance mazurkas in *Der Bettelstudent*; and Hungarians fill the stage in Strauss's *Der Zigeunerbaron* (*The Gypsy Baron*, 1885). Romberg was able to depict these various European ethnicities in his scores using preestablished musical stereotypes. One of the best examples of this is in *Maytime*, where Romberg evokes different cultures in an act 2 dance. Another impressive instance is the song "Where Else But Here" from the wartime propaganda film *Let Freedom Ring* (1939), in which Nelson Eddy tells people from various countries how wonderful it is to be in America, addressing each in their own ethnically clichéd musical idioms.

Disguise and impersonation are frequent plot devices in Viennese operetta. Fatinitza in the operetta of the same name is actually a man; the principals in *Die Fledermaus* come to Orlofsky's ball in act 2 dressed as people they are not; and the romantic leads in *Der Bettelstudent* fabricate identities. In von Suppé's *Boccaccio* (1879), the title character travels undercover, and in the same composer's *Donna Juanita* (1880), a male army cadet cross-dresses to become the female title character. Impersonation and cross-dressing are of course nothing new in the history of musical theater, but the Viennese creators and audiences, with their intense fascination with façade, endorsed and enjoyed these stage behaviors. Concealment of various sorts figures prominently in many Romberg operettas, including *The Student Prince*, *The Desert Song*, and *The New Moon*. In each of these operettas, the male lead employs impersonation or disguise to achieve his goals—the prince is an ordinary student in *The Student Prince,* Pierre dresses and acts like an Arab in *The Desert Song,* and the aristocrat Robert works as a bondservant in *The New Moon.*

A fundamental paradigm shift in Viennese operetta took place in 1905 with the appearance of Franz Lehár's *Die lustige Witwe.* Here, the setting was Pontevedro, an imagined land that provided a cultural and political mirror for Western Europeans that, according to the vocal score, was a foil for Montenegro.[6] Lehár was not the creator of such domains, but *Die lustige Witwe* solidified their place in the world of operetta. These invented geographic areas—collectively known as Ruritania—were usually Balkan domains populated with dimwitted royals and colorfully dressed locals. The name comes from the illusory setting of Anthony Hope's novel *The Prisoner of Zenda* (1894). Ruritania became synonymous with the created mythological Balkanesque regions that quickly became popular in both literature and music.[7]

The romances set in these kingdoms almost always include royals who impersonate ordinary people. They travel freely, meet their subjects unrecognized, and dress in various national costumes. The ease with which all the characters travel and visit royal palaces undermines any claims to historicity that these tales might possess.[8] One needs only to recall Karl Franz's attendance at Heidelberg University in *The Student Prince* and his desire to join in student activities to see this aspect of Ruritania in Romberg's work.

At the turn of the twentieth century, the physical discovery of the Balkans through travelogues and journalistic literature went hand in hand with the further fictional development of Ruritania. The processes were inseparable; truth and imagination were carefully manipulated and balanced.[9] Especially significant in these creations was the perceived inherent superiority of Vienna when compared to outlying parts of the Dual Monarchy.

At the center of these depictions was Lehár's *Die lustige Witwe.* Though set in Paris, it was the Ruritanian domain of Pontevedro that was at the heart of the drama. Pontevedro's economy is in financial disarray, and Hanna, the wealthy widow of the banker Glawari, must marry a countryman in order to save her nation's finances. She does so, and thus rescues Pontevedro from economic collapse. This depiction of the country's financial basis fits comfortably with the Ruritanian narrative. People marry out of national duty, and a country whose finances are completely dependent upon a single marriage could not have solid fiscal management. Citizens of Pontevedro (e.g., the Balkans) are shown to be comparatively slow and uncivilized because of their economic system, but, in their defense, they dress marvelously and sing and dance with great vigor. Pontevedronians are a created Balkan people who embody the characteristics imposed on them by travel writers, journalists, and geographers.

Likewise, in Oscar Straus's *Ein Walzertraum* (*A Waltz Dream*, 1907), Princess Hélène of Flausenthurn, a non-Austrian part of the Habsburg Empire, is engaged to Lieutenant Niki, a Viennese officer. Much of the operetta's plot and music concerns Viennese and non-Viennese characterizations. At one point in the operetta, Niki and his friend Montschi listen to "music of their beloved Vienna" performed by a band whose repertory includes the waltz "Leise, ganz leise" ("Gentle, Completely Gentle").[10] The waltz melody emerges as a central aspect of the plot, for Hélène learns it in order to prove her love for Niki. Her decision to learn a waltz in order to win a man is filled with implications. First, she, like Niki, equates the waltz with Vienna, an element seen earlier in the work of Johann Strauss Jr. and later in that of Romberg. Second, her decision exposes her inherent belief that Viennese ways are superior to her own. She must learn Viennese ways, represented through the waltz, in order to make her husband happy and also to improve her own station in life.

These types of characterizations continued until World War I. Balkan peoples, real or imagined, were forced into cliché-ridden images. Their imposed qualities included both positive and negative aspects such as generous hospitality and living close to nature, but also backwardness and uncleanliness. They did not represent individual cultures, but rather a collective assembly. Like the term Oriental, Balkan became a keyword for the exotic Other against which European "cleanliness, order, self-control, strength of character," etc., could be viewed as inherently superior.[11] The Ruritanian domains of Pontevedro and Flausenthurn provided Viennese audiences with geographic locales in which their Empire still held superiority. They also represented a union between these people and themselves—the marriages of the principals were symbolic of those desired between the Viennese and real Ruritanians. Reality was far different, for although many found it difficult to admit, the glorious Habsburg Empire was in decline. The tragic events and results of the assassination of Archduke Franz Ferdinand in Sarajevo on June 28, 1914, hastened its downfall.

Ruritania, though an imaginary domain, was extremely significant for

Romberg. Because he grew up on the fringes of the Habsburg Empire, in a sense he lived and experienced firsthand the real-life inspiration for these fictional lands. He knew, and very well may have been at times, a "colorfully dressed local." He understood what it meant to be a citizen of Ruritania.

New York and the Shuberts

Romberg arrived inauspiciously in New York in 1909. Supporting himself at first by working in a pencil factory, the recently arrived immigrant began his professional musical activity playing piano in various Hungarian restaurants, including Café Continental and Pabst's Harlem Restaurant. He soon formed his own orchestra, which often played at Bustanoby's Restaurant on 39th Street. Their repertory included standard Continental fare, music that was reminiscent of Romberg's beloved Vienna.

One of the Bustanoby's patrons was Harry Carroll (1892–1962), a young composer of popular songs in the Tin Pan Alley style. Once, Carroll approached Romberg and criticized him for his lack of musical versatility. Romberg retorted that he could write a better rag in one day than Carroll had ever composed, and the next day, to prove himself, Romberg handed his critic the turkey trot "A Leg of Mutton" ("Le gigot"). The ragtime-style piano piece not only quieted Carroll but also helped establish Romberg's fame as a composer, for it was one of three piano works published in 1913 by Joseph Stern—the other two being "Some Smoke" ("De la fumée"), another rag, and "Le poème" ("The Poem"), a waltz.[12] All three were extremely popular with Romberg's restaurant clientele.

Another steady Bustanoby's customer was theater mogul J. J. Shubert, who heard the piano pieces and was especially impressed with the ragtime numbers. At the time, Shubert and his staff composer, Louis Achille Hirsch, were having a row that resulted in the latter not completing music for the revue *The Whirl of the World*. Urgently needing someone to write music for the show, Shubert asked Romberg, who quickly accepted the famous producer's offer. Romberg completed the score for *The Whirl of the World* (January 10, 1914, Winter Garden) while working at Bustanoby's, then left the restaurant to become a full-time staff composer with the Shubert Theatrical Corporation. He had been working in the restaurant music business for over four years before going to work for the Shuberts.[13]

The Shubert brothers, Lee (1875?–1953), Sam (1877?–1905), and J. J.

(1879–1963), collectively represented the major theatrical power in New York during the first half of the twentieth century. They also exerted their control in theaters throughout the United States. When they arrived in New York City in 1900 to begin their conquest of Broadway, commercial theater was ruled by the Theatrical Syndicate, a group of producers and theater owners who banded together to prevent any one of their productions from being closed. The Syndicate standardized (or, more precisely, sanitized) the material that appeared in their houses in an effort to avoid police interference because of "questionable moral content." Some independent producers, including the Shuberts, although not formally associating themselves with the Syndicate, nonetheless followed their practices.[14]

The Shuberts, keen businessmen and shrewd entrepreneurs that they were, challenged and broke the Syndicate's stronghold and replaced it with one of their own. They began with one theater, the Lyric, located on 42nd Street west of Broadway. From this their empire grew. At its zenith in the 1920s, the Shubert Theatrical Corporation owned over thirty houses in New York City and more than one hundred theatres nationwide. Additionally, they booked shows for nearly a thousand other venues.[15] During the course of the twentieth century, many of their properties were either demolished or sold because of financial hardship or antitrust legislation. In 2007, the Shubert Organization owns sixteen and one-half Broadway theaters (The Music Box Theatre is co-owned with the Irving Berlin Estate).

In the area of musical theater, the Shuberts were involved with all of the types of offerings available, but their reputation rested mainly on two genres: revue and operetta. These two types of musical theater, while certainly different from each other, share a number of features, the most important of which is innovation and spectacle in stage presentation, especially concerning sets and costumes. Opulent production values were the Shuberts' strong point, and perfectly matched the requirements of both revue and operetta.

Romberg's relationship with the Shuberts vacillated between extremely cordial and unbearably tense. The brothers were exceptionally strong-minded and even ruthless in their business dealings—they could not have dominated the theater industry as they did if they were not forceful. Romberg owed them a great deal; after all, they provided him with his first employment as a professional musical theater composer. But they also could be difficult when they felt they had been wronged. Romberg, like everyone associated with the Shuberts, had to walk a fine line.

Revues

The quintessential revue consisted of lavishly choreographed dances featuring beautiful long-legged female performers who could sing, catchy solo and choral musical numbers, breathtaking sets, and comical skits. With roots in vaudeville and burlesque, revues differed from their predecessors in that they usually were organized around some common theme that was often tied to current affairs and topical fads. Parodies of contemporary media personalities, news events, literary, dramatic, and operatic works, and anything else in the public's eye could appear on stage. Revues typically lacked dramatic plots, although thin stories were sometimes constructed as a way to provide unity between otherwise disparate scenes. Ronald Jeans, a writer of revues, called the genre "a form of entertainment so designed that it doesn't matter how late you get there."[16] Central to the revue were its stars. Legendary performers such as Fanny Brice, Will Rogers, and W. C. Fields were among the genre's most famous headliners.

Cultural lines were blurred or even ignored in most revues. In the early twentieth century, highbrow and lowbrow cultural attitudes were being created as a substitute for class: this was the time when specific cultural products were becoming closely identified with particular social classes.[17] The revue, however, was an egalitarian art form where anything was considered fair game for parody. Opera, sport, Shakespeare, prohibition: it was all viable source material for revues. Revues defied broader cultural hierarchies and relied on the concept of a shared culture. They sought to bridge and negate the emerging highbrow-lowbrow split.

Audience response was at the heart of the revue. The quality of the production was measured by its popularity, not by its aesthetic or artistic value.[18] This duality between the level of artistic product and its endorsement by the audience remains one of the central issues in any aspect of *popular* musical theater. Artistic qualities that would ensure the works' sustained reputation were not that important—ticket sales were what mattered. Commercial viability is an important benchmark for success when it comes to musical theater, as it is for any business enterprise.

Music by several creators for a single revue was common. One composer was generally responsible for the overall score, but there often would be several contributors. A song could be inserted either because the principal composer recognized its merits or because a star insisted upon its inclusion.

It was also common practice for the principal composer, usually a staff composer for the producing body, to share credit on songs he chose to include. The staff composer's name would appear as co-composer, thus entitling him to a share in the royalties if the song was a success.[19]

Composers who wrote for revues, including Romberg, had to create music that would have direct audience appeal. Its function, though, was to provide material for the chorus girls and big-name stars. Music was not a self-sufficient entity. People went to revues to see celebrities on stage and to be dazzled by the costumes, sets, and choreography, not to hear a particular composer's latest creation. Although, to be sure, many songs introduced in revues, such as Irving Berlin's "A Pretty Girl Is Like a Melody," from the 1919 edition of Ziegfeld's *Follies*, became immensely popular in their own right.

Songs for revues were typically in the Tin Pan Alley style, the trademark American popular song style of the early twentieth century. Verse-refrain form was the norm, and popular social dance styles were especially prevalent. Close ties existed between the theater and the music publishing industry, and music publishers often included a statement along the lines of, "as heard in such-and-such-a-show on Broadway," as a marketing ploy.

The Passing Show (1894) is generally credited as the first American musical revue.[20] It played at the popular Casino Roof Garden, one of several open-air performance spaces located on the rooftops of New York theaters.[21] Produced by George W. Lederer (1861–1938), the show spawned a variety of successors, either individual shows or annual series. The most famous and influential series was Florenz Ziegfeld's *Follies*, which ran uninterrupted from 1907 until the producer's death in 1932. Other noteworthy series of revues, following in the wake of Ziegfeld's success, included George White's *Scandals*, produced by George White, a former dancer in Ziegfeld's *Follies* and the series for which George Gershwin often contributed songs; Earl Carroll's *Vanities*; Irving Berlin's *Music Box Revues*; and several series produced by the Shuberts: *The Passing Show, Greenwich Village Follies*, and *Artists and Models*.

Although the flexibility of the revue approach allowed it to be manipulated for changing times, the archetypal model championed by Ziegfeld and the Shuberts faded in the early 1930s. This was due in part to the death of Ziegfeld, but it also had a great deal to do with the Depression and the rise of movie musicals.[22] Revues were expensive to mount, and many of the creative personalities associated with the genre moved to Hollywood.

The Shubert Revues

Revues were among the Shuberts' greatest achievements, and certainly one of their most lucrative. Between 1906 and 1943, the Shuberts staged a staggering 104 different revues, though productivity declined in the 1930s and 1940s.[23] The Shuberts understandably kept a team of creators on staff in order to maintain this extremely intense level of productivity. Romberg, Otto Motzan, and Jean Schwartz were their principal composers, but neither Motzan nor Schwartz achieved Romberg's level of fame. (Indeed, Romberg would not be remembered either, if he had not written operettas.)

Otto Motzan (1880–1937), an Austrian immigrant known primarily as a composer of Tin Pan Alley songs, wrote for the *Passing Shows* in 1916 and 1917, as well as for *The Show of Wonders* in 1917. Not limited to theatrical revues, Motzan also contributed songs to the musical comedies *Nobody Home* (1915, with a score by Jerome Kern) and *A Modern Eve* (1915, an adaptation of the German-language *Die moderne Eva*).

Jean Schwartz (1878–1956), like Romberg, was a Hungarian immigrant. He had been a major figure in vaudeville as part of the team Jerome and Schwartz: William Jerome was the duo's lyricist, while Schwartz was its composer. Their partnership resulted in the creation of over one thousand popular songs, including the extremely famous "Chinatown" and "Rock-a-bye Your Baby with a Dixie Melody" (first popularized by Al Jolson and later by Judy Garland) in addition to the World War I standard "Hello, Central, Give Me No Man's Land." In a further connection to musical theater, Schwartz was married for a time to Rosie Dolly, one of the Dolly Sisters, a popular dancing team that often appeared in revues.[24]

The principal librettist and lyricist for the Shubert revues was Harold Atteridge (1886–1938). Atteridge created over forty libretti for the Shuberts and wrote for several of the leading musical theater personalities of the day, including Al Jolson, Eddie Cantor, and Willie Howard. In addition to writing for revues and musical comedies, the genres in which he excelled, he also dabbled in operetta, collaborating with Rida Johnson Young on the book for *Dream Girl* (1924), Victor Herbert's last completed score. Atteridge based his humor on everyday lives of ordinary people, and wrote: "Most of the comedy dialogue comes from what I observe in everyday life—on the subway, in restaurants, on the street, in hotel lobbies, at church, in barber shops, in business offices, and almost any place where ordinary people are seen. During the day I watch people and at night I write about them."[25] The Shuberts' success in the genre was due in large part to Atteridge's ability to transfer his observations of real life to the stage in compelling and entertaining ways.

The Shuberts mounted three different series of revues, each with a different emphasis. *The Passing Show* was the crown jewel in the Shuberts' revue empire and in many ways epitomized their efforts. They took the name from Lederer's show that inaugurated the genre, hoping to capitalize on its fame and continue its legacy. The "editions," as the annual versions were called, were among the summer's most anticipated theatrical offerings. The *Greenwich Village Follies* series was presented in Greenwich Village, away from the Times Square–centered theater district, and was the only Shubert series for which Romberg did not contribute music. Finally, the *Artists and Models* series was noted for its inclusion of on-stage female nudity.

The Passing Show productions, like all successful revues, drew upon contemporary life as the basis for their songs and sketches. World War I, prohibition, dancing, the human body, and Orientalism were among the topics that appeared regularly throughout the series. Songs and scenes about dance, music, and the theater industry itself also figured prominently in several editions. The program for *The Passing Show of 1912*, the first edition in the series, described the production as: "A kaleidoscopic almanac in seven scenes presenting the comic aspect of many important events, political, theatrical and otherwise, and embracing the sunny side of 'Kismet,' 'Bought and Paid For,' 'Bunty Pulls the Strings,' 'A Butterfly on the Wheel,' 'The Return of Peter Grimm,' 'The Typhoon,' 'The Quaker Girl,' 'The Pirates of Penzance,' 'Oliver Twist,' etc. put into story and verse by George Bronson-Howard and Howard B. Atteridge."[26] This model continued in subsequent editions of the series. Romberg contributed to—or was the sole composer for—all the *Passing Show* revues from 1914 to 1919, except for 1915. He also contributed to the 1923 and 1924 editions.

Artists and Models had a different focus. In these "novelty revues" (as the first one, *Artists and Models of 1923* [August 20, 1923, Shubert] was called), "lightning sketch artists" drew quick portraits of characters; models took the caricatures and posed with them. It was not the art but rather the models who were remembered, for the female beauties appeared wearing little or no clothing. Hence, nudity became the trademark feature for *Artists and Models*. Romberg wrote for two editions of *Artists and Models*: *Artists and Models of 1924* (October 15, 1924, Astor) and the series' "Paris Edition" (June 24, 1925, Winter Garden).

In addition to their highly successful series, the Shuberts produced indi-

Advertisement for *Passing Show of 1914*. Courtesy of the Shubert Archive.

vidual revues that were not associated with a series. The format for these shows was essentially the same as that of the *Passing Show* revues, although sometimes there were very basic story lines that served as connecting devices between the songs and sketches. It was in one of these productions (*The Whirl of the World*) that Romberg's music was first heard on Broadway. The descriptor on the published sheet music for songs from that revue read, "As Introduced in the latest Winter Garden carnival of sensations *The Whirl of the World*." Because Romberg had not yet written for Broadway, he is identified as the "composer of 'La Poème,' 'Some Smoke,' 'Le Gigot,' etc."

Romberg also contributed to revues with such evocative titles as *Dancing Around* (October 10, 1914, Winter Garden), *Maid in America* (February 18, 1915, Winter Garden), and *A World of Pleasure* (October 14, 1915, Winter Garden). *Dancing Around* featured Al Jolson in blackface as his trademark character Gus and had a thin plot about a British military officer chasing after a prima donna. The opening scene of *Maid in America* took place at the "Made in America" exhibition then being held at Madison Square Garden, hence the homonymic title. The plot for *A World of Pleasure* was about a wealthy man who courts an heiress. The story lines were not important; the nonlinear scenes defined the shows and were the reasons why audiences flocked to the theaters.

The Shuberts produced two patriotic-themed revues, both with Romberg's music, during World War I. The pro-war effort attitudes promoted in the revues were the result of George Creel's Committee on Public Information, a government agency whose purpose was to manipulate American public opinion toward supporting U.S. intervention in Europe. Creel's activities had a significant influence on commercial theater. Support for the military was the focal point of *Doing Our Bit* (October 18, 1917, Winter Garden). Even the interior of the theater was transformed into a khaki military alcazar. Some of the overt military references included the act 1 finale, which presented a powerful visual spectacle showing the debarkation of American troops in France, and in act 2 the backdrop for "The Egyptian Rag" featured pyramids and a comic version of the Sphinx, explicit allusions to the Egyptian campaigns. *Over the Top* (November 28, 1917, 44th Street Roof) opened the following month. Its title suggested both the trenches in Europe and the location of the theater: over the top of the 44th Street Theatre.[27] The revue, which introduced to Broadway the brother and sister dance team of

Fred and Adele Astaire, included both frivolous sketches and more realistic scenes set in the trenches.

With the exception of *Over the Top*, all of the Shubert revues for which Romberg provided music played at the Winter Garden Theatre, a venue that was synonymous with lavish stage spectacle in the first quarter of the twentieth century.[28] Audiences who attended performances at the Winter Garden expected to be dazzled, and the Shuberts met, and often exceeded, the desires of their public. (This was still the case at the turn of the twenty-first century, when two highly visual shows that include elements of revue, *Cats* and *Mamma Mia!*, played at the Winter Garden.)

The physical appearance of the Winter Garden itself was transfixing. The house, which opened as a theater in 1911, was originally a horse exchange building: the auditorium had been the show ring. The proscenium arch, designed by William Albert Swasey, was unusually wide at forty-five feet (the largest of any Broadway house at the time), and the breadth of the auditorium allowed the audience to be closer to the stage than was the norm. The opulent interior included latticework-covered ceilings and walls, and a rose-pink plush curtain. Ornate painted moldings of garlands and leaves covered the box fronts and proscenium arch. Pompeian features included red floor tiles and wall spaces decorated with pottery, statues, shrubs, and flower boxes. The venue was a visual feast of treasures.[29] These sumptuous elements that filled the house complemented the live-action ones presented on stage.

Romberg's Music for Revues

Music for revues served the show's other elements. The only time music became the focus was when a star championed a particular song. This never happened for Romberg. For good or bad, Romberg did what he was paid to do: he wrote like a "hack composer" when it came to most of his revue scores. He created songs that were acceptable, but not exceptional, and this of course did nothing to enhance his reputation as a composer. It led to remarks such as "another commonplace score by Sigmund Romberg," "more forgettable tunes," "nothing memorable about the music," and so forth in the press. (Irving Berlin, by contrast, excelled at writing songs for revues.)

The revue's musical score, with its overall supportive role, focused on songs and dances. Onstage physical movement was paramount to the revue's visual splendor and spectacle: Ziegfeld epitomized this quality in his *Follies* with its famous precision dancing. Syncopated songs and social dances often derived from ragtime were central in forming Romberg's idea of the American Broadway idiom. These formed the basis of the musical language that Romberg grafted onto his Viennese sound world of waltzes and marches.

In his work for revues, Romberg not only assimilated American popular music styles but also learned the art of effectively combining music and words. Especially in revues, where topical references were essential elements, text declamation was vital. Musical settings had to allow for the clear articulation of lyrics. The revue was the arena in which Romberg learned how to achieve a practical and artistic synthesis of words and music.

It was not just the music but also the vocal styles that were changing. "Legitimate" singers, that is, those who formally trained in the fine art of singing and who focused their attention on matters of vocal timbre and refined technique, were now sharing stages with new types of singing stars who were more concerned about delivering individualized characterizations and humor. These were actors who had to sing, as opposed to singers who had to act. Furthermore, many of them were trained dancers and capitalized on their fancy footwork. Broadway composers needed to adjust their music to accommodate these new demands: melodic ranges became narrower and tessituras dropped into the same general register as speaking voices. The combined effects of these changes allowed for the clearer enunciation and declamation of texts. Among the performers most closely associated with this fundamental paradigm shift were Al Jolson (c. 1885–1950) and Fred Astaire (1899–1987). While the stage personas and vocal timbres of these two famous figures were vastly different, together they demonstrated the tremendous variety of allowable—and immensely popular—performance styles in early twentieth-century musical theater.

When it came to other aspects of musical style, ragtime, a style of syncopated instrumental music practiced and promoted by African Americans that flourished between the 1890s and the late 1910s, had a huge impact on American popular song.[30] When Romberg arrived on Broadway in 1914, ragtime was in full bloom. The style's most evident characteristic was a ragged—that is, syncopated—rhythm in the melody against a non-syncopated accompaniment.

Popular song, as a commercial enterprise, was quick to assimilate aspects of ragtime. Many of these songs, including Irving Berlin's immensely popular "Alexander's Ragtime Band" (1911), while not in true ragtime style, nonetheless incorporated some of its salient features. First was the name: a "ragtime song" possessed great marketing appeal. Second was the idea of a gently syncopated melody. Syncopation was of course nothing new in the history of music, but now it was a salient feature. Ragtime songs were certainly about more than syncopation, however. As Charles Hamm writes in *Yesterdays: Popular Song in America,* "Ragtime songs differ from other Tin Pan Alley songs more in spirit than musical style; they are brash, spirited, slightly syncopated, breezy, almost always humorous."[31] From a musical point of view, ragtime songs, in addition to being characterized by syncopation, also had more dotted rhythms than was typical in other styles of popular song. The tremendous popularity of ragtime songs proved the commercial adaptability of the style.

Similarly, syncopated dances, or "ragtime dances," become immensely popular. Dances with appealing animal names such as the turkey trot and the bullfrog hop appeared both in dance halls and on stages. The foxtrot, though it may sound like a syncopated animal dance, was not named for the sly mammal, but rather for the step's originator. Invented by Harry Fox (1882–1959), the foxtrot became one of the most important ballroom dances, and its popularity continues into the twenty-first century. Likewise, the Castle walk, developed by Vernon (1887–1918) and Irene (1893–1969) Castle, was also an important part of the social dance craze of the early twentieth century.

Ragtime songs and dances were perfect for revues, considering the genre's implicit hunger to capitalize on the most familiar aspects of popular culture. Hence, syncopated numbers were a requisite part of Romberg's compositional assignments. A handful of examples will suffice to show the significance of the style for Romberg, who used it in three fundamental and distinctive ways: 1) as a general popular music idiom; 2) as a musical means to set texts associated with sexual proclivity; and 3) as a means to bridge the gap between high and low art.

Romberg treats ragtime as a general musical idiom in three songs he wrote for *Whirl of the World* (1914), his first Broadway score: "The Twentieth Century Rag," "The Ragtime Pinafore," and "Ragtime Arabian Nights." Syncopation and displaced accents are not especially prominent in any of these songs, though they are present. Rather it is their breezy nature, one of Hamm's descriptors, that characterizes these songs. The most pronounced use of ragtime idioms in "Ragtime Arabian Nights," for example, occurs in the final measures of the refrain. Here, measures of strongly accented beats

Example 2.1. "Ragtime Arabian Nights" *(The Whirl of the World)*, refrain, mm. 29–32

alternate with those in which the third-beat stress is moved an eighth note earlier, creating an anticipation of the expected metric stress. (See example 2.1.) This type of metric shift was nothing extraordinary, and passages such as this are plentiful in Romberg's ragtime songs. Romberg had learned the formula for a ragtime motif and synthesized it accordingly.

When it comes to the association between ragtime and sexual proclivity, Romberg's finest example is the alliteratively titled "Sister Susie's Started Syncopation" (lyrics by Harold Atteridge) from *Maid in America*. According to the lyric, young Susie has rag fever and will not remain at home and sew, as she is told to do. She would rather go out and dance (and possibly engage in sexual activity, depending on how one interprets the morally ambiguous lyrics). Romberg's music for the song includes syncopated rhythms, as would be expected, but also has an unusually high number of chromatic passing tones. The rhythmic and pitch anomalies (when compared with nonsyncopated diatonic music) give the song a distinctively displaced character. Susie, like the music, is defying normative behavior. The song was a parody of the World War I comic tongue twister "Sister Susie's Sewing Shirts for Soldiers," popularized by Al Jolson in *Dancing Around*, the Winter Garden show that immediately preceded *Maid in America*. Sister Susie was no longer staying at home, as she did in Jolson's show; she was now out dancing and cavorting. Romberg, like many social commentators of the time, associated an increase in musical syncopation with the decay of Puritanical attitudes regarding sexuality. The coming of the Jazz Age was a dangerous thing when it came to morality.

Revues transversed the line between high and low art, and Romberg used ragtime to emphasize this mixing of styles. In "The Galli-Curci Rag," from *The Passing Show of 1918*, comics Willie and Eugene Howard, along with Violet Englefeld, describe what happens when an opera singer is asked to sing rag. The song's title and overall theme refer to Italian soprano Amelita Galli-Curci (1882–1963), who made her New York debut in January 1918 singing the title role in Meyerbeer's *Dinorah* in a touring production by the Chicago Opera. She was a singer in the news, and thus a good choice for parody. The syncopated song alluded to differences between opera and ragtime, musical styles at opposite ends of the high-low cultural continuum, and the disparity and mayhem that occur when a performer versed in one approach attempts the other. The song worked because revues embraced both opera and ragtime as viable musical styles and allowed them equal footing.

"The Galli-Curci Rag" was just one of many instances where Romberg refers to classical music in his revue scores. At the beginning of the refrain to "On a Modern Wedding Day" from *The Passing Show of 1914*, he quotes Wagner's famous wedding march ("Here Comes the Bride") with its famous ascending perfect fourth and distinctive dotted rhythmic motif. Five years later, for *The Passing Show of 1919*, Romberg collaborated with Jean Schwartz on "America's Popular Song," a list song that includes quotes of famous classical melodies alongside references to Tin Pan Alley. Textual and musical allusions to Mendelssohn's "Spring Song," Rubinstein's "Melody in F," Chopin's "Fantasie-Impromptu," and the operas *Pagliacci*, *Aida*, and *Carmen* appear in the number. Again, audiences for revues would have understood and appreciated the full range of musical citations. (Irving Berlin, in the act 2 finale of his first musical comedy, *Watch Your Step* [1914], offered a similar treatment through a succession of popular dance-style versions of operatic standards, including *Aida* and *Rigoletto* as rags, *Carmen* as a tango, and *Pagliacci* as a one-step.)[32]

Ragtime songs were certainly not the only type of original music Romberg wrote for revues. Waltzes and marches, as popular in America as they were in Vienna, were also present. In his revues (as in his operettas), Romberg associates the waltz with love, particularly its more heartrending aspects such as lost love or the parting of lovers. This association forms a strong part of the history of the Tin Pan Alley waltz, for even in an early famous example, "After the Ball" (1894, music and lyrics by Charles K. Harris), the idea of loss and separation is at its core.

Romberg continued this tradition in his waltz songs. In the *Passing Show of 1914*, for example, the refrain of "Dreams from Out of the Past," marked *Valse lento*, has a lyric that evokes the memory of lost love. One couplet of Atteridge's lyric reads, "Many years have now departed / Since that day when love first started." Similarly, "Only for You" from *Maid in America*, again with words by Atteridge, is sung by a man who is leaving his beloved to go off to war in a "far-off distant clime." Since this revue appeared during World War I, the wartime reference had special resonance for the audience. Yet another example of this association is "The Golden Pheasant" from *Over the Top*. Matthew C. Woodward's lyric compares a lover to the Golden Pheasant: both will come home to love. This was certainly the hope of couples in the audience soon to be separated by war, and the wish of women in audience whose partners were overseas.

Furthering the trend of wartime references in revues, Romberg contributed several marches that accentuated Harold Atteridge's military or patriotic lyrics. These songs promoted the public's duty in supporting the war effort (following the Committee on Public Information's mission) and worked to influence public opinion regarding America's approaching entry into the conflict. *The Passing Show of 1916*, for example, featured "Liberty Number" (called "Ring Out, Liberty Bell" on the published sheet music), a Sousa-style march that promoted American patriotism. Romberg's score for *Doing Our Bit* included "For the Sake of Humanity," another patriotic march, this one with lyrics about making the world safe for democracy. The song originally concluded the first act, but after one month was moved to the end of the second act.[33] It thus became the revue's closing number, and the production closed with appropriate wartime sentiment. Another march in the show, the almost-title song "Doing My Bit" by Romberg and Tierney, by contrast, is a comic feature marked *Tempo di marcia* in which a soldier "does his bit" by eating with people of different nationalities.

In addition to writing ragtime songs, waltzes, and marches, Romberg also evoked various ethnicities through musical means in his revues. *The Passing Show of 1916* was particularly eclectic in this regard, with three different musical traditions appearing on stage. "(I've) A Little Bit o' Scotch (in Me)" referred to the Johnnie Walker liquid variety, and included drone fifths in the refrain with the idiomatic half-step grace notes associated with Scottish bagpipes, while "The Willow Tree" had a waltz refrain with strummed chords in the accompaniment meant to evoke the sound of the traditional Japanese koto. "Bedouin Girl," about a man who desires a Bedouin woman, evokes desert exoticism through chromatic appoggiaturas and passing tones. "Bedouin Girl" was especially significant because it reflected a broader and deeper fascination with the Arab world, the cultural phenomenon known as Orientalism.

Orientalism, according to historian Bernard Lewis, was an artistic movement that portrayed the Middle East and North Africa in a romantic, extravagant, and sometimes even pornographic manner.[34] (More about the aesthetic, cultural, and political implications of Orientalism will be discussed in chapter 6 in connection with *The Desert Song*.) Orientalism was a significant part of popular culture in the early twentieth century, and references to the Arab world frequently appeared in revues, including the *Passing Show* series. In the *Passing Show of 1914*, the fourth scene takes place in "A Persian Garden. A Thousand Years Ago" and features Omar Khayyam as one of its characters. The specific musical numbers bore the titles "Omar Khayyam," "Dreams from Out of the Past," and "Way Down East."[35] The first act of the *Passing Show of 1919* took place at the court of King Solomon and included the number "Shimmy à la Egyptian."[36] Orientalism was also a prominent feature in Romberg's debut show, *The Whirl of the World*. The revue's final scene took place at "The Arabian Night Ball at Madison Square Garden, New York," and included three songs: "Oh, Allah," "My Cleopatra Girl," and "Ragtime Arabian Nights." A popular manifestation of Orientalism in New York, the Arabian Night Ball was the real-life source for this second-generation version of American Orientalism.

Orientalist musical identifiers in revues were not terribly sophisticated and were generally limited to dotted rhythms (also characteristic of ragtime songs) and an emphasis on the minor second interval. The Orientalist semitone generally appeared as a melodic ornament: a chromatic neighbor tone,

Example 2.2. "Ragtime Arabian Nights" *(The Whirl of the World)*, verse, mm. 1–4.

a passing tone, or an appoggiatura. Static harmonic rhythm was also a salient feature of Orientalist songs in revues.

A typical example of Romberg's early musical Orientalism is "Ragtime Arabian Nights," mentioned earlier with regard to its ragtime elements. When it comes to Orientalist musical identifiers, these are most pronounced at the beginning of the verse, where the first four measures of the melody consist entirely of half steps. The central melodic pitch, G, is surrounded by F-sharps and A-flats, all of which are half-step neighbor tones. This chromaticism provides musical interest above the unchanging C minor underlying harmony. Chromatic melodic embellishment and static harmony thus establish the created Oriental sound world. (See example 2.2.)

Romberg used this same technique in the waltz refrain of "Way Down East," where chromatic neighbor tones surround the otherwise diatonic melody, and again in "Bedouin Girl," where half-step passing and neighbor tones embellish the tune. These examples are exceptional, however. Most of Romberg's music for numbers with Orientalist titles are ordinary ragtime songs, with no discernible exotic musical identifiers. Occasional chromatic passing tones appear, but this is standard musical practice and does not suggest or signify any overt programmatic association. The syncopation and rhythmic anticipation of strong beats, inherent characteristics of ragtime songs, are the dominant musical properties of most of Romberg's Orientalist music for revues. Romberg hints at Orientalism but is not consistent in using Orientalist musical properties as a way to enhance a sense of place in his revues. This was accomplished instead through set design, costumes, and song lyrics.

Musical Comedy of the 1910s

The musical comedy of the 1910s is closely related to the revue. The genres share a similar musical language that is rooted in American popular song. Musical comedies differ from revues, however, by their greater emphasis on the narrative aspect of the production, or the "book." Songs are related to a plot, either tangentially or integrally, in a musical comedy, as opposed to existing as largely independent entities in a revue. The stories in musical comedy are based on humor, as the name suggests. They are typically set in the present and usually involve ordinary people who find themselves in extraordinary circumstances. While Romberg approached musical comedy in several different ways, he always considered the needs of the genre as a whole and the specific musical-dramatic requirements of each show.

Jolson's Musical Comedies

Al Jolson was undoubtedly the Shuberts' greatest star and the only one for whom they truly could take full credit.[37] During the 1910s and early '20s, he appeared in numerous Shubert-produced shows, usually at the Winter Garden, and in 1927 he starred in one of the first talking movie musicals, *The Jazz Singer*. Jolson and the Shuberts were well suited for each other, for they were fierce in all their business dealings but maintained strong mutual respect.[38]

Trained in the Jewish cantorial tradition, Jolson was best known on stage for his recurring role of Gus, a wisecracking servant drawn from minstrelsy. Consistent with its roots, the character was performed in blackface. Jolson first appeared as Gus in *Whirl of Society* (1912) and reprised the role in several shows, including four for which Romberg contributed music. The first, *Dancing Around* (October 10, 1914, Winter Garden), was a revue, while the other three, *Robinson Crusoe, Jr.* (February 17, 1916, Winter Garden), *Sinbad* (February 14, 1918, Winter Garden), and *Bombo* (October 6, 1921, Jolson's), were musical comedies.[39] The songs for Jolson's shows came from various authors, including Jolson himself. Songs were freely added and deleted at Jolson's will, even from performance to performance.

Each of the three Jolson-Romberg musical comedies incorporates an overarching framing story. This clever dramaturgical technique allows aspects of the show to remain in the present day while permitting various scenes that recall and emulate the splendor and spectacle of the revue to take place anytime and anywhere. Audiences now had a dramatic plot to follow, though not a terribly sophisticated or challenging one. The framing tales for *Robinson Crusoe, Jr.*, *Sinbad*, and *Bombo*, all by Harold Atteridge, remove these works from the world of thematically unified revues and place them into the realm of narrative-driven musical comedies.

The framing stories all involve contemporary fictional Americans, most of whom possess substantial wealth. *Robinson Crusoe, Jr.* features millionaire Hiram Westbury, who, exhausted after dealing with a film crew that wants to make a movie on his Long Island estate, falls asleep and dreams that he is Robinson Crusoe, Jr. His chauffeur, Gus (Jolson), becomes Good Friday, and together they visit several visually splendid locales (as opposed to staying on one deserted island, as in Daniel Defoe's novel). Similarly, *Sinbad* opens at a Long Island country club, where a wealthy socialite, Nan Van Decker, is trying to decide which of two men she should trust in a financial matter. She looks into a crystal ball and in it "sees" the extravagant locales of the Middle East and their inhabitants, including the porter Inbad (Jolson), an Arabian incarnation of the Long Island valet Gus. Finally, in *Bombo*, American explorer Jack Christopher and Gus, who is now a cook, are visiting Genoa. After participating in some magic tricks at Count Garibaldi's castle, they are transformed into Christopher Columbus and his servant Bombo. In all three shows, the innovative framing device provides dramatic narrative unity while still allowing ample opportunities for Jolson to display his talents as the show's unchallenged star.

As a staff composer for the Shuberts and the one most closely associated with the Winter Garden, Romberg was, at least on paper, heavily involved with all three shows. He was listed as a principal composer, which meant that he theoretically had control over the music. Jolson, though, was the one with the real power: the star did not perform any of Romberg's music in these shows, leaving that task to others in the cast. Instead, he sang specialty songs by other writers. Among the Jolson standards introduced in these musical comedies were "Rock-a-Bye Your Baby with a Dixie Melody" (*Sinbad*), "Swanee" and "My Mammy" (*Sinbad*'s national tour), "Toot, Toot, Tootsie! (Goodbye)" (*Bombo*), and "April Showers" and "California, Here I Come" (*Bombo*'s national tour).[40]

Romberg's music for these shows, therefore, was the aural backdrop for Jolson's legendary stage performances. Jolson's songs stood out because they were substantially different from Romberg's contributions. Romberg was of course aware of his role in the overall scheme of things, and knew that his music had to take a backseat to Jolson's song and dance routines.

When it came to the secondary role of Romberg's music in a Jolson show, *Bombo* constitutes the worst-case scenario. Although Jolson did not sing Romberg's music in the other two productions, he at least allowed others to do so. In *Bombo*, sadly enough, there were instances where *none* of Romberg's music was performed. On some nights, Jolson asked the audience if they wanted to hear him sing or see the rest of the show. When they voted in his favor, he dismissed the cast, lowered the curtain, and entertained them.[41] In his now solo act, Jolson performed five songs, none of which were by the show's "official" composer, Romberg.[42]

In the end, Romberg's lasting contributions to the Jolson musical comedies were modest, if not negligible, especially since the great star did not sing any of the official composer's music. Despite the less-than-ideal creative environment, Romberg still wrote some worthwhile music for these shows. His decisions regarding musical style reflected the same compositional choices he made when writing for revues. Since two of the three shows appeared at the revue-associated Winter Garden, and because plots for the Jolson shows were framing devices for revue-like skits, this similarity is indeed expected. Two examples from the Jolson shows prove this connection. In the first, from *Robinson Crusoe, Jr.*, a waltz functions as a musical depiction of emotional separation, while in the second, from *Sinbad*, Orientalist musical identifiers are used in order to establish a sense of place.

Robinson Crusoe, Jr.'s framing tale, as mentioned earlier, concerned filmmakers who exhaust a millionaire to the point that he falls asleep. Subsequently, his dreams appear onstage and constitute the bulk of the show. One of the musical numbers set on Long Island, "When You're Starring in the Movies," is an extended musical sequence for Howell Lauder, the director of "The Shameless Players' Film Co.," and "Leading Lady." Lauder's homonymic name ("Howl Louder") is indicative of the type of humor heard throughout the play, while "Leading Lady" is that character's only name in the show. The scene includes a melodrama during which the two performers enact various screen scenarios. In one segment, a husband is bidding farewell to his wife and baby as he leaves for war. The underscoring here, significantly, is a waltz, and Romberg ties the waltz to a particular dramatic function as an aural symbol of separation and loss.

In a similar technique of employing specific musical means to achieve certain dramatic ends, Romberg's use of Orientalist musical identifiers (namely ornamental minor seconds, syncopations, and dotted rhythms) in the music for *Sinbad* helps distinguish between the show's framing story and its crystal ball scenes. In "A Thousand and One Arabian Nights," for example, Jack (Franklyn A. Batie), a wealthy Long Islander, sings of his desire to be in the Arab world. His music is straightforward, unashamedly and blatantly void of syncopation and dotted rhythms. The song's lack of Orientalist musical identifiers tells the audience that it is not sung in the Orient but rather at a Long Island country club. On the other hand, "Bagdad" and "The Rag-Lad of Bagdad" are filled with Orientalist musical identifiers. "Bagdad," sung by Jack's Arab alter ego, The Cobbler, is a tribute to the city and has an overabundance of chromatic passing tones. The melody of "The Rag-Lad of Bagdad," a collaboration between Romberg and Jolson, emphasizes dotted rhythms and syncopations, just as any decent ragtime song should. But near the end of the verse a descending scale with an augmented second gives a strong sense of the musical Other. Romberg's Orientalist portrayals are not terribly sophisticated (there is no reason for them to be so—this is a Winter Garden show, after all) and come from a relatively basic use of chromaticism. Jack, incidentally, gains the trust and even becomes the beau of the Long Island socialite whose crystal ball–gazing drives the show's plot.

Emulating Revues

As the Jolson shows with their framing stories demonstrate, there is a strong relationship between revues and musical comedies. Both have star-centered specialty numbers, but the presence of a linear plot, or book, gives the musical comedies a narrative unity that is not part of the basic revue aesthetic.

Romberg never really seemed to make his musical comedies work. His musical comedy scores pale in comparison to those of his illustrious contemporaries Jerome Kern, George Gershwin, Harry Tierney, Vincent Youmans, and Richard Rodgers, all of whom succeeded in creating outstanding examples of the genre. In his musical comedies, Romberg never seemed to be able to connect the songs to the *spirit* of the libretto, as others were able to do. Instead, Romberg had to rely on aspects of the revue or the operetta in order to fulfill the musical-dramatic requirements. Of the seven musical comedies Romberg wrote between 1915 and 1923, not counting the Jolson vehicles, the music for five of them is in the style of revues, while that for the other two relies heavily upon operetta elements.

The musical comedies that bear strong resemblances to revues all have narrative plots, the element that distinguishes them from revues. With the exception of the two productions that appeared at the Winter Garden (*Monte Cristo, Jr.* and *The Dancing Girl*), Romberg collaborated with different lyricists and librettists on each show. (Harold Atteridge, the Shuberts' in-house lyricist, provided the words for the Winter Garden musical comedies.) If he had had a regular wordsmith well versed in the field of flashy and witty musical comedy, his reputation in the genre might have been greater; but then again, perhaps it would not have made any difference.

The plots of the musical comedies varied as well. *Hands Up* (July 22, 1915, 44th Street) is a detective yarn in which amateur sleuths are looking for a stolen ruby ring. Romberg collaborated with E. Ray Goetz, who was also the show's lyricist, on the score, and Edgar Smith provided the libretto for the self-described "musico-comico-filmo-melodrama." *Monte Cristo, Jr.* (February 12, 1919, Winter Garden) has a framing story similar to the Jolson shows, which is not surprising since Atteridge, who wrote the Jolson-Romberg libretti, was the show's lyricist and librettist. In this instance, Monte falls asleep and dreams that he is Dantes, an actor who is playing the title role in a stage version of Alexandre Dumas's *The Count of Monte Cristo*. Romberg collaborated with Jean Schwartz on the score, which closely resembles those for the Jolson vehicles. *Love Birds* (March 15, 1921, Apollo) is an Orientalist adventure tale with a book by Edgar Allen Woolf and lyrics by Ballard Macdonald, while *The Blushing Bride* (February 6, 1922, Astor), with book and lyrics by Cyrus Wood, revolves around a rotund millionaire and his romantic exploits.[43] Finally, *The Dancing Girl* (January 24, 1923, Winter

Garden), with book and lyrics by Atteridge, is about a Spanish dancer and her romance with a wealthy man. Each of these shows begins in the present in a place familiar to New Yorkers (a fashionable shop in *Love Birds* and a cabaret in *The Blushing Bride*, for example), thus endorsing the musical comedy's notion of having plots rooted in the present time and place.

All five shows include a variety of musical styles, as would be expected, but syncopated songs with prominent dotted rhythms, like the ragtime songs Romberg wrote for revues, are the most prominent. For example, Romberg's contributions to *Hands Up* include two songs with overt ragtime references. The first, "(On) The Levee Along Broadway," glorifies ragtime and its popularity on Broadway. Goetz's self-referential lyric and Romberg's syncopated music are well matched, especially in phrases such as "sweet plantation syncopation." The second, "Evolution of Ragtime (Evolution of a Rag)," concludes the first act and is another endorsement of the style's immense popularity.

Likewise, foxtrots pepper *The Blushing Bride*. Three songs from the show, "A Regular Girl," "Mr. and Mrs.," and "Rosy Posy," are all labeled "fox trot song" on the printed sheet music.[44] All three have melodies that emphasize smaller intervals; skips of more than a fourth are rare. Gentle syncopations alternate with passages of dotted rhythms, creating the relaxed, unhurried musical atmosphere associated with the dance.

Syncopated dances were not the only popular steps from the 1910s that Romberg appropriated for his musical comedies. The seductive tango, popularized in Buenos Aires and arriving in New York via Paris, where "tango teas" were in fashion among upper-class society, quickly made its way to Broadway. *Hands Up* featured "(Sing Sing) Tango Tea," the lyrics of which tell of crooks imprisoned at Sing Sing pouring themselves a formal tea. Then, in *Monte Cristo, Jr.*, the stylish tango "Marseilles" is an homage to the French city frequented by the wealthy—the very people who would dance the night away in the tight embrace of a tango.

Monte Cristo, Jr., *Love Birds*, and *The Dancing Girl* each have anomalies in their musical depictions that make them especially intriguing. Jolson's reputation haunted *Monte Cristo, Jr.*, since it immediately followed *Sinbad* at the Winter Garden. Some critics feared that the competition would be too fierce, especially since the overall format of the shows was the same.[45] This was not the case, for the show enjoyed a reasonably long run of 254 performances. The reason for its success was its star, Charles Purcell (1883–1962). Purcell had a strong reputation in operetta, having starred in *The Blue Para-*

dise and *Maytime*, both with Romberg scores, before appearing in *Monte Cristo, Jr.* His stage presence, which was that of a sentimental and gentle leading man, was radically different from that of Jolson, the supreme ego-driven showman. Most of the score, however, whether sung by Purcell or by someone else in the cast, has a relatively narrow range, basically stepwise motion, and gentle syncopations—the hallmarks of Jolson's style. Operetta-style numbers with their wide ranges and technical vocal demands, which one would expect in a show starring Purcell, are not present. This show gave its leading man the chance to show his flexibility at various musical styles, something he accomplished most admirably.

Just as operetta numbers were lacking in a show featuring an operetta singer, the chromatic inflections associated with musical Orientalism are notably absent from the Arab-inspired *Love Birds*. This is indeed surprising, for the musical comedy's libretto is part of a tradition of harem tales in which Western women find themselves in Eastern lands, a line that includes Mozart's *Die Entführung aus dem Serail* (*The Abduction from the Seraglio*, 1781) and Rudolf Valentino's film *The Sheik* among its most famous examples. (*The Sheik* appeared in 1921, the same year as *Love Birds*; both works are indicative of the marketability of harem tales at the time.) It is the visual dimension that sets the show in the Muslim world, for the musical numbers in *Love Birds*, clever as they are, reside squarely in the revue tradition.

Love Bird's principal song was "Two Little Love Birds," the melody of which bore a recognizably close resemblance to Christian Sinding's "Rustle of Spring" (discussed in chapter 1). This melody at the heart of this Orientalist musical sounded so inherently Western European that critics compared it to the work of a *Norwegian* composer. Sinding was not even among those usually associated with musical Orientalism such as Alexander Borodin (*Prince Igor, On the Steppes of Central Asia*) or Camille Saint-Saëns (*Samson et Delilah*). The immediate "here and now" aspect of the musical comedy took precedence over the inclusion of exotic elements in the musical score.

"Fat-Fat-Fatima" and "I Love to Go Swimmin' with Wimmin'" were two of the show's other principal numbers. (Both appeared in the film *Deep in My Heart*, though they were placed into different shows.) The three evenly accented driving beats of FAT FAT FATima, as performed in the show by the Emir and his guests, provide a vivid contrast to the short / short-LONG-short / short-LONG-short / short-LONG rhythmic pattern in the melody of "I Love to

Go Swimmin' with Wimmin'." The heaviness of the first song balances the buoyancy of the second.

Love Birds featured some fine performers, but it was the veteran vaudevillian Pat Rooney in a cameo role who stood out because of his acrobatic routines and vaudeville-based character dancing.[46] Rooney's rendition of "I Love to Go Swimmin' with Wimmin'," accompanied by the harem girls, was one of the show's highlights. After *Love Birds* closed on Broadway, Rooney and his vaudeville partner Marion Bent, who played the bit part of Mamie O'Grady, bought the rights to the show, rewrote the libretto to increase their roles, changed some of the music, and took the revised production on a national tour.

The third show in this "missing the obvious" subset of musical comedies is *The Dancing Girl*. A number of complex issues surrounded the show, not the least of which was the unusually large number of contributing composers. Although Romberg was the principal writer, the show also included music by George Gershwin, A. J. Carey, Alfred Goodman, and Cole Porter. Stylistic unity was not a concern. Second was the physical space, for the production also inaugurated a renovated Winter Garden house; the building's fine architectural details had been restored and the famous "Bridge of Thighs" removed. A great deal of attention was given to the Winter Garden itself, and less to the show that appeared on its stage. As if there were not already enough convoluted distractions, critics (and probably some audience members) could not agree as to whether *The Dancing Girl* was a revue or a musical comedy; in other words, they could not concur on the existence of a plot! Some called it a revue, since it appeared at the Winter Garden, while others pointed out the importance of the plot, calling attention to the very existence of a driving narrative as something unusual for a Winter Garden show.[47]

These confusions aside, the show's title character is Anna, a Spanish beauty (played by the dancer Trini) who is traveling steerage on board a ship to the United States. She dances her way through the show, mostly to flamenco-style numbers.[48] Her love interest, the wealthy Bruce Chattfield (Arthur Margetson), has no solo numbers and only two duets with Anna. But a musical needs a lead singer, and in *The Dancing Girl* it turns out to be one of Anna's fellow steerage passengers, an Italian tenor named Rudolpho. His music encompasses the full gamut of styles, from opera to street songs. (Nelson Eddy's character, Paul Allison, does the same thing in the 1937 film version of *Maytime*, discussed in chapter 9.) Just as Anna was danced by a real dancer, Rudolpho was sung by a real singer, Tom Burke (1890–1969). Burke was an English tenor who sang several times at Covent Garden both before and after his appearance in *The Dancing Girl*.[49] Known to opera audiences as Thomas Burke, he was, because of his appearance in that production, what in the early twenty-first century would be called a "crossover" artist, a person who sang comfortably in a variety of styles. So, the lead singer in this musical comedy was an opera singer, but one whose role in the plot was secondary. The fascinatingly ambiguous nature of musical theater genres in the early twentieth century is clearly evident here.

Romberg's revue-derived musical comedies hold historical interest as much for what they lack as for what they include. Some blame for the failure of these shows could be placed on the book writers, the all-too-often guilty party when Broadway musicals fail. But here, the music is also to blame. Romberg's musical comedy scores do not have the same modern exuberance as those of his contemporaries. Romberg was much more comfortable in the gentler ragtime-inspired music of the 1910s.

Nowhere is this assertion more obvious than in the film *Deep in My Heart*. Three musical comedy songs by Romberg appear in the film. They are included as independent songs, removed from their original contexts and placed on-screen into shows from the previous decade.

"Mr. and Mrs.," one of the foxtrots from *The Blushing Bride*, is credited as a song from *The Midnight Girl*. In the film rendition, the duple-meter ballad is followed by two dance repeats of the refrain. Its choreographic roots are thus maintained. When it comes to historical veracity, Romberg actually did contribute two songs ("On the Lonely Lagoon" and "Oh, You John") to *The Midnight Girl* (February 23, 1914, 44th Street), an adaptation of the German-language *Das Mitternachtsmädel*, with music by Adolf Philipp (1864–1936).[50] Both of Romberg's songs, however, were dropped during the show's run. *The Midnight Girl*, therefore, was not a high point for Romberg in his early Broadway career, but it appeared in *Deep in My Heart* nonetheless, with music from an altogether different show.

Two previously mentioned songs from *Love Birds* round out the film's musical comedy selections: "Fat-Fat-Fatima" and "I Love to Go Swimmin' with Wimmin'." "Fat-Fat-Fatima" is part of the *Jazzadoo* routine, while Gene and Fred Kelly (as the O'Brien Brothers) perform "I Love to Go Swimmin' with Wimmin'" as part of *Dancing Around*. This production was a revue from 1914, and, anachronisms aside, the fact that the song fit comfortably into a revue setting ably illustrates the similarity between musical styles for revues and musical comedies. The sailor costumes and stage-prop waves as seen in *Deep in My Heart*, not to mention a performance by two men, are a far cry from the harem setting of the original with a vaudeville dancer and Arab-clad female chorus. Despite the complete change in staging and dramatic placement, the song still entertains.

The actual shows from which the songs originate, *Love Birds* and *The Blushing Bride*, appeared in 1921 and 1922, respectively. In the film the featured shows, *The Midnight Girl* and *Dancing Around*, are historically much earlier—both are from 1914—while *Bombo*, the historical counterpart to *Jazzadoo*—is from 1921. This temporal adjustment is telling, for the film's creators easily make two musical comedy songs ("Mr. and Mrs." and "I Love to Go Swimmin' with Wimmin'") appear as if they are from the previous decade. Romberg's writing for musical comedy is thus shown to be old-fashioned, too dated for "modern" musical comedies from the 1920s. Even with "Fat-Fat-Fatima" appearing in *Jazzadoo*, this was the Jolson-inspired routine, and Jolson was associated with the earlier style of musical comedy.

Operetta in Musical Comedy

Romberg preferred the "old type of musical comedy" with the gentle and occasional syncopations of ragtime to more "modern" varieties. But holding even more appeal for Romberg than revue-style numbers was the genre with which he fell in love during his youth—operetta. Romberg incorporated operetta elements in two bona fide musical comedies: *The Melting of Molly* (December 30, 1918, Broadhurst) and *Poor Little Ritz Girl* (July 28, 1920, Central). Both shows are set in the present, a musical comedy trademark, and both have plenty of duple-meter ragtime-inspired numbers, another musical comedy sign. Romberg's music for the shows, however, rather than consistently endorsing the jaunty here and now, often evokes the sound and spirit of operetta in very powerful ways.

In the late 1910s, Americans were increasingly concerned about their weight and physical appearance; hence, a dieting craze was sweeping the country.[51] *The Melting of Molly* capitalized on this fad. Romberg collaborated with librettist Maria Thompson Davies and lyricist Cyrus Wood to tell the story of Molly Carter (Isabelle Lowe), a Virginia woman of means who is obsessed with appearances. While Molly's fiancé, Alfred, is away on a four-year (!) diplomatic mission to London, she gains an enormous amount of weight. She also meets a physician, the athletic and handsome

Dr. John Moore (Charles Purcell), who just happens to specialize in weight loss. When Molly hears that Alfred's return is imminent, she begins a fierce diet regimen under the direction of Dr. Moore and sheds her unwanted pounds. All is well until Alfred returns and Molly is shocked to see that *he* is now obese. Disgusted by his appearance, she breaks off the engagement and instead marries the muscular Dr. Moore.

Operetta star Charles Purcell played the physician with the physique, and likewise sang some of the show's most romantic waltzes, including "Darling" and "You Remember Me," the central love duet. The vaulting, expansive, and sentimental "You Remember Me" has strong vestiges of "Will You Remember?," the principal waltz from the previous year's operetta *Maytime*, in both title and musical style. Not coincidentally, Purcell was also the star of *Maytime*. Dr. Moore's music is firmly entrenched in operetta, befitting the fame and reputation of the actor who played the role.

Since the romantic male lead is a doctor, several numbers in the score refer to his profession, but in a musical comedy vein rather than an operetta one. He is an operetta character—his occupation, though, appears as pure musical comedy. "Jazz All Your Troubles Away," with lyrics by Augustus Barratt, is an ensemble number that endorses early Jazzercise: dancing to jazz music is a good way to keep fit. Marked "slow fox trot," the song includes a prevalence of dotted rhythms and syncopations. "Oh! Doctor, Doctor" is a lighthearted and bubbly comic number in duple meter, replete with dotted rhythms, in which the female chorus members proclaim their ardent desires to have an appointment with the medical professional. The titles of both numbers have double entendres, jazz and playing doctor both being euphemisms for sex. These songs refer back to Romberg's practice in his revues of using syncopation as a musical indicator of sexual prowess. Romberg's ability to write revue-style musical comedy is apparent in these specialty numbers; however, the waltzes—the operetta-style numbers—are without a doubt the strongest songs in the show.

Similarly, elements of both operetta and musical comedy appear in *Poor Little Ritz Girl*. Here, aspects of the generally plotless revue join the stylistic pair, making it a trio and paving the way for works such as the seminal *Show Boat* (1927), where again all three genres coalesce.

Poor Little Ritz Girl is unfortunately remembered primarily as the Rodgers and Hart show whose book was rewritten and whose score was largely replaced with one by Romberg, all without the knowledge of its original creators. While this is certainly true, the show also represents a significant change in the conceptualization of musical comedy.[52] Lew Fields (1867–1941), the show's producer, articulated an idea as early as 1904 for a type of musical comedy with a believable plot, characters who develop over the course of the show, and a true integration of music and story. He came very close to realizing this concept with *Poor Little Ritz Girl*.

The show drew together several strands of musical theater practices. At its heart was a Cinderella story: the ingénue Barbara (Eleanor Griffith) arrives in New York to find fame and fortune on stage and "rents" a luxury apartment for next to nothing from an unscrupulous janitor. Unbeknownst to Barbara, the apartment she supposedly rented already has a tenant, the wealthy William "Billy" Pembroke (Charles Purcell), who returns home to find Barbara in his bedroom. In the end, after the plot becomes a humorously innocent "bedroom comedy," and after plenty of rehearsal and performance sequences of the farce in which Barbara is appearing, entitled *Poor Little Ritz Girl*, Barbara and Billy marry. George Campbell and Fields, who created the story, modeled the show on the Princess Theatre musicals of Guy Bolton, P. G. Wodehouse, and Jerome Kern, where humor arose from the situation and from the characters. The "show within a show" approach was one of its other innovative elements, as well as the idea of having a musical based on the life of a chorus member, something that was epitomized over a half century later in *A Chorus Line* (1975, conceived and directed by Michael Bennett, music by Marvin Hamlisch, lyrics by Edward Kleban). Furthermore, Fields was a firm believer in the power of stagecraft. As such, he employed huge "jackknife wagons" that swung away to reveal the Frivolity Theater stage (home of the farce) behind them.

While the final version of the show was a great public success, playing to packed houses for 119 performances and deemed by critic Heywood Brown "an amusing and ingenious musical comedy," the show and its creative team underwent massive changes from what it had been when rehearsals began in early April.[53] At that time, a songwriting team from the Winter Garden, Al Bryan and George Meyer, were to create the score, and Adeline Leitzback was to be the librettist. Bryan and Meyer's score proved unsatisfactory, and since Fields was already over budget, he hired Richard Rodgers and Lorenz Hart, whose musical theater experience to date had been as creators of Varsity shows at Columbia University, to write their first professional score. The result was a combination of earlier songs with new lyrics by Hart and original songs written expressly for *Poor Little Ritz Girl*. (One additional recycled song that appeared in the show, "Mary, Queen of Scots," had music by Rodgers and lyrics by Herbert Fields, Lew's son and later an important Broadway producer.)

The production underwent almost daily rewrites: new librettists, Henry B. Stillman and William J. O'Neil, were brought on board, and the show's pre-Broadway tryout began at the Shubert-Wilbur Theatre in Boston on May 28. Critics were unimpressed, and Fields demanded a complete reworking. Concerned about the show's New York reception, he brought in yet another new book writer, George Campbell, and yet another songwriting team, this one—like the first—with experience at the Winter Garden: Sigmund Romberg and Alex Gerber. The final result, unlike the Boston tryout, was a resounding success.

All was not wonderful at the opening night, however, for Rodgers and Hart had not been told that eight of their songs—half of their contribution—had been cut. They came expecting to hear their own score, but instead, were shocked and humiliated to hear songs by Romberg and Gerber along with *some* of their music. The experience devastated Rodgers, who was spending the summer as a counselor at a boy's camp. He related his response to the events in his autobiography, *Musical Stages:* "[E]ven now, more than fifty years later, I can still feel the grinding pain of bitter disappointment and depression. I didn't want my parents at the opening, but since there was no way to keep them out, we sat and suffered together until they took me to the train to go back to camp—one badly bruised unconquering hero."[54]

Though many of his songs were cut, Richard Rodgers received strong attention from the press. His modernity of style was recognized, as was the difference between his musical approach and that of Romberg. Heywood Brown wrote in the *New York Tribune*, "The more serious and sentimental songs are from Sigmund Romberg, and they are pleasing but hardly as striking as the lighter numbers."[55]

Even in 1920, the "new" style of Rodgers and the "old" one of Romberg was beginning to be identified—and neither composer had even begun to reach the pinnacle of his career. Rodgers's melodies have plenty of the dotted rhythms and gentle syncopations typical of the era, but his harmonic language shows signs of tremendous ingenuity. "Love's Intense in Tents," for example, has a wonderful harmonic surprise at the words "rents increase" when a tonally foreign G-flat chord appears in the D-major context.[56]

Romberg's contributions to *Poor Little Ritz Girl* are much less daring and consist largely of sentimental and nostalgic numbers that recall the sound world of the operetta. Several critics noticed this, including the one who wrote: "There is nothing particularly inspiring in the music, but it has a pleasant lilt, that by Sigmund Romberg being in his best Viennese style."[57]

Romberg's "best Viennese style" meant waltzes. The most prominent waltz in *Poor Little Ritz Girl*, "When I Found You," constitutes the act 1 finale. Sung by Romberg's by-now-familiar leading man Charles Purcell, this was at first his only solo song in the show. (A second song, "Dear Heart My Heart Sweetheart," with music and lyrics by Bide Dudley and Fred [Ted] Barron, was added during the second week of the run.)[58] Considering that this was a musical comedy and that the title role did not belong to the operetta-singing Purcell, his relatively minor part in the show is understandable. Furthermore, Purcell's stilted performance was one of the few things in the show to receive negative criticism.

The refrain of "When I Found You" contains the most overt Viennese waltz reference in the entire score: a caesura after the second beat. Viennese waltzes are known for their idiosyncratic elongation of the second beat; but here, Romberg prolongs the second beat even further by completely stopping the musical flow immediately afterward. He does not do this in every measure, only before the final measures of each phrase. By having steady, predictable rhythmic motion prior to the break (a melody consisting initially of only dotted half notes before moving into even quarter-note motion), Romberg is thus able to draw even more attention to the disruption. (See example 2.3.)

Romberg also wrote two songs and an instrumental number to be performed as part of the farce's New York opening night. The slow ballad "In the Land of Yesterday" was a celebration of nostalgia. The past is idealized in the lyric, and the musical language is decidedly uncomplicated. The other song, "The Bombay Bombashay," though filled with textual references to India and a syncopated dance seen in Bombay, is a characteristic ragtime song with gentle syncopations and dotted rhythms. The spirit of the lyrics and the musical setting are curiously at odds at one point in the verse, where the Oriental jazz band is being described as "playing melodies, freaky harmonies." One might expect something bizarre to be happening in the music at this moment, but instead, the harmony simply alternates between dominant seventh and tonic chords. This is a prime example of where Romberg's exclamation regarding the synthesis of text and music, "It fits," might apply to the syllables, but certainly not to their meaning.

The instrumental number is the graceful ballet "The Phantom Waltz." Danced by Dolly Clements (as Mlle. Lova) and Michael Cunningham (as

Example 2.3. "When I Found You" *(Poor Little Ritz Girl)*, refrain, mm. 1–8

M. Mordky, her partner), the dance garnered great praise from the critics, one of whom wrote, "'The Phantom Waltz,' an entirely lovely and melting fantasy presented by Dolly Clements and Michael, alone makes 'Poor Little Ritz Girl' worth your idle hour."[59] Another wrote, "One of the best numbers of the evening was 'The Phantom Waltz' . . . Mlle. Lova [using the character's name] proved that even in this era of handspring dancing the traditional technique of the real dancer is productive of grace and skill which will still be popular when the modern gymnast of the spotlight are all suffering from the gout."[60] Romberg's expansive music perfectly matched the sublime choreography.

While Romberg certainly does not employ any sort of Asian musical exoticism in "The Bombay Bombashay," he does so in "Pretty Ming Toy," another song from the farce. In the story, Barbara is describing the number for Billy when the jackknife wagons open to reveal it in a fully staged production. Romberg suggests the song's Chinese theme through an initial stream of parallel triads. After the introduction, though, all such indicators disappear and a typical ragtime song emerges.

Although *Poor Little Ritz Girl* was extremely popular, its production costs exceeded its potential profit. Lee Shubert, owner of the Central Theatre, the house where the musical played, decided that a film would bring in more money for the theater and closed the show.[61]

Romberg's work in musical comedy and revue, though not something he continued beyond the mid-1920s, nonetheless constitutes a significant part of his career. It was here that Romberg acquired his working knowledge of American popular song idioms as well as notions of creating distinctive music for specific dramatic requirements. Ragtime songs, basic Orientalist identifiers, and plots set in the time and place of the audience that alluded to contemporary affairs: these were the basic elements of revue and musical comedy that Romberg infused into his operetta scores.

Romberg's operettas were rooted in the Viennese approach to the genre, but—because of the composer's experiences with revue and musical comedy—they were not mere pastiches of the Continental style. They were something quite distinctive: a masterful blend of Old and New Worlds. It is this synthesis of European and American principles that constitutes Romberg's approach to operetta.

CHAPTER 3

Staging Nostalgia: The Road to *Maytime*

ALTHOUGH ROMBERG ESTABLISHED HIMSELF ON BROADWAY IN THE 1910s as a composer of revues and, to a lesser degree, of musical comedies, he undoubtedly found his truest voice in the realm of operetta. Romberg's close involvement with the Viennese-inspired art form began less than two years after his Broadway debut with *The Whirl of the World* in January 1914. Knowing of his expertise and love of the genre, the ever-resourceful Shuberts asked Romberg to contribute new songs for an English-language adaptation of Edmund Eysler's *Ein Tag im Paradies* (*A Day in Paradise*, 1913), which they produced on Broadway as *The Blue Paradise* (August 5, 1915, Casino). This show, for which Romberg wrote his first notable operetta waltz, "Auf Wiedersehn," endorsed many of the precepts that defined operetta in America at the time. These included a shift away from European-based nomenclature (due to World War I), a detachment from Ruritania, and, most importantly, a simultaneous embrace of nostalgia and stage realism.

American operettas were certainly nothing new when Romberg's first original work in the genre, *Maytime*, appeared in 1917. Drawing on a long and varied history dating from the eighteenth century and featuring forms as diverse as burlesque, pantomime, opera comique, ballad opera, and grand opera, many notable operettas graced American stages in the latter decades of the nineteenth century—the same time that Romberg was acquiring his love and knowledge of Viennese operetta in Europe.[1] One of the most successful was *Robin Hood* (1891) by Reginald de Koven (1859–1920) and Harry B. Smith (1860–1936). This show not only proved the popularity and viability of the genre but also introduced the perennial wedding song "Oh, Promise Me."

"Royal" operettas that extolled some sort of Ruritanian roots were often seen on American stages during the early years of the twentieth century. Among the most famous was *The Prince of Pilsen* (1903), with music by Gustave Luders and lyrics by Frank Pixley. The tale concerned a Cincinnati brewer who, while vacationing in Nice, is mistaken for a German prince. Other works followed in the wake of the alliteratively titled triumph, including *The Duke of Duluth* (1903) and *The Duchess of Dantzic* (1905). When Lehár's *The Merry Widow* appeared in English translation in New York in 1907, audiences were already familiar with imaginary European realms and their disguised and misidentified royals.

The Shuberts adored operetta. It was one of the genres, along with the revue, upon which they built their musical theatrical legacy. The Shuberts' operetta productions successfully integrated the glamour and showmanship of the revue with the gentleness and sentiment of Viennese operetta. Numerous critics noticed their efforts, including an unnamed one who wrote in 1925, "During the last three seasons the Shuberts have developed a type of opera comique which may easily become our national musical expression."[2]

American operetta in the first quarter of the twentieth century was a multifarious affair, one that was strongly shaped by the eventualities of World War I and the end of the Habsburg Empire. Changes in the real world greatly affected those in the created realm of Ruritania, the favored setting for Viennese operetta at the turn of the century (discussed in the previous chapter). What continued, though, was the concept of a show focused on its musical score. Spoken dialogue separated the various types of musical numbers, many of which were still in the style of waltzes, marches, and assorted dances. The primary plot usually involved love between or across class lines, and a secondary love story between comic characters (foils for the high romantics) was common. Significantly, settings were somewhere other than the present time and place: operettas were glorious escapist works whose wondrous sets, costumes, and music made them feasts for the eyes and the ears.

Operetta certainly faced many challenges in the early twentieth century, the very name of the genre being among them. Romberg's works, especially those from the 1910s, were often called something other than operettas, though they were examples of the style. This avoidance of the term operetta was due largely to the association of the genre with Vienna: in the years surrounding World War I, this was not an alliance to be celebrated. The most common appellation was some version of "play with music." For example, *The Blue Paradise* (1914) was "a musical play in a prologue and two acts," *Maytime* (1917) was "a play with music in four acts," and *Blossom Time* (1921) was "a musical play in three acts."

By the 1920s, it again became acceptable to call works operettas, especially when they had European settings or characters. *The Student Prince* was "a spectacular operetta," while *Princess Flavia* (1925) was simply "an operetta" and *My Princess* (1927) "a modern operetta." *The Desert Song* (1926), though, was "a musical play," as were *The Love Call* (1927) and *Nina Rosa* (1930). *My Maryland* (1927) was "a musical romance," and *The New Moon* (1928) was billed as "a romantic musical comedy (musical romance)." This latter group of works, from *The Desert Song* on, did not have European settings but were operettas in all other respects. During the 1920s, the term operetta was synonymous with these other descriptors, for many of the works that were not called operettas on their playbills were referred to as such in the press and among the public.

World War I affected more than the nomenclature of operetta; it also transformed its spiritual core. Ruritania was no longer the land of dim-witted colorfully dressed inhabitants who were politically and economically inferior to the Viennese. These kingdoms were now lands filled with danger and evil foreboding. With the assassination of the Archduke Franz Ferdinand in Sarajevo, the geographic region that inspired the creation of Ruritania could no longer be imagined as a blissful land suspended in some sort of eternal dream state.

Just as Ruritania's initial creation took place in the literary realm, so did its postwar reinvention. First, the geographic area was no longer limited to the Balkans; it was now a pan-Slavic world. For example, Agatha Christie's novel *The Secret of Chimneys* (1925) takes place in Herzoslovakia, a country whose name is a fusion of Herzogovina and Czechoslovakia—two locales that are not next to each other on the physical map.[3] Second, the region now had inherent menacing qualities. Although from later in the century and filled with Cold War allusions, the created domain of Vulgaria, a play on Bulgaria, in the film version of *Chitty Chitty Bang Bang* (1968) alludes to this construction. Operetta writers such as Romberg, therefore, had to be much more careful in their choice of locales, for Ruritania was no longer an exclusively benign region of Europe.

Aside from the malevolent transformations, Ruritania still retained aspects of its benevolence in the form of a European *Volksmuseum*. This staging involved locals who were suspended in the nineteenth century, impervious to the realities of postwar Europe.[4] They were the same types of representations of the Balkans that permeated Ruritanian operetta before World War I—created place names and cultures happily existing in highly decorative isolation. The classic Peter Sellars film *The Mouse That Roared* (1959), again from the Cold War era, offers a superb example of this slant on Ruritanian life. The most significant result of these *Volk* incarnations, as far as operetta was concerned, was a powerful evocation of nostalgia for prewar Ruritania and its ideals.

The *Oxford English Dictionary* gives two definitions for nostalgia: "1) *Path* (Pathological): A form of melancholia caused by prolonged absence from one's own home or country; severe home-sickness. 2) *transf* (transferred sense): Regret or sorrowful longing *for* the conditions of a past age; regretful or wistful memory or recall of an earlier time."[5]

Both definitions are relevant to Romberg and his work. For this Hungarian, who spent a significant amount of time in Vienna, the psychological effects of World War I, not to mention the death tolls, were profound. In 1920, as a result of the Treaty of Trianon, Hungary lost two-thirds of its territory and one-third of its Hungarian-speaking population. The effects on the Hungarian psyche were immense, especially in a country with an already extraordinarily high suicide rate.[6] Romberg, proud of his Hungarian heritage, surely empathized with the suffering that was taking place in his native land.

It was not just the loss of Hungary but also of Vienna itself that deeply affected Romberg. Prewar Vienna had now joined the illusory realm of the imagination. In his romanticized biography of Romberg, *Deep in My Heart*, Elliott Arnold imagines a conversation between Franz Lehár and Romberg during which the Viennese composer tells his friend, who now lives in America: "We can live, we Viennese, only in art now. The world will know us only through the dreams of artists who remember. When you go back to America, do not forget Vienna. And through your eyes and through your art thousands of others will know how we once were."[7]

Whether or not this conversation actually took place, the alleged words capture the spirit of Romberg's nostalgia. Romberg yearned for the world Lehár described. As a magazine profiler related: "Sometimes, when he needed the refreshment of good companions and good conversation, he visits his friend, William R. Steinway, at Steinway Hall. . . . There he plays phrases from his new operetta and talks about the Europe of before-the-war.

And often his conversation turns to the world of the future—a world which he hopes will be a place of peace and beautiful music."[8]

Romberg's nostalgia for the past shaped his vision of the future: he longed for a world without the ravages of war. Although Romberg took his audiences to faraway places in his operettas, he was acutely aware of reality. In a heartfelt expression of his views during World War II, he wrote to Lt. Cdr. C. B. Cranford in September 1944: "Of course, it is very interesting today, to watch the Presidential campaign, (I am of course, a strong Democrat) and there is no doubt in my mind that Roosevelt will be re-elected. Nevertheless, with this terrible war going on, the masses of people are up in their education to the extent that they realize that all the things Dewey and Bricker say, is being said because of their desire to be elected, and nobody is paying much attention to any of the complaints the opposition may bring up. The only thing I am worried about as a private citizen, is how the powers to be will make peace, because unless the peace is properly established nothing can stop a third World War."[9]

Romberg, in his operettas, strove for a mixture of nostalgia and utopia. He attempted to purify the past, make it better than it was, in order to create a model for a future free from the menace of war. This is readily apparent in works such as *The Student Prince*, where it is nearly impossible to imagine that the idyllic Germany portrayed in the operetta was capable of being involved in two World Wars. This was Germany both how it *should have been* and how it *should be*.

Idealistic as he was, Romberg also possessed a keen sense of reality that gives a rational underpinning to his fundamentally nostalgic music and keeps it from becoming too maudlin. Reality was not something that could easily be eschewed. His concerns about Central Europe give extra poignancy to the music he created for lyrics such as "You will remember Vienna" (*Viennese Nights*) and "Give me some men who are stouthearted men, who will fight for the right they adore" *(The New Moon)*.

There is no question that nostalgia was a significant force in Romberg's creative mind. As a musical practitioner of nostalgia in the early twentieth century, he was certainly not alone. The attitude also figures prominently in the work of Antonin Dvořák, Gustav Mahler, and Charles Ives, among others.[10] Like his contemporaries, Romberg drew inspiration from nostalgia's inherent longing for the past in creating some of his finest music.

While nostalgia can and does operate on private, psychological levels, it is in the public sphere where its effects are most pronounced. As Svetlana

Boym asserts, "Nostalgia is about the relationship between individual biography and the biography of groups or nations, between personal and collective memory."[11] In this context, nostalgia operates as a communal experience, and, as such, becomes a social phenomenon. Audiences flocked to operettas to participate in this collective encounter with the world of the imagination. It is no wonder that operettas were among the most popular musical theater offerings during the 1920s: they provided the necessary impetus for audiences to indulge in their collective nostalgic feelings for a prewar society.

Robert Davis and B. Scully, in their review of a revival of *The Student Prince* that took place in Boston in 1941, noted this longing: "There is nothing like a well-loved melody to revive nostalgic memories, and the songs in this Romberg operetta are guaranteed to bring back a Germany of romance, legend and beauty. One forgets the Nazi empire of 1941 in the idealistic Heidelberg of the golden days of which Dr. Engel and his royal pupil sing so glowingly."[12]

The same writers noted in the *Christian Science Monitor*: "In these days of disaster in Europe, too, 'The Student Prince' not only brings back happy recollections of personal experience for many people, but for many others it recalls with equal glamour, an earlier, happier, and more colorful era."[13]

Nostalgic yearning was balanced in American operetta by the new direction of dramatic realism and theatricality associated with David Belasco (1853–1931). Belasco, nicknamed the "Bishop of Broadway," dominated New York theater as playwright, actor, director, and impresario in the early years of the twentieth century. Richard Eyre and Nicholas Wright call him "a combination of the opportunistic showman and the artistic adventurer."[14] Belasco wanted everything on stage—the actors as well as the sets—to appear as real as possible. Theatrical veracity was paramount.

Belasco and the Shuberts had a common history, for it was supposedly Belasco who provided Sam Shubert's entry into show business. As the story goes, Belasco was stage manager and casting director for a show called *May Blossoms* in Syracuse in 1885. He needed an extra, and hired the young Sammy Shubert. Belasco's grandiose manner impressed the young man, who began to emulate the impresario not only in speech and gestures but also in physical appearance. Lee and J. J. recognized the significance of Belasco in the early days of their brother's career, and memorialized the link in the titles of two of their most famous operetta adaptations, *Maytime* (1917) and *Blossom Time* (1921).[15] May and blossoms, the two words in the title of the 1885 play, appeared in the titles of these pivotal works, both—

not incidentally—with scores by Romberg. Belasco's spirit loomed large over the Shuberts' concept of operetta. The Shuberts, as producers, ensured that Belasco's approach to stagecraft was present in their shows.

This quest for authenticity, when combined with nostalgia and new concepts of Ruritania, certainly posed a challenge for operetta creators in America. Since the musical score was the centerpiece of an operetta, composers, including Romberg, needed to write music that enhanced these new dramatic requirements.

Adaptations

In the early years of the twentieth century, many Viennese composers began to write specifically with exportation in mind, particularly to the English-language stages of the world, including those in North America.[16] New York producers, including the Shuberts, subsequently engaged their staff creators to adapt these imported works for American audiences. The Shuberts, knowing that Romberg was intrinsically familiar with Viennese operetta, assigned him this responsibility for their shows. (While working on these adaptations, Romberg continued writing for the Shuberts' revues and musical comedies.) Romberg's knowledge of the original repertory and its dramatic and musical style, along with his experience with revues and musical comedies, made him an ideal choice for this sort of work. Before the huge successes *Maytime* and *Blossom Time*, Romberg redressed four European works for the American stage, the results being *The Blue Paradise*, *The Girl from Brazil*, *Her Soldier Boy*, and *My Lady's Glove*. In each of these works, Romberg's music appeared alongside selections from the original German-language productions as well as those by other American interpolators.[17] (See Table 3.1.)

What really transpires in these works, though, is another facet of the ongoing metamorphosis of operetta. While notions of Ruritania, Vienna, nostalgia, and realism deeply affected the genre, so did its physical transfer to New York. In the four adaptations to which Romberg contributed music, each show's European setting and fundamental plot is retained. Romberg's music, because of its Viennese base, fits comfortably with selections from the original scores. But at the same time, Romberg's music is generally not as effusive as that of his European counterparts. There is less recitative and more spoken dialogue, and choral scenes are simplified in their vocal and ensemble demands. The modified scores thus endorse realism, Belasco's creed, in ways that the original scores do not.

Table 3.1 Adaptations by Romberg, 1915–1917

American adaptation	European original
The Blue Paradise (August 5, 1915, Casino) Book by Edgar Smith, lyrics by Herbert Reynolds (Romberg is credited for eight songs on the playbill, Eysler for six, Leo Edwards for three, and Cecil Lean for one.)	*Ein Tag im Paradies* (A Day in Paradise, 1913) Music by Edmund Eysler, book and lyrics by Leo Stein and Béla Jenbach
The Girl from Brazil (August 30, 1916, 44th Street) Book by Edgar Smith, lyrics by Matthew Woodward (Romberg is credited for seven songs on the playbill, and Winterberg for three.)	*Die schöne Schwedin* (The Beautiful Swede, 1915) Music by Robert Winterberg, book and lyrics by Julius Brammer and Alfred Grünwald
Her Soldier Boy (December 6, 1916, Astor) Book and lyrics by Rida Johnson Young (Romberg is credited for seven songs on the playbill, Kálmán for three, Clifton Crawford for three, and Augustus Barratt for one.)	*Az obsitos* (On Leave, 1910), then *Der gute Kamerad* (The Good Comrade, 1911) and *Gold gab' ich für Eisen* (I Gave Gold for Iron, 1914) Music by Emmerich Kálmán, book and lyrics by Victor Léon
My Lady's Glove (June 18, 1917, Lyric) Book and lyrics by Edward A. Paulton (Romberg is credited for five songs on the playbill, Straus for six, and both composers for one.)	*Die schöne Unbekannte* (The Beautiful Unknown, 1915) Music by Oscar Straus, book and lyrics by Leopold Jacobson and Leo Stein

Nostalgia and the desire to physically return to the past drive the plot of the first adaptation, *The Blue Paradise*. Rudolf Stoeger (Cecil Lean), a young man who frequents the Blue Paradise Inn in Vienna, goes to America to run a business venture for his father. Before he leaves, he sings the waltz "Auf Wiedersehn" [*sic*] with Mizzi (Vivienne Segal, in her Broadway debut), the flower girl with whom he is in love. Twenty-four years later, Rudolf returns to Vienna. Unbeknownst to him, Mizzi has married one of his friends and now lives in the Blue Paradise, which has become a private residence. Rudolf suggests a reunion with his friends at the inn of their youth—he wants to return to the world of twenty-four years ago, find Mizzi just as she was, and revel in her love. The Blue Paradise is restored to its former glory, and Rudolf, when he arrives there, imagines that he has physically traveled back in time. He embraces a woman whom he thinks is Mizzi, but who is in fact her daughter Gaby. Mizzi confesses to concocting the ruse in order to jolt Rudolf back to reality. The past is gone, and no amount of nostalgic longing can bring it back. To provide a happy ending, Rudolf learns that Gaby is engaged to his nephew and blesses their union. The next generation will consummate the lost love of Rudolf and Mizzi.

The nostalgia, farewell, and loss at the heart of the tale are unforgettably captured in the operetta's primary love duet, "Auf Wiedersehn." Romberg's waltz melody perfectly matches the lyric sung by lovers who tell each other that despite the present pain of separation, the memory of their first love will always remain. The waltz concludes the first act and is reprised as the operetta's penultimate number. The young Rudolf and Mizzi sing it the first time, as Rudolf departs for America, while their mature selves reminisce about the events of twenty-four years ago in its reprise (marked "Reminiscence" on the playbill).

Following a verse in common time (a standard practice for waltz songs), the refrain, a thirty-two-measure through-composed melody divided into eight phrases, becomes the operetta's ultimate expression of hope for the future in the midst of impending loss. The pain of separation expressed in the first part of the lyric is reinforced musically through the low tessitura and slow-moving melody. Furthermore, the "home pitch," the tonic, is not present in the opening measures. The emotional and physical distance expressed in the lyric is echoed in the music through this lack of a tonic pitch — the melody is separated from its tonic. (See example 3.1.)

By contrast, at the end of the refrain, a hope for the future through the power of past love is enhanced through a chord progression employing an Italian, then a French, augmented sixth chord (at the words "on thro' the") and a melodic ascent in the final measures in which the lovers say goodbye *auf Deutsch*. (See example 3.2.) Since the two characters are alone on stage singing to each other, the music itself is all there is to amplify their heartfelt sentiments.

"Auf Wiedersehn" brought Romberg his first glimpse of fame as a Broadway composer. It was his first successful song, and proved that he was more than a utilitarian staff composer for the Shuberts. This waltz, with textual

Example 3.1. "Auf Wiedersehn" *(The Blue Paradise)*, refrain, mm. 1–8

references to loss, nostalgia, and Vienna, is a fine example of one of the song types for which Romberg remains best known.

In *The Blue Paradise*, Rudolf wants to travel back in time not only to recapture young love but also to experience prewar Vienna. This was a desire shared by many in the audience. To that effect, one of Edmund Eysler's original songs, a waltz entitled "Wien, Wien" ("Vienna, Vienna"), was retained on Broadway. Waltzes thus were employed in *The Blue Paradise* to signify the passing of both young love and the essence of Vienna.

The show did not celebrate only the past, however. The present was also an integral part of the plot. Just as the past was portrayed through the waltz, so was the modern world through duple-meter musical comedy styles. "One Step into Love," performed by the secondary characters

Example 3.2. "Auf Wiedersehn" *(The Blue Paradise)*, refrain, mm. 25–32

Gladys Wynn (Frances Demarest) and Hans Walther (Robert G. Pitkin), is a ragtime-derived one-step dance that establishes the present day of 1915. The song's title incorporates a clever dual interpretation of the words "one step": one choreographic and the other dramatic. Text painting in the song's lyric occurs on the word "hesitate," for when the word is uttered in regard to deciding to marry, the music also pauses. This characteristic element of the one-step dance—the hesitation—is evident in the music and reinforced by the lyrics.

Similar musical-dramatic techniques appear in *The Girl from Brazil*. Although billed as a musical comedy, the show has characteristics of an operetta in its foreign setting (Stockholm and Rio de Janeiro), plot (which has strong echoes of *The Merry Widow* with its tale about financial dealings), and overall musical style. The story centers on Hilma (Beth Lydy), the "beautiful Swede," who wants to marry the German Baron Heinz von Reedigan (John H. Goldsworthy). However, her brother, Sven Liverstol, a Stockholm banker, is in dire financial straits that need to be resolved before a wedding can take place. His situation worsens when his bank's biggest client, Edith Lloyd (Frances Demarest), arrives from Brazil (not London, although her surname connects her to Lloyd's of London) and withdraws her fortune. Later, back in Brazil, Edith's own business is in trouble due to growing competition from a certain Señor Camberito. When it is discovered that Camberito is a fiscally recovered Sven Liverstol, all ends happily, with a wedding for Hilma and Heinz, and another, accompanied by a corporate merger, for Sven and Edith.

In *The Girl from Brazil*, Romberg uses musical means to distinguish between the two leading ladies. Hilma, the title character in the Viennese original (*Die schöne Schwedin*), requires an operatic soprano, while the part of Edith, who assumes the title role in the American adaptation, does not. In Hilma's "Come Back, Sweet Dreams," for example, a demanding coloratura cadenza precedes the waltz refrain, and during the final statement of the refrain Hilma must sing a highly decorative obbligato while the orchestra plays the melody (a Viennese operetta practice). Edith, on the other hand, has much simpler music. "The Right Brazilian Girl," her only solo number, is a duple-meter song set in the middle register and has a mostly stepwise melody. Edith is a mature businesswoman, not a young girl in love, and her music, by being controlled and ordered, tells us this.

The score includes three love duets: "Bachelor Girl and Boy," "Stolen Kisses," and "My Señorita." The first, sung by the secondary Swedish characters Olaf Nansen (Stewart Jackson) and Lona Cedarstrom (Dorothy Maynard), is a gently syncopated song that emerged as one of the show's most successful independent numbers. The other two duets belong to Hilma and Heinz. The first act's "Stolen Kisses" is a waltz, while the show's penultimate number, "My Señorita," though it begins with triple-meter underscoring, turns out to be a lyrical duple-meter ballad.

Several factors contributed to *The Girl from Brazil* being called a musical comedy in the playbill, despite the fact that the original Viennese production was labeled an operetta, even appearing at the legendary Theater an der Wien, long a home to operetta. First, Romberg's score resides firmly in the Tin Pan Alley style and avoids "exotic" Latin American musical references and idioms. Second, comedy was central to the show's concept: George Hassell, as the money-lending Torkel, received many critical accolades for his performance, far outshining the male principals. Third, the show's title alluded to the musical comedy practice of having female references in the title, evident in works such as *The Pink Lady* (1911, music by Ivan Caryll, book and lyrics by C. M. S. McLellan) and especially *The Girl from Utah* (1914, music by Jerome Kern, lyrics by Harry B. Smith, book by James T. Tanner and Smith; with musical interpolations by other composers and lyricists).[18] What makes *The Girl from Brazil* noteworthy in Romberg's output is not its generic classification, though, but rather the manner in which Romberg uses music to distinguish between various character types.

The third adaptation, *Her Soldier Boy*, of 1916, instead of allowing audiences to escape from the Great War, took them directly and unashamedly into it. This was the first show to address the war in such an overt manner.[19] (The war-themed revues to which Romberg contributed music, *Doing Our Bit* and *Over the Top*, both appeared in 1917.) This was a second-generation adaptation, for the operetta was originally produced in Budapest, then altered for Vienna (in two different versions) and revised yet again for New York. In *Her Soldier Boy*, Alain Teniers (John Charles Thomas), a young French officer, travels to the home of one of his friends, Frantz Delauney (Frank Ridge), to tell Frantz's mother of her son's death. The mother, who is nearly blind, has not been in contact with her son for many years and mistakes Alain for Frantz. Alain maintains the deception in order to placate the elderly woman, but falls in love with Marlene (Beth Lydy), his supposed sister, in the masquerade. All ends happily when Frantz is found among a group of missing soldiers and Alain and Marlene marry.

In a similar fashion to what he did in *The Girl from Brazil*, Romberg employs contrasting voice types to highlight differences between the primary and secondary leads. Alain and Marlene have legitimate voices, as does Frantz, while the newspaper reporter Teddy McLane (Clifton Crawford) and his love interest Amy Lee (Adele Rowland) sing more in the style of revue and musical comedy.

Noted American baritone John Charles Thomas (1891–1960), who later enjoyed a successful operatic career, played Alain. Thomas made his Covent Garden debut in 1928 and was on the roster at the Met from 1934 to 1943. Back in 1916, though, the young star of *Her Soldier Boy* was heralded as a Broadway matinee idol.[20] Likewise, Beth Lydy reprised her role as an operatic leading lady on Broadway singing Romberg's music, having just played Hilma in *The Girl from Brazil*.

Three waltzes form the foundation of Romberg's contributions to the score. The first is the poignant "Mother,"[21] which occurs in the prologue. The scene takes place, according to the playbill, "Behind the Lines. Somewhere in Belgium." In the song, Frantz yearns for the comfort and loving embrace of his mother. The idea of looking to the past for strength in the present—a similar sort of transtemporal sentiment to that of "Auf Wiedersehn"—recurs here. Romberg's melody, like that of "Auf Wiedersehn," amplifies the text. The refrain, in AA'BB form, is more expansive than that of "Auf Wiedersehn." It opens quietly with largely stepwise motion and a predictable half-note–quarter-note rhythmic gait. Here, Frantz is thinking of his mother. By the latter part of the refrain, however, Frantz's whispered urgency for protection (the passage is marked *pp*) is portrayed musically by large leaps in the melodic line—a marked contrast to the opening—as well as a much fuller instrumental accompaniment. The harmonic language also becomes more chromatic, and hence emotive, particularly in the final cadence, where a iv-I progression, a mixed-mode version of a plagal cadence, concludes the refrain. Romberg thus transforms the song's fundamental atmosphere from respite to fear, aurally animating the experiences of not only Frantz but also of many soldiers in Europe and their loved ones in America.

In "Mother," Romberg employs the waltz to express feelings of separation, in this instance, between a young man on the Belgian front and his mother. In the two other waltzes from *Her Soldier Boy*, though, the moods are much more joyous. When Marlene learns that news of her brother's death was a mistake and that he is returning (or so she thinks, though it is actually Alain who is about to arrive), she responds with the wistful "He's Coming Home." Later, Marlene and Alain express their love in the sweeping "The Kiss Waltz." As was becoming the norm for Romberg, *The Girl from Brazil* notwithstanding, the principal love duet of the operetta is a glorious waltz. The expanded duple-meter verse is a musical and textual exchange between the two lovers, while the refrain's gentle rise in tessitura culminates in the final phrase as the lovers continue their journey upward toward musical and emotional ecstasy.

Her Soldier Boy included far more than operatic singing. Clifton Crawford and Adele Rowland sang Tin Pan Alley–style songs to the audiences' great delight. Crawford, in addition to singing the comic revue-style Romberg number "All Alone in a City of Girls" with the female chorus, performed three of his own creations: "Slavery," "History," and "Military Stamp" (the third as a duet with Rowland). One of the show's most memorable moments, though, was Rowland's inspiring rendition of the World War I standard "Smile, Smile, Smile" (also known as "Pack Up Your Troubles in Your Old Kit Bag," music by Felix Powell, lyrics by George Asaf). It was not just the performance but also the social resonance of the song that led to its rousing reception night after night.

Although the operetta's music was generally praised, the appropriateness (or inappropriateness) of presenting a sentimental dramatic work with a war background was on many people's minds. Echoing many of his contemporaries, the unnamed critic for the *Christian Science Monitor* described its effect on an audience member: "So, when he finds the scene of a Shubert musical play laid in a land where suffering and ruination rule, and is asked to distort his perspective and obscure the vista of a world tragedy with the puny love affairs of a musical comedy, the bad taste and the incongruity of it all strike him, and the applause he is wont to bestow on a 'Shubert show' is not started so easily as usual by the vigorous and hard-working claque. . . . Not that it is in itself bad entertainment. The fault lies in the bad taste of the setting relied on to carry the slender plot interest."[22]

Was the setting too unnerving? The incongruity between it and the romantic theatrical style obviously caused discomfort for many. Operetta, whose reputation rested on escapist sentiment, was being employed to offer a human interest story with a happy ending that was set amid the horrors of war. It offered a tale of hope for audiences filled with fear. Furthermore, operetta's reputation was changing: the genre was proving itself to be a viable style for shows set in the present. Current affairs had again entered the operetta domain, just as they had done in John Philip Sousa's *El Capitan* during the Spanish-American War in 1898 and would do so again in Romberg's *The Desert Song* in 1926.[23]

Her Soldier Boy transferred to London as *Soldier Boy* (without the possessive pronoun), opening at the Apollo Theatre on June 26, 1918, where it ran for nine months. Romberg's name appeared on the playbill as "Rombeau." The Frenchification of his surname was certainly due to the war—a pseudo-French composer was much more welcome than a pseudo-German one. For the British production, Frederick Chappelle also contributed songs to the score, and Rida Johnson Young and Edgar Wallace shared billing as authors.

The final pre-*Maytime* adaptation, *My Lady's Glove*, was the tale of a philandering soldier (Charles Purcell) who falls in love with his colonel's daughter (Vivienne Segal), the "beautiful unknown" of the Viennese title *(Die schöne Unbekannte)*. The original operetta took place in Austria, but due to the war in Europe and the fact that the Americans were fighting the Austrians, the setting was changed to France in 1913. The work was unexceptional, as the reviewer for the *New York Times* noted: "[I]t differed little, if at all, from dozens of Viennese operettas made over for American consumption that have gone before."[24] It is not at all surprising that it closed after a mere sixteen performances. For Romberg, though, the show's importance lies in the fact that it featured two singers known for their interpretations of his music: Charles Purcell, who played the title role in *Robinson Crusoe, Jr.* the previous year and who would star in *Maytime* a few months later, and Vivienne Segal, the lead actress from *The Blue Paradise* who in 1926 would star in *The Desert Song*.

Romberg's contributions included, among others, the opening scene's marches "Officers of the 25th" and "Keep Repeating It." Considering the military backdrop of the show, the marches added to the overall realistic atmosphere of the production. The masculine duple-meter numbers were set off by Elly's effervescently captivating "Foolish Little Maiden, I," a "valse grazioso," according to the score. Another of Elly's numbers was "The Daughter of the Regiment—Czardas," in which she was accompanied by the Hussar chorus. Marked "Tempo di Czardas," the musical style of the song had nothing to do with the characteristic Hungarian form with which Romberg was intimately familiar, but rather was firmly in the Tin Pan Alley style.

Romberg's operetta adaptations endorse and promote the general transformations taking place in the genre. None of the four works have Ruritanian settings—all exist in real places, and none of the locales are in the Balkans, Ruritania's real-life model. Romberg, like operetta in general, had left Ruritania. Furthermore, nostalgia figures prominently into the dramatic plots, especially in *The Blue Paradise*, where Romberg uses the waltz as a symbol for loss and remembrance. Realism also plays a part, especially in *Her Soldier Boy* and *My Lady's Glove*, where the actuality of the world situation serves as a backdrop for the plots. In *Her Soldier Boy*, the war is integral to the story, while it is incidental to *My Lady's Glove*. Romberg's additions contributed to the overall musical-dramatic framework for each show, but the fact remains that the scores had several contributors. In 1917, though, an adaptation appeared that included music by Romberg only: *Maytime*.

Maytime

As Romberg's first complete operetta score, *Maytime* (August 16, 1917, Shubert) was proof positive that the Hungarian immigrant possessed extraordinary abilities and a deep affinity for the genre. The show was an overwhelming commercial success and established Romberg's reputation as an operetta composer.

On February 19, 1917, the Shuberts acquired legal permission to revise Rudolf Schanzer and Rudolf Bernauer's popular operetta *Wie einst im Mai* (*As Once in May*, 1913), with music by Walter Kollo and Willy Bredschneider, for New York.[25] The producers hired Rida Johnson Young, who had written the book and lyrics for *Naughty Marietta* (1910, music by Victor Herbert), and with whom the Shuberts and Romberg had collaborated on *Her Soldier Boy*, to adapt the book and write lyrics for this show.[26] For the music, they called upon their staff composer Sigmund Romberg, just as they had done in the past. World events, however, interfered with their plan to bring a version of *Wie einst im Mai* to New York.

On April 6, 1917, six weeks after the Shuberts acquired the rights to *Wie einst im Mai*, the United States entered World War I by declaring war on Germany, which just happened to be the home country of their new theatrical property. The Shuberts knew they had a potential hit with the American version of the show and, instead of merely adapting the operetta for Broadway, decided to radically transform it. The reworking meant that all German references had to be removed: after all, this was the era of songs with strongly worded titles such as "We're Going to Take the Germ Out of Germany" (1917, music by Frederick V. Bowers, lyrics by Arthur J. Lamb). Young moved the action from Berlin to New York, and none of Kollo and Bredschneider's original music was retained. The risk of having any music by living German composers appearing in a glorious Shubert production and possibly destroying its commercial viability and the producers' reputation was too great. Fearing negative publicity, J. J. Shubert did not even refer to the origins of the new "play with music" in any publicity materials or in the playbill, although some reviewers discerned the plot's source. Hans Bartsch, the agent from whom the producers secured the rights to adapt and produce *Wie einst im Mai*, pressured the Shuberts to include a credit for the German source material as well as to incorporate Kollo and Bredschneider's original score; the producers, though, vehemently opposed the idea and refused to meet Bartsch's demands.[27] They would not even call the work an operetta because of the term's inherent Central European associations.

This was an unprecedented opportunity for Romberg: for the first time in his operetta career, he would not have to hear his music sung alongside that by his European contemporaries. He was moving from an interpolator to the sole creator of a complete operetta score. The prospect undoubtedly thrilled him.

The story of *Maytime*, like that of *The Blue Paradise* from two years earlier, concerns the enduring power of first love, a memory that can be both pleasant and painful. In both shows, a future generation consummates the love of its ancestors, providing a compromise ending with elements of both sadness and joy—sadness that the romantic leads are not together but joy that their descendents are.

In addition to the grand arch of the story, the aural centerpiece in both operettas is a genre-defining waltz. In *The Blue Paradise*, this is "Auf Wiedersehn," while in *Maytime* the role belongs to "Will You Remember," also known by the first words of its refrain, "Sweetheart, sweetheart." In both shows, the young lovers first sing the waltz as they are about to part. They realize that all that can and will remain of their present rapture is its lingering memory. Whereas the lyrics of "Auf Wiedersehn" are rooted in the present pain of separation, those of "Will You Remember" point toward the future and the joy of remembering what once was.

After a brief orchestral introduction, the verse of "Will You Remember," in 6/8, begins with Ottilie and Richard (or Dick), the romantic leads, exchanging musical phrases in which they declare how "love is so sweet in the springtime." As the verse progresses, the harmonic language becomes increasingly chromatic and the singers realize that their present state of ecstasy is quickly coming to an end. The growing tonal instability parallels the mounting emotional distress of the words, as the lyrics pass from the present tense at the beginning, "love *is* so sweet," to the past tense at the end, "the thrill it *knew*."

The refrain of "Will You Remember" is one of Romberg's most memorable waltzes. In thirty-two-bar ABAC form, the A periods are sung as solos (the first by Ottilie and the second by Richard), while the B and C ones are duets in which the lovers express their ardent passion for each other. This intensity culminates midway through the final period, where the singers sustain two successive high notes, both indicated with fermatas, on the final syllables of "will you re-*mem-ber*."

Example 3.3. "Will You Remember" *(Maytime)*, refrain, mm. 1–4

Every bit as haunting as these climactic skyscraping pitches is the distinctive rhythmic motif that pervades the refrain. Whereas the rhythm of a typical waltz melody, such as Lehár's "Gold and Silver Waltz," is LONG-short / LONG-short (half note–quarter note), Romberg inverts the pattern, resulting in short-LONG / short-LONG (quarter note–half note). (See example 3.3.) This reversal accomplishes two things. First, it creates a distinctive, and therefore more memorable, melody. Since the entire song is about remembering, the lyric and the music need to operate in an extremely effective symbiotic relationship. One must remember the music as well as the sentiment. Second, Young's lyric, the simple yet immortal words "Sweetheart, sweetheart," ideally matches Romberg's music from a text-setting standpoint and practical performance requirements. The sustained "a" vowel on "heart" is much more pleasant for both the singer and the listener than the piercing long "e" of "sweet." By having the preferred vowel on the longer note, the text is easier to sing and to comprehend. Especially in an era before amplification, the need for singers to project on open vowel sounds was critical in musical theater.

This distinctive rhythmic figure reappears at the end of the refrain, providing respite after the passionate high notes. The idea of remembrance operates on two different levels in the song's final measures. The lyrics state what will be remembered, "springtime, lovetime, May," while the music recalls the distinctive opening motif and its text. It likewise confirms the heartfelt feelings between the lovers, the "sweethearts."

"Will You Remember," the musical centerpiece of *Maytime*, captures

Peggy Wood (as Ottilie) and Charles Purcell (as Dick) in the original production of *Maytime*. Courtesy of the Shubert Archive.

the essence of the operetta: a tale of forbidden love, a love that is unselfish and giving, and one that is finally realized through the grandchildren of the protagonists. Johnson's libretto spans more than sixty years, with over a decade transpiring between each act. The playbill descriptor "in four acts (or episodes)" is thus wholly accurate—these are glimpses into an epic story. Act 1 is set in 1840, act 2 in 1855, act 3 in the 1880s, and act 4 in the "twentieth century," meaning the present day (1917).[28] (A decade later, *Show Boat* also presented an expansive tale that took place over fifty years and two generations and which also ended in the present day.)

In act 1, Ottilie Van Zandt, daughter of a wealthy colonel who lives with her family in fashionable Washington Square, and Richard (Dick) Wayne, son of the poverty-stricken foreman of a copper shop owned by Colonel Van Zandt, are childhood sweethearts. They pledge to marry, but know that this cannot be, for they are from different social classes. Ottilie's father ensures that they are both painfully aware of this fact when he commands Ottilie to marry her cousin Claude, a chronic gambler. To make matters worse for Ottilie, it is her birthday, and a group of gypsies providing entertainment for her party prophesy that Dick will marry one of the guests at the party, Alice Tremaine. The relationship between the Van Zandt and Wayne families becomes more complicated when Dick's father, John, who is in debt to the Colonel, gives him the deed to the family mansion on upper Fifth Avenue. The paper blows out the window and lands in the hands of Ottilie and Dick, who are alone in the garden. Knowing they must part, they declare their love in song ("Will You Remember"), writing the poetic words on the back of the deed. They bury a box containing the deed and Dick leaves, promising Ottilie that he will earn his fortune and return to marry her, despite any protestations from her father.

Act 2 takes place in a nightclub fifteen years later. Since his marriage to Ottilie, Claude has been squandering her fortune, and she, heartbroken, has also been living a careless existence. Dick returns from South Africa a wealthy man, just as he promised Ottilie at the end of act 1. He finds her at the club, and, reunited, they sing another romantic waltz duet, "The Road to Paradise." Ottilie's jealous husband witnesses the meeting and accuses them of reigniting their romance. Since they have been singing words such as "In your loving eyes, there my Paradise lies" to an expansive, flowing melody, his suspicions are certainly justified. He responds by threatening to sue Dick and Ottilie for alienation of affection. Ottilie's cousin Matthew, the comic character who has a different wife in each act, offers the only possible solution: Dick must immediately marry Alice Tremaine, who just happens to be at the nightclub. He proposes, she accepts, and Ottilie is saved the anguish of court action. An Italian singer, Signor Vivalla, brought to the club by none other than P. T. Barnum, brings the act to a close with a solo rendition of "Will You Remember," a painful reminder that this song is no longer the property of Dick and Ottilie, who now more than ever are forbidden to sing it. (This is reminiscent of Koko and Katisha's marriage in order to avoid a legal wrangle in Gilbert and Sullivan's *The Mikado*.)

When act 3 opens, we learn of the awful tragedies that have beset Ottilie. Claude died, leaving her penniless. Then her daughter died in childbirth, so Ottilie is raising her granddaughter, also called Ottilie, alone. She is in the midst of auctioning off her belongings when Dick and his five-year-old grandson, Dicky, arrive at the auction, not knowing why it is taking place. The thwarted lovers meet, once more realize the depth of their love, and yet again have to deny their feelings, this time because Dick is married to Alice. A mysterious buyer purchases the house and all its contents. The buyer, it turns out, is Dick's secretary acting on his behalf. As Dick leaves, he gives Ottilie the deed to her house and the bill of sale. Even if he cannot be with her, he can at least provide her with financial security. Dicky brings the act to a close by singing his grandfather's song, "Will You Remember."

In act 4, Ottilie's now-grown granddaughter has opened a dress shop in what was her grandmother's home. Business is booming, largely because Dicky Wayne, now a handsome young man, sends Broadway chorus girls there to shop and then pays their bills. He is in love with the young Ottilie, and she with him, although she does not approve of his carefree spending habits. The same actors who played Richard and Ottilie in the first three acts now appear as their respective character's grandchild, a physical embodiment of the power of the love so passionately expressed in act 1 and subsequently denied in acts 2 and 3.

Workmen digging in the back garden unearth the box that Ottilie and Dicky's grandparents buried there in 1840. They discover the love song of their ancestors and the deed that John Wayne gave to Colonel Van Zandt. The Fifth Avenue property, which according to the deed now belongs to the younger Ottilie, has soared in value, making her very wealthy. Dicky proposes to his beloved, and she accepts. The couple sings the love song of their grandparents, "Will You Remember," and likewise fulfills the promise of love that their grandparents were denied.

"Will You Remember" is the unforgettable musical centerpiece of the show, for it appears in each act and holds the multigenerational storyline together. Richard and Ottilie, the grandparents, sing it in act 1, and Richard and Ottilie, the grandchildren, in act 4. But in the internal acts, other characters sing the waltz, with differing dramatic effects. At the end of act 2, Signor Vivalla sings it as an expression of love denied. By contrast, at the end of act 3, young Dicky sings it to his grandfather and Ottilie, reminding them that their love was strong in the past and remains so in the present. He also promises them that it will live on in a future generation, namely his.

Maytime is filled with splendid music. The nature of the story allowed Romberg to insert various specialty numbers, especially in the first two acts, as a means of providing the variety of styles necessary to maintain musical interest and contrast. Act 1's gypsy music fits nicely into the libretto since gypsies provide entertainment at Ottilie's birthday party, while act 2's nightclub setting allows the opportunity for a wide variety of song types.

Act 1's "Gypsy Song" begins with a quasi-improvisatory flourish before the appearance of its verse and refrain, both of which are waltzes. A hint of exoticism is present in the minor-mode verse, but is dispelled at the arrival of the major-mode refrain. Significantly, the refrain employs the archetypal LONG-short / LONG-short (half note–quarter note) waltz rhythm on the words "[So] COME, my OWN, a-LONE with ME" (with a quarter-note anacrusis on "so"), thus establishing the pattern before the appearance of "Will You Remember," with its reversal of the rhythm, soon afterward. Romberg thus prepares the distinctive nature of "Sweetheart, sweetheart" by stating the norm in the preceding waltz. The "Exit music" for the gypsies, the only music that separates "Gypsy Song" and "Will You Remember," is a lively dance in D minor in which parallel thirds and strong accents on various beats combine to suggest a stereotypical gypsy sound.

For the nightclub scene in act 2, Romberg incorporates several different styles that would have been known in 1855. The act opens with a mazurka, a Polish dance, before Matthew sings "Jump, Jim Crow," a ragtime song with direct roots in minstrelsy. Later, Amorita, a dancer brought by P. T. Barnum, provides a "Spanish Dance."[29] This "show within a show" was of course nothing new and demonstrated a connection with both Viennese operetta (for example, Orlofsky's party in act 2 of *Die Fledermaus*) and the revue, with its series of specialty numbers.

The music for the final two acts is more closely tied to the plot than that of the first two. Act 3, the shortest of the four, contains only two musical numbers, a unison chorus sung by buyers at the auction who are dismayed at the poor quality of goods for sale, and young Dicky's rendition of "Will You Remember." Act 4, however, contains a great deal of extremely worthwhile music that functions to establish a sense of the present, as well as the final reprise of the principal waltz.

Act 4's opening chorus pulls the audience immediately into 1917 with its opening line, "Since the war in Europe, I have been so busy."[30] In this dual ode to capitalism and immigration (for which Cyrus Wood contributed lyrics in English and French), Ottilie tells how she sells dresses to ladies from different countries by relating to each customer's ethnicity. Romberg depicts the culturally diverse nature of New York in 1917 through various musical means in the verse. A Spanish habanera, a French waltz with a legato melody, and a Russian mazurka (!) filled with rests that create a sharply articulated texture all appear as the proprietress tries to sell dresses to her array of immigrant customers. Romberg was conflating the Slavic world by using a Polish dance to depict Russia, but the text makes it clear that the song is about Russia. (This is not the same mazurka from act 2.) The sequences depicting Spain and France are sung in Spanish and French, demonstrating the shop owner's multilingual abilities.

German shoppers are notably absent from the shop. The operetta appeared during World War I, after all, and the Shuberts, who eliminated all German references from the show, certainly would not want them to enter this scene.

During the refrain, a 2/4 march, Ottilie is helping an English customer. The occasional second beat accents suggest the sound of a grand British march, such as Elgar's *Pomp and Circumstance* marches. The British are not mentioned in the song's verse but receive full treatment in the refrain. Ottilie concludes the refrain by telling her customer that the dress will cost only fifty pounds—a large sum of money indeed. We know we are in an exclusive shop.

Romberg thus depicts three of America's allies in World War I—France, Russia, and Britain—in the song, reinforcing its present-day setting and political allegiances and keeping the Creel Commission satisfied. Spain was neutral during the war, but was important to the United States, and hence is included in the miniparade of nations.

Other notable numbers in act 4 include the waltz "Dancing Will Keep You Young" and the comic march "Go Away, Girls." The waltz's dramatic function is prepared when cousin Matthew, now an old man, arrives at the shop looking for wife number four. He succeeds, and with his new love, Ermintrude d'Albert, sings and dances the number. The physical benefits of dancing are the basis for the lyric, set in the refrain to a slow waltz melody. Matthew is by now very elderly, and though still capable of marriage, cannot quite negotiate a fast-paced dance routine.

Matthew Van Zandt, importantly, is the romantic foil for Ottilie and Dick. He freely searches for love in many places, yet never finds a true soul mate. By contrast, his cousin and Dick find true love but can never be together. Perhaps Matthew finally finds love in old age, for his music in act 4 is a waltz, a musical symbol of love, rather than a lighthearted number such as the syncopated "Jump, Jim Crow," his song in act 2.

The other notable song in act 4 is "Go Away, Girls," sung by the virile and attractive Dicky Wayne.[31] In this fast-paced comic march, he tells the shop's patrons to leave him alone, for he is interested only in one girl, the proprietress. The song is in the style of a revue or musical comedy number, and endorses the present-day setting of the act.

After all this fine music, Romberg ends the operetta in a curious manner. Following the reprise of "Will You Remember" and the consummation of Dick and Ottilie's ill-fated romance by their grandchildren, the operetta ends not with a gloriously sentimental finale, but rather with a seemingly bizarre reprise of Ottilie's shopkeeper's march. There are two possible interpretations of this curious choice. First is that the march, being in duple meter, indicates that the characters are modern individuals living in 1917, and are not their grandparents. In this interpretation, the musical comedy trait of present-day settings and the style's penchant for duple-meter numbers trump the dominance of old-fashioned waltzes. Second is that the wartime sentiment and patriotic obligations necessitated ending the operetta (or, "play with music") with a rousing march rather than with a romantic waltz. Whatever the reasoning behind the decision, the emotional highpoint of the operetta, the realization of a forbidden love set to a stunning waltz melody, is cut short by the march reprise.

Although *Maytime* initially received mixed reviews from the critics, it was a success with the public, playing 492 performances in its original New York run. John Corbin, writing for the *New York Times*, disliked the "Winter Garden" elements in the show, likely referring to songs such as "Jump, Jim Crow" and "Go Away, Girls." He felt that they detracted from the multigenerational tale and otherwise sentimental music of the score.[32] But audiences flocked to see *Maytime*. Its basic tale offered hope for the future and spoke directly to the thousands of people who saw it. Peggy Wood, who played Ottilie, said that it was the show all the soldiers who were about to be sent overseas wanted to see.[33] This is ironic considering the play's German source material, but it proves the viability and appeal of the story and its music, regardless of it origin.

A large part of *Maytime*'s success was due to its stars. The handsome Charles Purcell, who played lead roles in most of Romberg's shows from the 1910s, was Dick, while the charming Peggy Wood established her career as a Broadway star in the show, moving from chorus roles in earlier operettas to a principal part in *Maytime*. (Decades later, Wood played the Mother Abbess in the 1965 film version of *The Sound of Music*.)

In January 1921, a production of *Maytime* opened in Montreal at His Majesty's Theatre. Less than four years after its premiere, the nostalgic glow of the show was already firmly entrenched. As the critic for the *Star* remarked: "The charm of 'Maytime' seems perennial. No matter how many times you see it, there is always some new feature that moves you, some new appeal that delights. The romantic beauty of the story has much to do with this. The unusual freshness and fragrance of the musical setting is an element that can never be overlooked."[34]

Maytime was one of the most beloved shows of its day. The only book musical to play longer during the 1910s was *Irene* (1919, music by Harry Tierney, lyrics by Joseph McCarthy, book by James Montgomery). Broadway lore has it that *Maytime* was so successful that the Shuberts had to open a second company at the 44th Street Theatre, across the street from the Shubert Theatre, to meet audience demand. This did not happen; the perpetuators of the legend, including the screenwriters for *Deep in My Heart*, confused *Maytime* with the similarly titled *Blossom Time*, which did have two companies playing across the street from each other for several weeks in 1923. The confusion is certainly understandable, given the closeness of the titles of the two shows. However, the Shubert Theatre production did move to the 44th Street Theatre on February 18, 1918. When the show started appearing at the 44th Street Theatre, it stopped playing at the Shubert, and the play *The Copperhead* took its place. The show's transfer from one theatre to another is the most likely source of the erroneous legend—the fact that it stopped playing at the Shubert was probably overlooked.

The confusion about *Maytime*'s run does not end there, however, for two separate companies did in fact constitute the first New York run, the one on which tallies for the number of performances are based. On August 5, 1918, the original "New York Company" went to Boston and was immediately replaced in New York at the Lyric Theatre by the "Chicago Company," headed by baritone John Charles Thomas, star of *Her Soldier Boy*, and Carolyn Thomson. Having these two companies both playing in New York also contributed to the fable that they appeared at the same time, even though they did not.[35] However messy, the complexity and convolution of *Maytime*'s performance history is ultimately indicative of one thing: this show was a phenomenal popular success. Romberg had arrived.

Maytime was much more than a commercial success for its composer. The show established a paradigm for operetta that Romberg would follow for the next seven years, through *The Student Prince*. First, the libretto is a sentimental and nostalgic story that ends with some sort of unhappiness or loss—the principal romantic leads are not together at the final curtain. Second, a glorious recurring waltz duet is the centerpiece of the score while, third, other musical styles orbit around this emotive and memorable tune. Last, nostalgia was a driving force in the libretto—the unregainable past was a central dramatic theme. The design worked for *Maytime,* and Romberg and the Shuberts knew that they had found a distinctive approach to American operetta, one they would emulate in future shows.

CHAPTER 4

Continued Success: *The Magic Melody* and *Blossom Time*

AFTER THE INITIAL SUCCESS OF *MAYTIME*, ROMBERG LEFT THE SHUbert fold (for a time) and founded the short-lived Wilner-Romberg Productions with Max Wilner. Thanks to the financial windfall of *Maytime*, he now had enough capital to start his own business. Although Wilner-Romberg Productions ended up being a commercial failure, the enterprise gave Romberg the chance to produce original works according to his own dictates. He did not have to answer to anyone, particularly J. J. Shubert, on any aspect of the musical score. The only operetta produced under the auspices of Romberg's company was the evocatively titled *The Magic Melody* (November 11, 1919, Shubert). Although the show played at the Shuberts' flagship house, the legendary impresarios were not involved with the production, other than leasing their theater.

Romberg's next operetta after *The Magic Melody* was the immortal *Blossom Time* (September 29, 1921, Ambassador). Produced by the Shuberts, *Blossom Time* became one of the producers' greatest successes and, especially after the success of *Maytime*, cemented the prominence of Romberg and the Shuberts in post–World War I American operetta. Both shows continue the formula so successfully applied in *Maytime*: a recurring waltz duet unifies the multifaceted score to a tale with a bittersweet, if not outright sad, ending. Separation and loss are set to unforgettable, glorious music. In the cases of *The Magic Melody* and *Blossom Time*, curiously, the male leads are both composers: the fictional Beppo Corsini in *The Magic Melody* and the real Franz Schubert in *Blossom Time*.

The Magic Melody

Called a "romantic musical play" on the playbill, *The Magic Melody* was deemed a reasonable success with its 143 performances. Frederick Arnold Kummer wrote the book and lyrics, and J. C. Huffman and J. Clifford Brooke staged the production.

The sentimental libretto was a tale of tragic separation and joyous reunion, not of lovers, however, but of a young man and his mother. The libretto thus echoed *Her Soldier Boy* more than *Maytime*. The prologue, which takes place twenty years before the operetta's two acts, is set in a Sicilian fishing village. Beppo Corsini has just learned that the Milan opera house rejected his new opera. Gianina, his loving and supportive wife, nevertheless arranges a deal with one of her wealthy admirers to bring her husband's opera to the stage. However, through a window shade Beppo accidentally sees the silhouettes of his wife being kissed inappropriately by the unbeknownst-to-him benefactor and suspects the two of having an affair. Distraught by the double tragedy of the denunciation of his opera and the supposed infidelity of his wife, Beppo leaves with his young son and is lost at sea.

Twenty years later, in the then present (1919), the Russian Prince Vladimir Potemsky is hosting a party at his home in Paris. Two of the guests are Madame Jessonda, Beppo's widow who now owns a villa in Versailles, and Arthur Stanley, a captain in the British navy. Jessonda comes to the party seeking revenge on her former suitor, now the Marquis de Vernon, who kissed her and subsequently ruined her family. Arthur, an attractive young man, is in love with the Marquis's daughter Isabel. Potemsky invites his guests to offer entertainments, recalling Prince Orlofsky's ball in act 2 of *Die Fledermaus* and also the act 2 nightclub scene from *Maytime*.[1] Arthur sings a love song, a waltz (this is an operetta, after all) entitled "Once Upon a Time" that he remembers from childhood. Madame Jessonda recognizes the melody—it is the principal theme from her late husband's unperformed opera. Through the "magic melody," she realizes that Captain Stanley is her long-lost son. He tells her how an English couple rescued him at sea and adopted him. The operetta ends amidst great rejoicing at the reunion of mother and son, but is tinged with a bit of sadness at the fact that Beppo is not there as well.

The refrain of "Once Upon a Time," like that of "Will You Remember," is in ABAC form. "Once Upon a Time" relies on the repeated LONG-short (half note–quarter note) rhythmic motion, a typical and predictable waltz pattern, for its forward motion.

While the primarily conjunct melody and its rhythmic regularity may be commonplace, its harmonic underpinning certainly is not. Since Romberg wrote the music first, it was up to the lyricist to match key words to specific musical events, whether they are generated by the melodic line or by the harmonic structure. Kummer possessed innate abilities for this difficult task. In the first phrase, for example, Kummer's words "Once upon a time in May," a happy, carefree image, are set to purely diatonic (I-V-I-V) music. However, when he gets to the phrase "How can I forget, dear," the shift in the text corresponds to a disruption in the music. At this point Romberg begins an extremely chromatic (when compared with the opening passage) sequence of chords that is resolved through linear chromaticism in the outer parts.

"Once Upon a Time" is not only the principal love song in *The Magic Melody* but also a constituent part of the dramatic action. Were it not for this song, Madame Jessonda may never have found her long-lost son. As such, the song needs to be memorable and have strongly discernable features. Romberg achieves this recognizability harmonically, rather than melodically or rhythmically. The tune is pleasant enough, though not exceptional. Jessonda remembers the past as her son sings "How can I forget," and realizes that she, too, has not forgotten the love she had for her family twenty years earlier.

The Magic Melody had a great deal in common with *Maytime*, including a plot that concerned the passing of time and a waltz as the musical focal point. This waltz, though, had another overt *Maytime* reference in the opening line of the refrain, "Once upon a time in *May*."

In addition to *Maytime* references, *The Magic Melody* draws together several strands of Romberg's writing to this point, including the musical depiction of ethnicity, Orientalism, and musical comedy. Romberg's ability to portray various ethnicities, something he developed in his revue scores and ably demonstrated in *Maytime*, is evident in the prologue's "Gianina." With its various combinations of dotted rhythms and high notes with fermatas, it is a pastiche of an Italian street song. Furthermore, the opera composer Corsini, who just happens to be a trademark Italian tenor, sings it. This is Romberg's tribute to Italian tenors, and, in the song, Romberg defines Corsini's role as that of an Italian singer. It is a male version, if you will, of Herbert's "Italian Street Song" in *Naughty Marietta*, though without the coloratura runs.

Romberg's continuing interest in musical Orientalism appears in act 2 numbers such as "I am the Pasha" and "Down by the Nile." Chromatic passing and neighbor tones, devices that are becoming Orientalist clichés for Romberg, are present in both songs. These fit comfortably into the dramatic story line as diversionary numbers performed by guests at the prince's party, the same occasion where Arthur sings his waltz.

Romberg also gives a nod to musical comedy in "The Little Church Around the Corner" (with lyrics by Alex Gerber), a duple-meter song whose melody consists primarily of alternating thirds. The comic leads, a newspaper reporter (Earl Benham) and a young girl from Utah (Carmel Myers) chaperoned by her mother, sing the gentle ballad about wanting to get married. These characters have direct musical comedy allusions, for *The Girl from Brazil* also featured a comic newspaper reporter, while Kern's "girl," *The Girl from Utah*, had a female Utahan in its title role.

The Magic Melody was conceived as an operetta, and as such, it required a legitimate singer for the male lead. Romberg's leading man from the 1910s, Charles Purcell, fresh from receiving laurels as the costar of *Maytime*, played the dual role of Beppo Corsini and his son. Romberg knew Purcell's voice and wrote the fine male showcase numbers such as "Once Upon a Time" and "Gianina" for the exceptional tenor.

By contrast, and defying expectation, Gianina/Madame Jessonda is a speaking role. Julia Dean received tremendous critical acclaim for her emotional portrayal of the revenge-seeking heroine. Apparently the actress looked exactly the same in the main parts of the operetta as she did in the prologue, even though she should have aged twenty years.[2] The presence of a nonsinging leading lady kept the musical focus squarely on the male star, Purcell.

Arthur's romantic interest, Isabel, is a smaller role than that of his mother, suggesting Oedipal elements in the operetta. Nevertheless, Arthur and Isabel do sing several duets, including the recurring waltz "Once Upon a Time," at the prince's party.

Following in the path of *Maytime*, *The Magic Melody* has textual references to some of America's allies in World War I, this time Italy, England, Russia, and France. The prologue takes place in Italy and the central family in the story is Italian; Stanley is in the British navy; a Russian prince hosts the act 2 fete; and the entire present-day action takes place in France. Allusions to the German-speaking world are carefully avoided, just as they were in *Maytime*.

Critics liked *The Magic Melody*, especially its lavish sets and costumes. One called the production "a triumph of gorgeous costume colors."[3] Another commented that the Russian prince's reception room had "draperies of various tones of purple embroidered in color and contrasted with hangings of yellow and orange" and that it was "the most striking of the young season."[4] This extravagant visual treatment was due to J. C. Huffman's involvement with the show, for he was a veteran of numerous Winter Garden productions and brought the colorful spectacle of that legendary house to the Shubert Theatre.

The music was also praised, especially because it was not jazz-based. The reviewer for the *Globe* concluded his remarks by stating: "Altogether 'The Magic Melody' will be delightful entertainment to those who are tired of jazz, ragtime, and the shimmy. It is clean and wholesome and the haunting music will linger long with you."[5] His counterpart at the *World* wrote that most of the score "is of a potent warmth and melody, . . . some of which rises to the standard of a genuine opera comique."[6] The writer for the *Sun* had a similar opinion, stating, "All the characters moved to the melodious music of Sigmund Romberg, who has already proved his skill as a composer in the Viennese modes. Last night his waltzes lingered longest in the memory of the audience."[7]

Oscar Radin's orchestrations also drew attention because they required an extraordinarily large orchestra. The pit was so crowded that Charles Previn, the conductor, barely had room to move his baton.[8] Surely Romberg's role as producer allowed him the chance to have a bigger ensemble than was the norm.

The only element that received consistent criticism was the book. Writers generally found the plot too confusing, a common complaint of that era, and something that occurs again and again in the history of musical theater.

But all in all, *The Magic Melody* was a success.

Blossom Time

After Wilner-Romberg Productions went bankrupt, a sheepish and repentant Romberg returned to the Shuberts. The producers welcomed their "prodigal son" back to the fold. After all, he had helped make them a huge amount of money with *Maytime*. For his next project, they assigned him to write music for a sad tale, something they knew he could handle because of the sentimental nature of *Maytime* and *The Magic Melody*. While the plots of *Maytime* and *The Magic Melody* ultimately had somewhat happy endings (though not for the lovers in the works' opening scenes), the new endeavor would not. For this was *Blossom Time* (September 29, 1921, Ambassador), a fictional story based loosely on the life of Franz Schubert and ending with the composer's death on stage at the final curtain.

The Shuberts took a chance here: the tale not only ended tragically but, because of its historical basis, it had to be set in Vienna. Whereas Germanic locales were strenuously avoided in *Maytime* and notably absent from *The Magic Melody*, there was no choice here: this operetta had to take place in the former Habsburg capital. The Shuberts were right, as they often were, for *Blossom Time* turned out to be even more successful than *Maytime*, playing over one thousand performances in its first two years. It firmly established the Shuberts and Romberg as leaders in the world of American operetta and proved that *Maytime* was not a fluke. To have two monumental successes within four years was a major accomplishment. Because of *Blossom Time*, Romberg and the Shuberts were also recognized as a powerful and lucrative creative alliance. Additionally, the Shuberts saw a tremendous marketing ploy based on the homonymic sound of their name (without the "c") and that of the famous Viennese composer (with the "c").

As important as the show was for both Romberg and the Shuberts, it also inaugurated a significant working relationship for Romberg and wordsmith Dorothy Donnelly (1880–1928). Romberg and Donnelly created three more operettas after *Blossom Time*: *The Student Prince* (1924), *My Maryland* (1927), and *My Princess* (1927). The two enjoyed a strong, productive, and friendly, though relatively brief, collaboration.

The Donnellys were great thespians. Dorothy's parents were both involved with the theater. Her father, Thomas Lester Donnelly, was manager of the Grand Opera House in New York, and her mother, Sarah Williams Donnelly, was an actress. Dorothy began her acting career in 1898 with the Murray Hill Stock Company, which was directed at that time by her brother, Henry. She garnered attention from audiences and critics alike in 1903, when she created the title roles in the American premieres of W. B. Yeats's *Kathleen ni Houlihan* and George Bernard Shaw's *Candida*. Her greatest stage triumph, though, was in the title role of Henry W. Savage's production of *Madame X* in 1910.

However, it was not on stage but rather as a librettist that Donnelly is best remembered. *Flora Bella*, which she co-wrote with Cosmo Hamilton, opened at the Casino Theatre on September 16, 1916, and played for fifteen weeks. Lina Abarbanell, Charles Cuvillier, and Milton Schwarzwald composed the musical score. Although Donnelly's most memorable works were her collaborations with Romberg, she also wrote two other musical libretti: *Poppy* (1923, music by Stephen Jones) and *Hello, Lola* (1926, music by William Kernell). Donnelly suffered from kidney disease for the last five years of her life, and passed away from nephritis-pneumonia on January 4, 1928. Romberg was devastated at her passing; in addition to providing him with some of the best libretti for his shows, she was also a close friend.

When the Shuberts learned that they could obtain the rights to the American version of the extremely successful Viennese operetta *Das Dreimäderlhaus* (*The House of the Three Maidens*, 1916), they wasted no time in closing a deal.[9] The original Viennese production included music by Heinrich Berté based on selected themes by Franz Schubert. Berté chose both well-known and less-familiar pieces by the Viennese composer for his score, with more of the former than the latter. *Das Dreimäderlhaus* was immensely popular, and its Schubert-derived music made it marketable for export. And exported it was. Each international version differed slightly in its title and musical score. It traveled to Paris as *Chanson d'amour* (*Song of Love*, May 7, 1921, Théâtre Marigny) in a version by Hugues Delorme and Léon Alric, and then appeared in London as *Lilac Time* (December 22, 1922, Lyric) in an adaptation by Adrian Ross, with music arranged by G. H. Clutsam. The tale also made it to the screen four times. Three film versions of the German original appeared, in 1917, 1936 (as *Drei Mäderl um Schubert* [Three Girls for Schubert]), and 1958. The fourth film, an English version entitled *Blossom Time*, although using music and plot details from *Lilac Time*, appeared in 1934 and starred Richard Tauber, Paul Graetz, and June Baxter. Whatever the language, the sad tale of Franz Schubert in a Vienna that no longer existed—one that had been forever destroyed—tugged at the heartstrings of audience members throughout Europe and the United States, and they loved it.

They loved it so much in New York that *Blossom Time*'s original run lasted a stunning 516 performances, according to the standard counting practice (from opening night to closing night).[10] But the story is actually much larger than this. Although the original production closed on January 27, 1923, a second company started playing in Philadelphia on October 23, 1922, within a month of the New York company's first anniversary. This Philadelphia company moved to Chicago, opening there on March 12, 1923, while another group of performers took its place in Philadelphia. The second Philadelphia company moved to New York's Shubert Theatre on May 21, 1923, and on the same night another cast opened across the street at the 44th Street Theatre. (These dual productions are the ones sometimes erroneously attributed to *Maytime*.) The 44th Street company closed after only a few weeks on June 2, and the Shubert one the following week, on June 9. Thus, the first production of *Blossom Time* included twenty out-of-town tryout performances, 516 shows in its "official" first run, and 576 more by the two companies just described. In the end, the operetta played for a remarkable total of 1,112 performances between March 21, 1921, when audiences first saw its tryout in Atlantic City, and its closing on June 9, 1923. This level of success was astonishing.

And it did not stop there, for *Blossom Time* played continuously in at least one Shubert house from its premiere in 1921 until 1943, fifteen years after the death of its librettist. The unbroken production sequence of over two decades made Foster Hirsch wonder if the so-called revivals that took place in New York in 1924, 1926, 1931, 1938, and 1943 should really be considered as true revivals.[11] To further complicate matters, the 1931 Broadway revival was a New York production by one of the road companies, not an original re-production of the 1921 operetta.

These road companies form a major part of the *Blossom Time* legacy. Four different traveling productions took the operetta throughout the United States. In another clever marketing ploy, the Shuberts had each of these companies play one night on Broadway so that they could advertise the road production, with all honesty, as "direct from Broadway." The road tours operated on very small budgets. Their tattered costumes and dilapidated sets made "a road tour of *Blossom Time*" synonymous with theatrical shabbiness. It is unfortunate that *Blossom Time* became known more for its threadbare touring companies that for its fine music.

Blossom Time defies all conventions of a successful Broadway musical. First, the story ends tragically: the hero dies of a broken heart. Second, the songs are intentionally derivative: they are supposed to sound like modern versions of some of Schubert's finest work. Third, the plot is set in Vienna, the capital of the former Habsburg Empire, one of the European powers the United States had recently fought in a major war.

These elements actually became the key to the work's success. Audiences no longer required a happy ending in a Broadway musical; a tragic one could also be extremely effective and satisfying. They also knew that the story was largely fictional and was not intended to be a documentary. Although Schubert purists scoffed at the idea of "cheapening" the great master's music (much less concocting biographical elements), the show's music nonetheless proved to be extremely popular with the public. A great tune is a great tune, no matter who wrote it. Finally, nostalgia for a prewar Vienna and the remembrance of Vienna as it once was overshadowed more recent events in the city's history. *Blossom Time*'s Vienna is the city of dreams, a place where creative artists and their friends meet in restaurants and cafés to sing, enjoy music, and revel in each other's company. It is an idealized past filled with nostalgic remembering.

Critics and audiences alike adored *Blossom Time*. The wistful return to early nineteenth-century Vienna captured their attention. Critics appreciated the approachable nature of the score, finding it neither too modern nor too classical. Alexander Woollcott, writing for the *New York Times*, had this to say: "After jazz, what? They tried a new answer on Broadway last evening, when 'Blossom Time' was produced at the Ambassador. . . . The immortal melodies, of a beauty that often lies near to tears, were perhaps necessarily sophisticated a bit by successive adapters, even at certain points 'syncopated' for Broadway."[12] Woollcott's descriptors "sophisticated" and "syncopated" likely refer to the refrain of "My Springtime Thou Art," to be discussed below.

Others shared his enthusiasm. George S. Kaufman, also writing for the *Times*, especially admired the "songs of passionate longing that illuminated 'Blossom Time' like pictures in a Christmas book."[13] Alan Dale described the show in the *New York American* as "a veritable avalanche of exquisite melody . . . nothing more musically titillate has been heard in ages. . . . It is a relief to sit through such a musical play as 'Blossom Time.' Melody was showered upon you opulently; one number was followed by another of even greater beauty."[14] Similarly, Kenneth Macgowan praised it effusively in the *New York Globe*: "A triumphantly lovely score with the success of a hundred years behind it, and of how many more in front!"[15]

The unsigned reviewer for the *New York Herald* dismissed fears about the show possibly being too stuffy, and highlighted Romberg's contributions: "Nobody need be afraid of the name of Schubert in connection with the score. The most popular numbers have in every case been selected. Sigmund Romberg has occasionally come to the assistance of the famous song writer but he has done it expertly since he is proficient in the Vienna modes."[16]

Audiences flocked to see *Blossom Time*. As a musical about Franz Schubert, the show had a unique marketing opportunity less than four months after its opening, for January 31, 1922, was the 125th anniversary of the composer's birth. The Shuberts established a Schubert Memorial Committee to create interest in the music of its namesake and sponsored a Schubert Memorial Week from January 29 to February 5. The committee had its headquarters at the Ambassador Theatre, home of *Blossom Time*. The producers wrote on an advertising card for their Schubert-based show:

> We extend felicitations to the Franz Schubert Memorial Committee upon this the beginning of Schubert memorial week and are happy to lend our co-operation and that of our theatres in the nation-wide celebration of the 125th Anniversary of the Composer's birth.
>
> We are, indeed, proud of "Blossom Time" in which Franz Schubert is the principal and the fundamental figure. We believed that there was a place in New York for an operetta of superior quality in which the beautiful melodies of the "greatest song writer who ever lived" would be heard and the character of the immortal Schubert himself would be embodied.
>
> Our faith has been approved enthusiastically and sincerely by the public. (Signed) LEE and J.J. SHUBERT[17]

The Shuberts were right. New York needed and wanted a show like *Blossom Time*. Its nostalgic properties drew audiences away from their present-day worries and concerns into a fantasy world filled with laughter, joy, and springtime, but one that had a significant dose of reality, that is, a love story without a happy ending.

The operetta's underlying plot is basically a modified version of Cyrano de Bergerac. Franz Schubert (Bertram Peacock) is in love with Mitzi Kranz (Olga Cook), one of the crown jeweler's three daughters, but is too shy to let her know. He expresses his feelings through the show's recurring waltz, "Song of Love." Schubert implores his friend, Baron Franz Schober (Howard Marsh), to sing Mitzi a song that he himself has written ("Only One Love Ever Fills the Heart"). The Baron obliges, and Mitzi, thinking the sentiments are the Baron's, falls in love with the messenger.

Several secondary plots surround and intersect with the story. In one of these, Count Scharntoff wants to win back the affections of his wife, Bellabruna, an operatic soprano, and asks Schubert to write him a song. The composer, in a sudden burst of inspiration, immediately writes his "Serenade."[18] Bellabruna, in turn, is in love with Schober, who has no interest in the married woman, a realization that only angers the prima donna.

Meanwhile, Kranz's two other daughters, Fritzi and Kitzi, have secret lovers. In act 1, they come to Domayer's Restaurant, along with their sister Mitzi, happily singing "Three Little Maids" and looking forward to meeting their beaus. Unbeknownst to them, their father has followed them, suspicious of their plans. The resourceful Schober tells Kranz that they accompanied Mitzi, who has come to the café in order to ask Schubert for music lessons. Schober then leads four of his friends in the stunning male quintet "My Springtime Though Art." (They also sing the "Serenade" that Schubert wrote for Scharntoff.) The plan works even better than expected, for Schober and his friends get Kranz drunk, and the jeweler not only acknowledges his daughters' sweethearts but also allows them to marry.

The second act takes place three months later, on the double wedding day of Fritzi and Kitzi. Bellabruna, angry with Schober, tells Mitzi about an awful man with the initials "F.S." Bellabruna jealously thinks that Schober is interested in Mitzi and wants to slander his name in front of the object of his affection. Mitzi has just finished singing a duet with Schubert ("Tell Me Daisy"), and infers that Bellabruna is talking about the composer, since his initials are also "F.S." It is at this point that Schober sings the song Schubert wrote for Mitzi, "Only One Love Ever Fills the Heart," and of course, after hearing horrible things about "F.S.," Mitzi focuses her romantic attention on Schober, whom she really does love more than Schubert. The composer is devastated.

In the final act, Schubert is too ill to attend the premiere of his Eighth Symphony and sits alone at home. Ever since Mitzi fell in love with Schober, all inspiration has left him. Scharntoff storms in and demands his song back. He tells Schubert that Bellabruna is not worthy of such beautiful music and, furthermore, that he has challenged Schober, whom he suspects is his wife's secret lover, to a duel. Schubert informs the Count that this cannot be the case, for he knows that Schober loves Mitzi. When the heartbroken composer thinks of Mitzi, inspiration returns for a fleeting moment, during which he writes the emotive and serene "Peace, Peace to My Lonely Heart." Schubert's friends arrive from the concert, telling him that the new symphony was a great success. It ultimately does not matter, for Schubert dies as a chorus of angels sings his final creation.

For the score to this musical version of Schubert's life, Romberg com-

Bertram Peacock (as Franz Schubert), Olga Cook (as Mitzi), and Howard Marsh (as Baron Franz Schober) in the original production of *Blossom Time*. Courtesy of the Shubert Archive.

bined Schubert's music with that of his own. The playbill says it best: "Music adapted and augmented by Sigmund Romberg from the melodies of Franz Schubert, selected and arranged by Heinrich Berté." Romberg, like his fellow *Das Dreimäderlhaus* adapters, followed Berté's general musical plan and focused his energies on creating new renditions of well-known Schubert melodies. When it comes to specific parallels between Berté and Romberg, only five of the songs appear with the same music in both works. (See Table 4.1.) Four of these are in act 1 and include the opening and the finale. Romberg rearranged the order of the Berté borrowings in act 1 so as not to have a direct song-by-song reworking. He departed further from Berté in act 2, the only parallel music being the finale.

More important than Romberg's treatment of Berté, though, is his treatment of Schubert. Schubert's music appears throughout the operetta and

Table 4.1 *Blossom Time* numbers and their parallels in *Das Dreimäderlhaus*

Blossom Time song and number in vocal score	*Das Dreimäderlhaus* source and number in vocal score
"Opening Ensemble—Hail, Let Us Greet the Spring" (1)	"Lied"—refrain, "Licht senkt es sich von Himmel nieder" (6b)
"Three Little Maids" (3)	"Auftritts-Terzett" (2)
"My Springtime Thou Art," refrain (5)	"Duet"—verse, "Bin so glücklich" (5)
"Finale Act 1—Opening" (7)	"Quintett" (4)
"Finale Act 2" (14)	"Finale 2" (12)

Table 4.2 Principal *Blossom Time* numbers and their sources in the works of Franz Schubert

Blossom Time song	Schubert source
"Three Little Maids"	*Rosamunde* ballet music
"Serenade"	"Ständchen" from *Schwanengesang*
"My Springtime Thou Art"	Ecossaise, D. 735, no. 2 and "Trauerwalzer," D. 365, no. 2
"Song of Love"	Symphony No. 8, first movement
"Love Is a Riddle"	"Heidenrößlein"
"Tell Me Daisy"	Symphony No. 8, second movement
"Only One Love"	"Die Forelle" and Piano Sonata, D. 568, first movement
"Thou Art My Love"	"Ungeduld" from *Die schöne Müllerin*
"Peace to My Lonely Heart"	"Ave Maria"

forms the basis of its major songs and ensembles. (See Table 4.2.) The inclusion of Schubert's music in a show about the composer would be futile if the audience did not recognize the quotes.

Romberg's treatment of Schubert's music varies greatly. In some instances, such as "Serenade" and "Peace to My Lonely Heart," Romberg leaves the originals basically intact, and Donnelly creates new words for the well-known melodies. Other times he transforms the melodies into entirely new entities that, while still recognizable as Schubert, are substantially changed. Romberg focuses his alterations on the linear dimensions of rhythm and meter, leaving the vertical harmonic structures largely unchanged. Three instances of this treatment are the refrains of "My Springtime Thou Art," "Only One Love Ever Fills the Heart," and "Song of Love."

Example 4.1. Schubert, "Trauerwalzer," D. 365, no. 2, mm. 1–4

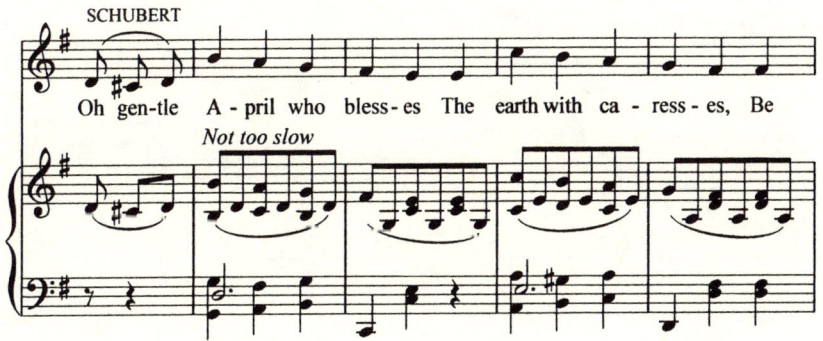

Example 4.2. "My Springtime Thou Art" *(Blossom Time)*, verse, mm. 25–28

Romberg bases the refrain of "My Springtime Thou Art" on "Trauerwalzer," D. 365, no. 2, and eventually transforms the "mourning waltz" into a duple-meter, moderate-tempo testament to love. Prior to the appearance of the metamorphosis, however, he quotes the original waltz version, though with an ornamented anacrusis, in the final part of the verse. (See examples 4.1 and 4.2.) Schubert sings his melody before Schober leads the quintet in its cut-time rendition. Off-beat stresses infuse buoyancy into the melodic line (for example, on the word "laughs") and rests likewise forbid a legato melodic line from being constructed. The joyous nature of the text is thus ensured, removing all references to the piano piece's nickname. (See example 4.3.)

The song's vocal scoring also merits attention, for the existence of five independent parts is far more complex than was typical in a Broadway number, even in an operetta. Romberg's idea for this treatment comes from Berté's original music for *Das Dreimäderlhaus*. At this point in the score, the German composer also has a quintet based on "Trauerwalzer," but one with

Example 4.3. "My Springtime Thou Art" (*Blossom Time*), refrain, mm. 1–4

Example 4.4. Schubert, Piano Sonata, D. 568, E-flat version, first movement, mm. 186–87

Example 4.5. "Only One Love Ever Fills the Heart" *(Blossom Time)*, refrain, mm. 1–8 (melody line only)

a different musical effect, for Berté kept the original waltz for the refrain. Romberg and Donnelly clearly modeled "My Springtime Thou Art" on this concerted number, which, not incidentally, also refers to spring in its title, "Es soll der Frühling mir künden" ("Spring is telling me").

Reversing the process from "My Springtime Thou Art," in "Only One Love Ever Fills the Heart," the song Schubert asks Schober to sing to Mitzi on his behalf, Romberg significantly alters the second theme of the first movement of Schubert's Piano Sonata, D. 568, by transforming it *into* a waltz. Although the source material is in 3/4, it is not a waltz. Romberg slows the overall tactus of the melody, lengthening eighth notes into either quarter notes or, more distinctively, dotted half notes. (See examples 4.4 and 4.5.) Furthermore, he articulates each eighth-note pulse of Schubert's initial dotted quarter note as three successive dotted half notes on the same pitch. Donnelly then provides one syllable of text for each measure ("On-ly one"). The basic melodic line is preserved, but because of the rhythmic elongations, its character is changed—a gentle triple-meter idea becomes an expressive waltz.

The third example of Romberg's thematic transformation of a Schubert melody is the operetta's primary waltz, "Song of Love." Here, as in "Only

Example 4.6. Schubert, Symphony No. 8, first movement, mm. 44–47

One Love Ever Fills the Heart," Romberg lengthens certain notes of the original in order to create a waltz. The Schubert source material is the opening of the second theme from the first movement of the Eighth Symphony, a triple-meter melody that has the character of a waltz, although its syncopated accompaniment creates some ambiguity as to whether or not it truly is one. Romberg triples the value of the melody's first note and places its second pitch on the downbeat of the second measure. In doing so, he immediately creates the impression of a waltz through the readily discernable OOM-pah-pah accompaniment that appears against the single melodic note. (See examples 4.6 and 4.7.) Romberg alters the end of Schubert's melodic line so that the phrase ends with a 9–8 appoggiatura (G-F) set as two dotted half notes, thus emphasizing the word "im-mor-tal."

This song, derived from one of Schubert's most popular compositions, is the operetta's principal number. Donnelly's lyric is notably different from those of Romberg's earlier love waltzes. Here, the time is the present and the character's emotional response is immediate. There is no sense of parting, no hint that the only thing that will remain of this present love is a memory. Elation will continue forever exactly as it is at this moment—this is a song rooted in the present tense: "You *are* my song of love."

Romberg employs "Song of Love" in various dramatic situations, as he did with the main waltzes in *The Blue Paradise*, *Maytime*, and *The Magic Melody*. Schubert and Mitzi first sing it in act 1, shortly after they meet; it is an expression of their mutual attraction, their belief in love at first sight.

Example 4.7. "Song of Love" (*Blossom Time*), refrain, mm. 1–8

By contrast, the song's direct, present-tense nature makes its reprise at the end of act 2 especially poignant. Mitzi and Schober have just left together, leaving Schubert alone on stage. Sitting at the piano, he sings the love duet, but this time, obviously, as a solo. He is still deeply in love with Mitzi and is absolutely devastated that she has gone off with another man. Schubert is suffering from lovesick despair as he intones his heartrending rendition of "Song of Love."

Schubert and Mitzi sing two duets in *Blossom Time*, "Song of Love" in act 1 and "Tell Me Daisy" in act 2. Schubert cognoscenti in the audience would have realized that these were the only two Romberg songs derived from Schubert's Eighth Symphony, the "Unfinished," the one that receives its premiere in act 3. According to *Blossom Time*, Schubert leaves his Eighth Symphony unfinished because of Mitzi. She is his inspiration for the work, and once it becomes obvious that she is not in love with him, he loses the will to complete it. Schubert, Mitzi, and the Eighth Symphony are brought together through the choice of source material for the two duets. In the operetta's chronology, these songs are in effect the "working sketches" for the symphony. The symphony is Schubert's tribute to Mitzi and their love; therefore, in the context of the operetta's plot, it makes perfect sense that it should include the two songs he sang with her.

Lost love in an operetta was of course nothing new to either Romberg or the Shuberts: the theme was central to *The Blue Paradise, Maytime,* and *The Magic Melody.* Now it appeared again in *Blossom Time* but intensified to the point where the lead character dies on stage of a broken heart. Romberg continued to create shows with a formula that worked—a tale of lost love with a score centered around a nostalgic waltz. Thanks to *Blossom Time*'s success, operetta proved to be a commercially and artistically profitable enterprise for the Shuberts. They cemented their dominance over American operetta with *Blossom Time,* and the genre, along with their theaters, became their longest-lived legacies. *Blossom Time* survived in productions of all sorts, from road tours to summer stock to junior high school productions, and, as of 2007, it is the only operetta for which the Shubert Theatrical Corporation still controls the performance rights.

Blossom Time, importantly, was the first in a long line of Broadway musicals to recount the lives of classical composers and to have scores derived from their works. This legacy includes *The Love Song* (1925) and *The Happiest Girl in the World* (1962)—Offenbach; *Najda* (1925) and *Music in My Heart* (1927)—Tchaikovsky; *White Lilacs* (1928) and *Polonaise* (1945)—Chopin; *Song of Norway* (1944)—Grieg; *Rhapsody* (1944)—Kreisler; *Kismet* (1953)—Borodin; and *Anya* (1965)—Rachmaninoff.[19] This does not include Hollywood's biopics, for which the list is even longer.[20] *Blossom Time* showed that there was commercial viability and strong public interest in the lives, whether real or imagined, of great classical composers.

After the success of the *Maytime, The Magic Melody,* and *Blossom Time,* Romberg returned briefly to his previous Shubert-appointed task of writing additional songs for European operetta imports. In 1922, the year after *Blossom Time* appeared, Romberg wrote interpolations for three Shubert adaptations: *The Rose of Stamboul* (March 7, 1922, Century), based on *Die Rose von Stambul,* by Leo Fall; *The Lady in Ermine* (October 2, 1922, Ambassador), after *Die Frau im Hermelin,* by Rudolf Schanzer and Ernst Welisch; and *Springtime of Youth* (October 26, 1922, Broadhurst), derived from *Sterne, die wieder leuchtet,* by Walter Kollo. Among the outstanding numbers from these works are the expressive waltz "My Heart Is Calling," from *The Rose of Stamboul*, and the gentle ballad "When Hearts Are Young," from *The Lady in Ermine*.

For Romberg, these interpolations—as well as his work in revue and musical comedy—were diversions from his central career path as an operetta composer. They were not worthless endeavors, by any means, for they provided him opportunities to create various types of music for specific dramatic contexts. But with *Blossom Time* and its immediate predecessors, Romberg's reputation as an operetta composer was solidified. He discovered the types of stories that inspired him the most, and at the centerpiece of these scores was a waltz, not just any waltz but one that was integrated into the plot. In *Maytime* it was written on the back of a deed; in *The Magic Melody* it was the theme to an unperformed opera; and in *Blossom Time* it was the creation of the male lead. By tying these waltzes to the dramatic plot, Romberg was establishing an important precept of American operetta—the union of music and drama. Furthermore, he was establishing the waltz, the Viennese paradigm, as the fundamental musical basis of an American-based genre. Romberg's operettas were praised for their glorious waltzes; other song types were certainly present as well, but waltzes formed the musical core of Romberg's distinctive approach to operetta.

CHAPTER 5

Young Love in Old Heidelberg: *The Student Prince*

IN THE YEARS SURROUNDING WORLD WAR I, GERMAN ELEMENTS IN Broadway musicals had to be handled very carefully. In *Maytime*, the Shuberts were so concerned about any German associations that they completely removed all Teutonic elements from the production. After the United States entered the war, performances of German-language plays, operas, and operettas were forbidden. But by the early 1920s the situation had changed considerably.[1] German composers such as Richard Wagner were enjoying a renaissance in New York. The Metropolitan Opera, for example, mounted productions of *Lohengrin*, *Parsifal*, and *Tristan und Isolde* during the 1920–21 season, after not performing any of the composer's music in 1918 and 1919. Additionally, the Manhattan Opera House sponsored a four-week Wagner festival that began in February 1923.[2] As a strong endorsement of the rehabilitation of German music and culture, a concert "For the Benefit of the Richard Wagner Bayreuth Festival Theatre Restoration Fund" was held at the Metropolitan Opera House on February 10, 1924. Siegfried Wagner, son of the great composer, conducted music by his father and Franz Liszt, his grandfather (Cosima's father), as well as his own works. German music and culture had once again become acceptable in New York City.

It was in such an atmosphere that the Shuberts, keenly aware of popular tastes, decided to create a musical version of one of the most successful German-language plays of the early twentieth century, Wilhelm Meyer-Foerster's *Alt-Heidelberg* (1901). First produced in Berlin, the play quickly crossed the Atlantic. Its U.S. premiere took place on March 5, 1902, at the Pabst Theatre in Milwaukee, Wisconsin. The first New York production (still in German) took place seven months later, on October 21, at the Irving Place Theatre.³ The play was performed for the first time in English at the Princess Theatre in New York on December 15, 1902. This version, prepared by the actor Aubrey Boucicault for his own use, was titled simply *Heidelberg*. Another actor, Richard Mansfield, saw Boucicault's production and created his own version, called *Old Heidelberg*, to open the Lyric Theatre on October 12, 1903. It was one of the highlights of his career.

In the play, Prince Karl Heinrich of Karlsberg leaves his kingdom to study at the University of Heidelberg, accompanied by his tutor Juttner and his valet Lutz. He wants his life as a student to be as normal as possible and does not want people to know that he is heir to the Karlsberg throne. He falls in love with Kathie, a waitress at the Inn of the Golden Apples, and is supported in his youthful romantic efforts by the fraternal Saxon Corps. All is well until he is summoned back to Karlsberg when his grandfather the king is dying. Duty calls in another way as well, for he must enter into an arranged marriage with a princess. In the final scene, Karl Franz returns to Heidelberg to bid a sad farewell to Kathie. The lovers part, realizing that all that remains of their young love is its memory.

The sentimental drama was popular with audiences. It was revived twice, in 1904 and 1910, and two mute Hollywood film versions appeared, the first in 1915 and the second in 1927. Both films were called *Old Heidelberg*, after Mansfield's title. John Emerson directed the 1915 Griffith-Triangle Film Company release that starred Wallace Ried and Dorothy Gish. Erich von Stroheim (1885–1957) was assistant director and technical adviser for the film and also played Lutz. The young assistant had many duties, including overseeing the actors who played the Saxon Corps. Von Stroheim's legendary heavy-handed directorial approach was already evident: he demanded that all the members of the student group have German-style haircuts and forced them to appear in military fashion on an open stage for roll call, inspection, and drill. Neither actors nor bystanders appreciated the overtly martial and Teutonic nature of von Stroheim's activities, especially with the worsening tensions in Europe at the time.[4] Ernst Lubitsch directed the 1927 MGM remake, which starred Ramon Novarro and Norma Shearer. The film appeared three years after *The Student Prince* and relied on the popularity of the operetta for its own success, even appearing under the alternate title *The Student Prince in Old Heidelberg*.

The Shuberts were interested in creating a musical version of *Old Heidelberg* as early as 1919.[5] They owned the rights to the stage version, but these did not include creating and producing a musical adaptation. World War I was over, and German culture was being rehabilitated. The Shuberts certainly did not want to miss out on this money-making opportunity. Meanwhile, of course, they had produced *Blossom Time*, in which Vienna was re-created in a benign manner, void of any politics or danger, except that which occurs from a broken heart. A musical version of *Old Heidelberg* was poised to do the same for Germany—the Teutonic nation could be promoted as a domain of castles and beer where everyone is blithely unaware of any real politics and the only sadness or disdain results from ill-fated romances.

Not having the rights to produce an operetta based on *Old Heidelberg* did not stop the Shuberts from proceeding with the project. In August 1922, Dorothy Donnelly signed a contract with the Shuberts to write the libretto and lyrics.[6] It is likely that she had already done a fair amount of work, for J. J. Shubert commented on the prologue and first two acts in a letter dated August 21:

> Dear Miss Donnelly,
> I have read the Prologue and the first and second act of "Alt Heidelberg." While I think it is charming, I think a great many improvements can be made in the way of the prologue. I think the Princess whom Carl Franz is to be betrothed to should see him at Carlsburg before he leaves for Heidleberg [sic]. He should be very still and pompous, and she should be very cold. I think that would inject a little femininity into the play to show the difference between Katie [sic] and this girl. Bringing the Princess back in the second act is a very good idea.
> I should also have liked to have made Franz a sojourner in Heidelberg for about eight months to give him a chance to become entirely different, and also time for the Princess to have changed a little. In fact, it would help all the characters to have a little more time elapse between the prologue and the second act.
> Another idea which I had in mind was to make the prologue sort of a story between Carl Franz and his son and enact the entire play of Alt Heidelberg. He could tell him what happened to him and his grandfather, the same as they did in Romance.[7] Of course, that is merely a suggestion.
> I am sorry you did not consult me before going so far, as we could have gotten together on a great many things which might have improved it a whole lot. However, I am waiting for the third act, and it might change my entire idea of the play. I am only giving you my first criticism on the reading of same.
> I want this play to take the place of Blossom Time, and I am sure you are

on the right track. It is very well written and I know you are very enthusiastic, otherwise you could not have put so much in the play.[8]

Shubert made it clear in the final paragraph that he wanted the new operetta to be the successor to *Blossom Time*. Whether he meant this in terms of atmosphere or commercial viability is not absolutely clear, but he likely meant both.

Donnelly's final libretto followed the original play very closely, the notable changes being the names of the prince and his tutor. In the play they are Karl Heinrich and Juttner, while in the operetta they become Karl Franz and Engel. Engel means "angel" in German, and the new name is appropriate, for the tutor is in many ways his charge's guardian angel.

Romberg became interested in the project as early as spring 1922, several months after *Blossom Time* opened. Donnelly had already started creating the libretto before Romberg began writing music for the new show. Surely the working relationship he had developed with Donnelly contributed to him wanting to work with her again. Although Romberg completed sections of the score in February 1923, he did not sign a formal contract with the Shuberts to write the new operetta until July 11, 1924.[9]

The new operetta, entitled *In Heidelberg*, had its world premiere on October 27, 1924, at the Apollo Theatre in Atlantic City. Its pre-Broadway tryout continued the following week at the Shubert Theatre in Philadelphia, where it played for three weeks (November 3–24). It received strong reviews in both cities. Furthermore, Harms published sheet music selections from the new show imprinted with the title *In Heidelberg*.[10] The show was quickly moving toward a Broadway opening.

But there were still some concerns. Even though the coldness toward Germany and German culture was thawing, the Shuberts worried about the underlying Teutonic themes and setting of their new show. There are stories that they were also apprehensive about the large male chorus (the size of which would substantially increase the production costs) and the bittersweet ending.[11] Considering *Blossom Time*'s Viennese setting, operatic male quintets, and tragic conclusion, these claims are likely overstated. In any case, the producers need not have worried, as Romberg himself related: "They objected to the large male chorus, and were certain that the public would take exception to the German tale. But when we opened in Philadelphia the audience applauded so enthusiastically that the producers realized they had a success."[12]

The Shuberts also faced legal challenges, for even as the show was playing in Atlantic City and Philadelphia, the producers still did not have the rights to create a musical version of Meyer-Foerster's play. The situation had to be resolved before the operetta opened on Broadway. To summarize the complex sequence of events, Arthur Hirsch, the Shuberts' agent in Berlin, secured the rights for himself on October 9, 1924. The producers had great difficulty obtaining them from him, and as would be expected, J. J. Shubert was extremely irritated, even referring to Hirsch as "a dirty crook."[13] It was not until November 26, 1924, literally days before the work opened on Broadway, that the Shuberts finally acquired the legal rights to produce a musical version of the German play.[14] Details of the contract included, among other things, that the title *Old Heidelberg* could not be used in any form. This did not bother Shubert, for as he wrote to Hirsch: "Regarding Alt-Heidelberg, we are not producing Alt-Heidelberg and never called it Alt-Heidelberg. The title we started to use was 'In Heidelberg,' but we changed it because the people all thought it was a revival and it was effecting [sic] our business and hurting us to use that name."[15] The Shuberts finally decided that the show's name would be *The Student Prince in Heidelberg*, or simply *The Student Prince*.[16]

As J. J. Shubert wrote to Dorothy Donnelly, he wanted *The Student Prince* to replace *Blossom Time*. His wish was granted, for *The Student Prince* (December 2, 1924, Jolson's) became the longest-running Broadway musical to appear in the 1920s, with 608 performances in its initial run.[17] It was a phenomenal success and the pinnacle of Romberg's work with the Shuberts. The show harkened back to their previous successes in the operetta realm and—importantly—did not have a happy ending. The romantic leads are not together at the final curtain, following the trajectory of the ill-fated lovers in *The Blue Paradise*, *Maytime*, and *Blossom Time*. Furthermore, the musical score is unified through a recurring waltz. In the case of *The Student Prince*, it is "Deep in My Heart, Dear." The music will be discussed later; here we will focus on dimensions of the drama.

The show ends with the unfulfilled and unfulfillable love of the Student Prince and his first and only true sweetheart. Their romance is not resolved in a future generation. It ends with them. There is no compromise ending, as at the end of *The Blue Paradise* or *Maytime*, but on the other hand, at least one of the characters does not die, as occurs at the end of *Blossom Time*. *The Student Prince* ends with an overt outpouring of sentiment and a nostalgic yearning for the freedom and joys of youth.

Karl Franz and Kathie are not the only couple in *The Student Prince*—the show boasts three pairs of lovers. Princess Margaret loves Tarnitz, and must also forswear her feelings to marry the prince. Theirs is the gender-reversed counterpart to Karl Franz and Kathie. To offset these ill-fated tales, the romance between the show's comics, Lutz, the prince's valet, and Gretchen, a barmaid at the inn, provides the show's requisite humor. All of the interaction between these witty foils for the "serious" couples takes place during spoken dialogue: Lutz and Gretchen do not have any musical numbers to themselves. In fact, the singing requirements of both roles are minimal. Lutz has only a few solo phrases in the act 1 finale when he discloses the prince's identity and is chastised for doing so, but the rest of the time the pair sing only with the chorus. Lutz and Gretchen are sometimes cast with actors of physically larger stature than those who play the romantic leads. This choice allows for visual contrast, in addition to differences in character type and vocal writing (nonsinging versus singing), with the principal couple.

The shift away from Ruritanian operetta that characterized Romberg's work in the 1910s is also evident here. While *The Student Prince* has a royal-commoner romance at the heart of its tale, the male lead is not a dim-witted Ruritanian prince but rather a highly intelligent German one. He is going to historic Heidelberg, after all. The ethnic numbers in the show are not quasi-Balkan music (as in Lehár's *The Merry Widow*) but rather German-style songs, either real or created.

And who sings most of the German songs? The male chorus, of course. The male chorus in *The Student Prince* is central to the show's plot. The fraternal affection that they show toward the prince is accentuated in numbers such as "Drinking Song," "Students Marching Song" ("To the Inn We're Marching"), "Come, Boys, Let's All Be Gay, Boys," and "Serenade," as well as the actual student song "Gaudeamus igitur." Romberg's focus on the male chorus as a central dramatic force is far greater in *The Student Prince* than in any of his previous works, where its role is minimal. The male chorus remains one of the show's most memorable aspects.

The Student Prince's early success was due not only to the show itself but also to its stars, Ilse Marvenga and Howard Marsh. The German-born actress Ilse Marvenga (1896–?) played Kathie, the prince's love interest. Her association with the role was so strong that J. J. insisted that she play the opening of every major *Student Prince* company. Marvenga played Kathie in over three thousand performances, a phenomenal achievement. In addition to her role in *The Student Prince*, Marvenga starred in revivals of two operettas during the 1920s and '30s: Herbert's *Naughty Marietta* and Friml's *The Firefly*.[18]

Howard Marsh (1888–1969) was one of Broadway's most popular leading men during the 1920s, making his New York debut as Count de Cluny in *The Grass Widow* (1917), a musical with a score by Louis A. Hirsch. Subsequent Broadway credits before Karl Franz included *Greenwich Village Follies* (1920) and Baron Schober in *Blossom Time* (1921). After his success in *The Student Prince*, Marsh played Ned Hamilton in Romberg's *Cherry Blossoms* (1927) and created the role of Gaylord Ravenal in Jerome Kern's *Show Boat* later that same year.

The Student Prince was extremely popular with critics and audiences. Of the many reviews that appeared after its premiere, among the most enlightening was the one by George Jean Nathan that appeared in the *American Mercury*. Nathan was enthralled with the production, even though it lacked subtlety:

> I have mentioned the fact that "Old Heidelberg" is the kind of play that might be acted in a livery stable with Julius Marx in the role of Prince Karl and Robert Mantell in the role of Kathi [sic] and that it would still retain a great deal of its mood hypnosis and eternal charm. The tender fable told these years ago by Meyer-Foerster, a fable universal in the hearts of men, can successfully survive almost any assault that is made upon it in the theatre. Nothing can kill it; its pulse beats on and on. . . . The chief flaw in the presentation lies in the direction of the love scenes. The love story of "Old Heidelberg" is one of hesitant grace; there is to it the suggestion of a hundred forgotten twilights. It is like a lovely tune played upon a silent piano. In the present instance, this fragile and delicate story is given a fortissimo treatment. The Prince and Kathi do not simply embrace when they embrace; they make a mutual flying tackle. The Prince goes at Kathi on all occasions like a hobo after a free lunch, while Kathi meets his advances all too often like an Elinor Glyn book advertisement.[19]

The astute reviewer found the direction to be out of place with the sentimental nature of the work itself. His reference to Elinor Glyn (1864–1943), the novelist whose tales of sexual adventures scandalized Edwardian society, suggests that Kathie was portrayed not as an operetta ingénue but rather as a musical comedy heroine whose primary goal is to find a man.

By contrast, the unnamed reviewer for the *New York Times*, likely either Olin Downes or Stark Young, discussed the work in terms of an operetta, highlighting its romance, music, and style:

"The Student Prince" is a prodigious operetta. The play that was "Old Heidelberg" has been produced again in musical form, and on a scale that never would have been possible in the old days. . . . Not even the comparative absence of the comic element is of importance in "The Student Prince": the piece concentrates so successfully upon its prime ingredients that nothing more is needed.

The simple story of the Prince of Karlsburg and his love for a Heidelberg barmaid lends itself perfectly to this style of production—it requires a minimum of dialogue and so clears the decks rapidly for the business of an operetta, which is music. The score of this piece is by far the best that Sigmund Romberg has done. The clicking heels of the students and the high patent leather boots of the court are not alone on the stage of Jolson's; they are woven deep into Romberg's music.[20]

The Student Prince was not the only important show to open on Broadway in early December 1924, for two other impressive offerings appeared December 1, 1924, the evening before Romberg's operetta: *Lady, Be Good!* and *The Music Box Revue*. George Gershwin and Ira Gershwin's *Lady, Be Good!*, starring Fred and Adele Astaire, played at the Liberty Theater and featured the famous song "Fascinating Rhythm." Meanwhile at the Music Box Theatre, the final edition of *The Music Box Revue* had its debut. Grace Moore (later of Metropolitan Opera fame and still later of Hollywood renown) and Oscar Shaw sang Irving Berlin's "All Alone," and the legendary Fanny Brice dazzled her audience with her wisecracking humor and unforgettable stage presence. Thus, on two consecutive nights, December 1 and 2, new works that were epitomes of musical comedy, revue, and operetta opened on Broadway—all to strong reviews and enthusiastic audiences. Nostalgic operetta was every bit as welcome on Broadway as were its more modern cousins, musical comedy and revue.

Romberg and Donnelly's tale of unrequited love in nineteenth-century Germany was extremely popular with American audiences. The show exuded nostalgia for prewar Europe, a time and place unravaged by the horrors and realities of war. It also proved the rehabilitation of German themes in American popular culture.

This was not the case in London, however, where anti-German sentiment was much stronger than it was in the United States. The reader for the Lord Chamberlain's Office, G. S. Street, wrote: "I hope the German setting will not interfere with the success of the Play. There is nothing to find fault with."[21] Street's concerns were justified, for the operetta's German elements did not work in its favor, and the show played for a mere ninety-six performances in London.

The Student Prince opened at His Majesty's Theatre on February 3, 1926, with Allan Prior as Karl Franz and Ilse Marvenga in a reprise of her New York success. The London Bureau of the *New York Herald Tribune* wrote: "Some anti-German feeling, a hangover from the war, is also ascribed as one of the reasons for the cold reception to 'The Student Prince.' . . . Then, too, there is some prejudice against Ilse Marvenga, the prima donna, because she was born in Germany."[22]

Other factors worked against the London production of *The Student Prince* as well. British audiences were distraught at J. J. Shubert's decision to abolish unreserved pit seats, which were sold at cheaper prices. The Shuberts were eventually forced to reinstate the seats. This overt attempt at the Americanization of London theatrical practices, a cultural colonialism of sorts, justifiably annoyed London audiences. In addition to the controversy about the seating, the great influx of American musicals to London displaced the English revues, and this, too, frustrated audiences and critics.[23]

The Student Prince's tale of thwarted love in nineteenth-century Germany certainly had a great deal to do with its success. But the operetta's music is what made it immortal. *Alt-Heidelberg* and *Old Heidelberg* have not survived into the twenty-first century as standard repertory, unlike *The Student Prince*. The difference is, simply put, Romberg's remarkable score. From single numbers to large multisectional scenes, from German drinking songs to alluring waltzes, and from spirited marches for the male chorus to the operatic "Serenade," *The Student Prince* is undoubtedly one of Romberg's finest musical creations, and one of the most impressive operetta scores ever created.

The Music of *The Student Prince*

What makes *The Student Prince* so outstanding? First are its individual songs—primarily its extraordinary waltzes and marches. (See Table 5.1.) Second are its extended musical scenes. They are far more expansive than in Romberg's previous works, and follow Lehár and Kálmán's continental models in their integrated use of various musical styles. In *The Student Prince* Romberg and Donnelly employ music to substantially enhance and even drive the dramatic plot. Songs were treats in *Blossom Time*, pleasantries for the audience. But in *The Student Prince*, they were central to the story line.

Table 5.1 Musical program for *The Student Prince* (according to the opening night playbill)

Prologue: Ante-chamber in the Palace at Karlsberg, Spring, 1860
"By Our Bearing So Sedate" (Four Lackeys)
"Golden Days" (Prince, Dr. Engel)

Act I: Garden of the Inn of the Three Golden Apples. At the University of Heidelberg
"Garlands Bright" (Ruder, Gretchen, Flower Girls, Waitresses)
"Drinking Song" (Detlef, Students)
"To the Inn We're Marching" (Detlef, Von Asterberg, Lucas, Kathie, Students) [also known as "Students Marching Song"]
"You're in Heidelberg" (Prince, Dr. Engel)
"Welcome to Prince" (Kathie, Ruder, Gretchen, Girls)
Duet—"Deep in My Heart, Dear" (Prince, Kathie)
"Serenade" (Prince, Detlef, Lucas, Von Asterberg, Students)
Finale (Prince, Kathie, Detlef, Lucas, Von Asterberg, Ruder, Lutz, Dr. Engel, Gretchen, Hubert, Students, Girls)

Act II: Sitting Room of Prince Karl, at the Inn. Four months later.
Opening—"Farmer Jacob" (Detlef, Students)
"Students' Life" (Prince, Kathie, Dr. Engel, Gretchen, Detlef, Lucas, Von Asterberg, Eight students) ["Student Life" in the vocal score]
Duet—"Farewell, Dear" (Prince, Kathie) ["Farewell to Youth" in the vocal score]
Finale (Prince, Kathie, Von Mark, Dr. Engel)

Act III: A Room of State in the Royal Palace at Karlsberg. Two years later.
Opening—"Waltz Ensemble" (Ambassadors, Officers, Countess Leyden, Baron Arnheim, Ladies of the Court)
Solo Ballet (Premier Dancer)
"Just We Two" (Princess, Tarnitz, Officers)
"Gavotte" (Karl Franz, Princess, Countess, Baron Arnheim, Tarnitz, Officers, Ambassadors, Ladies of Court)
"What Memories" (Prince) [reprise of "Farewell to Youth"]
Finale (Prince, Kathie, Dr. Engel)

Act IV: Garden of the Inn of the Three Golden Apples. The next day.
Opening—"Sing a Little Song" (Students, Girls)
"To the Inn We're Marching" (Detlef, Von Asterberg, Students)
"Serenade" (Detlef, Students)
"Come Boys" (Students, Detlef, Von Asterberg)
Finale—"Deep in My Heart, Dear" (Prince, Princess, Kathie, Winter, Gretchen, Hubert, Lutz, Duchess, Detlef, Von Asterberg, Students, Girls)

Table 5.2 Waltzes in *The Student Prince*

Title	Number and title in vocal score
"Golden Days"	2. "Duet (Prince and Engel)" (act 1)
	Reprises: 6. "Entrance of Prince and Engel" (act 1)
	6b. "Reprise (Engel): Golden Days" (act 1)
	9. "Introduction" (act 2) [instrumental]
	12. "Finale" (act 2) [underscoring]
	16. "Finale" (act 3)
	18. "Finale" (act 4) [instrumental]
"Drinking Song"	5. "Chorus of Students and Concerted Number" (act 1)
	Reprises: 5a. "Reprise: Drinking Song" (act 1)
	8. "Finale" (act 1)
	9. "Introduction" (act 2) [instrumental]
"I'm Coming at Your Call"	5. "Chorus of Students and Concerted Number" (act 1)
	Reprise: 8. "Finale" (act 1)
"Deep in My Heart, Dear"	7. "Duet (Kathie and Prince)" (act 1)
	Reprises: 8. "Finale" (act 1)
	12. "Finale" (act 2)
	16. "Finale" (act 3)
	18. "Finale" (act 4) [instrumental]
	18. "Finale" (act 4) [finale ultimo]
"When the Spring Wakens Everything"	8. "Finale" (act 1)
"Farewell to Youth"	12. "Finale" (act 2)
	Reprise: 16. "Finale" (act 3)
"We're Off to Paris"	12. "Finale" (act 2)
"Just We Two"	14. "Duet (Princess and Tarnitz) and Chorus" (act 3)

Waltzes dominate *The Student Prince*. The operetta boasts eight distinct examples, nearly all of which are reprised in the course of its four acts. (See Table 5.2.) Most have sentimental lyrics that revel in aspects of nostalgia and nevermore. Numbers such as "Golden Days" and "Farewell to Youth" extol a sense of loss for a past that can never be regained. By contrast, "Drinking Song" is a fast-paced celebratory number that lauds camaraderie and solidarity. The operetta's principal love song, "Deep in My Heart, Dear," is an opulent extended waltz sequence, while "When the Spring Wakens Everything" is a joyful choral celebration of youth and vitality. "We're Off to Paris" endorses an optimistic hope for the future on the part of Kathie, while "Just We Two," the waltz for the secondary romantic leads, Margaret and Tarnitz, is the musical manifestation of their unrealizable love.

Five of the eight waltzes are introduced in act 1. They establish the overall musical setting of the operetta as a place where people can dance to their heart's delight. The waltzes provide the cornerstone of the show's underlying sense of nostalgia and romance.

Looking at each waltz in turn, the lyrics of "Golden Days" juxtapose happy memories of the past with the limitless possibilities of the present and the future. This duet between Engel, the elderly tutor, and Karl Franz, the young prince, allows the two characters to reflect on the wonders and joys of youth. Engel fondly recalls his student days in Heidelberg while the prince eagerly anticipates becoming a Heidelberg University student. In the song, Engel reminds his pupil that the nostalgic memories for the future are created in the joyous moments of the present.

Engel's idea of "Golden Days" is rooted in the past and endorses the ideals of nineteenth-century German Romanticism. In the opening of the verse, he muses on the Neckar River, a major tributary of the Rhine, "Down where the Neckar flows swiftly along." This type of river reference is central to German Romantic poetry and music, from which an entire genre of Rhine-related works emerged. In "Golden Days," Romberg and Donnelly allude to the German tradition of songs such as the immensely popular "Die Wacht am Rhein" ("The Guard on the Rhein"), which was published in many versions during the late nineteenth century. In the classical realm, "Im Rhein" ("On the Rhine") from Robert Schumann's *Dichterliebe* ("A Poet's Love," 1840) and *Das Rheingold* (*The Rhinegold*, 1851–54), the first of Richard Wagner's *Der Ring des Nibelungen* (*The Ring of the Nibelungen*), are just two examples of the river's widespread popularity and significance in nineteenth-century German music.[24]

Nostalgia is at the root of Engel's fond recollections, and memory is the agent. Donnelly and Romberg make this explicitly clear in the line "looking back through memory's haze." At these central words of the refrain, the principal E-major tonality sidesteps to D-flat minor, an enharmonic submediant. (See example 5.1.) The overriding concept of nostalgia, the past as viewed through memory, is affirmed textually and accentuated musically.

Karl Franz sings for the first time in "Golden Days"; it provides the first impression of the operetta's title character. In contrast to the formality of the opening choral number, which establishes an ordered sense of place at the Karlsberg court, "Golden Days," as a waltz, introduces the human side of

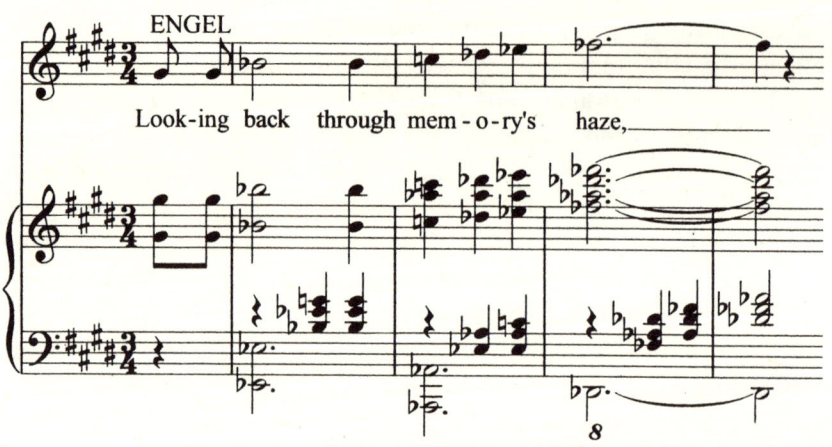

Example 5.1. "Golden Days" *(The Student Prince)*, refrain, mm. 21–24

Karl Franz. He is a prince who dreams of the future and its possibilities. He wants more out of life than the rigidity of court. He dreams of the "Golden Days" he will have in Heidelberg, and does so in a waltz.

"Golden Days" is reprised several times in the course of the operetta, each time emphasizing the passing of time and evoking nostalgic images. In this way, it functions like *Maytime*'s "Will You Remember." The opening motif of the refrain accompanies Engel's initial music upon his arrival in Heidelberg (no. 6 in the vocal score), "Heidelberg, beloved vision of my heart, the place of my dreams." Later in the same scene, following the student chorus's rendition of "Gaudeamus igitur," Engel sings a full reprise of the refrain, a testimony to his faith in the power of Heidelberg. The music appears in the orchestral introduction to act 2, and as underscoring in the same act's finale. Engel intones yet another reprise in the act 3 finale, providing contrast to the prince's minor-mode waltz bemoaning the passing of youth, "Farewell to Youth." The final appearance of the song is as an instrumental interlude in the operetta's finale. Here, it symbolizes not Engel's memories of the past, but rather those of Karl Franz. The song's nostalgic associations have passed from teacher to student.

In marked contrast to the backward-looking sentiment of "Golden Days," "Drinking Song" is a boisterous, carpe diem waltz in a fast tempo, befitting its dramatic function as an impromptu communal toast. The strong downbeats and diatonic arpeggiated melody give it a Teutonic underpinning, evoking the clichéd sound of a German band, and its lack of verse (being only a refrain) endorses its spontaneous spirit. (See example 5.2.) Furthermore, the song appears in a diegetic context—the Heidelberg students *do* sing drinking songs while imbibing beer.

This song was especially popular with audiences. The operetta appeared during Prohibition, and the vicarious experience of legally imbibing alcohol and the overt celebration of beer appealed to many sitting in the house. "Drinking Song" was part of the "brindisi" tradition associated with Italian opera, one of the most famous examples being in Giuseppe Verdi's *La traviata* (1853). It also followed the lead of popular Broadway drinking songs such as "Brown October Ale" from Reginald de Koven's *Robin Hood* (1891) and "Heidelberg Stein Song" from Gustav Luders's *The Prince of Pilsen* (1903).

Kathie, the waitress at the inn where the students drink, enters singing the waltz "I'm Coming at Your Call." Her waltz is graceful and charming, as befits her personality. Its largely stepwise melody, LONG-short LONG-short rhythmic pattern, and clearly delineated eight-bar phrase structure, all unexceptional qualities, complement Kathie's character. She is an ordinary waitress working at a student haunt owned by her uncle.

Significantly, both romantic leads enter to waltzes, Karl Franz to "Golden Days" and Kathie to "I'm Coming at Your Call." Although they are from different social classes, they can meet in the common ground of the waltz. After both characters have been introduced through their own waltzes, it becomes imperative for them to have a waltz duet. This song has to be expansive and luscious, for it is the musical centerpiece of the score, just like "Will You Remember" in *Maytime* and "Song of Love" in *Blossom Time*.

"Deep in My Heart, Dear" fulfills this need. One of Romberg's most famous songs, its title was used in abridged form for both Elliott Arnold's novelized biography of 1949 and MGM's 1954 biopic. It is a much more elaborate number than its predecessors in *Maytime* and *Blossom Time* and is also representative of Romberg's expansion of songs into scenes, one of the distinguishing features of *The Student Prince*. In "Deep in My Heart, Dear," this occurs in the verse, which has three distinct sections—a departure from the conventional one-section form—each of which is contrasting in terms of key or meter. (See Table 5.3.)

From a tonal perspective, the first two sections of the verse are linked through a typical ascending perfect fifth relation (I-V); however, the tonal

Example 5.2. "Drinking Song" *(The Student Prince)*, mm. 1–8

Table 5.3 Sectional construction of "Deep in My Heart, Dear," from *The Student Prince*

Text	Key	Tempo	Meter
"Of love I've often heard"	G	Moderato	C
"Oh, tell me if within your heart"	D	Valse moderato	3/4
"The magic of springtime"	F	Valse	3/4
"Deep in my heart, dear" (refrain)	F	Molto espressivo	3/4

relation between the second and third sections is a mediant one. In the first two sections, Kathie and Karl Franz explore their self-doubts about love; they are communicating with each other and do so in related keys. Once they dispel their fears ("The magic of springtime"), the tonality shifts to F major, the key in which they express their mutual love. The final section of the verse establishes the tonal center, which then remains for the refrain.

The refrain consists of four eight-bar phrases arranged in ABCA' form. The first half of each phrase has the exact same rhythm, and the dramatic effect of the passage is intensified through this repetition. It culminates in Kathie's realization in the third phrase that she and Karl Franz will never be able to be together ("Our paths may sever") and the concluding statement in which they promise always to remember each other, no matter what happens ("Deep in my heart, dear, always I'll dream of you!"), complete with a high-note ending that confirms the urgency of the moment. (See example 5.5 for the opening of the refrain.)

Like "Golden Days" and the principal waltzes in Romberg's earlier operettas, "Deep in My Heart, Dear" returns several times during the show. Most reprises take place in the midst of act finales.

According to the manuscript scores at the Library of Congress, "Deep in My Heart, Dear" replaced an earlier song, "For You." In 1928, four years after the appearance of *The Student Prince*, Harms published "For You," a lilting love ballad in 6/8, as an independent song, without any references to its source. The existence of the earlier song is significant, for it shows that Romberg was experimenting with idioms other than a waltz for his primary love duets. He must have realized that his use of the waltz was becoming formulaic and was at least attempting to do something different. However, he also realized that the waltz was still the best idiom for a principal romantic duet, especially for a show set in the nineteenth century. "Deep in My Heart, Dear," in addition to being a waltz, had another meaning for Romberg, for, as will be recalled from chapter 1, he wrote it especially for Lillian, calling it her love theme.

Waltzes appear not only as independent numbers but also within act finales. The act 1 finale includes the choral waltz "When the Spring Wakens Everything," an ode to the season of youth and love. The act 2 finale opens with the prince's "Farewell to Youth," a soliloquy on what he is losing. The waltz's minor mode — unique in the operetta — accentuates the prince's emotional distress. Kathie responds with the major-mode "We're Off to Paris," thinking that she and Karl Franz will spend the rest of their lives together. Karl Franz at this point tells her the truth of his situation, and the act concludes with a reprise of "Deep in My Heart, Dear." Two years separate the second and third acts, and in the course of the act 3 finale, Karl Franz and Engel sing reprises of "Farewell to Youth" and "Golden Days" as they recall their time in Heidelberg. The act 4 finale, the final sequence of the operetta, concludes with a reprise of "Deep in My Heart, Dear." Thus, this glorious operetta ends with the most quintessential of operetta forms, the waltz. (*Maytime*, by contrast, concluded with a reprise of a march.)

"Just We Two," the duet for Princess Margaret and Tarnitz, is a song of unrequited love, a waltz sung by people who know they can never be together. Its dramatic function recalls "Will You Remember" from *Maytime*. Donnelly's lyric includes a reflexive line that links the waltz with love: "Just we two, if they knew, how in the waltz we woo." They must be secret about their affections, and cannot express them in words but only through the physical gesture of the waltz. The music is extremely gentle and sensitive, as is the relationship it represents.

In addition to waltzes, marches constitute a significant part of the music in *The Student Prince*. (See Table 5.4.) "Students Marching Song" ("To the Inn We're Marching"), "Come, Boys, Let's All Be Gay, Boys," "Let Us Sing a Song," and the marches in the act 1 finale exude the boisterousness of the Heidelberg male student chorus. Karlsberg marches include "By Our Bearing So Sedate," which informs the audience of the rigid and formal life at court, and "The Flag That Flies Above Us," Karlsberg's noble national anthem. These are among the major numbers for the large male chorus, the noteworthy addition to *The Student Prince*. Like the waltzes, the most prominent marches, "Students Marching Song" and "Come, Boys, Let's All Be Gay, Boys," are reprised later in the operetta. The first reprises occur in act 1, and the second set in act 4, when the prince returns to Heidelberg and once again encounters the boisterous male students.

Table 5.4 Marches in *The Student Prince*

Title	Number and title in vocal score
"By Our Bearing So Sedate"	1. "Prologue" (act 1)
"Students Marching Song" ("To the Inn We're Marching")	4. "Entrance of Students and Kathie" (act 1) Reprises: 5b. "Exit of Students" (act 1) 19. "Finale" (act 4)
"Come, Boys, Let's All Be Gay, Boys"	5. "Chorus of Students and Concerted Number" (act 1) Reprises: 8. "Finale" (act 1) 19. "Finale" (act 4)
"Come, Sir, Will You Join"	8. "Finale" (act 1)
"Saxon Corps"	8. "Finale" (act 1)
"Karl Franz, Beat Him if You Can"	8. "Finale" (act 1)
"The Flag That Flies Above Us"	12. "Finale" (act 2) Reprises: 15. "Ensemble and Gavotte" (act 3) 19. "Finale" (act 4)
"Let Us Sing a Song"	17. "Opening Chorus" (act 4)

"Come, Boys, Let's All Be Gay, Boys" deserves further comment because in addition to showcasing the male chorus, Kathie has a lead part. Introduced in the course of a concerted number (no. 5 in the published vocal score), the waltz-singing waitress entreats her adoring young men to enjoy their youth and not to spend all their time with books, telling them, "In drinking you with honor graduate." By singing a march, she speaks (or literally sings) their language. The male chorus agrees with her in the B section of the number's ABA form, and in the reprise of the opening section she enthusiastically demonstrates not only her high sustained C (one of sixteen she has in the show, not counting any encores) but also her two-octave range in a descending coloratura arpeggio. (See example 5.3.) Kathie must be an operatically trained soprano in order to negotiate the demands of the score, as is clearly evident in this short passage. This is one of the operetta's especially memorable passages with its vocally virtuosic coloratura (although subdued when compared with Rossini, Donizetti, and sometimes even Johann Strauss Jr.) riding above and through a vigorous male choral march.

Although waltzes and marches dominate, they are by no means the only types of music in *The Student Prince*. Romberg added historical authenticity by interpolating the famous German student song "Gaudeamus igitur." This

Example 5.3. "Come, Boys, Let's All Be Gay, Boys" *(The Student Prince)*, version with Kathie and men's chorus, mm. 1–9

Ilse Marvenga (as Kathie) and the male chorus in the original production of *The Student Prince*. Courtesy of the Shubert Archive.

was the same student song Brahms quoted in his *Academic Festival Overture* (1880), and which was sung on university campuses across America in the 1920s. Here was an opportunity for Romberg to include a number that was familiar to his audience. An unaccompanied chorus performs the song, recalling the performance style of "Heidelberg Stein Song" in an earlier operetta about a beer-drinking royal, *The Prince of Pilsen*.

Act 3 takes place at the Karlsberg Royal Palace. To establish the formal atmosphere, Romberg not only uses the waltz ("Just We Two") and of course the Karlsberg National Anthem ("The Flag That Flies Above Us"), but also a gavotte. In fact, the act opens with a formal ballet sequence. Because of the way music is employed, we know that we have left the conviviality of Heidelberg for the reserve of a royal court.

The joy of Heidelberg life is immediately apparent in the first scene in the university town. The female chorus, in its featured number, sings "Garlands Bright," a lighthearted ode to spring. The carefree existence of youth, with the girls even ignoring their employer's commands to work faster, is effectively captured in the sprightly yet consciously unhurried number.

As far as comedy is concerned, two humorous songs, "Farmer Jacob" and "Student Life," open act 2. These clever foxtrots have their heritage not in European operetta but rather in American revue and musical comedy. They provide respite from the nearly fatalistic romantic plot and keep the score from being a complete pastiche of nineteenth-century styles. These are the songs that remind the audience that this is a work written in the 1920s. "Farmer Jacob" is a short feature for four-part male chorus about a fox who steals a goose from a sleeping farmer, while "Student Life" is a more extended number for the principals and male chorus. The lyrics for the gleeful main melody tell of drinking until dawn and the number even ends with the student leaders yawning and snoring. In the midst of the revelry, Karl Franz and Kathie sing about the immediacy of youth ("Youth is here today, so seize it while we may") to a lyrical melody in the style of a foxtrot. The two songs effectively capture the joys of carefree student life, the very things that the prince and Kathie will be forced to give up at the end of the act.

Although individual numbers are certainly memorable, the most significant musical aspects of *The Student Prince* are its extended scenes. Songs and choruses do not always appear in isolation, separated by spoken dialogue. Instead, they are often joined together to form larger structural units. Romberg was following the ideals of Gluck, Mozart, Weber, and Wagner in this regard. He also was reclaiming one of the precepts of Viennese operetta he altered in his adaptations during the previous decade, in which he abridged such scenes when they appeared in the European originals. In addition to the act finales, Kathie's entrance in act 1 and the entrance of the prince and Engel that follows soon thereafter are extended musical scenes. In each of these instances, the drama is developed using various musical techniques, including choral numbers, solo songs, spoken dialogue over orchestral accompaniment (melodrama), and recitative.

Of the extended musical scenes, the act 1 finale is the most impressive.[25] It features the principals, secondary leads, and chorus in the sequence that takes place immediately after the prince and Kathie fall in love singing "Deep in My Heart, Dear." Its music includes both reprises and new material, the most impressive of the latter being the immortal "Serenade." (See Table 5.5.)

The combination of vocal textures, musical styles, and dramatic functions makes this passage one of the most extraordinary in the entire operetta repertory. Significantly, the male chorus is onstage for the entire sequence—it is truly a central character in the drama. Its members, led by

Table 5.5 Sectional construction of the act 1 finale of *The Student Prince*

Musical Section	Key	Meter	Characters
1. Introduction (melodrama)	E	4/4	von Asterberg, Lucas, Detlef
2. "Come Sir, Will You Join"	E	12/8	Detlef, von Asterberg, Lucas, male chorus (Prince at end)
3. "Saxon Corps"	E, D	2/4	Prince, Detlef, von Asterberg, Lucas, male chorus
4. Scene (Engel's entrance)	E-flat	6/8, 4/4	Engel (Detlef, von Asterberg, Lucas, male chorus at end)
5. "Karl Franz, Beat Him if You Can"	E-flat	C	Detlef, von Asterberg, Lucas, male chorus
6. "Come Answer to Our Call" (reprise)	D	3/4	Kathie, Detlef, von Asterberg, Lucas, Engel, male chorus
7. Salamander toast	D minor	6/8, 4/4	Detlef
8. "Drinking Song" (reprise) [short dialogue]	B-flat	3/4	Detlef, von Asterberg, Lucas, male chorus
9. "Serenade"	F	4/4	Prince, Detlef, von Asterberg, Lucas, male chorus
10. "Gaudeamus igitur"	B-flat	3/4	Engel, Detlef, von Asterberg, Lucas, male chorus
11. Lutz's castigation scene	B-flat, C, B	4/4, 2/4, 4/4	Lutz, Prince, Engel, Ruder, Hubert, Gretchen, male chorus (Prince and Kathie enter at end)
12. "When the Spring Wakens Everything"	F	3/4	Prince, Engel, Kathie, Gretchen, Ruder, mixed chorus
13. "Come, Boys, Let's All Be Gay, Boys" (reprise)	F	2/4	Kathie, Gretchen, Prince, Ruder, Engel, mixed chorus
14. "Deep in My Heart, Dear" (reprise)	F	3/4	Kathie, Prince

Detlef, von Asterberg, and Lucas, invite Karl Franz to join their fraternity ("Come, Sir, Will You Join"), are there when he accepts their offer, and accompany him as he woos Kathie ("Serenade"). Secondary characters keep appearing throughout the sequence, first Engel, followed by Herr Ruder (Kathie's uncle), the prince's valet Lutz, Lutz's valet Hubert (yes, the valet has a valet), and Gretchen, a maid at the inn. The waitresses at the inn (the female chorus) join the ensemble in a choral celebration of love and springtime ("Hail, Youth and Love") near the end of the sequence. The students also demonstrate their nonsinging acting abilities in the castigation of Lutz, the only person who tries to curtail the prince's social and amorous activities.

The opening sections of the sequence progress tonally from E to E-flat to D, descending semitones, leading to the reprise of the "Drinking Song" in B-flat, its original key. Following the "Serenade," Romberg remains primarily in F major for the remainder of the finale, with a brief excursion to the subdominant (B-flat) for "Gaudeamus igitur." But in the midst of all this apparent tranquility, Lutz's interference and castigation disrupts the dramatic flow of the sequence and steals the emphasis from Karl Franz and Kathie. Likewise, the tonal center shifts to B, a tritone away from the principal key of F. Once Lutz is removed from the situation, the stability of F major returns. Romberg employs large-scale tonal motion to emphasize important moments in the dramatic plot.

A number of song types appear during the sequence. In addition to the expected waltzes and marches and the interpolated "Gaudeamus igitur," the lyrical "Serenade," one of Romberg's greatest achievements, appears in the course of the finale.

"Serenade," a late addition to the score, is introduced musically after the strong V-I cadence of the reprise of "Drinking Song."[26] At this point, Romberg and Donnelly bring the music to a screeching halt and insert a brief line of dialogue in which Engel tells the students to sing "Serenade," his favorite song and one he taught to Karl Franz. Through these few words of spoken introduction, the audience is reminded of the inherent topics of nostalgia, memory, and young love that permeate the show.

"Serenade" is texturally the most advanced number in the operetta. Scored for a male quartet accompanied by full male chorus and orchestra, no single vocalist monopolizes the number. The trio of leaders of the Saxon Corps, Detlef (tenor), von Asterberg (baritone), and Lucas (bass), who sang as a trio in earlier numbers, including "Drinking Song," become a quartet with the addition of Karl Franz as first tenor. He has more music than the rest, not just because he is the operetta's title character but also because he is the newest member of the Saxon Corps. Furthermore, he is able to provide a high C on the final chord. (In this way, he also shows his connection to Kathie, for she also sings prominent high Cs.) Karl Franz does not have to declare his love for Kathie by himself; he now has the support of his fellow students. As a solo song (the setting in which it is almost always performed outside of the operetta), "Serenade" is a consummate and beautiful love song; in its original context, it is also a dramatic statement of the acceptance of a new member into a student society and a stirring depiction of camaraderie.[27]

Constructed in a large ABA' form, "Serenade" begins with the prince singing the arpeggiated opening phrase that spans an octave and a fourth and gives the song its alternate title, "Overhead the moon is beaming." The prince must earn his place as the operetta's title character in this difficult passage. The moon might be beaming overhead, but the attention of the entire cast and audience is squarely focused on Karl Franz. At the end of the first phrase, the texture becomes that of a male quartet with the addition of Detlef, von Asterberg, and Lucas. Karl Franz is no longer on his own; his new friends have joined him. (See example 5.4.) When the opening material reappears ("Overhead the moon is beaming"), the male chorus is now present, enhancing the sound of the solo quartet. The entire Saxon Corps now supports Karl Franz, both musically and dramatically, in his quest for Kathie's heart.

The tonally stable outer sections are contrasted by the central B section, which is much more chromatic than the framing A sections. Dominant seventh chords, along with a modulation to the chromatic submediant key of D-flat major (in the overall F-major tonal plan), with its alternation between V7 and I 6/4 chords, create harmonic tension.

The relative tonal stability and instability in "Serenade" mirror the dramatic action of the number. Karl Franz begins confidently in his expression of love for Kathie and does so firmly in F major. In the middle section, however, doubts about their ultimate fate arise, and Romberg moves to the chromatic submediant in order to emphasize this unrest. These doubts are alleviated as Karl Franz gains strength from his fellow students during the reprise of the opening material and a return to the tonic.

"Serenade" proved to Romberg and others that he could write a dramatic

Example 5.4. "Serenade" *(The Student Prince)*, mm. 1–10

love song that was *not* a waltz. Although the waltz was still the dominant medium for his love songs, "Serenade" demonstrated that he was not exclusively limited to triple meter in his depictions of passionate romance. This was a significant development for Romberg, for it opened the way for impassioned songs such as "One Alone" in *The Desert Song,* and "Lover, Come Back to Me" in *The New Moon.*

The musical demands of *The Student Prince* are considerable, as are the acting requirements. Experienced singers need to play the parts of young adults. These are college students and barmaids, after all. John Hanson, the British singer who popularized Romberg's operettas in the United Kingdom during the 1950s and 1960s, said of the title role: "I found the 'Prince' a difficult part to play. To begin with, no young man of twenty could ever sing what is really an operatic tenor part. I tried to act the part of a shy, sensitive young man, but it just didn't work, so in the end, I just played myself, and hoped for the best!"[28]

Emil Gerstenberger, who orchestrated most of Romberg's shows from the 1920s, effectively captured the stereotypical sound of nineteenth-century Germany in *The Student Prince*. While his typical 1920s operetta scoring emphasizes the strings, he gives the brass, particularly the low brass, plenty of moments to shine. The German brass band sound is especially evident in "Drinking Song" and "Students Marching Song." Gerstenberger also scored some beautiful solo woodwind passages, such as the evocative flute solo at the beginning of "Deep in My Heart, Dear."

Romberg reached the pinnacle of his operetta formula with *The Student Prince*. All the necessary ingredients were present, elements that also existed in his previous operettas with the Shuberts, including *The Blue Paradise*, *Maytime*, and *Blossom Time*. First is a story with a fundamentally unhappy ending. The romantic leads who sing the impassioned waltz duet in act 1 are not together at the end. Second is the waltz duet itself. These are the centerpieces of their scores and are reprised in various dramatic guises throughout their respective operettas. Third are the other types of music that surround the recurring waltz, either other waltzes, marches, or even foxtrots. Fourth is the idea of nostalgia, for in each of these operettas, characters reflect on the past and its happy memories, things that are gone forever.

But in *The Student Prince*, new elements were added. From a structural point of view, there was a reliance on extended musical scenes. Also, the male chorus with its rousing marches ("Students Marching Song," for example) became a fixture, and the female chorus, which took second place to its male counterpart, would also have a featured number ("Garlands Bright"). The song for women's chorus, though, was lighter in style and sentiment. It existed to provide gender-based musical and dramatic contrast to the machismo assertiveness of the male choral numbers and, in the case of *The Student Prince*, to establish the carefree atmosphere of student life in Old Heidelberg.

The Student Prince further established Romberg's reputation as a significant Broadway composer. His place would have been secured if he had written nothing else, for *The Student Prince* was an unqualified success commercially, musically, and dramatically. In the work, Romberg, with librettist Dorothy Donnelly, set a benchmark against which all subsequent American operettas would be judged.

After *The Student Prince*: *Annie Dear, Louie the 14th,* and *Princess Flavia*

Romberg's activities around the time of the premiere of *The Student Prince* were not limited to that seminal work, for the composer also contributed music to two shows during the same season. Both were produced by the Shuberts' archrival, Florenz Ziegfeld: *Annie Dear* (November 4, 1924, Times Square) and *Louie the 14th* (March 3, 1925, Cosmopolitan). Ziegfeld had not yet turned his attention toward the world of operetta (he produced Friml's *The Three Musketeers* in 1927), as he was still focused on presenting revues and musical comedies. Romberg's music for Ziegfeld, therefore, resembled his work for the Shubert revues and musical comedies.

Clare Kummer wrote the original book, music, and lyrics for *Annie Dear*, basing the musical on her comedy *Good Gracious, Annabelle*. The show was a vehicle for Billie Burke (Ziegfeld's wife at the time) and had a lighthearted plot about a runaway bride who masquerades as a maid. Ziegfeld, unhappy with Kummer's songs, hired Romberg and Clifford Grey to create additional music for the production, but Kummer insisted that the original material be restored. Although *Annie Dear* opened with Romberg and Grey's interpolations, reconciliation with Kummer could not be reached, and Ziegfeld eventually closed the show (after 103 performances). Romberg's songs, most of which were lyrical, gently syncopated songs, were called "gratifying to the ear" and consisted largely of solos for secondary characters accompanied by various choral ensembles.[29]

Louie the 14th, like *Annie Dear*, was a star vehicle, this time for the comedian Leon Errol, who was especially known for his visual humor.[30] The show's plot concerned Louie Ketchup (Errol), a U.S. Army cook who remains in France after World War I. He meets the wealthy and superstitious socialite Paul Trappman, who is giving a dinner party. When Trappman realizes that there will be thirteen people at dinner, he superstitiously invites Louie to avoid having a supposedly unlucky number at the table. Louie arrives posing as a rajah and provides great comic amusement for the guests (and for the audience).

Romberg's score is firmly in the musical comedy vein, but not in an overtly syncopated style. This was old-fashioned musical comedy. Foxtrots are plentiful in the score, including the refrains of "Little Peach," "My First Love Letter," and "Edelweiss." But nostalgia is also present. The hymnlike "Homeland" begins with a fanfare, after which a group of doughboys, an unaccompanied male chorus, tell of their upcoming return home to America. During the final refrain the orchestra plays Stephen Foster's "Old Folks at Home" while the chorus sings Romberg's song.[31] The soldiers are nostalgic for home, as we know from the Foster allusion.

Romberg still worked with the Shuberts, however, and the producers wanted to repeat the success of *The Student Prince* with their next operetta, *Princess Flavia* (November 2, 1925, Century). This was authentic Ruritania, for the production was a musical version of Anthony Hope's *The Prisoner of Zenda*, the novel that gave the aesthetic construct its name. The show was in some ways a gender-reversed remake of *The Student Prince*, and Romberg's score was squarely based on the previous year's success.[32]

In *Princess Flavia*, the Englishman Rudolf Rassendyl is a virtual double for the crown prince of Ruritania. When the real prince is unable to appear at his coronation as king, Rassendyl agrees to take his place. The prince's cousin, Princess Flavia, falls in love with the foreign impersonator, thinking him to be the true prince. When the truth is revealed, Flavia transfers her affections to the rightful monarch. While in *The Student Prince* a disguised prince falls for a commoner, in *Princess Flavia* a princess falls for a disguised commoner.

Pageantry and visual spectacle dominated the production. In act 1, a forest clad in autumn foliage led to a raised road over which the large, uniformed male chorus bellowed their way onstage. The palatial set in act 2 featured illuminated stained-glass windows, tapestries, and arched doorways. The coronation scene, modeled after the real investiture of King Nicholas I of Montenegro in 1910, was described as "an orgy of beauty and luxuriousness."[33]

Reviews from the opening night were uniformly strong. Not only did the critics praise the singing of the leads, Evelyn Herbert and Harry Welchman, and the chorus, they also reveled in the work's overall spectacle. Stephen Rathburn giddily wrote in the *New York Sun*: "It is the most ambitious operetta ever produced in America. The chorus numbers one hundred or more and that the choristers did not raise the roof when they sang must have been due to the fact that the roof was fastened securely."[34]

Popularity slackened, however, and the show soon entered the graveyard of forgotten musical theater. The main reason why *Princess Flavia* lost favor was its all-too-obvious closeness to *The Student Prince*. Why see a copy when the original is still playing strong? *Princess Flavia*'s huge male chorus was the progeny of the Saxon Corps in *The Student Prince*; both were even clad

Example 5.5. "Deep in My Heart, Dear" *(The Student Prince)*, refrain, mm. 1–8.

in military-style uniforms, and both sang rousing marches. Furthermore, the primary love duet in *Princess Flavia*, "I Dare Not Love You," bears an uncanny resemblance to *The Student Prince*'s "Deep in My Heart, Dear." Both numbers are musical scenes with multisectional verses and have refrains that begin with nearly identical musical material. Although "I Dare Not Love You" is in duple meter, the opening melodic gesture, repeated notes and an ascending fourth, and its harmonic underpinning are basically the same. In "I Dare Not Love You" the upward leap in the melody occurs one measure later than in "Deep in My Heart, Dear," but the nearly identical harmony creates an unmistakable link between the two refrains. (See examples 5.5 and 5.6.)

Example 5.6. "I Dare Not Love You" (*Princess Flavia*), refrain, mm. 1–8

"Only One," a song for Flavia and the male chorus, was a reincarnation of "I'm Coming at Your Call" from *The Student Prince*. Like Kathie's number, Flavia's is a waltz, and both move into features for the male chorus. In *The Student Prince* it was a march ("Come, Boys, Let's All Be Gay, Boys"); here, it is a czardas. We are in Ruritania, after all, where male choruses are as familiar with the czardas as German students are with the march.

Although its concept was unquestionably derivative, the operetta provided starring roles for two singers who would be closely identified with Romberg in future years: Evelyn Herbert and Harry Welchman. Herbert, called "the queen of light operatic prima donnas," was one of the leading musical theater actresses of the era.[35] After *Princess Flavia*, she starred in three other Romberg operettas: *My Maryland*, *The New Moon*, and *Melody*. Welchman created the role of Karl Franz in the London production of *The*

Student Prince and made his New York debut in *Princess Flavia*. He returned to his native England, where he created the lead roles in *The Desert Song* and *The New Moon* in their British premieres.

Although *The Student Prince* was a phenomenal success, the works that immediately followed it were not. There are some similarities, however, between *The Student Prince*, *Louie the 14th*, and *Princess Flavia*. Aside from the European settings, the male leads in each work engage in impersonation and disguise: Karl Franz wants to be a normal university student in *The Student Prince*, Louie Ketchup dresses like a rajah in *Louie the 14th*, and Rudolf Rassendyl becomes Ruritanian royalty in *Princess Flavia*. This idea of impersonation, certainly nothing new in the history of operetta, was an important part of these three works. But in Romberg's next operetta, *The Desert Song*, it became one of the plot's driving features.

CHAPTER 6

Romance and Exoticism in North Africa: *The Desert Song*

THE DESERT SONG (1926) WAS A RADICAL DEPARTURE FROM ROMberg's established operetta mold. The show was set in French Morocco, not Europe or even New York, and its action was entirely present-day. This musically and dramatically compelling operetta was not a nineteenth-century tale, nor even one that spanned a broad expanse of time and ended up in the present. Although the title song was a waltz and there were ample marches for the male chorus, it was a long way from *The Student Prince* of just two years earlier. In *The Desert Song* there is a genuine happy ending to the romance, something that had not happened in Romberg's three previous hits (*Maytime, Blossom Time,* and *The Student Prince*). Whereas nostalgia and young love were driving forces in Romberg's operettas to this point, Orientalism permeates *The Desert Song* in both the libretto and the music. More liberal views of sexuality are also portrayed, making it a theatrical reflection and refraction of the Roaring '20s. *The Desert Song* incorporates more aspects of contemporary culture than does any other Romberg operetta, and as such demonstrates that Romberg was able to create a show that had deep social resonance for its time, one that was rooted in something other than nostalgia and ill-fated love stories.

The tremendous advance in musical dramaturgy was due in large part to the operetta's principal wordsmiths: Otto Harbach (1873–1963) and Oscar Hammerstein 2nd (1895–1960). The pair crafted the show's lyrics, and was joined by co-producer Frank Mandel in writing the book. Harbach was one of the most important Broadway lyricists of the first quarter of the twentieth century and worked with Rudolf Friml on all of his important Broadway shows from his debut hit, *The Firefly* (1911), through the legendary *Rose Marie* (1924). He thus had a great deal of experience writing for operetta when he joined the creative team of *The Desert Song*.

Hammerstein was also a familiar name to Broadway audiences, for he came from a well-established theatrical family. His grandfather, after whom he was named, owned and managed the Manhattan Opera House, which for a time rivaled the Metropolitan Opera. His uncle, Arthur, was an important Broadway producer, while his father, William, managed the Victoria Theatre. Thus, Oscar Hammerstein 2nd was truly a child of the theater. He was acutely aware of its traditions, limitations, potentials, and possibilities.

The composers with whom Hammerstein collaborated constitute the core of American musical theater creators in the first two-thirds of the century; in addition to Romberg, Hammerstein also worked alongside Friml, Jerome Kern, and Richard Rodgers. The shows for which he wrote words after *The Desert Song* include *Show Boat, The New Moon, Sweet Adeline, Music in the Air, Carmen Jones, Oklahoma!, Carousel, South Pacific, The King and I,* and *The Sound of Music,* among others. Many of these, especially those written with Rodgers, have become canonic repertory of the American musical theater.

Hammerstein's importance in the American musical theater cannot be overstated. In addition to creating words for classic songs, he also envisioned the musical as more than a succession of songs. Hammerstein advanced the notion of extended musical-dramatic scenes in which words, music (both songs and underscoring for dialogue), and sometimes dance are combined and integrated with the expressed goal of accentuating the drama.

Romberg and Donnelly had approached *The Student Prince* with this same idea, and Romberg and Hammerstein continued developing it in their collaborations. Scene finalettos, act finales, and other numbers such as Margot, Paul, and Pierre's trio with chorus "I Want a Kiss" (in which their love triangle is illustrated against waltz and foxtrot refrains) and the concerted "Eastern and Western Love" are conceived and executed as large, multisectional scenes. In these cases, Hammerstein and Romberg utilize spoken dialogue above music (melodrama) to a great degree, exploring and exploiting its theatrical possibilities. The act 1 finale becomes a focal point of the work's dramaturgy in which several strands of the plot come together in a powerful way. Hence, the Rodgers and Hammerstein paradigm of driving the first act's action to a gripping dramatic peak just before intermission is already evident in *The Desert Song*, a work that appeared seventeen years before *Oklahoma!*

In addition to the creators, the producers were also responsible for the show's remarkable success. Frank Mandel (1884–1958) and Laurence Schwab (1893–1951) first worked together as librettists on *No, No, Nanette* (1925, music by Vincent Youmans), the musical comedy that included "Tea for Two" and the title song among its outstanding numbers. The team then turned to producing shows, and after *The Desert Song*, their first major triumph, they mounted the sports-themed musical comedies *Good News!* (1927) and *Follow Thru* (1929), both with music by Ray Henderson and lyrics by Buddy De Sylva and Lew Brown, as well as several notable operettas by Romberg and Hammerstein, including *The New Moon* (1928), *East Wind* (1931), and *May Wine* (1935). From their work in musical comedy, Mandel and Schwab learned how to infuse their productions with references to popular culture, whether it was college football in *Good News!*, golf in *Follow Thru*, or Orientalism in *The Desert Song*. While the Shuberts excelled at mounting nostalgia, Mandel and Schwab stood out for their abilities to stage contemporary life.

Like many works that preceded and followed it, *The Desert Song*, which was called *Lady Fair* during its tryout in October and November 1926, demonstrated an inseparable bonding of music and drama.[1] The program for Poli's Theatre in Washington, D.C., during the week of October 25 included the disclaimer "Owing to the fact that the music of the play is so thoroughly interwoven with the story, it is impossible to enumerate the numbers in the exact order in which they are rendered." This was nearly identical to the phrasing that appeared in the playbill for *Rose Marie* two years earlier, and that would be used again in the playbill for Rodgers and Hart's *Chee-Chee* in 1928. The statement did not make it into *The Desert Song*'s Broadway playbill. Either the creators thought it was too close to what had already been said about *Rose Marie*, or they used it as a means of suggesting that *Lady Fair* was a work in progress and that the final order of musical numbers had not yet been set.

The Desert Song, with its alluring title finalized, opened in New York on November 30, 1926, at the Casino Theatre. The initial run lasted 471 performances. Robert Halliday and Vivienne Segal played the romantic leads, Pierre/Red Shadow and Margot, while other principal cast members included Eddie Buzzell, William O'Neill, Lyle Evans, and Pearl Regay.

Critics were generally favorable toward *The Desert Song*. The music and the singing, especially that of the male chorus—a carryover from *The Student Prince*, were praised. Charles Brackett wrote in *The New Yorker*: "A great, roaring, splendid musical show . . . The music is Romberg's best, and in the book it seemed to me that the sheik plot has found at last its really happy medium."[2]

The Desert Song was the most popular of Romberg's operettas in the United Kingdom. Its impressive 432-performance run at the Drury Lane Theatre began on April 7, 1927. Harry Welchman and Edith Day played the lead roles, and Romberg himself traveled to London to conduct the opening night performance. The show's numerous Orientalist elements accounted for its tremendous success in Britain. Orientalism was a fashionable commodity on London stages, proven by the unprecedented popularity of Oscar Asche and Frederic Norton's *Chu Chin Chow*, which played 2,235 performances from its opening on August 31, 1916, to its closing on July 22, 1921, and held the record as the longest-running West End musical when *The Desert Song* appeared in London.[3]

The overt sensuality of *The Desert Song* came to the attention of the Lord Chamberlain's Office when it reviewed the play for licensing. The examiner, George Street, remarked that "Act II . . . begins with dancing business, etc. of a company of rather dubious Spanish women." He continued: "I do not think there is anything to offend anyone. The scenes at Ali ben Ali's include a good deal of voluptuous dancing and so on, but we can be sure that kind of thing will be kept within bounds at Drury Lane. The comic man, Bernie, and a female comedian Susan are sometimes a little vulgar but nothing to matter." The Lord Chamberlain himself, then Lord Cromer, countersigned the report in his customary red ink and added the remark, "Drury Lane should be sufficient security for good taste in this production."[4] His trust in producer Alfred Butt and the solid reputation of the Drury Lane Theatre alleviated his concerns about the content of *The Desert Song*.

The story focuses on Margot Bonvalet, a Frenchwoman, and her romantic relationships. She is engaged to Paul Fontaine, son of the former French governor of Morocco, but really is in love with the mysterious Red Shadow, an amalgamation of Rudolf Valentino, Lawrence of Arabia, and Abd-El-Kim, who helps the oppressed Moroccans (the Riffs) rise against their French colonial rulers. Pierre Birabeau, son of the present governor, is the complete antithesis of the Red Shadow. He is completely inept at everything, including love. He is enthralled with Margot, but she will have nothing to do with him: her eyes are set on the Red Shadow. What the audience learns in the first scene is that the Red Shadow is Pierre (the Red Shadow discusses his dual identity with Sid El Kar, his lieutenant, and Hassi, a member of his band), although none of the central characters in the play has yet discerned this vital piece of information.

Several secondary characters add various subplots to the central drama. Benjamin "Bennie" Kidd, a reporter for the *Paris Daily Mail*, and Susan, his secretary, provide comic diversions. (Bennie's character has precedents in *The Girl from Brazil* and *The Magic Melody*, both of which include newspaper reporters as comic characters.) Bennie and Susan are kidnapped by the Riffs and subsequently find their way back to the French compound. Azuri is a native girl who had an affair with Captain Fontaine and who still is in love with the Frenchman. She wants Margot, Fontaine's current love interest, to suffer, and when she spies Pierre taking off the Red Shadow's garments and discerns his dual identity, knows that she has found leverage to counter the French imperialists. Completing the list of principals are General Birabeau, Pierre's father and the new French governor in Morocco; Ali Ben Ali, keeper of a large harem and Pierre's friend; and Clementina, a courtesan who is among a group of imprisoned Spanish dancers.

Margot's romantic feelings for the Red Shadow are not one-sided, to be sure. The Red Shadow woos Margot to the strains of the title waltz, and, after the Riffs invade Government House, he takes her to his desert lair, the palace of Ali Ben Ali, for her own safety (in the act 1 finale).

While held captive by Ali Ben Ali, Margot tells Pierre (whom she believes has also been captured by the Red Shadow) that she wishes the Red Shadow would appear and take her away by force. So, fulfilling her request, the Red Shadow returns, along with General Birabeau and the treacherous Azuri. The General challenges the Red Shadow to a duel, but the Red Shadow refuses, and thereby forfeits his position as leader of the Riff band.

Birabeau and Margot return unharmed to Government House. Paul is unnerved when he recognizes Margot's love for the Red Shadow and swears revenge against his romantic rival. The General encourages him to kill the Arab freedom fighter. Azuri, filled with hatred, then tells Birabeau that the Red Shadow is really Pierre, and that he has just ordered his own son to be killed. Pierre enters with the clothes of the Red Shadow and surprises everyone when he tells them that he, the inept and cowardly Pierre, has just slain the mysterious Riff leader. Only the General and Azuri know the truth. Margot, Pierre, and the General are left alone on stage. Margot, upset at the news of the death of her true love, realizes his dual identity when Pierre, standing behind her, dons the Red Shadow's costume and begins singing. The lovers embrace as the General leaves and the curtain falls.

Vocal characterization is central to *The Desert Song* and is one of its most important aspects. Margot is the central focus of the show—her romantic pursuits motivate the main plot and affect the subplots. As such an important dramatic character, she must have commanding music, which she does. She leads the chorus in both the "French Military Marching Song" and "Romance," sings the enticing title waltz with Pierre, and bears her soul to the Red Shadow's sword in the emotive "Sabre Song." Similarly, the Red Shadow has extremely alluring music, for it is his voice as much as anything else that attracts Margot. She seeks the perfect partner for her high-intensity music making.

Other principals provide vocal foils for Margot and the Red Shadow. Clementina and Azuri are both antitheses of Margot. They are progeny of Carmen, the title character of Georges Bizet's 1875 opera.[5] Clementina is a mezzo who is not only Spanish but also dances (her "Song of the Brass Key" has the same habanera rhythm as the famous "Habanera" from *Carmen*), while Azuri is a dancer who seeks revenge on men who have wronged her. Both women are much more liberal in their sexual attitudes than is Margot. Bennie and Susan are musical comedy characters whose music and dialogue provide humorous diversions from the romantic plot. Their music sits midrange, in the same register as their speaking voices. The two principal Moroccan males, both of whom need operatic voices, are at the extremes of the male vocal range: Ali Ben Ali is a bass while Sid El Kar is an exceptionally high tenor. Voice types are used to indicate the exotic nature of these characters, for they possess neither the oft-heard baritone of Pierre/Red Shadow nor the familiar-sounding speech-range intonations of Bennie. Finally, the music of Paul, and even that of Pierre when he is not the Red Shadow, has a relatively narrow range and hardly any glorious sustained notes. A large part of the Red Shadow's allure, and what sets him apart from the other European male characters, is his ability to sing.

Disguise and impersonation are central to the plot of *The Desert Song*. This would have been familiar to 1920s audiences, for they were used to the idea of non-Arabs donning desert attire. Thanks to Lawrence of Arabia and Rudolf Valentino, two well-known Westerners known for wearing Arab clothing, the idea of Pierre impersonating an Arab was completely plausible. But in *The Desert Song*, the hero's alter ego is a bespectacled nerd, following the Romantic model of Baroness Orczy's *The Scarlet Pimpernel* (1905), where the title character also leads a double life. The most famous example of this severe difference in personality between the "real" person and his disguised role in twentieth-century popular culture is undoubtedly Superman, created by Jerry Siegel (1914–1996) and Joe Shuster (1914–1992). Superman entered the world in *Action Comics* #1 in 1938, twelve years after the premiere of *The Desert Song*. Whereas it takes Margot only a few hours to learn the truth about Pierre and the Red Shadow, it took Lois Lane over half a century to come to the same realization about Clark Kent and Superman.[6]

Closely related to impersonation and disguise in *The Desert Song* is Orientalism, the dominant aesthetic of the operetta in both its plot and its music. Orientalism of course was nothing new on the American musical stage or in Romberg's work, but the impact of this construct was nowhere more evident in 1920s musical theater than in *The Desert Song*.

Orientalism in the 1920s

When Howard Carter first peered into King Tutankhamen's tomb on November 26, 1922, a new wave of Orientalism was sweeping across Europe and North America. That same year, Grauman's Egyptian Theater opened in Hollywood and Ernst Lubitsch's film *Das Weib des Pharaohs* (released in the United States as *Loves of Pharaoh* and also *Pharaoh's Wife*) had its American release. This fascination with all things Egyptian made Carter's discovery all the more exciting and captivating.[7]

One aspect that made the discovery of King Tut's tomb different from other events in the North African world was its media coverage. This was a true news event, and the media played an important role in creating an image of ancient Egypt that was both remote, because of its time, and modern, because of the manner in which people learned about the discovery, complete with photographs. Two contrasting cultures coalesced in the event, just as they did in *The Desert Song:* the local and the foreign. Benjamin (Bennie) Kidd in *The Desert Song* is an homage to the foreign press corps of the 1920s; he is in Morocco to tell the world of the Red Shadow's exploits.

The fascination with Egypt permeated many aspects of culture and style, including architecture. A particular Egyptian art deco style that combined elements of 1920s chic with Arabian sheik was especially popular. Notably evident in movie theaters, the approach endorsed the blend between reality and fantasy that also characterized early cinema. Many Egyptian-style theaters were built throughout the United States, one of the most famous being Grauman's in Hollywood.[8]

It was not only the Egyptian motifs but also other Arab identifiers that enhanced the fantasy quality of the lavish movie palaces built during the 1920s. The exterior of the State Theater (1927) in Kalamazoo, Michigan, for example, has Moorish terra cotta ornaments, while a Moorish spire dominates the façade of the Palace Theater (1928) in Louisville, Kentucky.

In addition to movie palaces, stage theaters also included Oriental motifs in their design. New York's Casino Theatre, where *The Desert Song* played, was loaded with Moorish elements in its exterior and interior. Erected in 1882, the building was modeled after the Newport Casino in Newport, Rhode Island, built two years earlier by Stanford White as the clubhouse for the resort's lawn tennis courts. During the 1880s, French and German operettas in English translation appeared on its stage, as did many English-language originals, making the Casino Theatre the premier house for operetta in New York. Significantly, Romberg's *The Blue Paradise* played there in 1914. With its rich heritage as a home for operetta, along with its Moorish design, the theater was the ideal venue for *The Desert Song*.[9]

The 1920s' movie palaces with their Arabian architectural features were the home of films, a burgeoning type of entertainment that presented created locales and fantastic and adventurous tales with a sense of documentary and cinematic realism. Just as the opening of King Tut's tomb was a media event because of its film coverage, Hollywood capitalized on its ability to bring visual images to a large audience. One type of production that played into this creative possibility, and the one that concerns us here, was Orientalist film.

The desert was the topographical domain of Orientalist cinema. It was an unchangeable terrain that exuded permanence. The desert subsequently became a symbol for underdevelopment—the Westerner, by contrast, became the productive, proactive, and creative redeemer of the arid wilderness. An East/West axis dominates many Orientalist films, thus endorsing a culturally determined geographic-symbolic polarity. This was part of the larger construct of Orientalism so passionately discussed by Edward W. Said in his highly influential *Orientalism*. The desert locale presented the Orient as a land of "irrational primitivism and uncontrollable instincts."[10]

The Colonial Gaze is a central feature of Orientalist cinema. The genre sees a need for the West to rescue the Orient from itself, and frequently includes literal rescue narratives. A typical plot concerned a Western woman who is kidnapped by an Arab and rescued by a Western hero. This scenario fit comfortably within the established seraglio abduction tradition, one of the most famous examples in music being Mozart's *Die Entführung aus dem Serail* (*The Abduction from the Seraglio*, 1782). As Ella Shohat asserts: "The figure of the Arab assassin/rapist, like that of the African cannibal, helps produce the narrative and ideological role of the Western liberator as integral to the colonial rescue fantasy. This projection, whose imagistic avatars include the polygamous Arab, the libidinous black buck and the macho Latino, provides an indirect apologia for domination."[11]

This method of characterization based upon culturally determined stereotypes exists in *The Desert Song*. The French are portrayed as having some sort of inherent right to be colonial rulers in Morocco. They are there, according to the stage and subsequent film narratives, to help the Moroccans reform their allegedly violent and uncivilized mannerisms. In *The Desert Song*, though, the kidnapper and the rescuer are the same person.

In Orientalist cinema, the white woman was the object of desire of both protagonists and antagonists. She has to be "lured, made captive, and virtually raped to awaken her repressed desire."[12] This is an apt description of what happens to both Margot and Susan in *The Desert Song*.

Orientalist films typically carry theological overtones related to sexuality. The Western, Christian world of monogamy overrides the Eastern, Islamic world of polygamy, showing the latter to be inferior to the former.[13] This attitude motivates the "Eastern and Western Love" sequence in *The Desert Song*, where Ali Ben Ali and the Red Shadow exchange their views on women. The Red Shadow, Pierre in disguise, sings "One Alone," an ode to monogamy, in response to Ali Ben Ali's "One Flower Grows Alone in Your Garden," a sonnet to polygamy. The justification of monogamy, like that of colonialism, is part of a larger promotion of Western (Christian) values.

Rudolph Valentino (1895–1926) was the star who, more than any other, epitomized Hollywood's creation of the Arab world. He was one of the most prominent celebrities of the 1920s—the first dark-skinned male to become a romantic hero in Hollywood. He embodied forbidden sexual fantasies for women (and some men) and helped redefine masculinity in the 1920s. Valentino's untimely death from a ruptured ulcer on August 23, 1926, at age thirty-one caused mass hysteria and even some suicides. Crowds outside and inside Campbell's Funeral Parlor, where Valentino's body lay in state, were riotous. Over one hundred people were injured in the hysteria, necessitating medical personnel to set up a temporary hospital on the ground floor of the

Rudolf Valentino and Agnes Ayres in *The Sheik*. Licensed by Getty Images.

funeral home.[14] The line of mourners to pay their respects to the deceased actor stretched for eleven blocks.

Romberg and Hammerstein were working on *The Desert Song* at the Hotel Marie Antoinette, located across the street from Campbell's Funeral Parlor, and saw firsthand the triple line of people waiting to see Valentino's body.[15] They were acutely aware of the popularity of Valentino and fully intended to ride the wave of Sheikmania.

The Sheik (1921), one of Valentino's most famous films, told the story of Ahmed, a North African chieftain who kidnaps, woos, and wins Lady Diana Mayo. At the end of the film, Diana learns that Ahmed is of English and Spanish, not Arab, ancestry; it turns out that he is even the son of an English Lord. Both Diana and Ahmed, therefore, are Europeans, and an interracial romance is conveniently averted. This was the same premise and resolution Hammerstein used in *The Desert Song* five years later: the supposed Arab is really a European in disguise.

The film was the inspiration for one of the most popular Orientalist songs of the century, "The Sheik of Araby" (1921, music by Ted Snyder, lyrics

Pearl Regay (as Azuri), Edmond Elton (as General Birabeau), Vivienne Segal (as Margot Bonvalet), and Robert Halliday (as the Red Shadow) in the original production of *The Desert Song*. Licensed by Brown Bros.

by Harry B. Smith and Francis Wheeler). Described as an "Arabian foxtrot," the song later became a favorite with jazz musicians and was even recorded by the Beatles. In the refrain, the title character promises a woman that he will steal her away to rule the desert with him. The song thus follows the basic premise of *The Sheik*. Snyder's music emphasizes the minor mode and diminished chords, giving the song a hint of exoticism. Romberg also employed the minor mode to evoke the Arab world in *The Desert Song*, as will be discussed below.

Because of Valentino's death at a young age, the actor's iconic image as the kaffiyeh-covered Sheik became enshrined in the American popular consciousness. He personified lust and violence, and popularized sideburns as a symbol of male virility.[16] Through the screen personas of actors such as Valentino, the desert became, metaphorically, the "world of the out-of-control id" and overt sexuality. It allowed Hollywood filmmakers narrative license to film flesh without risking censorship, making the Orient the locus for eroticism in an industry bound by a moralistic code.[17] This imagery is strongly present in the character of the Red Shadow in *The Desert Song*.

Central to the sexual imagining of the body was stylized physical gesture, primarily that of dance. Valentino was a dancer before he began his acting career and employed physical gesture as a central aspect of his screen persona. Film scholar Gaylyn Studlar suggests that it was the dance element of Valentino's on-screen performance that allowed audiences to enjoy "the full potency of his sexual persona."[18] This attribute was particularly evident in the rape scene in *Son of the Sheik* (1926), where Valentino's libido was choreographed in a highly stylized sequence.

Valentino's style of dance was not the only one to endorse Orientalism by any means. The Arabian dance popularized by "Little Egypt" at the 1893 World's Fair in Chicago continued to enter the American imagination in the 1920s: this "belly dance" became the most famous depiction of Orientalist choreography.

In *The Desert Song*, the image of the sensuous harem dancer appears in the character Azuri. Azuri is the villain, for she is the one who tricks General Birabeau into ordering his son killed. Azuri is sensual and alluring, and she uses physical gestures to endorse her sexuality. In a review of the operetta's tryout in Boston, the writer called Pearl Regay, who played Azuri, a "lady contortionist." He continued, describing her unforgettable performance: "Then, when tribal musicians drummed and piped, she wove Azuri's body into writhings, whirlings, bendings, archings wondrous to see. On the floor, in the air, wherever there might be such motion, she bent and unbent, strung and unstrung, her bow of flexile flesh."[19]

Phoebe Brune must have been equally captivating as Azuri in the London production, for a reviewer extolled the merits of the actress's "animated snake. In this there was distinct *allure*."[20]

Azuri is just one of the harem dancers in *The Desert Song*. Act 2 opens in a harem with an extended dance sequence. A writer in Boston compared the scene to a Ziegfeld's *Follies* number, calling it superior to the revue: "In the second act, tawny-clad and short-skirted, they likewise had a dance to themselves. Faster and faster whipped the music; swifter and swifter they tossed their gambollings. No Charleston might outfling or outrace this young frenzy of motion . . . in October, Mr. Ziegfeld's youngsters in the newest Follies seemed the nonpareil. . . . [T]he flappers of 'Lady Fair' outdo them hands down—or rather feet up."[21]

Another Boston reviewer found the entire operetta to be a raison d'être for Orientalist dance: "Of course they had to have a plot for an excuse to stage so munificent a festival of Oriental costume dancing and such an extravagance of catching song hits."[22]

The union of Orientalist dance and *The Desert Song* was further endorsed in the Romberg biopic *Deep in My Heart*. *The Desert Song* sequence features Cyd Charisse and James Mitchell in a stylized, veil-filled Arabian ballet to an instrumental rendition of "One Alone."

The Colonial Gaze, a critical component of Orientalism, was strongly promoted in the telling of the desert exploits of Thomas Edward Lawrence (1888–1935), better known as Lawrence of Arabia. Lawrence's campaigns in the Arab world during World War I were well known in the English-speaking world; he was a real-life hero who had seen adventure in the nearly mythical North African desert. In many ways, his image was a media concoction delivered by the clever entrepreneur and journalist Lowell Thomas (1892–1981).

Thomas created a lantern slide lecture show, "With Allenby in Palestine and Lawrence in Arabia" (1919–26?), that brought the exploits of Lawrence to British and American audiences. He toured extensively throughout the United States with his intentional propaganda piece. Thomas's audience was a war-weary public that was far more interested in the Eastern Front, about which they knew very little, than the Western Front, about which no one wanted to hear more after the Armistice. The mystique of the Arab world held great potential for the media entrepreneur: audiences were enraptured by the show, and, as Steven C. Caton asserts, Thomas's goal was to displace the popular memory of the Western Front, a gruesome one, with a more romantic acknowledgment of the Eastern one. Orientalism was essential in this construction; after all, Lawrence of Arabia in his dashing robes was a far more glamorous hero than his counterparts on the Western Front.[23]

In addition to the lecture show, Thomas promoted Lawrence's self-created Arabic vision in his book *With Lawrence in Arabia* (1924), complete with photographs of Lawrence in various types of robes. Impersonation was central here: Lawrence was supposed to pass for Arabian but was Nordic in appearance. As Thomas describes him: "But this young man was as blond as a Scandinavian, in whose veins flow Viking blood and the cool traditions of fiords and sagas. The nomadic sons of Ishmael all wear flowing beards, as their ancestors did in the time of Esau. This youth, with the curved gold sword, was clean-shaven. He walked rapidly with his hands folded, his blue eyes oblivious to his surroundings, and he seemed wrapped in some inner contemplation."[24]

Lawrence was a resounding emblem of British imperialism. He was cast as "the Uncrowned King of Arabia," and helped organize, according to British standards, the Near East. He was deified, and his own feelings of racial superiority, along with those of his countrymen, coupled with his individual brilliance, certainly helped his cause.[25]

Lawrence himself fed into his media image by privately publishing his autobiography, *The Seven Pillars of Wisdom*, in 1926, the year in which *The Desert Song* appeared. His personal account of his adventures as a guerrilla leader had the flavor of a heroic epic.

It is this same attitude of a "racially superior" European being able to help the Arabs when they cannot help themselves that is at the heart of *The Desert Song*. Pierre, in his work as the Red Shadow, leads the Riffs, even though he is European. He is completely accepted for his military prowess and inherent knowledge of Arabian ways, unlike the real-life Lawrence of Arabia, who garnered only a partial following.

News from Morocco during the first half of the 1920s centered on the exploits of Abd-El-Kim, a Riff leader who detested foreign rule. In 1904, France and Spain divided Morocco into spheres of influence, and in 1920, Abd-El-Kim led a revolt against the Spaniards. Within four years, his forces had driven the Spaniards out of Morocco. He then turned his attention toward the French. France and Spain formed an alliance in 1925 to repel the Riff forces. The Europeans achieved victory the following year, 1926, although it took twenty-five thousand French and Spanish troops to defeat Abd-El-Kim. The Red Shadow's efforts paralleled those of Abd-El-Kim, although the Riff leader was not a disguised European.

Margot, as a European traveling in the Orient, also had models in popular cinema, such as Lady Diana Mayo in *The Sheik*, and in real life. The Englishwoman Gertrude Bell (1868–1926) was famous for her travels in the Arab world and the books she wrote about her experiences.[26] Bell died on July 12, 1926, in Baghdad, and her contributions to Arab culture, including her efforts toward founding the Baghdad Archaeological Museum, were lauded and remembered in the five and a half months leading up to the premiere of *The Desert Song*. In the Francophone world, Isabelle Eberhardt (1877–1904) was another European who traveled in North Africa, but that is where the similarity between her and Margot ends. Eberhardt was known for her cross-dressing and sexual escapades, attributes completely foreign to Margot.

The Desert Song, therefore, was textually and philosophically rooted in Orientalism. It played upon broader cultural notions such as the Colonial

Gaze and integrated real-life figures such as Rudolf Valentino, Lawrence of Arabia, Abd-El-Kim, and Gertrude Bell into its discourse. For this treatment to be effective, it required a musical score that operated on similar principles. Romberg's music was extremely effective in accomplishing this purpose.

The Music of *The Desert Song*

Romberg's score for *The Desert Song* is one of his finest and most cohesive creations. (See Table 6.1.) Nearly operatic in conception, and certainly eclectic, it includes rousing marches, lyrical waltzes, and numbers firmly rooted in Tin Pan Alley. Elements of a distinctive Orientalist musical aesthetic appear as well. In the score, Romberg endorsed the role of major and minor that he offered in his 1928 article, "A Peep into the Workshop of a Composer," quoted earlier but worth repeating here: "Music is in two categories: major and minor. Hungarian, Russian, and Balkan States, Persia, and India take music in the minor key; Anglo-Saxon and Latin countries are written in major."[27] In *The Desert Song*, songs performed by the French characters, such as "Romance" and "French Marching Song," are in major, while Moroccan numbers, such as the opening of "The Riff Song," are in minor.

Romberg presents the Riff band as decidedly non-European in "The Riff Song."[28] The male choral number begins in D minor, but with some added chromatic tinges. The melody centers on a sustained G-sharp, a raised fourth scale degree and a tritone away from the tonic. This emphasis is unusual for European tonal harmony and immediately establishes an exotic aural atmosphere. Its accompanying harmony is likewise atypical, for the fully diminished seventh chord built upon the enticingly alien G-sharp (G-sharp-B-D-F, vii°/V in D minor) returns immediately to the tonic the first time the motif appears, and to another pre-dominant chord, E dim (E-G-B-flat, ii° in D minor), the second time. The normal resolution to the dominant is cleverly averted in both instances. (See example 6.1.) After the two prolonged G-sharps, the music returns to functional harmony based on strong root movement (ii-V-I). Once the sense of the exotic has been established, regular tonal function can resume.

This relatively simple use of harmony creates an immediate sense of the Other, one of the hallmarks of musical Orientalism. We are immediately aware that the Riffs are not Western Europeans. Even in the refrain, when the music has moved to the relative major (F major), D minor continues

Table 6.1 Musical program for *The Desert Song* (according to the opening night playbill)

Time: One year ago. Place: North Africa

Act I
Scene 1: Retreat of the Red Shadow in the Riff Mountains Evening
Opening—"High on a Hill" (Sid, Riffs)
"Ho!" (The Riff Song) (Red Shadow, Sid, Riffs)
"Margot" (Paul, Soldiers)

Scene 2: Garden outside General Birabeau's Villa. That Night
"I'll Be a Bouyant Girl" (Susan)

Scene 3: Drawing Room of General Birabeau's Home. A Few Minutes Later
"Why Did We Marry Soldiers?" (Soldiers' Wives)
"French Marching Song" (Margot, Ensemble) [also known as "French Military Marching Song"]
"Romance" (Margot, Soldiers' Wives)
"Then You Will Know" (Pierre, Margot)
"I Want a Kiss" (Paul, Margot, Pierre, Ensemble)
"It" (Bennie, Susan, Girls)
"The Desert Song" (Red Shadow, Margot)
Finale (Company)

Act II
Scene 1: The Great Hall of Ali Ben Ali. Afternoon of the Following Day
Opening—"My Little Castagnette" (Clementina, Girls)
"Song of the Brass Key" (Clementina, Girls)
"One Good Boy Gone Wrong" (Bennie, Clementina)
"Eastern and Western Love"
    "Let Love Go" (Ali, Men)
    "One Flower Grows Alone in Your Garden" (Sid, Men)
    "One Alone" (Red Shadow, Men)

Scene 2: A Corridor. A Few Minutes Later

Scene 3: The Room of the Silken Couch
Opening (Margot, Girls)
"The Sabre Song" (Margot)
Dramatic Finaletto (Pierre, Margot, General Birabeau)

Scene 4: The Edge of the Desert. The Following Morning a Half Hour before Dawn
"Farewell" (Red Shadow, Riffs)

Table 6.1 Continued

Scene 5: Courtyard of General Birabeau's House. Two Days Later
Opening—"All Hail to the General" (Margot, Paul, General Birabeau, Girls)
"Let's Have a Love Affair" (Bennie, Susan, Girls) [dropped in January 1927, replaced by a reprise of "It"]
Dance (Azuri)
Finale (Company)

to exist as a secondary tonal region, endorsing the dual identity of the Riff leader. Modal identifiers provide aural clues to the Red Shadow's true identity as well as to his disguise.

The disparity between the Orient and the Occident is central to the scene "Eastern and Western Love." In this integrated musico-dramatic sequence, Romberg represents these cultural differences through his choice of mode. The first part of the scene, "Let Love Go" and "One Flower in Your Garden," constitutes Ali Ben Ali's *Eastern* view of women (the necessity of a harem) and is in F minor. The Red Shadow (the *Frenchman* Pierre) responds with "One Alone"—an ode to monogamy, the *Western* view—in A-flat major, the relative major to Ali's discourse. Ali and the Red Shadow not only disagree about women philosophically but also sing in different languages—Ali in minor and the Red Shadow in major. Furthermore, "One Alone" is in verse-refrain form, the archetypical Tin Pan Alley design, while "Let Love Go" and "One Flower in Your Garden" are not, for they are integrated into a larger ABA' design.

"One Alone," introduced in act 2, becomes one of the Red Shadow's principal songs. (See example 6.2.) In it, he expresses not only his philosophy regarding love but also his love for Margot alone. The tune is tonally stable and firmly grounded in the major mode, reflecting Pierre/Red Shadow's assuredness of the validity of his words. He sings it again as he bids farewell to his desert allies, telling them he must be with the one person he loves, and the operetta concludes with Margot intoning the tune and remembering her mysterious lover on the words "All alone, to be my own," when Pierre, his true identity revealed, responds with the second half of the phrase, "At her call, I'd give my all."

The same modal identification observed in "Eastern and Western Love" occurs in the act 1 finale, during Azuri's dance sequence. The French revel-

Example 6.1. "The Riff Song" (*The Desert Song*), mm. 1–9

Example 6.2. "One Alone" *(The Desert Song)*, refrain, mm. 1–4

ers implore Azuri to dance, and do so in E major. "Azuri's Dance," performed by the Moroccan dancer, follows in G minor.

These modal associations are also present in the music of the male lead. The character's double identity is mirrored in his songs, especially in the operetta's title song, the principal love duet. Pierre is disguised as the Red Shadow when he begins singing to Margot. The verse is in two parts, the first of which Pierre sings while hidden from Margot's view. He is Pierre, the European, and sings, in D-flat *major*, "Why waste your time in vague

Example 6.3. "The Desert Song" (The Desert Song), "Tempo di valse," mm. 1–8

romancing." When he emerges and continues into the second part of the verse, he is disguised as the Red Shadow, and sings "My desert is waiting" in C-sharp *minor*, the enharmonic parallel minor to the key of the opening section. The vocal line is largely pentatonic, creating an alternative exotic sound world. (See example 6.3.) The refrain, "Blue heaven and you and I," returns to the major mode as Pierre expresses his true feelings for Margot. (See example 6.4.) He is now being truthful in all things—his love for Margot and his European heritage—and as such, sings in the major mode.

Azuri, the prominent Oriental female in the operetta, does not sing, but rather is represented by an instrumental identifier, or leitmotif. (See example 6.5.) Her musical signature is monophonic and slitheringly chro-

Example 6.4. "The Desert Song" *(The Desert Song)*, refrain, mm. 1–4

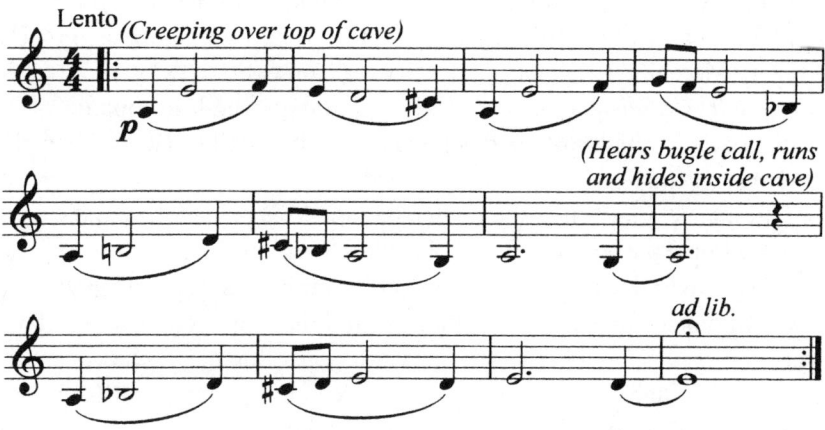

Example 6.5. "Entrance of Azuri" *(The Desert Song)*

matic. Half steps and augmented seconds characterize the passage, along with a pronounced use of G-natural, rather than G-sharp, as the seventh scale degree of the A-centered tonality. This is especially evident in the latter part of the passage, when Azuri runs to hide in the cave. Additionally, Romberg emphasizes the lowered second scale degree, suggesting the warlike and alien-sounding Phrygian mode. Azuri's music is every bit as exotic for Western audiences as she is.

Azuri's inability to sing arises from two distinct factors. First, her overtly deceitful intentions may prevent her from having the ability to sing, for only good and morally strong people are usually allowed to sing in an operetta. (An exception in *The Desert Song* is General Birabeau, which is a speaking role. In his case, though, not singing suggests his ineffectual leadership abilities.) Second, she is fundamentally a dancer, and physical gesture is more important than vocal utterance. This final point carries over into casting: since Azuri has to be able to dance and present herself physically on stage, eliminating the need to have her sing makes finding someone to play the role much easier.

In contrast to the Moroccans with their minor mode or chromatic music, the French characters all sing assuredly and diatonically in major. The march for female chorus, "Why Did We Marry Soldiers?" and its male counterpart, the "French Military Marching Song," resolutely follow standard Western harmonic procedures. The latter march includes trumpet fanfares on a B-flat triad that solidifies its rooting in the major mode, thus making it musically impossible to confuse the Riffs and the French. Furthermore, the "French Military Marching Song" hearkens back to "Come, Boys, Let's All Be Gay, Boys" in *The Student Prince*, for in both numbers, the lead soprano must demonstrate her high sustained notes and coloratura abilities while the male chorus sings the refrain.

"Romance" constitutes the French heroine Margot's cavatina and scena, to borrow operatic terms, in which she offers to the audience her most heartfelt desire: to find true love. The number is in two parts: a 4/4 allegretto followed by a graceful waltz. Both the verse and the refrain emphasize octave leaps followed by scalar passages and arpeggios. Romberg achieves musical unity through this common gesture. (See examples 6.6 and 6.7.) The music is firmly rooted in the major mode—Margot is European, after all. Her music endorses triadic harmony as much as Azuri's eschews it. This musical treatment clearly articulates the character differences between the two women.

In "Romance," Margot tells of her heartfelt dream to find romance. She is dissatisfied with her current romantic state and, since reality is barren, turns to fantasy. She is not alone in her desire, for the women's chorus enters to support her yearning. This is similar to the scoring in *The Student Prince's* "Serenade" (for men rather than women in "Serenade," though), but not in such sophisticated musical and dramatic terms. Additionally, it foreshadows Marianne's waltz "One Kiss" in *The New Moon* in terms of musical and dramatic content, but again in not as developed a manner.

Example 6.6. "Romance" (The Desert Song), Allegretto, mm. 3–4

Example 6.7. "Romance" (The Desert Song), Tempo di valse, mm. 33–36

In act 2's "The Sabre Song," Margot's feelings have changed. She truly loves the Red Shadow, and admits it, in song, to his sword. Reality has set in, and Margot sings in duple meter, rather than triple. She has achieved her dream, and no longer needs to sing fantasy-laden waltzes.

Continuing with the idea of reality, Romberg portrays the contemporary world through songs in the style of musical comedy or revue. The prime example of this treatment is the comic song "It." Here, Romberg gives a musical rendition of modern views of sexuality as endorsed by Elinor Glyn (1864–1943), author of the novel *It*, which was first published serially in *Cos-*

mopolitan magazine in 1926, the same year *The Desert Song* appeared.[29] Glyn defined the title of her book as follows: "To have 'It,' the fortunate possessor must have that strange magnetism which attracts both sexes. There must be physical attraction, but beauty is unnecessary." "It" and *It* are central to Bennie and Susan's number "It." Elinor Glyn is mentioned in the lyric, and the significance of the press in the novel (they are critical in shaping public attitudes) is emphasized by the choice of characters who sing the song—the journalists.

Romberg's musical setting, in A-flat major, is in the syncopated style of his revue numbers, many of which also had lyrics about sexuality. Frequent pauses interrupt the refrain, prohibiting it from being sung in the same luxuriant style as the music of Margot and the Red Shadow/Pierre. (See example 6.8.) Romberg thus shows through musical means that Bennie and Susan's "modern" syncopated view of love is very different from the fantasy-driven one of Margot.

In the film *Deep in My Heart*, "It" appears in the *Artists and Models of 1925* sequence rather than in *The Desert Song* one. The creators of the film, who were not overly concerned about historical accuracy, used the song to endorse the sexual themes and musical style of *Artists and Models*—a match that, although "It" did not actually appear in that particular revue, is nonetheless appropriate.

Romberg's operettas before *The Desert Song* typically end with a reprise of the show's principal waltz duet. This is not the case here, for "One Alone" is the last music heard. While the text allows for this to be extremely effective dramatically—Margot is afraid her heart will be alone after the death of the Red Shadow—it also was a successful attempt at ending the operetta with a duple-meter number. This of course had happened previously in *Maytime*, but the song was not a love song in that instance. Now, it is.

In the previous operettas that conclude with waltz reprises, such as *The Student Prince*, the stories end unhappily. The lovers are not together at the final curtain. In *The Desert Song*, they are. For a show with a happy ending, a sentimental waltz may not be the best artistic choice for the final musical utterance, for waltzes were often associated with lost love and nostalgia, neither of which is present here. Perhaps Romberg realized that he had connected the waltz to unrequited love to the point where this had become the style's only plausible meaning when it was reprised in one of his operetta finales. Therefore, in a work where the romance actually does have a happy ending, he knew that something other than a waltz needed to be sung at

Example 6.8. "It" (*The Desert Song*), refrain, mm. 1–8

the final curtain. "One Alone" fulfilled that purpose. A new formula for an operetta had emerged: one that included a happy ending and a recurring duple-meter love duet whose dramatic importance was equal to (or perhaps even greater than) the glorious waltzes.

Whether or not Romberg was conscious of it, Orientalism may also have played a part in this decision. The Orient was often envisioned as female, and femininity is often associated with the waltz, especially in operetta. *The Desert Song* is no exception, for the refrain of Margot's "Romance" is a waltz. So is "The Desert Song," which is sung initially by the Red Shadow. The song represents the Oriental side of the male lead from a metric perspective, while "One Alone," his overtly Western number, is in 4/4. In Orientalist discourse, the West is masculine, and musically, masculinity is often portrayed through duple-meter songs, especially marches, a genre associated with male power and dominance. By ending the operetta with a reprise of "One Alone," Romberg is subtly asserting a pro-Western view at the end of the operetta: European masculinity prevails over Oriental femininity. The operetta's music, as well as its libretto, can be interpreted as endorsing many tenets of the era's unapologetic Orientalist discourse.

The Desert Song is justifiably one of Romberg's most popular and important works. It includes marches and waltzes in the operetta style, along with glorious parts for its singing principals. Romberg uses simple but effective means in establishing a sense of place and ethnicity. Orientalism, a salient feature of 1920s popular culture, enters strongly into the work, simultaneously infusing it with a sense of exoticism and relevance. A timeless tale of the triumph of love, the operetta's setting in the "forever constant" realm of the Moroccan desert was a perfect backdrop for its evocative score and libretto. Here was escapist, romantic adventure that had just enough reality in it to keep it from being pure fantasy. The creators drew upon news events of 1926—the deaths of Rudolf Valentino and Gertrude Bell and the publication of *It*—in grounding the show in 1920s popular culture. Women in the audience could dream about being taken away by the Red Shadow, just as they had the same fantasies about Rudolf Valentino. Likewise, men had Azuri's physical allure and bodily gestures to keep their interest. The show inaugurated a strong working relationship between Romberg, Hammerstein, and the producing team of Mandel and Schwab, one that resulted in further successes, most notably *The New Moon*. But before that show appeared in 1928, Romberg produced five other works, all of which dealt with the same basic theme as *The Desert Song* and *The New Moon*: a dashing young hero finds true love.

CHAPTER 7

Exploring New Possibilities: From *Cherry Blossoms* to *The New Moon*

THE DESERT SONG PROVED THAT OPERETTA COULD BE SET IN places other than Europe (or a substituted New York City, as in *Maytime*) and wholly in the present. The possibilities for the genre, at least in Romberg's eyes and ears, expanded immensely. Romberg was liberating himself from the operetta model he had solidified with the Shuberts, where nostalgia was a powerful dramatic force and an unfulfilled love story was told through a musical palate dominated by a recurring waltz duet. He continued this shift away from his orthodox Shubert model in the works that followed *The Desert Song*: four new operettas in one year for the Shuberts, and *Rosalie*, a collaboration with George Gershwin. These led to another landmark success with *The New Moon*, the last of the great American operettas of the 1920s. In this genre-defining piece, Romberg effectively synthesized many elements drawn from not only his own work but also the rich history of comic opera and operetta.

Return to the Shuberts: *Cherry Blossoms*, *My Maryland*, *My Princess*, and *The Love Call*

After the success of *The Desert Song*, Romberg returned to the Shuberts in 1927 for a series of four operettas: *Cherry Blossoms*, *My Maryland*, *My Princess*, and *The Love Call*. J. J. succeeded in luring Romberg back with a promise of greater creative independence.[1] Romberg used this freedom to experiment with geographical settings, for each of the four shows takes place in a radically different time and place: Japan in modern times (the playbill is not specific as to exactly when the action occurs), Maryland during the American Civil War, New York City in the present day, and Arizona in 1869. None of the stories takes place in Europe, the traditional setting of operetta plots. *Cherry Blossoms* has a bittersweet plot resolution, while the others have happy endings, a notable departure from the earlier Shubert-Romberg model. However, each tale is radically different from its companions: *Cherry Blossoms* is about East-West relations, *My Maryland* is a historical romance, *My Princess* is a riches-to-rags-to-riches story, and *The Love Call* is a Wild West adventure.

Romberg, knowing what the Shuberts wanted and expected as far as music was concerned, placed a waltz duet at the center of each score, following the model he developed in the works leading up to and including *The Student Prince*. He also infused local color into each show, just as he had done in *The Magic Melody*, *The Student Prince*, and *The Desert Song*. Given the diversity of geographic locations, Romberg had an unprecedented opportunity to experiment with creating a sense of place and ethnicity through musical means. But he also maintained many of the precepts of operetta and musical comedy, and used them for focused musical-dramatic purposes. These four operettas, therefore, combine the idea of the formulaic Shubert-produced works with an intentional effort to create something new and innovative, a trajectory that led to *The New Moon*.

Of the group, *My Maryland* was the sole critical and commercial success. It played for 312 performances in its initial New York run and had a record-breaking forty-week tryout in Philadelphia (from January 24 to October 29), its run in Philadelphia continuing after its New York premiere on September 12. It remained extremely popular in Philadelphia and was revived there many times during the 1920s and 1930s.[2] The other three shows closed within months of opening. *Cherry Blossoms* ran a modest fifty-six performances, and *The Love Call* eighty-eight. *My Princess* was the greatest failure of the group, playing an embarrassingly few twenty times.

Before investigating the musical elements of these shows and what the scores reveal about Romberg's approach to operetta at the time, a brief look at the plots and background of each show is in order. Romberg tied his music to the particular needs of each story, and continued to foster a close bond between the shows' musical and dramatic elements.

Harry B. Smith's libretto for *Cherry Blossoms* (March 28, 1927, 44th Street) was based on J. H. Benrimo and Harrison Rhodes's play *The Willow Tree* (1917). Both the play and the operetta recall David Belasco's drama

Madame Butterfly (1900) and Puccini's operatic adaptation (1904), but without the tragic ending. In *Cherry Blossoms*, American Ned Hamilton (Howard Marsh, who created the role of Karl Franz in *The Student Prince*) goes on a world tour to recover from a broken marriage engagement.[3] While in Japan, he buys a statue of a young maiden carved from the heart of a willow tree. Seeing a gullible lovesick American in his shop, the malevolent shop owner, George Washington Goto, plays a trick on his customer. In a Pygmalion-like ploy, the carving magically becomes the living shop-girl Yo-San (Desiree Ellinger). Yo-San's father sold her to Goto, and the salesman is exploiting both her and the young American. Ned and Yo-San immediately fall in love and soon thereafter engage in conjugal relations. When Ned's ex-fiancée appears, Yo-San realizes the interracial relationship she shares with her American lover cannot succeed. She wants him to leave with his honor intact, and in a self-sacrificial act, gives herself fully to Goto. In an ending reminiscent of *The Blue Paradise*, Ned returns to Japan seventeen years later. He learns that Yo-San has died and that their daughter (also played by Ellinger), whom he did not know existed, has grown up to be a virtual double for her mother.

Cherry Blossoms portrayed a stylized Japan and followed well-known models such as Gilbert and Sullivan's *The Mikado* (1885) and Sidney Jones's *The Geisha* (1896) in this regard. The costumes for *Cherry Blossoms* endorsed this imaginary view of Japan for, according to one reviewer, they were closer to French variations of Japanese motifs than to actual Japanese specimens. One significant aspect of the staging, however, reflected actual Japanese theatrical performance: chroniclers recited the action that occurred between the acts. (Stephen Sondheim and John Weidman applied a similar technique in *Pacific Overtures* [1976], but with a single Reciter.) Thus, elements of invented stylization appeared alongside authentic theatrical practice in the show.[4]

My Maryland (September 12, 1927, Jolson's) was the third collaboration between Romberg and Dorothy Donnelly.[5] Its story originated with the real-life Barbara Hauer Fritchie (1766–1862), who supposedly waved a Union flag in front of Confederate troops as they passed through Frederick, Maryland, on September 10, 1862. The legend is almost certainly untrue, for Fritchie would have been in her nineties, very ill, and probably bedridden. However, John Greenleaf Whittier wrote a poem, which was published in the October 1863 issue of *Atlantic Monthly*, that immortalized the heroine. In the poem, Fritchie, aged "four score and ten," leans out of her window as

Evelyn Herbert (as Barbara Fritchie) and Nathaniel Wagner (as Capt. Trumbull) in the original production of *My Maryland*. Courtesy of the Shubert Archive.

Confederate General Stonewall Jackson rides by and utters the immortal words: "Shoot if you must this old gray head, but spare your country's flag." Out of respect for her outspokenness, Jackson leaves her house intact. The tale was embellished in Clyde Fitch's play *Barbara Fritchie* (October 23, 1899, Criterion), where the title character became a young Southern belle living with her widowed father, and her married name becomes her maiden one.

Fitch's play was the basis for *My Maryland*. In the operetta, Barbara Frietchie [sic] (Evelyn Herbert), a Southerner, and Captain Will Trumbull (Nathaniel Wagner), the commanding officer of the occupying Union army in Frederick, are in love. Jack Negley (Warren Hull), who has been courting Barbara, is jealous of Trumbull's amorous advances toward Barbara and joins the Confederate army, hoping to kill his rival. Barbara and Trumbull elope just before Trumbull is called away to his regiment. Barbara's brother Arthur ends up shooting Trumbull in battle, and the injured captain is secreted into the Frietchie home. Barbara's father discovers the recovering soldier and demands that he leave, until Barbara pleads with him to allow her *husband* to remain in his house. As Jackson's troops march through the town looking for Union soldiers, Barbara goes to the balcony and waves the Union flag, to which Jackson responds, "Who touches a hair of that woman's head—dies like a dog!" In true Broadway fashion, Fritchie's modest home became a palatial antebellum mansion. Although historical accuracy was discarded, the mansion's interior and especially its exterior allowed for spectacular sets.

My Princess (October 6, 1927, Shubert), Romberg and Donnelly's fourth and final show together, was their only failure. Donnelly based the libretto on the play *Princess Zin-Zin* by her and Edward Sheldon. Although the work appeared at the Shuberts' flagship house, Alfred E. Aarons was its producer. Albertina Rasch provided the extended dance sequences that appeared throughout the show.[6]

The title character is Minnie Johnson (Hope Hampton), a Long Island socialite nicknamed Mimosa who attempts to impress her friends by telling them that she will marry an Italian prince.[7] Not knowing any Italian princes, she goes to an Italian neighborhood in New York and finds a recent immigrant, Giuseppe Ciccolini, or Chick (Leonard Ceeley). She gives him a princely makeover and then marries him. Mimosa fails to climb the social ladder, and instead is forced to live with her new husband in his New York tenement. At the end of the operetta, Chick makes a confession: he is an Italian prince who wanted to experience the life of an Italian-American immigrant incognito but is now ready to reclaim his identity.

My Princess endorsed the Central European operetta paradigm of royals who disguise themselves as ordinary people, but it also looked to the present, for its setting was New York in the 1920s. It had the typical musical comedy setting, but with operetta conventions. The show was even called a "modern operetta" in the playbill—it was something different, a hybrid of traditional operetta tropes (waltzes, royalty, and fantasy) and modern musical comedy conventions (set in the time and place of its audience). As a reviewer during the Boston tryout observed, "It is not, as those who remember its predecessors 'The Student Prince' and 'Blossom Time' might expect, in the vein of Viennese operetta."[8]

The 1927 operetta quartet concluded with *The Love Call* (October 24, 1927, Majestic).[9] Harry B. Smith was the show's lyricist, and Edward Locke and Smith wrote the libretto, basing it on Augustus Thomas's popular play *Arizona* (1899). The musical resonated strongly with J. J. and Lee Shubert, for *Arizona* was their deceased brother Sam's initial success in New York. Set in Arizona, as one would expect from the title of Thomas's play, the action centers on the conflict between Indians led by Black Hawk (Stanley Jessup) and the white residents of the Canby ranch. The renegade Captain Hodgman (John Rutherford) incites an Indian attack on the ranch that is thwarted by Lieutenant Denton (John Barker) and his rangers. Not surprisingly, the heroic Denton also falls in love with Bonita (Berna Deane), the head rancher's daughter.

Taken as a group, these four operettas share several important features. All exhibit manifestations of three fundamental musical decisions on Romberg's part. First, waltzes, especially the recurring waltz duet, are important elements in each score. Second, musical numbers whose primary purpose is to establish a particular sense of place appear in all four operettas. Third, Romberg writes numbers squarely in the Broadway styles of the 1920s, either foxtrots or, in the case of *My Maryland*, dramatic scenes for a coloratura soprano, as he did in *The Desert Song*, reminding the audience that these are Broadway musicals of the 1920s, not historical or exotic pageants.

Waltzes and Shubert operettas went hand-in-hand. This was the case as far as Romberg was concerned ever since "Auf Wiedersehn" in *The Blue Paradise* from 1914. The idea of a recurring waltz duet was part of the Shubert-Romberg operetta paradigm, and continued in these four works. Here, the waltz duets—*Cherry Blossoms*'s "My Own Willow Tree," *My Maryland*'s "Silver Moon," *My Princess*'s "Follow the Sun to the South," and *The Love Call*'s "Eyes That Love"—are all in a luxuriant, lyrical style. Only "My Own Willow Tree" has any ethnic identifiers, as will be discussed below.

In two of these operettas, Romberg assigns the waltz a further dramatic function: it becomes an aural symbol of fantasy in *My Maryland* and *My Princess*. Not only is the principal duet between Barbara and Trumbull in *My Maryland* a waltz, but so is Jack's song, in which he seeks Barbara's hand in marriage, "Won't You Marry Me?" The recurring waltz refrain depicts not only Jack's steadfastness (or obsession), since it keeps returning throughout the song, but also the realization that he is wishing for something that cannot be. The waltz idiom represents Jack's fantasy about Barbara. The duple-meter verses that separate the refrains prove that Jack knows that she is not interested in him, although the waltz refrain keeps overriding the reality of impending rejection. The reprise of the song in the final act is especially poignant, for it becomes a mad scene of sorts for Jack, who by this point in the operetta has become delusional.

Likewise, waltzes in *My Princess* emphasize subtle elements of the story line concerning fantasy. "Follow the Sun to the South" is the operetta's principal waltz, but two other waltzes, "Prince Charming" and "My Mimosa," also figure prominently in the score. "Prince Charming" is Minnie's fantasy waltz in which she sings about wanting to find the perfect man. Similarly, "My Mimosa" is first heard when Chick, as a street-grinder, sings it, hoping to find true love. Both waltzes are heard several times in the early part of the show but fade as "Follow the Sun to the South" gains prominence. Once Minnie and Chick discover true love they can sing their waltz duet and no longer have to fantasize about finding the perfect mate through their individual songs.

Romberg surrounded his waltzes with music that suggested the particular setting of each show. He established a musical sense of place through orchestration, direct quotation of familiar songs, or synthetic versions of particular ethnic musical styles.

The Japanese music in *Cherry Blossoms* is more suggestive than authentic. In the refrain of "My Own Willow Tree," for example, Romberg alludes to the musically exotic world of Japan through an abundance of parallel fourths and augmented triads with added sevenths. He was not concerned about quoting actual Japanese music; he merely wanted to create something that sounded different and was not in a purely diatonic tonal idiom. Orchestration was also used to evoke the non-Western world, particularly muted cornets and gongs.[10] (No orchestrator is named for the show, but since Emil Gerstenberger scored the other three shows, as well as *The Student Prince*, he is the most likely candidate.) Romberg also placed the chorus in the orchestra pit, thus creating the aural effect of disembodied voices. In this regard, he follows the model of Igor Stravinsky's *Les Noces* (*The Wedding*, 1914–17, rev. 1921–23), a ballet-cantata about a Russian folk wedding that also calls for the chorus to be in the pit.

Music suggestive of the Civil War era dominates the score of *My Maryland*. The trademark male chorus sings the operetta's principal march, "Your Land and My Land." At the end of the refrain, Romberg quotes the final phrase of "Battle Hymn of the Republic" with slightly altered words. (Donnelly substituted "Glory, glory, hallelujah, we'll sing as we go on" for the original "Glory, glory, hallelujah! His truth is marching on.") The coda adds authenticity to Romberg's synthesized Civil War march. At the appearance of the "Battle Hymn" quote, Romberg shifts the meter from 4/4 to 2/4 and adds percussion riffs, giving the aural illusion of a faster tempo. The march became one of Romberg's most famous works and was even suggested as a replacement for "The Star-Spangled Banner" as the American national anthem![11]

In addition to the "Battle Hymn," Romberg quotes three other well-known Civil War songs in the show: "Dixie," "The Bonnie Blue Flag," and "Maryland, My Maryland."[12] Audiences during the 1920s would certainly have recognized these famous tunes from the Civil War era. In addition to incorporating actual music from the 1860s, Romberg created songs in the nineteenth-century popular style such as "The Mocking Bird," "Strawberry Jam," and "Old John Barleycorn." He also wrote three heroic marches for the chorus, in addition to "Your Land and My Land": "Song of Victory," "Boys in Grey," and "Hail Stonewall Jackson," the last of which includes "Dixie" as a countermelody.

Synthesis and quotation also appear in *My Princess*. Since the operetta concerned Italian-Americans, it is not surprising that Romberg created pseudo-Italian music for the score. The most impressive number is "Eviva," a saltarello in 6/8 that appears several times in act 2. Romberg also interpolated the well-known Italian song "Santa Lucia" into the score, providing the audience with a familiar favorite.

The Love Call was set in the American West, and its score has many allusions to Friml's *Rose Marie* (1924). The similarities begin with the title of the show and that of one of *Rose Marie*'s most famous songs, "Indian Love Call." Other striking coincidence-defying similarities appear throughout the show: for instance, the lyrics for the rousing male march "The Ranger's Song" are very close to those of *Rose Marie*'s "The Mounties."[13] Furthermore, the act 1 finale begins with a tom-tom dance that is highly reminiscent of *Rose Marie*'s act 1 finale, the "Totem Tom-Tom."

Romberg includes more Indianist identifiers in *The Love Call* than Friml did in *Rose Marie*. (Friml was also establishing musical characterizations for French Canadians and the Royal Canadian Mounted Police in *Rose Marie*, so there was no direct dramatic need to infuse the entire score with Indianist identifiers.) These identifiers (which were in many ways general features of musical exoticism) included drone fifths, pentatonic melodies, chord planing, dotted rhythms, and strongly accented downbeats.

According to a note in the playbill, the Indian music in the score was based on authentic Chippewa themes.[14] This becomes extremely problematic for those familiar with Native American cultures, for Chippewa (or Ojibway) were from the northern United States (especially Minnesota, Wisconsin, and Michigan) and southern Canada (especially Ontario, Manitoba, and Saskatchewan), and not Arizona. Navajo, Hopi, Tohono, and O'Dham are native to Arizona, but not Chippewa. But for Romberg and his audience, this conflation of cultures probably went unnoticed.

The Love Call also includes a Mexican element, as did *Arizona*.[15] This kept the show from being a virtual pastiche of *Rose Marie*. It is most evident in the colorful choral "Fiesta" that begins act 3. Romberg later returned to Mexican themes in the film operetta *The Girl of the Golden West* (1938). (See chapter 9 for a discussion of the film and its music.)

While Romberg used music in each of these shows to establish a sense of place, he also included music squarely in the styles of either musical comedy or operetta. These numbers filled a variety of dramatic purposes, whether to remind the audience that the show was created in 1920s America or to emphasize specific features of character development.

Cherry Blossoms offered a view of modern Japan, a country that had experienced strong Western influences. The opening chorus told the audience that they were in "the new Japan" in which temple bells still ring, "but only play jazz."[16] This is reminiscent of the opening number in Gilbert and Sullivan's *The Mikado* (1885), where the chorus of nobles sings, "We are the gentlemen of Japan / On many a vase and jar — On many a screen and fan." In *Cherry Blossoms*, as in *The Mikado*, a documentary view of Japan is not evoked, but rather an imaginary one that is closer to the audience's own experiences, whether it is Victorian England in *The Mikado* or 1920s Broadway in *Cherry Blossoms*.

In *My Maryland*, Romberg writes for the gamut of styles, from the high operatic to the low comic. The act 2 finale is an extended solo passage for Barbara that places tremendous musical and acting demands upon the lead soprano. It takes place at the end of the wedding scene, just after Trumbull has been called away to war. Understandably, Barbara is despondent about the future and the act 2 finale is in effect her soliloquy of lovesick despair. Colgate Baker, reviewer for the *New York Review*, said the finale "would fit nicely into any romantic grand opera as the 'grand aria dramatique.' Indeed there is nothing more intense in the Metropolitan repertory."[17]

At the other end of the spectrum are songs such as "When You're in Mexico." This number is a musical version of one of many tall tales told by Zeke, the local drunk and town gossip who claims to be a veteran of wars in Mexico. The triplet-dominated melody appears over a ragtime-based dotted figure. This metric incongruity shows that Zeke's stories are at odds with the real world — just as he cannot prove the validity of his yarns, he cannot match his music to that of the orchestra. Also in the realm of comedy is the fast-paced "Ker-Choo," a sneezing song sung by a trio of Barbara's friends. On a more sentimental note are the foxtrot "Something Old, Something New," which appears during the wedding sequence, and "Mother," Barbara's gentle ballad, a duple-meter plea to her deceased mother for peace and comfort. The various styles of these songs plant the show in the 1920s and keep it from being a historical pageant of Civil War–era music, real or created.

My Princess also includes references to 1920s popular music styles. For example, "Gigolo," "Nightlife," and "Dear Girls, Goodbye" are syncopated foxtrots, while a tango appears in the final scene. But the show also has many operetta characteristics, particularly the concept of musical scenes. The multisectional act 1 finale recalls that of *The Student Prince* and culminates in "Follow the Sun to the South." Other sections throughout the operetta are also conceived as larger constructions, with melodrama being used as the primary means to provide continuous music while advancing the plot.

In *The Love Call*, Romberg also integrated individual numbers into extended musical sequences. One of the most impressive of these is the opening, which contains five distinct musical numbers linked through melodrama or recitative.[18] Of these songs, two are waltzes, the mainstay of operetta—"You May Drink to My Wedding Day" and "'Tis Love"—and another is a tango—"You Leave My Girl Alone." The tradition of the waltz is coupled with the contemporary adoration of the tango.

Rosalie

When Florenz Ziegfeld asked Romberg and English lyricist and humorist P. G. Wodehouse (1881–1975) to create the score for *Rosalie* (January 10, 1928, New Amsterdam), the composer expressed interest in the project. Ziegfeld wanted *Rosalie* to be a vehicle for the actress and dancer Marilyn Miller (1898–1936), who, after making her debut in the 1918 version of Ziegfeld's *Follies*, had triumphed in *Sally* (1920) and *Sunny* (1925) and was at the height of her fame in the late 1920s.

William Anthony McGuire and Guy Bolton devised a plot for *Rosalie* about the love between a Ruritanian princess and an American pilot. (Early in the show's development, McGuire telegraphed a forty-two-page treatment to Ziegfeld, who liked both the story and the extraordinary manner in which it was received.)[19] If Romberg had written *Rosalie*, he could easily have combined Old World operetta with New World musical comedy: operetta for the European aspects and musical comedy for the American ones. But Romberg did not have time to write all of *Rosalie*, for he was revising *The New Moon* at the time. He told Ziegfeld that if the show included both operetta and musical comedy styles, he could provide the former and suggested that the producer hire George Gershwin (1898–1937) for the latter. Ziegfeld took Romberg's advice, and arranged for Gershwin and Romberg to co-write *Rosalie*. Like Romberg, Gershwin was unable to write a complete score for *Rosalie* because he also was involved with another project, *Funny Face*. Gershwin made one stipulation: he wanted to work with his brother Ira as lyricist, as was his custom. Ziegfeld agreed.

In the show's modern Ruritanian plot, Lieutenant Richard Fay (Oliver McLennan), a West Point cadet, is in love with Princess Rosalie of Romanza (Miller). Rosalie, according to Romanzan law, cannot marry a commoner unless her father (Frank Morgan) abdicates. Richard makes a solo flight to Romanza to be with Rosalie, but the queen of Romanza, contrary to the name of her country, does everything she can to halt her daughter's love affair with the American. Soon thereafter, the Romanzan royal family makes a state visit to America, where Richard and Rosalie are reunited and the queen continues to object to her daughter's involvement with a commoner. Eventually, everyone ends up at the Ex-King's Club in Paris. After Rosalie dances an elegant "Ballet of the Flowers," the king abdicates so that his daughter can marry the man she loves.

The story, like that of *The Desert Song*, alluded to current news events. Queen Marie of Romania visited the United States in 1926 on a mission to garner support for her country. Her activities during the U.S. tour made her fair game for musical comedy and parody. She carried herself in a grandiose manner, giving speeches with lines such as "Life could be very glorious if people loved each other a little more and hated each other a little less."[20] She traveled throughout the United States on her lavish private train, the *Royal Romanian*, and was the beneficiary of a ticker-tape parade in New York City. The press chronicled her exploits, and not always in the most glamorous fashion. She was a real-life operetta character, and Ziegfeld wanted to be sure to capitalize on Queen Marie's visit by modeling the Queen of Romanza on her.

It was not just Queen Marie but also Charles Lindbergh who is a recognizable presence in *Rosalie*. Lindbergh made his famous solo flight across the Atlantic in 1927, the year before *Rosalie* appeared. As the first person to accomplish this feat, Lindbergh became an American and international hero. The lieutenant in *Rosalie* recreated Lindbergh's courageous deed, but this time in the name of love.

Rosalie was an immense success, running for 335 performances. The production's popularity rested primarily on its star, Marilyn Miller. Her radiance and star quality kept drawing audiences to the theater. Many creators contributed to the show, recalling the days of the revue. There were two composers (Romberg and George Gershwin), two lyricists (Wodehouse and Ira Gershwin), and two librettists (McGuire and Bolton). Furthermore, since Ziegfeld wanted the show completed quickly, six orchestrators were engaged: Hans Spialek, Emil Gerstenberger, Max Steiner, Maurice B. DePackh, William Daly, and Hilding Anderson.[21] Joseph Urban, designer for Ziegfeld's *Follies* who was lauded for his work on *Show Boat* the previous year, was responsible for the opulent sets. The musical and visual dimensions of the show were resplendent, befitting a Ziegfeld production.

Romberg and Gershwin never collaborated directly on any of the show's musical numbers. As far as the lyricists were concerned, Wodehouse worked with Romberg and Ira with his brother, but the two coauthored several numbers.[22] The Gershwins' most significant contributions included "How Long Has This Been Going On?" (cut from *Funny Face*) and the show's principal duet, "Oh Gee! Oh Joy!"

Romberg's music featured marches, waltzes, a ballet, and a comic number. Because of the royal and military references in the plot, marches were of course an essential element of the score. Following the models of marches in *The Student Prince, The Desert Song,* and *My Maryland,* Romberg created celebratory numbers for the now-familiar male chorus, most importantly "West Point March" and "Hussar March." "Hussar March" also features a part for the princess, recalling "Come, Boys, Let's All Be Gay, Boys" from *The Student Prince,* but without the elaborate coloratura passages. Marilyn Miller, after all, was a musical comedy singer and dancer, not an opera star. The show's big waltz was "Kingdom of Dreams," sung by Rosalie as she dreams of love.[23] Since Gershwin's "Oh Gee! Oh Joy!" was the show's principal love duet, Romberg did not have to supply a lavish waltz number to function as the score's centerpiece. Two of Romberg's other significant contributions were at opposite ends of the spectrum of musical style: "The Ballet of the Flowers" and "The King Can Do No Wrong." The ballet, arranged by Mikhail Fokine (credited as Michel Fokine in the playbill), was the show's penultimate number and a showpiece for Miller's classical dance abilities.

"The King Can Do No Wrong," on the other hand, was a comic number for the king and a chorus of showgirls.

Although *Rosalie* was a commercial success, it did not represent the best efforts of either Gershwin or Romberg. Critics complained about the disunity of the score, something that would not have been such a significant factor in 1920, when *Poor Little Ritz Girl*, with a score by Romberg and Rodgers and Hart, appeared. As with *Poor Little Ritz Girl*, Romberg's contributions to *Rosalie* were largely in the operetta vein, while those of the other contributors exuded the spirit of musical comedy. When MGM filmed *Rosalie* in 1937, the Gershwin-Romberg score was discarded and replaced with an entirely new one by Cole Porter. (Dancer Eleanor Powell and baritone Nelson Eddy starred in the film.)

The New Moon

Romberg could not devote himself exclusively to *Rosalie* because he was busy revising what would become his final hit show of the decade and the last great romantic operetta of the age, *The New Moon* (September 19, 1928, Imperial). *The New Moon* opened in previews in Philadelphia on December 22, 1927, but closed after just a few weeks. It underwent extensive rewrites before opening on Broadway nine months later.[24] The show was a tremendous success and enjoyed a very long run (for the day) of 509 performances.

Broadway lore tells that *The New Moon* was almost completely rewritten after it closed in Philadelphia and that "Stouthearted Men" was one of the very few songs to be retained. While the book was extensively revised, this was not the case as far as the musical score was concerned. Although a substantial amount of music was cut, eight of the original musical numbers made it to Broadway, either in their entirety or in a recognizable form.[25] (See Table 7.1.) Some numbers were retained with only minor modifications, including changes in their titles ("An Interrupted Love Song," "Shoulder to Shoulder," "Try Them Out at Dancing," "The Marriage"). Others were trimmed considerably ("Sea Chanties," "Musical Scene"), and the opening and finale of act 1 were substantially reworked, though a significant amount of original material was retained.

The greatest change took place in the final scene. In the original, the romantic leads, Robert and Marianne, are alone in a dinghy singing what had been the show's principal love waltz duet, "'Neath a New Moon." (The song was eventually cut, although it already been published by Harms.) In

Table 7.1 Musical numbers in *The New Moon* retained from the original Philadelphia production

Philadelphia title	New York title*
Act 1 Opening	Act 1 Opening
"An Interrupted Love Song"	"Interrupted Trio"
"Shoulder to Shoulder"	"Stouthearted Men" (also called "Liberty Song")
Act I Finale (sections)	Act 1 Finale (sections)
"Sea Chanties"	Act 2 Opening
"Musical Scene"	"Sea Battle"
"Try Them Out at Dancing"	"Try Her Out at Dances"
"The Marriage"	"Marriage Number"

*Titles as they appear in the vocal score; some numbers are not listed on the opening night playbill.

the revised version, there is a large-scale choral finale. The emphasis was shifted from the romantic intimacy of the two principals to a communal celebration of democracy and freedom.

The same team that created *The Desert Song*, with the exception of Otto Harbach, wrote *The New Moon*. Oscar Hammerstein 2nd was lyricist, Hammerstein, Frank Mandel, and Laurence Schwab crafted the book, and Schwab and Mandel reprised their roles as producers. The operetta starred Evelyn Herbert (the original Barbara Frietchie in *My Maryland*) as Marianne and Robert Halliday (the first Red Shadow/Pierre in *The Desert Song*) as Robert. During the show's run, Herbert and Halliday married. Romberg said several times that he liked to think they fell in love because they sang his love songs to each other night after night.

As with *Rosalie*, a team of orchestrators worked on *The New Moon*. Emil Gerstenberger, who scored most of Romberg's shows from the 1920s, orchestrated the majority of the numbers. Alfred Goodman, who conducted the premiere, also contributed several orchestrations, as did Max Spialek, who was not credited in the playbill. Spialek's efforts were discovered among the Romberg materials at the Library of Congress when New York's City Center Encores! was preparing their 2003 semistaged production.[26]

The story begins in Louisiana in the 1790s, where Robert Misson (whose surname is frequently corrupted to Mission), an escaped French aristocrat accused of murder, falls in love with the headstrong Marianne Beaunoir, daughter of the plantation owner for whom he is working as a bondservant. The opening scene, a celebration of eighteenth-century French culture and colonialism, takes place at the Beaunoir mansion ("Dainty Wisp of Thistledown"). Historically, Louisiana was under *Spanish* rule at the time. The French gave up Louisiana to the Spanish in the 1760s, and although it was retroceded to them in 1800, they never reoccupied it. French culture maintained a strong presence in late eighteenth-century Louisiana, as is evident in *The New Moon*'s opening scene. Vicomte Ribaud, "the secret eye of the King of France," arrives from Paris to arrest Robert. Robert, meanwhile, has been serenading Marianne from behind a lilac bush ("Marianne"). Sailors from the ship *The New Moon*—the obligatory male chorus—offer to take Marianne to sea so that she does not fall prey to the mysterious singer ("The Girl on the Prow"). Georges Duval, captain of *The New Moon*, is also in love with Marianne and tries in vain to sing a love song to her ("Interrupted Trio"). Every time he begins the feeble waltz refrain, Robert intrudes with increasingly humorous excuses, finally causing Duval to give up on his serenade.

Later, at the Chez Creole, a Spanish dancer entices her customers, among whom are Robert and his dispossessed colleagues. Philippe (William O'Neal), one of Robert's friends, determined not to be seduced by the dancer's advances, tells of his ill-fated amorous experiences in the tango "Softly, As in a Morning Sunrise." Ribaud enters, hoping to find Robert, but Robert, aware of Ribaud's plan, ends up fighting him and steals his aristocratic clothing. Philippe encourages Robert in his utopian dream of establishing a democracy on the Isle of Pines, and the two of them lead the male chorus in the rousing march anthem "Stouthearted Men."

That same evening, Marianne is hosting a ball at which she will raffle a prize of "one kiss" in the song of the same name. Alexander (Gus Shy), Robert's second, rigs the contest so that Robert, who appears dressed in Ribaud's clothing, will win. Meanwhile, Clotilde Lombaste (Esther Howard) and a group of wannabe brides arrive. Clotilde, it is learned, is married to both Alexander and Besac, boatswain of *The New Moon*. This does not sit well with anyone, especially Julie (Marie Callahan), Marianne's maid, who is engaged to Alexander. Robert wins the raffle and implores Marianne for a moment alone with her. She agrees, and they sing the impassioned duet "Wanting You." Their budding romance is shattered when Ribaud enters and exposes Robert's identity. Marianne is furious, and Ribaud orders *The New Moon* to be prepared for immediate departure to France—with Robert traveling in the brig. In a sudden shift of plot, Marianne severs her feelings toward Robert (at least outwardly) and shifts them to Duval.

Act 2 opens on board *The New Moon*. The ship will stop at Martinique to drop off Clotilde and her brides before heading for France. Marianne, who came on board feigning adoration for Duval, sings of her love for Robert in "Lover, Come Back to Me." Although she loves Robert deeply, she still refuses to admit it publicly. When pirates fire on *The New Moon*, Robert escapes from the brig and takes control. The attacking ship, it turns out, is under the command of Philippe, who has arrived to free Robert. With Ribaud now in the brig and Robert serving as captain, *The New Moon* arrives at the Isle of Pines, where Robert establishes a democracy. In true operetta fashion, there are just enough brides for each member of the male crew, and a mass wedding takes place. Robert marries Marianne, but she allows only a legal union. The headstrong bride demands that they live apart. Though she loves Robert, she also follows her family motto, "Always win." One year later, the island and its inhabitants are prospering ("Marriage Number"/"Try Her Out at Dances"); however, Robert and Marianne still have separate houses. When French ships are seen entering the harbor, Ribaud thinks they have arrived to capture Robert and return him to France. Instead, they bring news that the monarchy has fallen, the *tricolore* has replaced the *fleur-de-lys*, and France is now a republic. Marianne now openly declares her love for Robert as "citizen Marianne," and the operetta ends on a celebratory note with a grand reprise, begun by Marianne, of "Stouthearted Men."

The "romantic musical comedy (musical romance)," as the show was called in the playbill, has a varied pedigree. In *The New Moon* Romberg was able to integrate aspects of *The Desert Song*, Beaumarchais's Figaro plays and their operatic adaptations, the European tradition of maritime operettas, Gilbert and Sullivan, and landmark American operettas from the 1910s.

Since the creative team of *The New Moon* was identical to that of *The Desert Song* (except for Otto Harbach), it is not surprising that the two shows share a number of dramatic features, even though they are set in different times and places. Robert is a democracy-loving hero who, like Pierre in *The Desert Song*, helps people overcome oppression and finds true love along the way. Both Robert and Pierre woo their respective leading ladies while impersonating someone else — Robert as a bondservant and Pierre as the Red Shadow. Furthermore, Margot in *The Desert Song* and Marianne in *The New Moon* are both headstrong women with strong senses of entitlement. Neither confesses her love for their dashing hero until the final scene. Margot should be forgiven for this, however, since she does not realize until the end of the operetta that Pierre is the Red Shadow. But Marianne is extremely self-centered, sings of her love for Robert in "Lover, Come Back to Me"—after knowing his true identity—but still will not live with Robert as his wife until the final scene.

Regarding the secondary, comic leads, Alexander and Julie in *The New Moon* are descendents of Bennie and Susan in *The Desert Song*. They provide foils for the romantic leads. "Gorgeous Alexander" and "Try Her Out at Dancing" in *The New Moon*, with their comparatively narrow vocal ranges, have an antecedent in "It" from *The Desert Song*. "It," however, has a much more sophisticated lyric and is halting in nature, as opposed to the light-hearted, forward-moving comic numbers in *The New Moon*.

Other characters also provide humor in *The New Moon*, particularly Clotilde. The seasoned marriage entrepreneur has a policy of tattooing her name across the chest of her multiple husbands. When Alexander opens his shirt and exposes her name during act 1, Clotilde reminds him that he is her property. Alexander's fiancée, Julie, cannot believe what is happening and physically attacks Clotilde. The rivalry between Julie and Clotilde recalls that of Susanna and Marcellina in *Le nozze di Figaro* (*The Marriage of Figaro*), whether it is Beaumarchais's play or Mozart's opera, where the two women fight over the title character. Besac is also one of Clotilde's husbands, and when he and Alexander discover that they have a common wife they embrace, calling each other "brother-in-law."

Ribaud also provides a great deal of comic relief as the lecherous old man who has his eyes on a much younger woman, the show's heroine. In another Figaro comparison, Ribaud is the counterpart of Don Bartolo in *Il barbiere di Seviglia* (*The Barber of Seville*). Just as Figaro tries to keep Bartolo from marrying Rosina, Robert does everything he can to thwart Ribaud's advances toward Marianne.

In addition to the commonalities with *The Desert Song* and the Figaro allusions, *The New Moon* is part of a legacy of operettas with maritime references. Numerous operettas with nautical themes appeared in nineteenth-century Vienna, including Franz von Suppé's *Flotte Bursche* (*Navy Lads*, 1863) and Ivan Zajc's *Mannschaft am Bord* (*Men on Board*, 1863).[27] More famous, though, are Gilbert and Sullivan's seafaring works from the 1870s: *H.M.S. Pinafore* (1878) and *The Pirates of Penzance* (1879). Romberg was familiar with these works and the tradition they represented, for scores of all four operettas were in his legendary music library.

In another Gilbert and Sullivan connection, Clotilde is a direct descendent of Katisha in *The Mikado* (1885). Both women, usually played by actresses with a great deal of comic stage presence and commanding low voices, enter during the first act finale and interrupt wedding plans. Just as Katisha claims Nanki-Poo but ends up with Ko-Ko at the end of *The Mikado*, Clotilde gives up Alexander and is with Besac at the conclusion of *The New Moon*.

The New Moon also has precedents in American operetta from the 1910s in its New Orleans and Caribbean settings. *Naughty Marietta* (1910, music by Victor Herbert, book and lyrics by Rida Johnson Young) was set in eighteenth-century New Orleans, while *The Firefly* (1912, music by Rudolf Friml, book and lyrics by Otto Harbach) included shipboard scenes and ended in Bermuda, which, like the Isle of Pines, is in the Atlantic. Thus, in this new work, the creators alluded to operettas by two of the most famous American operetta composers of the previous decade. Additionally, *Naughty Marietta* and *The Firefly* were both written for soprano Emma Trentini, and Marianne's virtuosic music in *The New Moon* is in many ways reflective of Herbert's and Friml's music for the famous singer. Arthur Hammerstein, Oscar 2nd's uncle, produced *The Firefly*, creating a Hammerstein family link between *The Firefly* and *The New Moon*.

As in *The Desert Song* and *Rosalie*, a historical figure inspired aspects of the leading male character in *The New Moon*. In the opening night playbill, the following note appeared: "The authors wish to state that the basic story of the play is founded on the life of Robert Misson, a French aristocrat whose autobiography was written in the late eighteenth century."

This statement, like the operetta's plot, is fictitious. There is no autobiography of Misson, and the only mention of him is in Captain Charles Johnson's *A General History of the Robberies and Murders of the Most Notorious Pyrates* (London, 1728). According to Johnson, Misson was an enlightened pirate of French birth who founded Libertalia, a free pirate colony on Madagascar. Since Johnson's book is the only mention of Misson and Libertalia, the authenticity of the tale is certainly spurious.[28] But the idea of Misson founding a democracy on an island made its way into *The New Moon*.

The real Isle of Pines, the imaginary site of Robert's democracy, lies just off the coast of Cuba. The island has been known as Isla de la Juventud (Isle of Youth) since 1978. But in the eighteenth and nineteenth centuries, it was the legendary *Isla de Pinos*, a famous pirate lair.[29] It inspired the pirate scenes in Robert Louis Stevenson's *Treasure Island* (1882) and J. M. Barrie's *Peter Pan* (1904) before appearing in *The New Moon*.

Pirate imagery appears at its strongest in the iconography used in advertising the show and on the covers of its published sheet music. Here, a woman dressed in pirate attire is sitting on a rock with a male pirate and a pirate ship in the background, even though this image never appears in the actual stage production.

Historical authenticity notwithstanding, the tale of a democracy-seeking individual was just what Broadway ticket holders of the late 1920s wanted. Many of them were worried about the rise of fascism, and a story about a freedom fighter who overcomes tyranny and oppression was certainly welcomed. Three shows that appeared shortly before *The New Moon* had similar themes: Friml's *The Vagabond King* (1925), Romberg's *The Desert Song* (1926), and Friml's *The Three Musketeers* (1928). In Friml's shows, the heroes were French, just like Robert. The creators of *The New Moon* were continuing a successful commodity on Broadway—a show that celebrated freedom and democracy.

Regarding the exact time frame for the action of *The New Moon*, the opening night playbill states that the action occurs in 1788 and 1789. This poses two major continuity problems. First, the opening line of the verse of the song "One Kiss," which reads, "In this year of seventeen ninety-two," makes no sense. Second, France was not declared a republic until 1792, and news might not have reached Caribbean islands until the following year. These temporal anomalies were rectified by moving the play a few years later and printing the line "The whole action of the play takes place in the years 1792–1793" in the published score and libretto as well as in later playbills.

The Songs of *The New Moon*

The New Moon contains some of Romberg's most famous songs, including "Stouthearted Men," "Lover, Come Back to Me," and "Softly, As in a Morning Sunrise." (See Table 7.2.) Although *The New Moon* has several extended musical-dramatic sequences along the lines of those in *The Student Prince* and *The Desert Song*, it is the individual songs that stand out in this show. This is due mostly to the revisions made to the show during its tryout and to the influence of *Rosalie*, especially Gershwin's contributions. Romberg's focus in *The New Moon* shifted from large integrated musical scenes to songs in verse-refrain form separated by spoken dialogue. Romberg maintained a legitimate style of singing (as opposed to the character-driven style typical of musical comedy) for most of the cast of *The New Moon*, the exceptions being the purely comic characters.

Sheet music cover for *The New Moon*. © 1928 (Renewed) WARNER BROS. INC. Rights for the Extended Renewal Term in the United States Controlled by WARNER BROS. INC. and BAMBALINA MUSIC. All Rights Reserved. Used by Permission.

The show's appealing music and its fine performances drew the attention of critics and audiences alike. The reviewer for the *Brooklyn Daily Eagle* expressed an opinion shared by many: "For a change we have here musical entertainment without jazz or jagged rhythms, free of cheap comedy, played and sung by pleasant people, sprightly without being noisy, swift and trim and spontaneous. Sigmund Romberg has written lilting tunes for it, with here and there a melody of the rousing variety."[30]

Waltzes and marches dominate *The New Moon*, but a tango and songs in the style of musical comedy or revue are also present. This multiplicity of styles does not detract from the unity of the score; rather, Romberg and Hammerstein utilize the various song types at their disposal to define characters and regulate the show's dramatic action.

Marianne's two principal numbers in act 1, "The Girl on the Prow" and "One Kiss," are both waltzes. In both instances, the lyrics tell of Marianne's wish for attention, but each song has a different focus: she wants to be adored by *all* men in "The Girl on the Prow" and by *one* man in "One Kiss." Both numbers include the chorus, a mixed one in "The Girl on the Prow" and the ladies only in "One Kiss." Everyone endorses Marianne's desire to be the center of attention in "The Girl on the Prow," while she confesses her secret longing only to her female companions in "One Kiss." In both songs, Marianne's fantasy of love and adoration dominates her thoughts, and this is depicted musically through the waltz. (Romberg did a similar thing in *My Princess* and *Rosalie*.)

Robert, on the other hand, sings in duple meter throughout act 1. "Marianne," with its dotted rhythms, is an ode to the woman of his dreams, while "Stouthearted Men" is one of Romberg's most stirring marches. The refrain of "Stouthearted Men" concludes with a coda in 2/4 (as opposed to the 4/4 of the remainder of the march) that implies an intensification of musical pacing. The tempo does not actually increase, but there is a sense that it does. (Romberg employed a similar technique in "Your Land and My Land" in *My Maryland* when he quoted "Battle Hymn of the Republic" at the end of the refrain.)

In many operettas, but especially in *The New Moon*, women waltz and men march. Gender is related to meter.[31] This is certainly the case for Marianne and Robert, and the axiom is also practiced in the opening number. The women enter to the strains of a waltz, "Dainty Wisp of Thistledown," in which they tell of wanting to be kissed. The men follow with a march,

Table 7.2 Musical program for *The New Moon* (according to the opening night playbill)

Act I
Scene 1: Grand Salon of Monsieur Beaunoir's Mansion near New Orleans (1788)
Opening—"Dainty Wisp of Thistledown" (Ensemble)
"Marianne" (Robert)
"The Girl on the Prow" (Marianne, Ensemble)
"Gorgeous Alexander" (Alexander, Girls)
"An Interrupted Love Song" (Duval, Marianne, Robert)

Scene 2: Entrance to Chez Creole

Scene 3: Interior of Chez Creole ·
"Tavern Song (Red Wine)" (Flower Girl, Dancer, Ensemble)
"Softly, as in a Morning Sunrise" (Philippe, Ensemble)
"Stouthearted Men (Liberty Song)" (Robert, Philippe, Men)

Scene 4: Entrance to Chez Creole

Scene 5: Grand Salon of Monsieur Beaunoir's Mansion. Evening
"Fair Rosita" (Girls, danced by Rosita and Ramon)
"One Kiss" (Marianne, Ensemble)
"The Trial (Ladies of the Jury)" (Alexander, Julie, Lombaste, Girls)
"Wanting You" (Marianne, Robert)
Finale (Ensemble)

Act II
Scene 1: The Deck of "The New Moon." Late Afternoon, Three Days Later
Opening—"A Chanty" (Besac, Men)
"Funny Little Sailor Man" (Lombaste, Besac, Ensemble)
"Lover, Come Back to Me" (Marianne)
Finaletto (Marianne, Robert, Philippe, Men)

Scene 2: The Road from the Beach. Two Days Later
"Love Is Quite a Simple Thing" (Lombaste, Besac, Alexander, Julie)

Scene 3: The Stockade. One Year Later
"Try Her Out at Dancing" (Alexander, Julie, Girls)

Scene 4: The Road from the Beach. That Evening
"Softly, as in a Morning Sunrise" (Philippe, Men)

Table 7.2 Continued

Scene 5: Marianne's Cabin. That Night
"Never for You" (Marianne)
"Lover, Come Back to Me" (Robert, Men)

Scene 6: The Road from the Beach. Midnight

Scene 7: The Stockade. Daylight, Next Morning
"Finale" (Company)

---

marked "Grandioso" in the score, in which they introduce the "Great Monsieur Ribaud," servant of the king.

There are of course exceptions to this axiom in *The New Moon*, but they can all be related back to the basic idea. In fact, the exceptions demonstrate subtleties in musical characterization on the part of Romberg and Hammerstein. Ribaud's "Interrupted Trio," for example, is a waltz. Here, the difference in meter accentuates the disparity between Robert and Ribaud. Ribaud cannot win Marianne's love because he cannot sing in duple meter. He is in fact effeminized through his triple-meter music, and so is obviously not the right man for strong-willed Marianne.

"Lover, Come Back to Me," the act 2 love song sung first by Marianne and later reprised by Robert and Marianne, is a quadruple-meter ballad. It is Marianne's music but is in 4/4 rather than 3/4. Here, Romberg employs meter as a means of representing fantasy and reality; waltzes are associated with fantasy, as they were in *My Princess*, leaving duple meter to signify reality. In her earlier 3/4 numbers, Marianne was wishing for something she did not have; now she sings about something that she had but lost. It is not a fantasy number on her part, and therefore is not a waltz. She has met her true love, and in order to sing about the reality of the situation, has to do so in a nonfantasy way. In her instance, she must do so in something other than a waltz.

The twelve-bar verse, in AAB form, provides a dramatic introduction to the song. Marianne regrets her treatment of Robert and longs for his return. This is portrayed musically through the eighth rests at the beginning of every two-measure group in the A sections. Hesitation, perhaps caused by sobbing, is apparent. When she recalls happier times (in the B section), however, she sings on downbeats, indicating a sense of security.

The refrain is in a thirty-two-bar AABA form, a standard Broadway song construction. The A section is characterized by eighth rests on the downbeats of the first five bars, thus providing motivic unity between the verse and the refrain, which in turn reiterates her insecurity. When she reaches the title words of the song (mm. 7–8), however, she sings on downbeats, reflecting her inner resolve and strength, just as she did in the verse. (See example 7.1.)

The quadruple meter also indicates Marianne's underlying assertiveness, often considered a masculine trait. She is as sure of what she wants in this song as the male chorus is in "Stouthearted Men."

In her other act 2 solo, "Never for You," Marianne blames Robert for destroying their love. Since she is confessing her true feelings, she again sings in quadruple meter. There is no fantasy on her part, and hence no waltz.

Romberg thus employs the waltz in two different ways in *The New Moon*: first to represent femininity and second to suggest fantasy. By using the same musical means to indicate two different constructs, he in essence conflates femininity and fantasy. A gendered reading of the operetta, with fantasy-driven females and, by corollary, reality-aware males, is strongly substantiated through musical evidence such as this.

In "Wanting You," the central love duet introduced in the course of the act 1 finale, Robert's machismo meets Marianne's womanliness. They meet in meter as well as in spirit. Robert begins the verse with a waltz. He has entered Marianne's musical realm. The refrain is in 12/8 meter: compound—triple divisions of each primary beat, as in a waltz—and quadruple—four beats per measure, as in a march. (See example 7.2.) Fantasy and reality coalesce. From a performance standpoint, the 12/8 meter should not allow the singers to enjoy too much rubato during the soaring music. In the B section of the AABA form, though, the music shifts to 3/4, allowing for more emotive flexibility on the part of the performers.

Romberg artfully combines the notion of Marianne singing in triple meter and Robert in duple in this central love duet. The singers find common ground, neither forfeiting their musical domain to the other. This parallels the family mottos of Marianne and Robert, which they articulate several times during the show: the Beaunoirs' "Always win," and the Missons' "Never surrender."

In Romberg's operettas up to this point, the primary love duet has been a waltz. In *The Desert Song*, an additional duple-meter love duet, "One

Example 7.1. "Lover, Come Back to Me" *(The New Moon)*, refrain, mm. 1–8

Example 7.2. "Wanting You" *(The New Moon)*, refrain, mm. 1–4

Alone," also occupies a place of high prominence, since it is the last music heard in the show. In "Wanting You," Romberg forges new ground in his love duets by integrating a waltz with a duple-meter ballad. This is the pivot that provides a direct link to his later duple-meter love duets, the most famous of which is "Close as Pages in a Book" from *Up in Central Park* (1945).

One of the most dramatic numbers in *The New Moon* is neither a waltz nor a march but rather a tango, or at least a song in the spirit of a tango: Philippe's "Softly, As in a Morning Sunrise." Philippe sings the impassioned number at the Chez Creole, a locale that contrasts sharply with the lavishness of the Beaunoir mansion. Chez Creole is decidedly nonaristocratic—

the patrons are victims of the French colonialist attitudes that were celebrated in the opening scene.

Tangos were extremely popular in the 1920s, due in great part to the iconic status of Carlos Gardel (1887–1935), described as "the tango made flesh." The French-born Argentine tenor was a remarkable popular culture figure whose tragic death in a plane crash at the height of his career immortalized his fame. Barbara Garvey, a *tanguera*, said of Gardel: "One of the reasons Carlos Gardel is so important is that he epitomized so many things about the tango. First of all, he was a bastard—he was just a little outside of respectability. Secondly, he was the image of the Argentine male: Dark, handsome, perfectly dressed, hair slicked back. Finally, he was a bachelor. He apparently had a mistress but was devoted to *'la barra y la vieja'*—to his circle of male friends and to his mother, Doña Berta."[32]

Gardel's importance and influence in the tango cannot be overstated. Gardel specialized in the *tango canción,* a sung tango whose lyrics concern the tragic aspects of love. This particular style of tango singing was extremely popular in New York in the late 1920s when *The New Moon* appeared.

"Softly, As in a Morning Sunrise" is marked "Tempo di Tango (very slow)" in the score. The characteristic tango rhythmic motif (♫♪) is present throughout the refrain, but the melodic line is much grander in scope and range than that of a true *tango canción,* where there is often a great deal of text declaimed on the same pitch. However, it was the spirit and general style of the tango, and not a detailed ethnographic copy of it, that Romberg and Hammerstein captured so effectively in "Softly."

The creators made three direct allusions to Gardel and the *tango canción* in "Softly" and used these for powerful dramatic effect. First, Gardel was a tenor, and it is this voice type that sings "Softly." Philippe's big song is heard from a voice that is different from Robert's baritone. Second, Hammerstein's lyric concerns the hardships and pitfalls of love, following that of a *tango canción*. The song provides dramatic contrast to the overt expressions of love and desire in numbers such as "Wanting You" and "Lover, Come Back to Me." Third, Philippe sings it to his male companions, following Gardel's example. By scoring the tango for a tenor and having a lyric about the perils of love sung to the male chorus, "Softly, As in a Morning Sunrise" becomes a riveting musical and dramatic foil for Robert, his music, and his romantic exploits.

Moving from the poignant to the comic, two songs, "Gorgeous Alexander" and "Try Her Out at Dances," are in the style of musical comedy num-

Example 7.3. "Gorgeous Alexander" (*The New Moon*), refrain, mm. 1–4

bers. Both feature solo sections for Julie and Alexander, and showcase the comic and dancing capabilities of the actors who play these roles. The vocal ranges are limited, and the orchestra doubles the melodic lines in order to provide musical security for the character actors, who sometimes must employ a sort of speech-singing technique to intone their songs. In "Gorgeous Alexander," Julie complains that she wants Alexander to be hers alone, while Alexander and the female chorus respond that he should be the property of all women. The song provides further dramatic and musical contrast to Robert and Marianne's waltzes and ballads as well as to Philippe's tango. The constant driving eighth notes provide a frenetic energy that distinguishes it from both the assertive moderate-tempo "Stouthearted Men" and the languid love songs. (See example 7.3.) At one point, the lyric mentions Alexander as having a "manly frame," a tongue-in-cheek remark, for in many productions, Alexander is played by an actor not especially known for traditional handsomeness but rather by one capable of comic antics. "Try Her Out at Dances" is marked "Tempo di Fox-trot" and, like "Gorgeous Alexander," concludes with an extended dance sequence. The self-reflexive lyric tells about the best way to choose a mate at a dance. Both songs rely more on strong downbeats than on syncopation for their rhythmic distinctiveness. Romberg eschewed the jazz-inspired approach to musical comedy in favor of the older one, with which he was more comfortable.

The music of *The New Moon* amplifies the show's drama. Characters are defined through their music, as are their shifting psychological states. The romantic leads sing in a nearly operatic style, while the comic foils are distinguished by their vocal styles, which need to be closer to speech-singing than vocal bravura. Additionally, Philippe's spurned attitude toward love is reflected through a *tango canción*, a song that also functions as a musical and dramatic alternative to the principals' overt expressions of love. Waltzes in *The New Moon* express either femininity or fantasy, while the choral numbers, whether comic, sentimental, or heroic, reflect the importance of community in this democracy-celebrating operetta.

Romberg's works from *The Desert Song* through *The New Moon* demonstrate a fundamental paradigm shift from his earlier works for the Shuberts. Happy endings become the norm, and none of the works have European settings (except for part of *Rosalie*), although they sometimes include displaced Europeans as characters. Waltzes and marches, the archetypical operetta forms, appear alongside other song types that either establish a sense of place or provide musical-dramatic foils for the vaultingly romantic or heroic music. Romberg expanded the definition of operetta in these works, taking it from an essentially European-focused genre to one in which there were far more possibilities. His efforts to explore further avenues for development were abruptly cut short in 1929 by the stock market crash and the subsequent Great Depression. It was no longer feasible for producers to mount large, lavish productions, hire massive choruses, and maintain the tradition of American operetta that had become a mainstay of Broadway during the 1920s. Seemingly undaunted by the economic realities, Romberg nonetheless continued to write beautiful and breathtaking Broadway scores, works that followed the trajectory of *The Desert Song* and *The New Moon*.

CHAPTER 8

Emulating the Past: Later Stage Works

Operetta was already being thought of as passé in 1928, when *The New Moon* appeared. As a critic for the *Brooklyn Daily Eagle* wrote: "Nevertheless, here despite its lapses is a romantic musical comedy in which music and comedy and manners are all things of grace and charm. That sort of thing was long ago supposed to have gone out."[1] Audience tastes were definitely changing. A show like *The Student Prince*, the longest-running musical of the decade, certainly would not have had its record-breaking run if it had appeared in 1928. Audiences no longer craved nostalgic sentiment like they did earlier in the decade.

One of the motivators for this change in taste was European travel. Americans began traveling to Europe at an unprecedented rate during the 1920s; some even lived abroad for extended periods. There, they drank what and when they wanted (Prohibition was in effect in the United States only), and found that they could live comfortably on relatively little money. European culture and its modernist trends had a notable impact on these sophisticates' world views, especially after they returned to America.[2] Operettas did not endorse their stylish, chic attitudes: they were reminiscent of the "old Europe." Audiences at the end of the decade favored things that were new and flashy. They enjoyed the cosmopolitan humor inherent in musical comedies by creators such as Cole Porter in *Fifty Million Frenchman* (1929) and *The New Yorkers* (1930), and George Gershwin in *Girl Crazy* (1930) and *Of Thee I Sing* (1931). Sentimentality no longer had the same luster and appeal.

Broadway musicals in general, not just operettas, were also facing another challenge: the emerging sound film. Live theater now had to compete with the "talkies," and the latter often won the battle. Movies became the nation's first choice for inexpensive entertainment and escapism, and, as a result, live theater lost a great deal of its former audience. In a curious case of self-reflexivity, the most popular musical films were based on Broadway tales. Movies such as *The Jazz Singer* (1927) were set on Broadway and had plots about an unknown performer overcoming obstacles to achieve stardom. Similarly, *42nd Street* (1933) extolled the merits of the Broadway musical by depicting it in a way that could hardly be accomplished in a live theater. Not surprisingly, because of the popularity of films and the huge expense involved with mounting live productions, many Broadway theaters were converted into movie houses. They had plenty of seats facing a focal point, and it was much cheaper to project a film night after night than to produce a play or musical.

Despite these challenges, operettas continued to appear on Broadway, although they appeared with less frequency and had shorter runs than did their predecessors. Three famous examples by creators other than Romberg are Noël Coward's *Bitter Sweet* (July 12, 1929, Her Majesty's, London; November 5, 1929, Ziegfeld, New York), Jerome Kern and Otto Harbach's *The Cat and the Fiddle* (October 15, 1931, Globe), and Kern and Oscar Hammerstein 2nd's *Music in the Air* (November 8, 1932, Alvin). In all three shows, traditional operetta styles appear in contemporary settings. In the Kern scores, part of the plot involves producing an operetta, so the musical style itself becomes an element in the drama.

Romberg wrote ten operettas after *The New Moon*, nine for Broadway and one for Paris. These works collectively demonstrate that Romberg was experimenting with the genre in an attempt to adapt it for new audience expectations in the 1930s and 1940s. The works fall into three broad categories, according to where they are set as well as when they were written: 1) Exotic locales—*Nina Rosa* (1930) and *East Wind* (1931); 2) European lands—*Melody* (1933), *Rose de France* (1933), *May Wine* (1935), and *Forbidden Melody* (1936); and 3) American settings—*Sunny River* (1941), *Up in Central Park* (1945), *My Romance* (1948), and *The Girl in Pink Tights* (1954, posthumous).

Nina Rosa and *East Wind* follow the model of *The Desert Song* in incorporating aspects of musical exoticism as a means of establishing an aural sense of place. For the middle group of works, from *Melody* to *Forbidden Melody*, the plots return to Europe, the traditional domain of operetta librettos. In these works, one of which was written for a Parisian theater *(Rose de France)*, Romberg reclaimed the heritage of his youth, but with some modern dimensions. His final set of works are all set in the United States during the nineteenth century, and likewise reflect a nostalgic yearning for the past.

The Last of the Exotic Locales: *Nina Rosa* and *East Wind*

Romberg knew from experience what it took to create a successful operetta in the late 1920s. He had already proven this with *The Desert Song* and *The New Moon*. In both shows, he achieved a new formula, something slightly different from what he had done with the Shuberts. Now, there was a rousing march for the large male chorus, a romantic waltz duet that is complemented by a duple-meter love duet, and specialty numbers, usually of an ethnic variety (such as "Azuri's Dance" in *The Desert Song* or "Softly, As in a Morning Sunrise" in *The New Moon*). In these newer operettas, significantly, the romantic leads are united at the final curtain—something that did not happen in *Maytime*, *Blossom Time*, or *The Student Prince*.

Romberg adhered to this precept for his first two shows from the 1930s, *Nina Rosa* and *East Wind*. In both operettas, lovers succeed in overcoming life-threatening obstacles in order to be together. Importantly, these two operettas were the last by Romberg to be set somewhere other than Europe and the United States. They were his last forays into musical exoticism.

Romberg looked to his own previous successes in creating these works: *The New Moon* for *Nina Rosa* and *The Desert Song* for *East Wind*. The two operettas are a continuation of his late 1920s style, though the plots are fraught with increased danger and villainy.

Nina Rosa (September 20, 1930, Majestic) was a splendid Shubert production in all its glory. Ethelind Terry, who played the title character, was the star of Ziegfeld's immensely successful *Rio Rita* (February 2, 1927, Ziegfeld), which ran for nearly five hundred performances. *Rio Rita* was a clear model for *Nina Rosa* (along with *The New Moon*), and the Shuberts spared no effort in outdoing their rival. They not only hired the star of *Rio Rita* but also secured its choreographer, Busby Berkeley. Romberg's music was complemented by Irving Caesar's lyrics and Otto Harbach's libretto. (Harbach had been part of the creative team for *The Desert Song*, and was the only contributor to that show who was not involved with *The New Moon*.) This was not the Shuberts' first attempt to capitalize on the popularity of *Rio Rita*, for *The Love Call*, Romberg's operetta that opened on October 24, 1927, also alluded to the Ziegfeld show in its southwestern flavor. (See chapter 7 for a discussion of *The Love Call*.)

The plot of *Nina Rosa*, which is remarkably similar to that of *Rio Rita* (except for its setting), takes place near Cuzco, Peru. (Cuzco is an impressive city with Spanish colonial architecture that was once an important center of Incan culture.) Don Fernando (Clay Clements), a rich Argentinean, is trying to cheat Nina Rosa Stradella (Ethelind Terry) out of her gold mine. The American mining engineer Jack Haines (Guy Robertson), who is in love with Nina Rosa, supports her claim to the mine. Don Fernando sends the assassin Pablo (Leonard Ceeley) to murder the interfering Jack. Jack leaves for his own safety, but Nina Rosa suspects that he has deserted her. Pablo attempts to seduce the heroine, but when Nina Rosa learns that Jack is hiding in Cuzco, she goes to find him. The reunited lovers go to Nina Rosa's mine, where they enter a golden chamber and witness a magnificent pre-Columbian sacred ritual. Pablo and his gauchos follow them into the chamber, abduct Nina Rosa, and wall Jack into the room. Jack and Nina Rosa both escape their fates, her claim to the mine is validated, and Jack ends up marrying Nina Rosa, who is now the wealthiest woman in Peru.

The Shuberts capitalized on the plot's exotic locale to create lavish spectacle. The sets included the resplendent "Café de los Gauchos," Don Fernando's sumptuous hacienda, and a richly decorated Incan ceremonial cave. Orry-Kelly (né Orry George Kelly) designed a vibrant drop curtain for the theater that included images of a woman offering a sacrifice to a god, a conch-shell player, and a mythological canine creature, all against a background of earth-toned geometric shapes.[3] The curtain was in the style of the great Mexican muralist Diego Rivera (1886–1957). Rivera was well known in the United States during the early 1930s, having completed important commissions for works in San Francisco, Detroit, and New York City. Like Rivera's murals, Orry-Kelly's curtain evoked a pre-Columbian visual aesthetic, but without the strong social commentary inherent in Rivera's work.

Romberg used two different musical means to establish the show's South American setting: 1) clichés associated with musical exoticism, and 2) a pan–Latin American approach, especially concerning the tango. The formulaic techniques of musical exoticism are most prominent in the music for the Incan cave ceremony in act 2. Here, Romberg combined hypnotic rhythmic ostinatos, the minor mode, augmented seconds, and chromatic inflections in the melodic line to give a sense of the musical Other. When placed in an Incan context through plot, costumes, and sets, these devices became indicative of not just exoticism but also primitivism. Though certainly not as original as Stravinsky's *Le Sacre du printemps* (*The Rite of Spring*, 1913), Romberg's primitivist evocation nonetheless captured the aural imagination just as the sets and costumes, along with the drop curtain, provided the visual dimension.

When it comes to South American musical styles and references, *Nina Rosa* is filled with incongruities. Argentine aspects, such as gauchos, payadors, and tangos, are applied to the geographically, topographically, and culturally different Peru. Gauchos, the famous cowboys, have their own march in *Nina Rosa*, even though they are foreign to Peru. Payadors, the guitar-playing troubadours who improvise verses to their songs, are also unrelated to Peru, as is the tango, which is the basis for two of the operetta's songs, "Payador" and "Serenade of Love."

The two tango evocations are used for drastically different dramatic purposes in the show. Nina Rosa leads the chorus in "Payador," which is marked "Tango argentino (slow)," as an expression of her love for her homeland, Peru. Just because the tango does not have immediate associations with Peru did not keep Romberg from employing it as a means to evoke the spirit of the country. The second tango evocation, which is much more sultry than the first, is a duet for Pablo and Nina Rosa during which Pablo tries to seduce Nina Rosa. The dance becomes an emblem of Pablo's sexual desire. The music returns in act 2 as the basis for a tango dance specialty.

Along with its place-specific numbers, the score has plenty of standard operetta fare: in this case a foxtrot, a march for the male chorus, a waltz duet and a duple-meter love song for the romantic leads, and musical comedy routines for the secondary leads. In *Nina Rosa*, these numbers are strikingly like their counterparts in *The New Moon*.[4] The exact melodies and harmonies may differ, but the tempos, meters, and general atmospheres of the songs are extremely similar. For example, the operetta's title song is a duple-meter foxtrot along the lines of *The New Moon*'s "Marianne." It even features the male chorus, which in this case consists of American engineers. "Gaucho March" is the machismo choral number, following the model of "Stouthearted Men." However, it is led not by Jack, the American hero, as one might expect, but rather by the villain, Pablo. Caesar's lyrics tell that the gaucho's motivation is not fighting for freedom but rather finding the love of a maid. A reprise of "Gaucho March" concludes *Nina Rosa* (this time led by Jack), just as a reprise of "Stouthearted Men" appears at the end of *The New Moon*.

"Your Smiles, Your Tears" is the requisite romantic waltz for the two leads, while their other duet in the operetta, "My First Love, My Last Love," is a lyrical duple-meter ballad in moderate tempo, akin to "Lover, Come Back to Me."[5] The music for Jimmy and Elinor, the comic characters, is in the style of that of Alexander and Julie in *The New Moon*. This is especially evident in "The Secret in Your Life," in which Jimmy asks the ladies of the chorus if he can be their clandestine lover, the secret in their lives. The song resembles "Gorgeous Alexander" in terms of both subject matter and musical style.

Additionally, the tango evocations, the ethnically distinctive feature of *Nina Rosa*, have a precedent in *The New Moon*'s "Softly, As in a Morning Sunrise." The dramatic functions of the numbers are different, however, for "Softly" is a song of unrequited love.

Nina Rosa played for only 137 performances. Even with this small number, the operetta was the Shuberts' most successful show of the era. (This is in contrast to the Gershwins' *Of Thee I Sing* [December 26, 1931, Music Box], which had an exceptionally long run of 441 performances.) *Nina Rosa* was Romberg's last operetta for the Shuberts for eighteen years, until *My Romance* in 1948. John Shubert, J. J.'s son, cited Romberg's departure as the impetus for the notable decline in the musical quality of Shubert-produced operettas during the 1930s.[6]

Although *Nina Rosa* was only moderately successful in New York, it nonetheless transferred to Europe. It opened on July 7, 1931, at London's Lyric Theatre, where it enjoyed a modest run. The production that opened at the Théâtre du Châtelet in Paris in 1932, however, was the most successful of any Romberg operetta in that city, and lasted for nearly two years. Its exotic sets, story, and music captivated audiences who relished the lavish spectacle of the *operette*. Its Peruvian setting continued a tradition in French opera, for *Les Incas de Pérou (The Incas of Peru)* from Rameau's *Les Indes galantes (The Gallant Indians*, 1735) and Offenbach's *La Périchole* (1868) were also set in the South American country.

The exotic splendor of *Nina Rosa* continued in *East Wind* (October 27, 1931, Manhattan). Set in Paris and Saigon, the operetta's most memorable moment occurred in the first-act finale, when the Saigon waterfront blossomed into a mass of tropical color as a flower boat arrived. The same team that created *The Desert Song* wrote *East Wind*: lyricist Oscar Hammerstein 2nd, librettist Frank Mandel, and composer Sigmund Romberg.

The plot concerns a Frenchwoman, Claudette Fortier (Charlotte Lansing), who is traveling to Saigon, capital of French-colonial Indochina. En route she meets Rene Beauvais (William Williams), a ladies' man and known philanderer. Although they really do not love each other, they are afraid they will never meet the ideal partner, and decide to marry. Upon arriving in Saigon, Claudette meets Paul (J. Harold Murray), Rene's brother, who is in the French army and stationed in Indochina. Claudette and Paul fall in love, but Rene remains adamant that he will still marry Claudette. After the wedding, Rene immediately returns to Paris with Claudette close in tow. Paul follows them, for he is worried about Claudette because of his brother's reputation. Paul's concerns are justified, for soon after arriving in Paris the newlywed husband leaves his wife for Tsoi Tsing (Ahi), an exotic dancer he met in Saigon before his marriage. Claudette has found a job singing in a music hall of questionable repute when Paul arrives and implores her to return to Saigon with him. Tsoi Tsing enters, murders Rene, threatens Claudette (who is saved by Paul), and commits suicide. After the overly melodramatic tragedy, Claudette and Paul are free to marry and the operetta ends with true love conquering villainy and deceit.

East Wind has a great deal in common with *The Desert Song*, which is not surprising since the exact same team created the two operettas. Orientalist traits are apparent in both shows, Arabian in *The Desert Song* and East Asian in *East Wind*. Furthermore, Romberg continues to employ extensive chromaticism and the minor mode to evoke the sound of the exotic Other. This is immediately evident in *East Wind*'s title song, a duple-meter ballad. (Romberg employed a similar technique in the "The Desert Song," where the verse, sung by the Red Shadow, is in minor.) In addition to the minor mode, the title songs of *The Desert Song* and *East Wind* share a dramatic theme, for both are enticements to enter the world of the exotic Orient. In both instances, the male lead, a Frenchman, implores a Frenchwoman to join him in his realm of sanctioned sensuality.

The romantic leads in both *East Wind* and *The Desert Song* are French citizens living abroad. French colonialism is certainly evident, especially with both works being set in the then present day. In *East Wind*, though, imperialism is not at the core of the operetta's plot, as it is in *The Desert Song*. In this show, the principal characters find true love outside of their native country. The Orient thus becomes first and foremost a region of love and sensuality, its most common portrayal in French literature, art, and music. (Consider, for example, in music, Saint-Saens's *Samson et Dalila* [1877] or Ravel's *Shéhérezade* [1903].) But it is also a primitive region fraught with danger.[7]

Tsoi Tsing, the principal Asian character, is the show's villain. She destroys Rene's marriage (though admittedly he was quick to leave his wife), murders her lover, tries to kill her lover's wife, and then commits suicide. She embodies the sexual dangers of the Orient and destroys the Western man who dares to love her. She is quite unlike her Oriental sisters Mimosa in *Cherry Blossoms* and Liat in Rodgers and Hammerstein's *South Pacific* (1949), both of whom are sympathetic characters. Tsoi Tsing is a vicious aggressor, and thus is the progeny of Azuri in *The Desert Song* and Wanda in Rudolf Friml's *Rose Marie*. These three women, Tsoi Tsing, Azuri, and Wanda, are all dancing operetta villains, though only Wanda and Tsoi Tsing commit murder. The dancing attributes of the role influenced its casting (as did that of Azur), for Ahi, a famous Hawaiian dancer of the 1930s, created the part. Her exotic dance in the show—the one that captures Rene's attention—was a hula, although the story takes place in Saigon. This curious conflation of Asian-Pacific cultures, while not dramaturgically sound, allowed the actress to showcase her dance specialty, which was cited as one of the show's most memorable moments.[8] It also followed the practice of cultural conflation observed in *Nina Rosa*.

Claudette, the female lead, is undoubtedly one of Romberg's most intriguing female characters. She possesses a wider variety of emotions and experiences than her predecessors Kathie, Margot, or Marianne. Her earnest optimism, which foreshadows that of Nellie Forbush in *South Pacific* and Anna in *The King and I* (other heroines transplanted to foreign cultures), is immediately evident in her opening number, "It's a Wonderful World" (not the song made famous by Louis Armstrong). Its infectious cheerfulness (this was an Oscar Hammerstein 2nd lyric, after all) prefigures "Cockeyed Optimist" in *South Pacific* and "Whistle a Happy Tune" in *The King and I*. Dotted rhythms permeate the buoyant refrain but are minimized in the bridge (B section of the AABA form), where the tempo slows down and true happiness is defined as "when the dreams you love fall in love with you."

Claudette's other solo feature is "I'd Be a Fool," a torch song and a rarity in Romberg's output. She sings this song as a cabaret feature, recalling Julie's rendition of "Bill," the torch song in *Show Boat* (1927). The refrain is extremely chromatic and oscillates freely between major and minor. It is as maudlin as "It's a Wonderful World" is joyful. Claudette's life has been difficult, and this transformation in her character is reflected in her music. The song is an autobiographical soliloquy, and another of the score's highlights.

In addition to her character-defining music, Claudette sings two passionate duets with Paul: "I Saw Your Eyes," a wistful waltz, and "When You Are Young," a lyrical duple-meter ballad. The couple sings the waltz as they meet and immediately fall in love. The ballad is the show's penultimate number, performed after the plot's denouement. Romberg again follows his new formula of including two principal love songs, a waltz and a ballad, in an operetta. The waltz represents the newfound lovers' hope that what is happening is real, while the ballad is a confirmation that true love has conquered all adversity. The fantasy associated with the waltz gives way to the reality symbolized by duple meter.

Another waltz, "Are You Love?," is especially important in the show's musical dramaturgy. The trio for Claudette, Rene, and Paul appears immediately after Claudette and Rene's wedding. Uncertainty and doubt are certainly present in the song's title and subsequent lyric. Here, Romberg employs the waltz idiom to represent the fantasy on the part of Claudette and Paul to be together, despite the reality of the current circumstances. The song's title is a telling turn of phrase from *Show Boat*'s "You Are Love," another waltz. Whereas "You Are Love" is a direct expression of love between the two principals, "Are You Love?" asks the all-important question. This is a fine example of Romberg and Hammerstein using song to create musical drama. What should be a glorious love song, according to traditional operetta dictates, instead becomes a trio steeped in uncertainty.

East Wind played for an undeservedly short twenty-three performances, a casualty of the Depression. It is unfortunate that it did not succeed, for like many of the operettas that were commercial victims of the time, *East Wind* contains some exceptionally fine music, especially the title song and Claudette's two solo numbers. The cast and crew believed strongly in the production, for after its closing was announced, the cast met to discuss ways of keeping the production alive, including either taking over the production or taking a pay cut.[9] Their efforts failed.

One humorous anecdote has survived concerning the show's music. Hans Spialek, the show's orchestrator, quoted Offenbach's "Can-Can" in the cabaret sequence where Claudette sings "I'd Be a Fool." During a rehearsal, Romberg ran to Spialek and exclaimed, "Hans! That's not my music—it's

Offenbach!" Hammerstein, who was standing nearby, replied dryly, "What's the matter with Offenbach?"[10]

Return to European Settings: *Melody, Rose de France, May Wine,* and *Forbidden Melody*

After the failure of *East Wind*, Romberg retreated to a more traditional, though still distinctive, approach to operetta. The next four shows, *Melody* (1933), *Rose de France* (1933), *May Wine* (1935), and *Forbidden Melody* (1936), are defined as a group by their European settings. Romberg was no longer experimenting with exotic locales and their musical invocations; he was writing music for operettas that took place in Europe, the genre's ancestral home. *Rose de France* exhibits this in its title, while the titles of the other works reveal a return to older, established practices. The word "melody" is in the title of two of the works: *Melody* and *Forbidden Melody*. In addition to being the primary focus of Romberg's compositional technique, the word hearkens back to the composer's early operetta *The Magic Melody*. Also, the title of his first big success, *Maytime*, is recalled in that of *May Wine*, though the plots of the two works are radically different. Romberg also reinforced the primacy of the waltz in this set of operettas, for waltzes are the musical centerpieces of the scores. As in his earlier operettas, these aural focal points are surrounded by a variety of other musical styles chosen for specific dramatic needs.

The four works are not clones of each other, nor are they part of yet another operetta formula for Romberg. They are distinguished from each other through specific dominant characteristics: *Melody* looks backward to the Shubert-Romberg model with unhappy endings, *Rose de France* is a French-language *operette* written for Paris, *May Wine* unfolds in an extremely innovative manner, and *Forbidden Melody* features a gypsy band as part of its novel orchestration and overall aural atmosphere.

Melody (February 14, 1933, Casino) was George White's entry into the Shubert-dominated world of operetta production. White was best known as a producer of revues, especially the series that bore his name, *George White's Scandals*. Romberg provided the music, Irving Caesar the lyrics, Edward Childs Carpenter the libretto, and Joseph Urban (who worked on Ziegfeld's *Follies*) the sets. The stellar cast included Evelyn Herbert, Everett Marshall, and Walter Woolf. Carpenter's libretto was a multigenerational love story similar to that of *Maytime*. Each act took place in Paris, but during a different time: act 1 in 1881, act 2 in 1906, and act 3 in 1933, the present day. Andrée De Nemours (Herbert) is forced to marry the Vicomte De Laurier (George Houston) rather than Tristan Robillard (Marshall), the composer whom she loves. Tristan dies in "the war" (though we never know which one), and decades later Andrée's granddaughter Paula (Herbert) marries George Richards (Woolf), the nephew of one of Tristan's friends.[11] The relations between the generations are not as straightforward as they are in *Maytime*, and this led to a lack of cohesion in the storyline—Andrée's granddaughter does not marry Tristan's grandson, but rather someone associated with Tristan. Of course, since Tristan is killed as a young man, it would be difficult for him to have children without being unfaithful to Andrée, and this would undermine the operetta's fundamental premise.

Melody is in many ways a compilation of elements from Romberg operettas through *Blossom Time*, and therefore in effect an anthology work of his pre–*Student Prince* shows. Its fundamental multigenerational story is very close to that of *Maytime*, going so far as to calling for Andrée and her granddaughter to be played by the same actress. However, since Paula does not marry Tristan's grandson, the actor who plays Tristan does not have to return in act 3 as Tristan's grandson, since that person does not exist. Another commonality with earlier shows is that Tristan is a composer, and composers appeared as major characters in *The Magic Melody* (1919) and of course in *Blossom Time* (1921).

As an operetta, *Melody* required a romantic waltz duet at its center. "You Are the Song" is this waltz. The romantic leads sing it in act 1, and it is reprised in act 3 first by the "new" romantic leads and then in a choral version as the operetta ends. The refrain includes sustained high notes near the end, recalling "Will You Remember" from *Maytime*.

The operetta also needed a march, ably filled by "Give Me a Roll on a Drum." There is a fundamental difference between this march and the male chorus numbers of the 1920s, which audiences had grown to expect in a Romberg operetta, for Andrée sings it as a solo number. This may be look like a male choral march on paper, but its context reveals it to be something quite different: a solo for the female lead. The number begins with fanfares, after which the verse tells that although the work of "Bizet, Massenet, and Debussy is fine," there is another type of music "for this café." Three *French* composers are mentioned in the lyric, a direct reference to the operetta's Parisian setting. The 2/4 refrain endorses the genre of the march both in its lyric and its musical style, especially in the line referring to a "rum-tum-a-tum by Monsieur Sousa." "Give Me a Roll on a Drum" recalls the act 4 opening of *Maytime*, where Ottilie the granddaughter sings a British-style march to one of her customers.

Again as in *Maytime*, slightly syncopated songs in the style of 1910s musical comedy appear in *Melody*. Most important is the act 3 opening, "Never Had an Education." The comic song establishes the time period as the present day and provides a foil to the sentiment that is to follow. It has the same dramatic purpose as the humorous "Go Away, Girls" in act 4 of *Maytime*.

In addition to the operetta's internal qualities, two of its performance aspects also were connected to Romberg's earlier successes. First was the actress who played the female lead, Evelyn Herbert. This was her fourth Romberg operetta, for she had previously starred in *Princess Flavia*, *My Maryland*, and *The New Moon*. Romberg knew her voice and wrote accordingly. Second was the venue, the Casino Theatre, the house where *The Blue Paradise* played in 1914 and *The Desert Song* in 1926. Thus, Romberg had a show appear at the Casino in the 1910s, '20s, and '30s.

Melody was set in Paris, a city whose audiences during the 1920s were captivated by American imports with their jazz rhythms, dance sequences, and extravagant scenery. In the 1930s, though, tastes leaned toward the sentimental, with waltzes and love songs returning to the fore. This was the virtual opposite of what was taking place on Broadway. Maurice Lehmann, producer at the Théâtre du Châtelet, brought spectacular stagings of American imports as well as original French works, most notably *Au Soleil du Mexique* (*In the Mexican Sun*, 1935, music by Maurice Yvain), to his stage. This native development of "opérette à grand spectacle" was an attempt to recapture the romantic spectacle of earlier days.[12] Lehmann was the French equivalent in the 1930s of the American Shuberts in the 1920s.

Lehmann commissioned Romberg to write his only French *opérette*, *Rose de France* (October 23, 1933, Théâtre du Châtelet, Paris). Albert Willemetz was the lyricist and André Mouëzy-Eon the librettist. (Lehmann, Willemetz, and Mouëzy-Eon were regular collaborators at the Théâtre du Châtelet.) Romberg's working method on the project was unusual but eminently practical. After receiving the libretto scene by scene, in French with a rough translation, Romberg set to composing the music. Since he was not fluent in French, he constructed his own lyrics with the aid of dictionaries. (These manuscripts are at the Library of Congress.) He wanted to provide

Willemetz with some idea of what he intended the music to express.[13] (This was another example of Romberg's credo that music and lyrics must form an integrated entity—"It fits"—but with additional challenges.) Another test that Romberg faced was to create a score that was three hours in length, the standard for the Théâtre du Châtelet. This was nearly twice the amount of music required for a Broadway show. According to the holograph score at the Library of Congress, Romberg did his own orchestrations for the show, yet another unusual practice. Romberg's extraordinary efforts on *Rose de France* were well received, for the show was extremely popular with Parisian audiences and played for two years.

Rose de France was the tale of Marie-Louise, niece of King Louis XIV of France. She is in love with Beauval, a sculptor, but must marry the king of Spain. Beauval declares his love to Marie-Louise, his "Trivolette," and is imprisoned for doing so. The sculptor escapes and heads to Spain, where he ultimately saves the life of the king and later Marie-Louise, who is now the queen. When the king asks Beauval what he wants as his reward for saving the lives of the royal couple, Beauval declares that he only wishes to be Marie-Louise's servant so that he can be near her.

The score is similar to Romberg's operettas for Broadway, although there certainly is a great deal more music. The recurring romantic waltz duet is "Pour vivre auprès de vous" ("I live only for you"). The waltz, marked "Valse lente," is a musical manifestation of Beauval's steadfast love for Marie-Louise, even though, in courtly love fashion, she is married to someone else. The couple sings another waltz late in the show, "Songez, songez que Trivolette" (Sing, sing like Trivolette). Having two waltzes follows the lead of *Maytime*, where "On the Road to Paradise" is a secondary waltz to the primary "Will You Remember." Choral marches are especially plentiful in *Rose de France*; among the most impressive are "Marche Militaire," "March of the Turkish Guard," and a "Marche Triomphale"—"Vive le Roi! Viva Louis" (Long live the King! Long live Louis!). Their presence follows not only the French tradition of populist marches (most famously *Le Internationale*) but also Romberg's practice of large-scale choral marches in his operettas from the 1920s.

Just as in his Broadway scores, Romberg added other song types to this basic framework of waltzes and marches. The title song is a tango duet for Marie-Louise and Beauval. The tango was extremely popular in Paris during the early decades of the twentieth century, and audiences were certainly captivated when they heard the dance in Romberg's *operette*. But there is also a dramaturgical reason for choosing the tango. One of the tango's extra-musical associations is unrequited love, as in *The New Moon*'s "Softly, As in a Morning Sunrise." This is the dance's function in "Rose de France"; although here, both members of the couple are in love; they just cannot be together. Like the waltz "Pour vivre auprès de vous," the tango is reprised throughout the work. The tango fulfills the same purpose as the duple-meter ballads in Romberg's Broadway operettas: it is a secondary love song that is not a waltz. A wide array of other song types appears in the score as well, including a foxtrot, a bolero, a gypsy number, and, since the work is conceived for the French stage, an extended "Ballet de l'Amour et Psyché" ("Ballet of Amor and Psyche"). Perhaps because of the language of its libretto or issues concerning performing rights, *Rose de France* was never produced in the United States.

Romberg's next show for Broadway was *May Wine* (December 5, 1935, St. James). While it was extremely traditional because of its Viennese setting, it was also his most original work as far as the manner in which the story is presented. *May Wine* had the same creative team as *The Desert Song* and *East Wind*: Romberg as composer, Hammerstein as lyricist, and Mandel as librettist. In addition to not having a chorus (certainly a new direction for Romberg), the show's curtain rose without an overture or opening number, thus beginning like a stage drama without music.[14] Hammerstein employed a similar technique, but with music, at the beginning of *Oklahoma!* eight years later, where Aunt Eller sits alone churning butter when Curly enters singing the glorious waltz "Oh, What a Beautiful Mornin'." In *May Wine*, however, the scene is not idyllic. An absentminded and very wealthy psychoanalyst admits that he has murdered his wife, and tells his tale, in flashback, to the police. The show is arranged in two acts containing fifteen discrete scenes. This design controls the play's action. Songs are appended to the plot and function as dramatic soliloquies. Mandel's experiment in operetta dramaturgy thus eliminated the singing and dancing choruses. Since musical numbers were in essence manifestations of the characters' psyches, he did not find them necessary. (This would be handled differently in shows such as Kurt Weill and Ira Gershwin's *Lady in the Dark* [1943], another show with psychoanalytic dimensions in its plot, and of course *Oklahoma!* with its "Dream Ballet," where the character's dreams are vividly portrayed onstage.) There were two solo dancers, however, who appeared in the second act to offer a choreographic interpretation of the narrative.

The story of *May Wine* was based on Erich von Stroheim and Wallace

Smith's novel *The Happy Alienist* (1936). The malevolent Baron Kuno Adelhorst (Walter Woolf King) encourages Baroness Marie von Schlewitz (Nancy McCord) to accept the marriage proposal of Professor Johann Volk (Walter Slezak), a psychoanalyst, in hopes of blackmailing him.[15] Johann is madly in love with Marie, but his shyness prevents him from confessing his feelings to her. To solve his dilemma, he makes a dummy model of Marie in order to practice his wooing. After the wedding, Marie realizes that she indeed loves Johann and will not follow Kuno's instructions regarding blackmail. Johann, meanwhile, discovers Marie's initial motivations behind the marriage and tries to shoot her, but hits the dummy instead. In typical operetta fashion, all is forgiven at the final curtain when Johann realizes that Marie is alive and that it was only a mannequin that suffered damage. Johann's murder confession in the opening scene emerges as being premature.

Despite its novel type of presentation, the production had many problems, nearly all of which stemmed from its experimental narrative structure. Reviewers had a difficult time classifying the show, stating that it had elements of operetta, musical comedy, revue, melodrama, and farce, without any one style being dominant.[16] Also to blame was the manner in which Johann was characterized. He is both timid and brilliant, which in itself is not terribly unusual or disturbing. But he invites Kuno to join him and his bride on their honeymoon, and has a sliding panel in his library, behind which he keeps his dummy wife. Was he tragic or comic? Whatever the verdict, the milquetoast and even slightly freakish romantic lead seemed extremely out of place in a play that involved attempted murder. One reviewer commented that Walter Slezak, who played Johann, "is so lamblike about his nuptials that you expect him to bleat rather than to sing."[17] He was certainly not the typical operetta hero.

Romberg's score was the unquestionable strong point of the show. Its Viennese setting allowed Romberg the opportunity to create exquisite waltzes. But instead of writing his customary waltz duet, he instead created separate waltzes for the romantic leads: "I Built a Dream One Day" for Johann and "Something New Is in My Heart" for Marie. Recalling the fundamental design of the show, the waltzes are private soliloquies for individuals rather than overt expressions of love between two people. Both songs are expressive, vaulting numbers with sustained notes at the end of their refrains, exactly what one would expect in a classic Romberg waltz. In *May Wine*, Romberg uses the waltz to represent Johann's idealistic world, a sound palate which the psychoanalyst establishes and which Marie does not enter until act 2, when she realizes that she loves him.

Prior to "Something New Is in My Heart," Marie sings exclusively in duple meter. One of her outstanding songs in act 1 is the sentimental ballad "Dance My Darling." The gypsy character of the song is enhanced through solo parts for cimbalom and solo violin. (Don Walker and Robert Russell Bennett provided orchestrations.) The refrain includes the wistful phrase "dance with your dreams while your dreams are still dancing with you," elegantly set to an ornamented cascading musical line with a gentle upward turn at the end.

Friedl (Vera Van), an artist's model, is the dramatic foil for Marie. Though Marie is certainly not a morally pure heroine, she nonetheless is an aristocratic woman with airs and graces. Friedl, on the other hand, wants love wherever and whenever she can get it. Her two songs, "Somebody Ought to Be Told" and "Once Around the Clock," reveal this aspect of her psyche. In "Somebody Ought to Be Told," Friedl tells how she wants a man, any man, to pay attention to her. One reviewer called it her "virginal lament."[18] The sweeping duple-meter ballad with its triplets, dotted rhythms, and slithering chromatic passing tones and appoggiaturas is ideal music for Friedl's self-expression of repressed sensuality. Baron Kuno gives Friedl the attention she wants, as she tells him in "Once Around the Clock," a song with lyrics of a sexually suggestive nature. The song's relatively narrow range and slow tempo are in marked contrast to Marie's music. The song is scored for a trio, with Friedl in the lead role and Baron Kuno and the sponging Uncle Pishka in secondary ones. A solo version of "Once Around the Clock" became a cabaret favorite with its unexpected advocacy of a one-night stand.[19] This is evident from the first two words of the verse, "No regrets," to the final line of the refrain, "Just as we met with the coming of the moonlight, we will part with the rising of the sun." This concluding line is intoned in a chantlike fashion, giving it additional emphasis.

Romberg and Hammerstein used music to distinguish between the two major female characters in *May Wine*. Marie's music is written for a legitimate soprano and is in the traditional operetta style. She is a baroness, and as such sings in a sophisticated manner. Friedl, on the other hand, wants and gets sex. Vera Van, a contralto who sang on the radio and was known for her husky tones, created the role of Friedl. The sultry singer brought a celebrity status to the show as well as offering a riveting portrayal of her character.

Marie and Friedl prefigure later musical theater females such as Laurie Williams and Ado Annie Carnes in Rodgers and Hammerstein's *Oklahoma!* (1943). Laurie, like Marie, is not without her faults, and Ado Annie loves to be with men, as she confesses in "I Cain't Say No." Laurie is a lyric soprano while Ado Annie is a belt role. This type of character-distinguishing vocal style, which also exists in Frank Loesser's *Guys and Dolls* (between Sarah Brown and Miss Adelaide) and *The Most Happy Fella* (between Rosabella and Cleo), has an important precedent in *May Wine*.

Although critics were generally negative toward *May Wine*, audiences enjoyed it and ensured it a solid run. As one reviewer commented, "Be it reported, however, that the first nighters disagreed with this play sampler. By their applause they cast an impressive ballot in favor of this new deal in musical plays."[20] The show ran for 213 performances, a strong number in a season that also included the premieres of the Gershwins' *Porgy and Bess* (October 10, 1935, Alvin, 124 performances), Cole Porter's *Jubilee* (October 12, 1935, Imperial, 169 performances), Rodgers and Hart's *Jumbo* (November 16, 1935, Hippodrome, 233 performances), and the latter team's *On Your Toes* (April 11, 1936, Imperial, 315 performances). The show's success proved that operetta and Romberg were still viable forces on Broadway.

The show was also significant in terms of its orchestrators, for it was the first show on which Romberg worked with Don Walker.[21] Walker orchestrated most of Romberg's later shows and also prepared the arrangements for Romberg's touring orchestra during the 1940s, orchestrated some of Romberg's orchestral miniatures, and completed the score to *The Girl in Pink Tights* after the composer's death.

Romberg was in his comfortable Viennese mode for *May Wine*. From Vienna, it was only a short jaunt back to Ruritania. And that is exactly where he went for *Forbidden Melody* (November 2, 1936, New Amsterdam). Otto Harbach was librettist and lyricist for this operetta that took place in Bucharest and Budapest and which was filled with quintessential Ruritanian mistaken identities and impersonations. The result, sadly, was a failure, for the show closed after only thirty-two performances with a loss of approximately $200,000.[22]

According to the date on Romberg's holograph score at the Library of Congress, he completed the operetta on June 9, 1935, in New York. At one point in its genesis, the show was going to include just five singers as its complete cast.[23] It thus would have followed the model of *May Wine*. Within several months, though, the concept changed, perhaps to avoid direct comparison with *May Wine*. The company grew to sixty, complete with dancers and a thirty-member singing chorus.[24]

Harbach's convoluted plot alluded to an actual news event: King Carol II of Romania's return to his throne after being exiled in Paris. Carol II (1893–1953) was known more for his romantic affairs than for his leadership skills. In 1925, he was forced to renounce his right to the Romanian throne and live in exile after becoming involved with a commoner, Elena Wolff (Magda Lupescu in Romanian). At the time, he was still married to his second wife, Princess Helena of Greece and Denmark. (He divorced Princess Helena in 1928.) In 1930, Carol returned to Romania to become king. His controversial and authoritarian reign ended with his abdication and subsequent exile in 1940. His life could have been the model for the operetta: a crown prince falls in love with a commoner, forfeits his throne in the name of romance, but ultimately regains it only to lose it again, this time for political reasons.

Forbidden Melody was not the first time the Romanian royal family figured into a Romberg work, for *Rosalie* (1928), Romberg's collaboration with George Gershwin, was based in part on Queen Marie of Romania's antics when she visited America. Queen Marie was Carol II's mother: the Romanian royal family seemed destined to inspire Broadway musical plots.

Direct references to King Carol II and his exploits, however, were marginalized in *Forbidden Melody*. The main story concerned a young army lieutenant, Gregor Fiorescu (Carl Brisson), who was photographed embracing an unknown woman in Bucharest. The woman turns out to be the wife (Ruth Weston) of his commanding officer, Colonel Geza (Arthur Vinton). The event provokes a scandal and a song, "Lady in the Window." This becomes the "forbidden melody," for it was against the law to sing the tune in Bucharest cafés because of its association with the compromising incident. Madame Geza tells people that the woman in the photo is not her, but rather Elene Constantine (Ruby Mercer), a young singer who is now in Budapest. (The singer's first name could be a reference to Elena Wolff, the woman with whom Carol had an affair.) Madame Geza is a Royalist and wants Crown Prince Carol II to return from Paris to assume the throne of Romania. She sends Gregor to Paris to convince the exiled royal to return, but he instead goes to Budapest to pursue Elene. Madame Geza is furious that Gregor is interested in another woman, but in true operetta fashion Gregor and Elene eventually end up together. Although Carol II is not a character in the play and only referred to in the plot, his romantic liaisons likely inspired the various affairs in the libretto.

Critics despised the story. John Mason Brown wrote in the *New York Evening Post*, "I shall be kinder to you than Mr. Harbach is and spare you its enervating details."[25] The *New York Times's* Brooks Atkinson stated that Harbach "has put together a plot that no one can solve, understand or win."[26] Burns Mantle, writing in the *New York Daily News*, had a difficult time believing that the prolific and talented Otto Harbach wrote the libretto: "If he is responsible, then something dire has happened to Herr Otto, for this undoubtedly is the most garbled of all the garbled libretti publicly exposed hereabouts during the last twenty years."[27]

Romberg's music did not fare well either. Arthur Pollack commented in the *Brooklyn Daily Eagle* that "This is not Mr. Romberg at his best. The music sounds like something he had lying around and hadn't ever used because in the knick [sic] of time better tunes came into his head."[28] While the score certainly had its share of lackluster numbers, particularly those in a musical comedy vein, it included innovative gypsy-style music with an onstage gypsy band, complete with solo violin, accordion, and cimbalom.

The gypsy band appeared in six of the fifteen musical numbers in act 1, according to the playbill.[29] It provided local color, whether the action was in Bucharest or Budapest. Romberg again employed orchestration to depict ethnicity, as he had done in *Cherry Blossoms* in 1927. In addition to the sound of a gypsy band, he also included gypsy scales (a major scale with raised fourth and lowered seventh scale degrees) and Hungarian forms (the two-part verbunkos) in the score. The opening number, for example, is a verbunkos, with a moderato *lassan* followed by a livelier *frissa*. A cimbalom cadenza separates the two sections.

But it is the sound of the gypsy band that permeates the first act. The band is featured in "The Lady in the Window," the "forbidden melody" of the operetta's title. The halting waltz is sung first by a café singer and later is reprised by Gregor. The gypsies accompany both renditions. They also appear in Gregor's first solo number, the fast-paced musical comedy number "Just Hello," and later in the show as background for Elene's "Hear the Gypsies Playing," which the actress sings as part of her performance at the National Variety Theatre in Budapest. The band added a great deal of aural atmosphere to the show, and was certainly its most distinguishing feature, though it seems to have gone largely unnoticed by the critics.

The operetta contained less memorable music as well—songs that filled Romberg's recipe for a made-to-order 1930s operetta. The primary love duet was Gregor and Elene's obligatory waltz "No Use Pretending," and their duple-meter love duet was "Moonlight and Violins." Gregor had a solo duple-meter ballad, "You Are All I've Wanted," characterized by a short-long rhythmic motive. Several songs in the style of musical comedy (without gypsy accompaniment) for secondary characters appeared in the score as well, including the perky "How Could a Fellow Want More."

The three principals in *Forbidden Melody* were all newcomers to the musical theater. Carl Brisson (1897–1958), who played Gregor, was a Danish-born boxer-turned-Hollywood-matinee-idol who was under contract to Paramount from 1933 to 1936. His most famous film was *Murder at the Vanities* (1934). He had a fine baritone voice and was a strong dancer.[30] Ruth Weston, who played Madame Geza, was known for her dramatic roles on Broadway. This was her first singing role, and critics noted her vocal insecurity. She later returned to the musical theater as a replacement Aunt Eller in the original production of *Oklahoma!* Ruby Mercer (1906–99), as Elene the singer, was an operatic soprano who made her Metropolitan Opera debut as Nedda in *I Pagliacci* the same year she appeared in *Forbidden Melody*. She married a Canadian, moved to Toronto, and became known as the "Grand Lady of Canadian Opera." Following exactly what one might expect to find in an operetta, the romantic lead chooses the opera singer rather than the singing actress.

In his operettas from the 1930s, Romberg kept looking backward to earlier models and practices. *Nina Rosa* was in some ways a musical remake of *The New Moon*; *East Wind* recalled many aspects of *The Desert Song*, and *Melody* was certainly reminiscent of *Maytime*. But the influence was stronger than recollections of past successes, for the fundamental aesthetic of waltz-centered scores remained firmly intact. Although duple-meter love duets were regular features in every one of these works except *May Wine*, they always appeared alongside waltzes. Nostalgia was certainly a driving force in these operettas, and Romberg was looking to his own past successes as models. But in the examples with European settings, nostalgia also had another face. Whether plots included historical settings, as did *Melody* and *Rose de France*, or were set wholly in the present, as were *May Wine* and *Forbidden Melody*, they all offered visions of a relatively peaceful Europe where conflicts were minimal and no real damage was ever done. The horrors of the rise of fascism, the fear of war, and the severe oppression of Jews were all erased. Romberg, as a Hungarian Jew, was acutely aware of what was happening in his homelands, and tried to create an alternative, peaceful vision of present-day Europe. Even when political intrigue was involved, as in *For-

bidden Melody, it was of an ultimately nonthreatening variety. The reality of King Carol II of Romania's pro-Nazi views that emerged in the late 1930s and his second exile were incongruent with the naïveté inherent in the plot of *Forbidden Melody*. This was escapism, to be sure, but the stage fantasies only served to emphasize the real-life crises in Europe. They were foils that were at such odds with reality that audience members, when comparing the portrayals of Europe in the operettas with those of the news media, realized that Europe was truly facing tremendous dangers and uncertainties.

Americana: *Sunny River, Up in Central Park, My Romance,* and *The Girl in Pink Tights*

In America, a different type of nostalgia was emerging—one that celebrated prewar America. This created American dream has perhaps its most famous incarnation in Rodgers and Hammerstein's landmark *Oklahoma!* (1943). Ideals of overcoming oppression and forming communities became part of what it meant to be American.[31]

Romberg's last four shows all have plots set in the American past. These visions of Americana offer portrayals of America not as it was, but as it should have been. The same restorative and reconstructive aspects of nostalgia that occurred for Europe after World War I appear here, but this time with America as their subject. The American past is idealized, even some of its less appealing aspects. Romberg's works from the 1940s all point back to the composer's first big success, *Maytime*. *Maytime*, of course, had an American setting, and Romberg certainly was thinking of that when he wrote *Sunny River, Up in Central Park,* and *My Romance* and when he began work on *The Girl in Pink Tights*.

The four shows all demonstrate how Romberg was attempting to combine tradition with modernity. Although waltzes appear in each operetta, Romberg challenges the supremacy of the style in his own output, for none of the principal love songs in *Up in Central Park*, Romberg's most successful show to appear after *The New Moon*, are waltzes. Innovative aspects of presentation are evident in the three completed shows from the decade, for *Sunny River* and *Up in Central Park* begin with choreographed scenes set to instrumental music while *My Romance* is told in flashback, as was *May Wine*. Romberg was certainly aware of new trends in musical theater during the 1940s and incorporated many of them into his work.

Sunny River (December 4, 1941, St. James), like Romberg's shows from the 1930s, looks backward to the 1920s.[32] The show failed on Broadway, playing for just thirty-six performances. This must have been especially disappointing for Romberg, for it was his first new show to appear on Broadway since *Forbidden Melody* five years earlier. In addition to being generally panned by the critics, the show saw its fate sealed by world events, for just three days after the operetta's premiere, on December 7, the shocking news of the attack on Pearl Harbor plunged the United States into the Second World War. Even though it closed quickly in New York, *Sunny River* transferred to wartime Britain. Its London run at the Piccadilly Theatre began on August 18, 1942, and lasted for eighty-six performances, surpassing its New York number.

Oscar Hammerstein 2nd's plot is set in early nineteenth-century New Orleans, although it could easily have taken place almost anywhere. A café singer, Marie Sauvinet (Muriel Angelus), falls in love with the upper-class gentleman Jean Gervais (Bob Lawrence). Cecilie Marshall (Helen Claire), a socialite, convinces Jean to marry her, causing Marie to leave for Paris. Marie returns to New Orleans years later as a prima donna (an obvious operetta ploy) wanting to rekindle her romance with Jean. She abandons her plan when she sees the true love that has developed between Jean and Cecilie. When Jean is killed in the War of 1812, both women mourn his passing. The plot involves several unusual aspects for an operetta—the male protagonist is killed, and, as a result of his death, the two female leads establish an emotional bond with each other.

Sunny River looked to the home front realities of World War II in that many women would lose husbands and former lovers in the war. The musical called for people to come together in mourning the human tragedies. It thus was similar to *Her Soldier Boy* in addressing a wartime audience, although the hero of *Her Soldier Boy* is only thought to be killed. *Sunny River*, by contrast, does not provide this happy resolution.

The show exudes its operetta heritage in its New Orleans setting, something its shares with *The New Moon* (1928, also by Romberg and Hammerstein), and, before that, Victor Herbert's *Naughty Marietta* (1910). Its title refers to the Mississippi River, the same river that is at the heart of Jerome Kern and Oscar Hammerstein 2nd's *Show Boat* (1927). Like these shows, *Sunny River* features a stunning waltz duet at the heart of its score. Marie and Jean sing "Along the Winding Road" early in the show as they dream of a happy and peaceful future amidst the turmoil of the present. Its slow tempo gives it an anthemlike quality that enhances its utopian lyric. The innovative song is more a plea on behalf of society as a whole rather than for two lovers from different social classes. The United States was just about to enter World War II when the show appeared, and the fears and concerns of the American public are reflected in the song. Hammerstein revisited this theme in the lyrics to "You'll Never Walk Alone" in *Carousel* and "Climb Every Mountain" in *The Sound of Music*.

The show's most inventive aspect was its ingenious "Pictorial Overture." The first part consisted of a "Symphonic Pantomime" in which actors strut along Levee Street in New Orleans on a late afternoon in 1806. The show's atmosphere was thus established before the actual story began. Both Romberg and Hammerstein revisited this type of opening in 1945—Romberg in *Up in Central Park* and Hammerstein in *Carousel*. After the "Symphonic Pantomime," the male lead, Jean Gervais, sings the solo ballad "My Girl and I," a slightly syncopated song reminiscent of Gershwin, before the battle for his affections begins.

Following a three-years hiatus from Broadway during which he was active with his touring orchestra, Romberg returned with *Up in Central Park* (January 27, 1945, New Century). At 504 performances, it was his most successful show since the late 1920s. *Up in Central Park* began with producer Mike Todd's idea to create a musical with the look and feel of a Currier and Ives lithograph print. In the wake of *Oklahoma!*, with its emulation of the work of artist Thomas Hart Benton, a created visual utopia—a world of peace— was a tempting prospect. The brother and sister team of Dorothy and Herbert Fields was consulted, and they proposed a story based on Central Park and the Boss Tweed scandal. They would tell the tale from the vantage point of John Matthews, the *New York Times* reporter who broke the ignominy, but not without having him fall in love with Rosie Moore, the daughter of one of Tweed's men. For the music, Dorothy Fields (1905–1974) suggested Romberg. Fields and Romberg had been friends for years, and Romberg was excited to work with Fields on what would be their only collaboration.[33]

In the plot, John Matthews (Wilbur Evans) is assigned to investigate and expose the crooked politics and money siphoning of Tweed (Noah Beery) and his cronies in the construction of Central Park. Rosie (Maureen Cannon) is romantically interested in the reporter, but prefers the extravagant life that results from ill-gotten gain. When one of Tweed's associates, Vincent Peters (Paul Reed), promises that he will further her singing career and make her an overnight success in New York, she marries him. After John exposes the corruption, and Rosie's husband (who is already married to someone else) runs away with a former mistress and is killed, the aspiring singer goes to Boston to resume her vocal studies. One year later, she returns to New York and meets John at a band concert in Central Park. They reaffirm their love against the backdrop of a cleaner, less-corrupt New York City with its "big back yard."

Up in Central Park did not open in a theater near Times Square, but rather at one next to Central Park, one of the show's central locales and the one promoted in not only its title but also in its grand anthem, "The Big Back Yard." The New Century Theatre, where *Up in Central Park* played, was located diagonally across from Central Park on Seventh Avenue between 58th and 59th Streets. For the opening night, Todd created a postshow spectacle equaling that which took place in the theater. He booked nearly every horse-drawn carriage in New York and carried the critics, press, cast, and invited celebrities through Central Park to Tavern on the Green, where 127 cases of champagne were consumed to the strains of two dance orchestras at an all-night extravaganza.[34]

Although the opening night festivities were certainly spectacular, the production itself was surprisingly modest. Todd decided not to mount a lavish extravaganza suggestive of either operetta or his previous show, *Mexican Hayride* (January 28, 1944, Winter Garden, music and lyrics by Cole Porter, book by Herbert and Dorothy Fields), but instead relied on painted backdrops for the set. Considering that the entire production was to resemble a Currier and Ives print, this made perfect sense. Todd was concerned about finances, and to minimize expenses did not feature any prominent stars in the show but rather used a talented ensemble cast.[35]

Romberg produced an effective score to complement the idyllic charm of the show's Currier and Ives look and overall theatrical aesthetic. (See Table 8.1.) He proved that he could write in a style akin to that of Rodgers and Hammerstein, who were beginning to make their distinctive mark on the concept, style, and future of the American musical theater. Romberg's music for *Up in Central Park* combines innovation and tradition. Ballads, rather than waltzes, dominate the score, though Romberg does include a fine waltz for the female lead. The show's other distinctive aspects include character-defining music, extended dance sequences, and novel ways of opening and closing the first act. Romberg's operetta heritage is evident not only through the evocation of nostalgic images from the past but also in the show's anthemlike marches.

The most obvious Rodgers and Hammerstein influences in *Up in Cen-*

Table 8.1 Musical program for *Up in Central Park* (according to the opening night playbill)

Act I
Scene 1: A Site in Central Park, June 1870
"Up from the Gutter" (Bessie)
"Up from the Gutter" (reprise) (Bessie, Rosie, Danny, Timothy)
Dance (Bessie, Rosie, Danny, Timothy, Singers, Dancers)
"Carousel in the Park" (Rosie) [spelled "Carrousel" in the playbill]
"It Doesn't Cost You Anything to Dream" (Rosie, John)
"It Doesn't Cost You Anything to Dream" (reprise) (Rosie, Bessie, John)

Scene 2: The Park Commissioner's Temporary Office in Central Park, July 1870
"Boss Tweed" (Tweed, Mayor Hall, Connolly, Sweeney, Monroe, Peters, Timothy, Men)

Scene 3: The Lounge of the Stetson Hotel (formerly McGowan's Pass Tavern), Christmas Eve 1870
Opening (Singing Girls and Boys)
"When She Walks in the Room" (John)
"Currier and Ives" (Bessie, Joe)
Dance (Bessie, Joe, Daniel, Dancers)
"Close as Pages in a Book" (Rosie, John)
"Rip van Winkle" (Rosie, Bessie, Tweed, John, Joe, Peters, Singers, Dancers)
Dance (Daniel, Dancers)

Scene 4: The Bird House in the Central Park Zoo, Next Day
"Close as Pages in a Book" (reprise) (John)

Scene 5: The Central Park Gardens, February 1871
Opening (Dancers)
"The Fireman's Bride" (Rosie, Bessie, Joe, Daniel, Dancers)
"The Fireman's Bride" (reprise) (Principals, Singing Girls and Boys)

Act II
Scene 1: The Annual Tammany Hall Outing, July 1871
"When the Party Gives a Party" (Singing Girls and Boys, Peters, Oakey Hall, Monroe, Sweeney, Timothy, Danny)
"Maypole Dance" (The Dancers)
Specialty (Joe, Ellen)
"The Big Back Yard" (John, Singing Girls and Boys)
"April Snow" (Rosie, John)
Finaletto (Dancers, Singing Girls and Boys)

Scene 2: Office of George Jones (owner of the *New York Times*), Later That Day

Table 8.1 Continued

Scene 3: Central Park West, Next Day at Noon

Scene 4: The Stetson Hotel, The Same Afternoon
"The Birds and the Bees" (Rosie, Bessie, Timothy, Danny)

Scene 5: The Mall in Central Park, July 4, 1872
Specialty (Bessie)

Scene 6: The Bandstand in the Mall, That Evening
"The Big Back Yard" (Orchestra)
"Close as Pages in a Book" (reprise) (Rosie, John)
Finale (Company)

tral Park are the show's lyrical ballads and extended dance sequences. More subtle aspects are present as well: for instance, Romberg employs vocal range and refrain forms to depict the changing relationship between John and Rosie. The dramatic structure of the show also follows the evolving R&H model—there is no lavish opening chorus for act 1, although there is for act 2, and the long first act concludes with a dramatic twist. (John leaves during one of Rosie's performances.) Romberg also uses musical style to emphasize certain character traits of the principal roles—this too was an R&H trademark, but Romberg had already developed the technique in his shows from the 1930s.

The show also differed from the R&H model in significant ways. The big love duets are just that—there are no conditions imposed as in "People Will Say We're in Love" from *Oklahoma!* Furthermore, reprises of act 1 music in act 2 (typical of R&H) are extremely limited in *Up in Central Park*, the only example being "Close as Pages in a Book" in the finale.

Up in Central Park includes four expansive love ballads, "It Doesn't Cost You Anything to Dream," "When She Walks in the Room," "Close as Pages in a Book," and "April Snow." These are the show's love songs and, significantly, none of them is a waltz.

The first two ballads, "It Doesn't Cost You Anything to Dream" and "When She Walks in the Room," take place in act 1, when John is trying to court Rosie. The refrains of both songs are in AABA form and have relatively narrow ranges. Both John and Rosie are afraid to express their love too extravagantly (as opposed to Ottilie and Richard in *Maytime*). John fears a romantic reprisal from exposing the scandal, while Rosie prefers to live a life of luxury. Thus, their music is restrained and reflective of their individual psychological states. "It Doesn't Cost You Anything to Dream," a duet in a moderately fast tempo, has mostly conjunct motion, and Fields's lyric avoids the direct mention of love altogether. Love is implied but not stated—theirs is still an unspoken love and longing. (Lerner and Loewe did a similar thing in "If Ever I Would Leave You" from *Camelot* [1960]. The word "love" is not mentioned in the overtly romantic song because the love of Lancelot and Guinevere had to remain secret.) John's solo number, "When She Walks in the Room," is filled with alternating thirds and slows down just before the singer identifies the exact moment his heart fills with love: when he hears the title phrase. His song is not fundamentally stepwise; he is beginning to take a chance on love by singing melodic thirds.

"Close as Pages in a Book," introduced in the same scene as "It Doesn't Cost Anything to Dream," is the song in which John and Rosie openly declare their love. Romberg portrays their change in attitude through musical means. The song has a much wider range than either of the previous two ballads, and Romberg also employs a different form for its refrain, AA'. Romberg expands each section to sixteen measures (as opposed to the usual eight), indicative of the characters' grand, sweeping love. The music is the most rhapsodic in the entire show, and Romberg constructs the refrain on a basic motif that is repeated at successively higher pitch levels in the opening passage to create both musical and dramatic intensity. Furthermore, the tonal language is much more chromatic than is Romberg's norm. This is immediately evident in the first measures of the refrain, for a lowered seventh appears in the melody on the downbeat of the second measure. Additionally, the smooth chromatic ascent in the bass line (E flat-E natural-F) provides conjunct counterpoint to the disjunct melody and thus contributes to the overall lyrical atmosphere of the song. (See example 8.1.)

After the overtness of "Close as Pages in a Book," the fourth ballad, act 2's "April Snow," is much more restrained. John and Rosie sing the largely stepwise number as they try to make amends. Since things are not ideal between them, Romberg returns to an AABA form for the refrain, the same construct as in the show's earlier ballads. For the ballads in *Up in Central Park*, this form implies some degree of uncertainty. Fields's lyric describes the special nature of love, a love that one dares not crush, for "forget-me-nots will not grow in an April snow."

In the final scene, however, Rosie and John act as if nothing had hap-

Example 8.1. "Close as Pages in a Book" *(Up in Central Park)*, refrain, mm. 1–4

pened since they first sang "Close as Pages in a Book." To prove this, they sing a reprise of what has emerged as the show's primary love duet.

A Romberg show needs a large-scale sentimental waltz, even if it is not a love duet. In *Up in Central Park*, "The Carousel in the Park" fulfills that requirement. It is not a love song between the romantic leads but rather is the vehicle through which Rosie gives her utopian view of Central Park and its carousel. With its wide range, fermatas on high notes, and flowing melody, it also demonstrates Rosie's love of singing and her desire to be an opera singer. This is her only solo number in the show, and its refined style helps define her character and career aspirations.

Since carousels are often associated with waltzes, Romberg's stylistic choice is perfectly in line with the song's subject matter. Months after the opening of *Up in Central Park*, another musical with a carousel in its plot that was filled with glorious waltzes, *Carousel* by Rodgers and Hammerstein, had its Broadway premiere on April 19 at the Majestic Theatre. There does not seem to be any extrinsic evidence that links these two shows—while they certainly do have similarities, their differences are far more pronounced.

In *Up in Central Park*, Romberg uses music style to distinguish between the personalities of the principal female roles. Rosie's operatic aspirations are in marked contrast to the motivations and desires of Bessie, the show's soubrette. Bessie is an Irish immigrant from the Lower East Side who wants to live among the wealthy. She is much more earthy than her opera-singing friend, and her music is indicative of this. Bessie's first song is the comic "Up from the Gutter," in which she expresses her life goal. Furthermore, she is not afraid to promote her sexual desires and does so in the song "Currier and Ives." She propositions Joe, on whom she has her sights set, with lines such as "May I show you my Currier and Ives?" (a play on the couch artist's "come up and see my etchings") and "If you show me where your hat is, I will show you where my flat is."[36] The song has a relatively narrow range and many words are intoned on the same pitch, facilitating the enunciation of the text. But more importantly, the song is in vivid contrast to Rosie's vaulting, nearly operatic music. Vocal style distinguishes the two friends.

Bessie is in many ways like Hildy, the randy taxi driver in *On the Town* (December 28, 1944, Adelphi, music by Leonard Bernstein, book and lyrics by Betty Comden and Adolph Green). *On the Town* opened only a month before *Up in Central Park*—this type of man-hunting female character was not unique on Broadway. "Currier and Ives" is in essence an 1870s version of Hildy's "Come Up to My Place" and "I Can Cook Too." Furthermore, both women are in some ways urban versions of Ado Annie in *Oklahoma!*, for they all chase after men and their musical numbers are rooted in musical comedy. Although the principal heroines in *Oklahoma!* and *Up in Central Park* certainly are not innocents, their ultimate dedication to the show's leading man is reflected in their lyrical and sometimes soaring music.

Another influence of *Oklahoma!* is *Up in Central Park*'s extended dance sequence, called simply "Dance" in the playbill, but commonly known as the "Currier and Ives Ballet." This was a *tableau vivant* in which a picture, in this case something resembling Currier and Ives's famous lithograph *Central Park, Winter: The Skating Pond* (1862), is recreated using real people who appear in still poses as the scene opens and then begin moving.[37] Helen Tamaris choreographed the exquisite sequence, which was considered to be the high point of the production. When the film version of *Up in Central Park* appeared in 1948 with Deanna Durbin, the tale was altered and much of the music changed. This scene, however, was kept intact. The look and atmosphere of Currier and Ives, so important not only in this ballet but also throughout the show, was the audience's first visual image of the show, for *Central Park, Winter: The Skating Pond* was on the playbill cover. Thus, even before the curtain rose, the audience had seen the iconic image that inspired the show.

Among the most original scenes in *Up in Central Park* are the act 1 opening and finale. The act (and the show) begins with a pantomime set to music in which various people, including bicyclists, balloon sellers, policemen, and

Playbill cover for the original production of *Up in Central Park*. Author's collection.

newsboys, are enjoying a day in Central Park. A long scene without music follows, giving the impression that this may be a straight play rather than a musical. Both aspects have precedents in Romberg's work: the pantomime in *Sunny River* and the dramatic scene in *May Wine*. The first musical number is Bessie's "Up from the Gutter," which is a solo song. Romberg and the Fieldses again followed the lead of *Oklahoma!*, with its opening number, "Oh, What a Beautiful Mornin'," although in *Up in Central Park* a secondary character sings a comic song, as opposed to the romantic male lead intoning a waltz.

The act's finale likewise held several surprises. It is set at the Central Park Gardens, where Rosie and Bessie are performing "The Fireman's Bride," a lively strophic comic waltz reminiscent of nineteenth-century popular music. The song tells the story of the "Fireman's Bride," who is a frequent guest at the firehouse and is the sexual partner of the entire brigade, not just her husband. Sexual innuendo is rampant in the lyrics, for the title character "clings to the hose," lies "flat on her hide," and is a "naughty Fireman's bride." The bawdiness of the song proves that Rosie is not the pure ingénue John expected her to be. By now, Rosie has become engaged to Tweed's business associate and is in essence John's enemy. John is about to expose Tweed and rushes into the Gardens to confer with a friend when he and Rosie spot each other. At that moment, which occurs during a reprise of "The Fireman's Bride," the music stops abruptly. During the uncomfortable silence that ensues, John gives Rosie a poignant ironic toast, puts down his glass, and leaves. With the stage still enshrouded in silence, the curtain falls.[38] This is one of the most dramatic first-act finales in any musical of the era, and certainly in any Romberg operetta. The large-scale finale sequences of shows such as *The Student Prince* and *The New Moon* are not present here. The power of silence envelops the sheer dramatic intensity of the moment.

Romberg did not completely eschew his operetta heritage for *Up in Central Park*. In addition to the fundamentally nostalgic atmosphere and effusive waltz, this legacy is evident in the show's two big marches: "Boss Tweed" and "The Big Back Yard." The first of these, act 1's "Boss Tweed," is a political endorsement for its namesake and is sung in clipped syllables. Tweed is the show's villain, and a broad lyrical melody for a song of support for him and his associates would be uncharacteristic and even inappropriate. By contrast, "The Big Back Yard" is the celebratory anthem for Central Park that appears in act 2. It affirms all that is good about the park, and likewise is a heroic march with plenty of sustained notes for John, who leads it, to show off his baritone voice. The song follows other heroic numbers such as "Your Land and My Land" from *My Maryland* and "Stouthearted Men" from *The New Moon*, and continues their dynamic vision of the power of community.

This celebration of New York followed on the heels of *On the Town*, the show from which the city got one of its most famous musical tributes in "New York, New York." Just as the entire city was promoted in that song, Central Park acquired its own musical advertisement in "The Big Back Yard."

Overall, *Up in Central Park* was a substantial departure from Romberg's typical operetta style, for the romantic leads sing ballads rather than waltzes. However, in the composer's next show, *My Romance* (October 19, 1948,

Shubert), he returned to the world of traditional operetta, complete with waltzes, nostalgia, a bittersweet ending, and the Shuberts.[39]

My Romance was the last operetta that the Shuberts themselves produced. It was the *finale ultimo* in their decades-long domination of operetta. A musical version of Edward Sheldon's play *Romance* (1913), *My Romance* was the tale of a prima donna, Rita Cavallini (Anne Jeffreys), who falls in love with an Episcopal priest, Tom Armstrong (Laurence Brooks). In an ending that recalls *The Student Prince* but with the genders reversed, the singer withdraws to a life of song so as not to hinder the cleric's career. The tale, set in New York City, was told in flashback—the show's most innovative aspect—with a then-bishop telling his grandson the tale of "my romance."

The old-fashioned operetta did not fare well with either critics or audiences. It appeared in an especially resplendent Broadway season that included Kurt Weill's *Love Life*, Frank Loesser's *Where's Charley?*, Cole Porter's *Kiss Me, Kate*, and Rodgers and Hammerstein's *South Pacific*, all of which were shows that demonstrated ingenious integrations of music and dramatic realism. This did not matter to J. J. Shubert, however, for *My Romance* represented his earnest hope to return to the theatrical limelight. It was an operetta in all its nostalgic and romantic glory as well as in all its potentially deadly trappings. The Shubert faithful came to see the operetta but were lukewarm in their response. Their support was more for the Shuberts and their legacy than for the new show. Anne Jeffreys, who played Rita Cavallini, remarked: "We ran for three months because some of J. J.'s operetta audiences from the old days came to see us. J. J. was heartbroken. He loved the show; he believed in it; he spent a lot of money on it. In New York he gave us the Shubert, one of his finest theatres. The show's failure helped to break him; it really contributed to his demise."[40]

Romberg returned to his pre–*Desert Song* paradigm for *My Romance*, which meant that in addition to the bittersweet ending and overall nostalgic sentiment, waltzes dominated the score. "In Love with Romance" is the obligatory recurring waltz love duet for the romantic leads, continuing a Romberg-Shubert convention dating back thirty-four years to "Auf Wiedersehn" from *The Blue Paradise*. "1898" is the operetta's opening number, and this choral waltz immediately establishes not just the time of the operetta but also its genre and fundamental aesthetic.

At the time of his death in 1951, the ever-productive Romberg was at work on *The Girl in Pink Tights*. Coming full circle with the history of Broadway theater, the musical's plot was loosely based on the production of *The Black Crook*, the 1866 extravaganza often cited as the first Broadway musical because of its permanent venue and long run. As such, *The Girl in Pink Tights* was a backstage musical about the creation of a real work. *The Black Crook*, though, was an incongruous mélange by 1950s (and also by 1866) standards, and its elements did not really coalesce, an attribute that added to the challenge of creating a musical based upon it. Don Walker, Romberg's orchestrator during the late 1940s, completed the score, and *The Girl in Pink Tights*, with a book by Jerome Chodorov and Joseph Fields, opened on March 5, 1954, at the Mark Hellinger Theatre. Agnes de Mille choreographed the show's impressive dance sequences.

How much of the score is by Romberg and how much is by Walker is a matter of speculation. The printed sheet music selections from the show include a footnote after Romberg's name, "Music developed by Dan Walker." It is extremely likely that Walker created the majority of the score for *The Girl in Pink Tights*.[41] Romberg apparently wrote some music for the show, including the main ballads, and left sketches for other numbers. However, the Don Walker qualifier appears on the sheet music for "Lost in Loveliness," the show's principal ballad, suggesting that it was not entirely Romberg's creation. In any event, the intensely chromatic harmonies and overall jazz-inspired flavor of the score is extremely different from anything Romberg had written earlier, including *Up in Central Park*. This leads to the conclusion that, although Romberg's ideas may have been the basis for some of the show's music, the result is largely Walker's handiwork.

The star of *The Girl in Pink Tights* was the French ballerina Jeanmaire (Renée "Zizi" Jeanmaire), who made her debut as a Broadway singer in the show. She was known to New York audiences not only because of ballet performances but also for her work opposite Danny Kaye in the 1952 film *Hans Christian Andersen*, in which she played the ballerina for whom the film's title character wrote a ballet version of *The Little Mermaid*. Her talents were showcased immediately in *The Girl in Pink Tights*, for the show's opening scene took place in a ballet studio and Jeanmaire's initial appearance was *en pointe*.

The show is set in New York just after the Civil War (an added bit of Americana). A French ballet troupe is scheduled to perform at the Academy of Music, across the street from Niblo's Garden, where a lurid melodrama entitled *Dick the Renegade* is about to open. When the Academy of Music burns down, the two companies merge and *The Black Crook*—along with the Broadway musical—is born.[42]

The Girl in Pink Tights addresses many of the dichotomies associated with not only musical theater but also Romberg's career. Most significant is the duality between "high art" (the ballet) and "low art" (the melodrama). Rodgers and Hart addressed this same theme in *On Your Toes* in 1936, where an ex-vaudevillian falls in love with a Russian ballet dancer. In *The Girl in Pink Tights*, the author of the melodrama falls for a French ballerina. The show includes formal ballet sequences, namely a pas de deux in act 1 and an evocative "Bacchanale" in act 2, as well as ensemble numbers rooted in a musical comedy vein, such as the energetic opening number "That Naughty Show from Gay Paree" and the comic waltz "Love Is the Funniest Thing," which features a laughing refrain.

The musical's finale, a created scene from *The Black Crook*, likewise juxtaposes multiple styles. It opens with a rousing march, "The Cardinal's Guard Are We," sung in praise of Cardinal Richelieu (of *The Three Musketeers* fame). This is in marked contrast to the next number, the high-energy jazz-inspired "Going to the Devil," performed by Jeanmaire, which in turn leads to a Broadway ballet, "Ladies from Hades." The ballet is based in part on the Faust legend, as is *The Black Crook*. Visually, it incorporated delights such as dancing bats, skyrockets, an American flag (this was World War II, after all), and the title character wearing a Civil War–era cap.

The Girl in Pink Tights is more musical comedy than operetta: the rousing opening number, the comic songs, and the gently syncopated ballads all evoke the spirit of musical comedy. The only operetta vestiges are the marches, such as the song of camaraderie when the two companies merge, "We're All in the Same Boat," and the show-within-a-show's "The Cardinal's Guard Are We." "We're All in the Same Boat" has the same dramatic function as many of Romberg's classic marches ("Stouthearted Men," for example), which is as musical endorsements of people coming together for a common cause.

What the score is missing, at least from the perspective of operetta, is a romantic waltz. This central feature of Romberg's work is notably absent in *The Girl in Pink Tights*, as it had been in *Up in Central Park*. It is hard to know whether or not Romberg would have written a sweeping waltz for the show if he had lived longer. Rather than a waltz, the show's main song is the languid ballad "Lost in Loveliness." The tempo of the refrain is exceedingly slow, allowing the singer and the audience to luxuriate in its highly chromatic language. Walker, in realizing the score for *The Girl in Pink Tights*, certainly maintained a great deal of Romberg's fundamental aesthetic, the notable absence of a waltz notwithstanding.

In his works from the 1930s and 1940s, Romberg was searching for a new voice—one that simultaneously embraced modernity and nostalgia. He kept aware of current trends in the musical theater, and several of his works, including *May Wine* and *Up in Central Park*, demonstrate some extremely innovative elements in their modes of presentation. Additionally, duple-meter ballads regularly appear alongside waltzes, a trend that he was already exploring in *The Desert Song* and *The New Moon*. The ballad even replaced the waltz as the principal musical style in *Up in Central Park*. Refrains frequently were in the conventional AABA form, and the large vocal ranges associated with his earlier operettas, especially in his soprano roles, were often decreased to accommodate a new type of singing actor, one without a trained coloratura and extensive range.

The move from non-European and non-American settings in Romberg's work from the early 1930s to European ones in the late 1930s and to American ones in the 1940s also reflects shifting paradigms in the composer's concept of operetta. The distant locales of Saigon and Peru continue the genre's opulent exoticism of the 1920s, while the European settings demonstrate a return to traditional Viennese models. With the works set in America, though, Romberg looked back to the operettas of the 1910s such as *Maytime* with their American settings while simultaneously glancing sideways to contemporary developments in the musical theater. In these works, he fused techniques from the past and the present and, in doing so, proved that operetta—with its fundamental sense of nostalgia, its stylized music, and its sentimental tales—was still a viable and sustainable genre on Broadway.

CHAPTER 9

Romberg in Hollywood

FILM CHANGED FOREVER ON OCTOBER 6, 1927, WHEN SYNCHROnized singing to on-screen images appeared in the much-publicized *The Jazz Singer* starring Al Jolson. A new multimedia form was emerging that was the result of a symbiotic synthesis of sound and visual image. From Hollywood's point of view, glorious film operettas, either new works or adaptations of stage pieces, were ideal vehicles to showcase the possibilities of sound on film. Cinema could also put bona fide opera scenes, familiar songs, choreographed spectacles, and much more on-screen.[1] Film operetta was the meeting place for this variety of styles—it was a place where opera met popular song.

In addition to being a forum for music, sound films provided new opportunities for singers. As Lawrence Tibbett remarked: "When my own talkies first came out, the M-G-M people were careful not to advertise me as 'baritone of the Metropolitan Opera Company.' There is a vast section of the country's movie public to whom such a billing would have meant 'something for the high brows—something for the swells—something to keep away from.' Instead, I was billed simply as Lawrence Tibbett—a new actor who sings! And those very people who might have been shy of a Metropolitan Opera baritone came to hear this Tibbett person and, I am grateful to say, liked him, too!"[2]

Tibbett was hopeful, as were many of his contemporaries, that operetta films would bring conservatory-trained singing to a wider audience. They hoped to entice the film-going public to attend operatic performances and other "highbrow" activities without feeling intimidated or undereducated;

they wanted to educate the public. Romberg echoed this view in his 1930 article "Screen Operetta": "Many people stay away from a picture advertised as a musical play, because they think they do not like music. The truth is they haven't heard enough music to find out whether they like it or not."[3]

Operetta films and their stars were extremely popular with audiences. Studios subsequently brought many opera singers to Hollywood to appear in screen operettas, creating an important chapter in film music history. These singing film stars became role models for many young singers during the 1930s and 1940s. For those not able to journey to a large metropolitan area to see live opera (or operetta), the film medium provided the means through which they experienced classical-style singing.

Like most of his Broadway contemporaries, including Rudolf Friml, Jerome Kern, Richard Rodgers, and George Gershwin, Romberg wrote for Hollywood. He composed music for four original film operettas, the first three of which, *Viennese Nights* (1930), *Children of Dreams* (1931), and *The Night Is Young* (1935), followed the general plan of his stage works from the 1910s and 1920s, while the fourth, *The Girl of the Golden West* (1938), showcased its stars, Jeanette MacDonald and Nelson Eddy.[4] Romberg also wrote songs for other films in the late 1930s that demonstrate his adherence to operetta norms.

Romberg's stage works were also transferred to the silver screen. Eleven film adaptations of Romberg's operettas exist. These include the famous films of *Maytime* (1937), *New Moon* (1940), *The Student Prince* (1954), and *The Desert Song* (1953), the incarnations in which these operettas are best known. These adaptations (and others) emulated original film musicals in approach, which in turn were modeled on stage musicals. Film versions of stage operettas, therefore, have a somewhat circuitous pedigree in that they are derived simultaneously from specific stage works and a film genre based on the general attributes of those same works.

Original Film Operettas

Romberg's entry into the world of Hollywood musicals came through his association with Oscar Hammerstein 2nd. The successful Broadway team wanted to continue their partnership in the film industry. Aware of the success of *Sweet Adeline* (September 3, 1929, Hammerstein's), for which Hammerstein was librettist and lyricist (to Jerome Kern's music), Warner

Brothers-First National commissioned Hammerstein and Romberg to write four musical films. Each collaborator was to be paid $100,000 per picture in addition to 25 percent of the net profits. Hammerstein, concerned about Hollywood's reputation for bastardizing films without the consent of their creators, insisted that the contract gave him final approval of the films, which it ultimately did. The Warner Brothers-First National scheme turned out not to be financially successful, and after the first two films, *Viennese Nights* and *Children of Dreams*, Romberg and Hammerstein were paid not to write the second two, although they had already begun planning their next feature, entitled *Heart Interest*.[5]

Viennese Nights (1930) was a self-described operetta film. Alan Crosland, director of *The Jazz Singer*, directed the movie, shooting it in just over three weeks.[6] In many ways a remake of *Maytime*, the libretto is a multigenerational love story. The film opens, according to titles, "In the days of youth and laughter—Austria under the monarchy." It immediately establishes itself as a nostalgic tale of Old Vienna. Elsa Hofner (Vivienne Segal), a cobbler's daughter, and Otto Stirner (Alexander Gray), a poor musician, fall in love. Otto writes a song for Elsa, "I'll Bring a Love Song." When Elsa is forced to marry Franz, the son of a wealthy Baron, Otto leaves for New York, where he becomes a violinist in a pit orchestra, marries, and has a son. Eleven years later, in 1890, Elsa goes to America and sees Otto, but once again the lovers are forced to part, since they are both married to other people. Still later, in the then-present day, Larry, Otto's grandson, and Barbara, Elsa's granddaughter, meet and fall in love on board a boat to Europe. Larry is going to Vienna to hear his *Poem Symphonic* played in concert. (The work receives a full performance in the film.) Barbara takes her grandmother to the concert, and Elsa recognizes the principal theme of the work, "I'll Bring a Love Song." She sees Otto's image above the stage as the music plays. After the concert, Elsa takes her granddaughter and Larry to the bench where she and Otto used to sit. Larry and Barbara then realize the love that their grandparents were denied, following the lead of young Ottilie and Dicky in *Maytime*.

The film ends with Elsa sitting on the bench as the ghost of young Otto appears. A youthful version of Elsa emerges from her elderly body and the phantom lovers sing a final reprise of "I'll Bring a Love Song." This is the same type of ending that appears at the end of the 1937 film version of *Maytime* with Jeanette MacDonald and Nelson Eddy. Thus, *Viennese Nights* not only recalls the final ending of the stage version of *Maytime* but also foreshadows the dramatic conclusion to its film adaptation.

The film's two most prominent songs, "You Will Remember Vienna" and "I'll Bring a Love Song," are reprised several times during the film. "You Will Remember Vienna" is a stereotypical Viennese waltz. Its dramatic function, however, is not a love duet between the romantic leads, as one might expect, but rather a love song for Vienna. The film's love duet is the duple-meter ballad "I'll Bring a Love Song." Romberg had already created duple-meter recurring love duets in *The Desert Song* ("One Alone") and *The New Moon* ("Lover, Come Back to Me"), so this was nothing new. But not giving the romantic leads a waltz duet to go along with the ballad was unusual. In *Viennese Nights*, Romberg reserves the waltz for Vienna, and in doing so makes the city a principal character in the film and nostalgia for prewar Vienna one of its central features.

Viennese Nights is also memorable in that it includes Romberg's largest instrumental composition, *Poem Symphonic*, which occupies a full eight minutes and forty-five seconds in the film. Its romantic style suggests Tchaikovsky, especially its turbulent opening and rich orchestration. The unrest gives way just over halfway through and the broad, legato melody of "I Bring a Love Song" soars from the orchestra. Romberg revised the work for piano and orchestra and included it on his touring concerts in the 1940s.

Multiple allusions to Romberg's stage operettas appear in *Viennese Nights*. Most obvious are *Maytime*'s multigenerational love story and ending. Otto is a composer, and composers are central characters in both *The Magic Melody* and *Blossom Time*. The beer-drinking students of *The Student Prince* reappear in an outdoor Viennese café singing "You Will Remember Vienna" while swaying their glasses, and the pirate ship associated with *The New Moon* appears in the "show within a show" for which Otto is in the pit orchestra. In another connection with stage operettas in general, a piano-vocal score for *Viennese Nights* was published.[7] This was unusual for film musicals, for only vocal selections typically appeared in print.

The second Warner Brothers film, *Children of Dreams* (1931), trades its Viennese setting for one in California. Unfortunately no print of the film is known to have survived.[8] Seasonal apple pickers Molly (Margaret Schilling) and Tommy (Paul Gregory) fall in love, but in order to save her father from going to jail Molly agrees, with the help of a wealthy socialite, to embark upon an opera career. The son of the woman who helped Molly wants to marry her, but she returns to the orchards and to Tommy. The tale was reminiscent of the familiar "poor girl makes good in grand opera" and "rags to riches" stories, but was unusual in that Molly gives up her fame and money to return to the man she loves.

Children of Dreams includes several operatic scenes, including one from the fictitious *Antonia*, described as "a new opera at the Metropolitan."[9] The highbrow-minded Romberg thus had the opportunity to create an opera scene, just as he had written a symphonic poem the previous year for *Viennese Nights*.

Other song styles also exist in the work. "That Rare Romance" is the normative waltz duet, while the duple-meter ballads "Children of Dreams" and "My Sleeping Beauty" exude lyricism. Both ballads have nocturnal themes, evident from their titles. The "Fruitpickers Song" is an exuberant march that establishes a sense of place. Just as he was doing in his stage operettas, but not in *Viennese Nights*, Romberg placed a waltz duet at the center of the score, surrounding it with duple-meter love songs and marches.

Hollywood, like the rest of the entertainment industry, entered a period of retrenchment in the early 1930s. Extravagant musical films became cost-prohibitive, and the film industry focused on making pictures with casts under long-term studio contracts.[10] It was in such a climate that Romberg began his association with Metro-Goldwin-Mayer (MGM), which by 1934 had become the leading studio for the production of movie musicals. Its impressive list of singing stars included Lawrence Tibbett, Grace Moore, Jeanette MacDonald, Nelson Eddy, Evelyn Laye, Maurice Chevalier, and Sophie Tucker, among many others.

In 1934, Romberg and Hammerstein renewed their collaborative efforts in Hollywood, this time with MGM. Hammerstein negotiated an agreement with the studio that would give him $2,500 per week to write a film with Romberg. It was thus an open-ended contract, rather than a "per picture" one.[11]

The only film Romberg and Hammerstein wrote for MGM, however, was *The Night Is Young* (1935). After Hammerstein created the screenplay and Romberg the music, the producer, Harry Rapf, called in screenwriters Edgar Allen Woolf and Franz Schulz to rewrite the scenario. Although they changed the plot and characters, they retained a great deal of the score.[12] The plot, strongly reminiscent of *The Student Prince*, concerns Archduke Paul Gustave, nephew of Emperor Franz Joseph, who falls in love with Lisl, a ballerina. Since the archduke must marry a princess, Paul and Lisl have to end their romance. The film starred British operetta star Evelyn Laye and matinee idol Ramon Novarro.

Romberg, in typical fashion, places a recurring waltz duet at the center of the film's score. The waltz for *The Night Is Young* is "When I Grow Too Old to Dream," which quickly became one of the composer's most famous songs. It is fitting that it appeared as the finale to the *Deep in My Heart* film, although, not surprisingly, its origins were completely obscured. The refrain's swaying LONG-short / LONG-short rhythmic motion and fundamentally stepwise melody create an immediately accessible and memorable tune that recalls Lehár's "Merry Widow Waltz," one of the most famous of all Viennese operetta evergreens.

Hammerstein fretted over the ambiguous title "When I Grow Too Old to Dream," asking himself, "Is anyone ever too old to dream?"[13] (He could have asked a similar question regarding his fine lyric to "Softly, As in a Morning Sunrise," for what kind of sunrise is there other than a morning one?) Hammerstein biographer Stephen Citron asserts that the lyricist was facing numerous personal challenges while writing the words. In 1934, Hammerstein found himself spending most of his creative life working with people who were substantially older than he was, facing his own fortieth birthday, and struggling with feelings of "selling out" to Hollywood. Perhaps Hammerstein believed that it *could* be possible to be "too old to dream" when one has lost hope for the future and cannot create new dreams.[14]

Romberg's second film for MGM was written not with Hammerstein but rather with Gus Kahn, a staff lyricist at the studio. *The Girl of the Golden West* (1938) possesses a level of artistic achievement that is often understated. Written for Jeanette MacDonald and Nelson Eddy, Hollywood's reigning operetta stars at the time, the film merged aspects of Romberg's stage operetta style with a modern melodramatic tale and MacDonald-Eddy conventions.

Herbert Stothart (1885–1949), MGM's music director since 1929, was heavily involved with the film and its musical construction. Although perhaps best known for his Academy Award–winning score for *The Wizard of Oz* (1939), Stothart already was a central figure in the film music industry and one of the leaders in the creation of film operetta.[15] He served as music director for all eight MacDonald-Eddy collaborations, works which are considered canonic in the film operetta genre. His involvement with his operetta films was substantial, as the title of Ronald Rodman's article "Tonal Design and the Aesthetic of Pastiche in Herbert Stothart's *Maytime*" reveals—not Romberg's *Maytime* but Stothart's *Maytime*.[16]

The Girl of the Golden West is a film musical version of David Belasco's 1905 play of the same name. *Girl* is often cited as the playwright's finest work. Belasco (1853–1931), discussed in chapter 3, arrived on the theatrical scene as traditional melodrama was in decline. With the ever-increasing regard for cinema, vaudeville, and realistic drama, melodrama was forced to change and provide a "higher class" of entertainment. In *Girl*, Belasco created new types of melodrama characters. For example, there is no true villain. Rance, the antagonist, does not represent any force of evil. The polarity of good and evil inherent in melodrama is merged into one character with a dual identity: Johnson/Ramerez. The plot revolves around the redemptive power of the "Girl," as she is called, to reconcile the rift in the central male character—Johnson, the basically good guy, and Ramerez, his bandit alter ego. The Girl herself is a new type of heroine, one who is strong and self-supportive, neither a helpless damsel nor a transplanted European aristocrat.[17]

Romberg and Kahn were not the first to create a musicalized version of Belasco's play, for Giacomo Puccini saw it in 1907 and made it the basis for his 1910 opera, *La Fanciulla del West*. "La Girl," as Puccini nicknamed the opera, opened at the Metropolitan Opera on December 10, 1910, with Enrico Caruso and Emmy Destinn (who was for a time romantically involved with Rudolf Friml in Prague) in the lead roles. Arturo Toscanini was the conductor and Belasco the stage manager. Although important aspects of characterization were changed, the libretto basically followed Belasco's play.

Girl was the fourth film starring "America's Singing Sweethearts," the first three being *Naughty Marietta* (1935), *Rose Marie* (1936), and *Maytime* (1937).[18] By 1938, several conventions for the screen couple had been established: Eddy would wear some sort of uniform during the film and sing a rousing march, while Jeanette MacDonald would be given ample opportunity for coloratura singing early on, often in an interpolated operatic sequence. Finally, background visual imagery for love songs consisted of either water or forests.

Importantly, of the eight films in which MacDonald and Eddy costarred, three of them (*Maytime*, *The Girl of the Golden West*, and *New Moon*) featured music by Romberg. He was the most-represented composer in their screen collaborations. Additionally, Eddy sang Romberg's music in two other films, *Let Freedom Ring* and *Balalaika*. "America's Singing Sweethearts" and Romberg had a fine, mutually beneficial relationship. The singers were famous because they performed Romberg's music and Romberg's music became increasingly well known because they sang it.

Screenwriters Isabel Dawn and Boyce DeGaw significantly altered Belasco's play for the film, causing the Romberg film operetta to have a substantially different plot than Puccini's opera. The film's story begins with a young Mary Robbins singing a tune that a young Ramerez (the Hollywood misspelling of Ramírez), an orphan known as "Gringo," hears. The scene changes and Ramerez the bandit (Eddy), for whom a ransom is offered, leads a quest for social justice. Mary (MacDonald), now an adult, owns the Polka Saloon. She has two suitors, the sheriff Jack Rance (Walter Pidgeon) and the uneducated Alabama (Buddy Ebsen). On the way to Monterrey, Ramerez attacks Mary's coach and immediately falls in love with its only passenger. Ramerez hears of a fiesta where Mary will be performing and decides to attend. He appears disguised as Lieutenant Johnson, a military officer. (This gave Eddy his chance to sport a uniform in the film; the costume does not exist in Belasco's play.) Meanwhile, Rance tries to capture Ramerez and Mary invites Johnson to her cabin, unaware of his dual identity. Rance shoots Ramerez as he makes his way to Mary's snow-encased abode and Mary hides the wounded man in her loft. When Rance arrives looking for Ramerez, Mary, now aware of who her lover really is, says he is not there. At that precise moment, blood falls from the ceiling and lands on Rance. The truth is revealed and Mary, knowing that Rance is a poker shark, challenges the sheriff to a game. If she wins, Ramerez goes free; if she loses, she will marry the lawman. She cheats and is caught; immediately, Rance leads her to the Mission. Ramerez follows and approaches his lover. Rance spies his nemesis with the heroine, and realizing that they truly love each other, leaves them to spend their lives together. Mary and Ramerez ride off together in a covered wagon as the film ends.

The film received mixed reviews. While the stars, the singing, and the music were praised, the plot was criticized. Frank S. Nugent wrote in the *New York Times*: "You just know that the sheriff will relent at the last terrifically anti-climactic minute and that the regenerate Ramerez, who answers to the name of Eddy, will somehow be enabled to sing duets with his soprano for life. There's no point in being nasty about these things. Either you like tapioca or you don't. A purely personal reaction is that it is as dated as a tin bathtub in its story and presentation, but redeemed by the singing of its singing stars. At best, we give it a fair rating and suggest that Mr. Belasco's Golden West Girl be permanently retired from now on."[19]

In order to portray Eddy's masculine persona, marches were essential. He led a male chorus in "Tramp, Tramp, Tramp" in *Naughty Marietta* and in "Song of the Mounties" in *Rose Marie*. Significantly, these rousing marches were Eddy's first appearances in their respective films. "Soldiers of Fortune," the opening march in *The Girl of the Golden West*, like its predecessors, promotes a machismo heroism achieved only through brute strength. The number was intended to appear in the film version of *Maytime* the previous year as "When Love Comes a Marching Along," but was cut.[20] Kahn wrote new lyrics, and "Soldiers of Fortune" was born. It follows the legacy of operetta marches such as "The Riff Song" in *The Desert Song*, "Your Land and My Land" in *My Maryland*, and especially "Stouthearted Men" in *The New Moon*. (Eddy would lead the male chorus in the 1955 television version of *The Desert Song* and again in a nighttime rendition of "Stouthearted Men" in the 1940 film version of *The New Moon*.)

Importantly, this is the guise in which Ramerez first appears in the film. In Belasco's play and in Puccini's opera, the hero appears *first* as Richard Johnson, his dual identity as a bandit as yet unknown. In the film, we are presented with the reality of the situation immediately. This is the heroic Nelson Eddy who leads a fight against injustice. Therefore, Nelson Eddy's bandit is not just a robber, as in Belasco, but is closer to *The Desert Song*'s Red Shadow, a champion for the oppressed. In the film, Johnson/Ramerez regularly gives gold to the mission church. Belasco's concept of the hero who truly is divided between good and evil is redefined: his supposed evil side is softened, for he gives money to charity. After all, how could Nelson Eddy be anything but a hero, even with a few flaws?

Just as Nelson Eddy had to be introduced through a rousing march, Jeanette MacDonald required a coloratura tour-de-force for one of her early musical numbers. "Italian Street Song" in *Naughty Marietta* and various opera sequences fulfilled this need in the pre-*Girl* films. In *The Girl of the Golden West*, "The Wind in the Trees" is the requisite coloratura number. With a flute obbligato synched by none other than Buddy Ebsen on a fife (!), the song allowed MacDonald to display her vocal agility. The lighthearted song shows Mary's carefree attitude early in the film, something that becomes less prominent as the film progresses and Mary matures.

The requisite love waltz, "Señorita," is not Viennese but pseudo-Mexican. It is an atmospheric number, akin to "Drinking Song" in *The Stu-*

dent Prince in its evocation of ethnicity. In true operetta fashion, it reappears as the final music of the film, sung by MacDonald and Eddy as they ride off in the closing scene.

Mary Robbins, MacDonald's character in the film, is closer to Belasco's self-sufficient heroine than to Puccini's incarnation. In the film, strong dichotomies exist in her personality. She is practically illiterate, having read only three books, but yet she sings words (by Gus Kahn) to Liszt's *Liebestraum* in her saloon and the Bach-Gounod "Ave Maria" at the fiesta. Thus, despite her illiteracy, Mary fulfills a typically female role as a keeper of culture. Two intellectuals are responsible for this high-culture knowledge — a blind professor for the Liszt and an elderly priest for the Bach-Gounod, neither of whom exerts overt masculinity in the same manner as Nelson Eddy's character. They represent the American East (civilization) in the American West (wilderness).

Additionally, Mary's completely untrained voice is capable of negotiating both coloratura and lyrical passages. Believability was suspended more than usual in these instances, for they existed largely as opportunities for Jeanette MacDonald to delight her audience.

Quintessential musical numbers for the leads were not the only instances of MacDonald-Eddy conventions in *The Girl of the Golden West*. Another is the physical setting of a love song near water. In *Naughty Marietta*, "I'm Falling in Love with Someone" has a lake in the background, as does "Will You Remember" in *Maytime*. In *Rose Marie*, "Rose Marie," "Just for You," and the famous "Indian Love Call" all appear against watery backdrops. Two songs in *The Girl of the Golden West* continue this tradition: "Señorita" and "Who Are We to Say." "Señorita," furthermore, takes place during the fiesta, so Nelson Eddy is in military uniform, as he is in "Indian Love Call."

MGM's proclivity for production numbers is also readily apparent. The lavishness of the opera and party scenes in *Rose Marie* and *Maytime*, as well as *Rose Marie*'s "Totem Tom-Tom," are all outdone in the "Mariache" (Hollywood's misspelling of "Mariachi") sequence in *The Girl of the Golden West*. Dancers, staircases, and even bowing horses enhance what is the visual focal point of the film. The sequence is pseudo-pseudo-Mexican music. Virtually nothing about it is authentic — it is first and foremost an MGM production number. Mariachi became popular as an urban form in the mid-twentieth century and originated in the Mexican state of Jalisco. It did not exist in this form in nineteenth-century California, but that did not stop MGM from incorporating its version of Mexican popular music into the film.[21] To make matters even more convoluted, the song is marked "Tempo di Rhumba," a reference to a *Cuban* dance. Romberg's pan-ethnic use of Latin styles recalls that of *Nina Rosa* from eight years earlier, where various Hispanic musical idioms were used to suggest a general sense of place.

The Girl of the Golden West was Romberg's fourth and final original film operetta. Many of his operetta conventions from the previous decade, namely a recurring waltz duet and a heroic march for male chorus, are central to the film. They appear alongside other musical numbers that either establish a sense of place ("Mariache") or provide insight into the personality of the film's heroine ("The Wind in the Trees," "Ave Maria"). The work is an important achievement in the legacy of not only Romberg but also film operetta.

Songs for MGM Films

Romberg contributed individual songs to several MGM films during the late 1930s, three of which (*Let Freedom Ring, Balalaika,* and *They Gave Him a Gun*) had wartime themes. As Jennifer R. Jenkins observed, wartime musicals fulfilled the dual roles of "providing escapism and instilling a sense of duty for all, not just for those in uniform."[22] This sense of duty is immediately evident in *Let Freedom Ring* (1939), for that film begins with a placard that states, "The greatest battles for Liberty and Human Rights are not fought on the Battlefields of History but in the Hearts of a Nation's People."

Let Freedom Ring was Eddy's first film where he was the sole singing star. The baritone plays Steve Logan, a Harvard-educated singing lawyer who foils the plans of villainous railroad tycoon Jim Wade (Edward Albert). Wade wants to steal land in the name of "progress" in 1868 by burning people's homes and farms and exploiting immigrant workers. Eddy reprises the Western righteousness of *The Girl of the Golden West* in *Let Freedom Ring*. Released on the eve of World War II, the film promoted and endorsed American patriotism and extolled the principles of freedom and democracy as being unequivocally American.

Romberg, who was not credited in the film's titles, contributed the rousing march "Where Else but Here" to lyrics by Edward Heyman (1907–1981). In the song Eddy, accompanied by a trademark male chorus, extols the merits of freedom. The march continues the tradition of Romberg's freedom-fighting choruses in his stage operettas. Romberg quotes a phrase of "The Star-Spangled Banner" in the final part of the refrain, similar to his treatment of "Battle Hymn of the Republic" in "Your Land and My Land." The nocturnal setting of the song foreshadows that of "Stouthearted Men" in the film version of *The New Moon* the following year.

Eddy's character tells immigrant workers about the glories of (American) freedom. In the middle section of the number, between the two refrains, Eddy approaches specific immigrants—Tony the Italian, Fritz the German, and Ivan the Russian—and tells them that they can enjoy their own national pleasures in America. Eddy sings each imploration in an appropriate accent with stereotyped ethnic references in both text and music.

An instrumental version of "Where Else But Here" accompanies the opening credits, setting the stage for the patriotic zeal of the film through its march style and quotation of "The Star-Spangled Banner." The song's rousing refrain also appears in the film's theatrical trailer, overlaid with the titles "Patriotism and adventure strike a thrilling chord . . . in this *All-American* drama of the late sixties!"

The strong sense of American patriotism and values was a direct response to events in Europe at the time. Immigrants in the film, whether Irish, Russian, German, Italian, or Jewish, can all find freedom from oppression, thanks to Nelson Eddy, in America. Eddy was fashioned into an icon of all that was good about America, and Romberg's single contribution to the score, a march, was an overt symbol of America as a nation that provided freedom from oppression.

By contrast, *Balalaika* (1939), another Eddy film, was set in Russia on the eve of World War I and the Bolshevik Revolution. The meandering plot relates the saga of Peter Karagin (Eddy), a Russian prince and military officer who travels incognito, and Lydia Marakova (Ilona Massey), a singer whose family supports the revolution. Romberg wrote three numbers for the film, all with Gus Kahn as lyricist, although only one, "Soldiers of the Czar," a rousing march for male chorus led by Eddy, made it onto the screen.[23]

As a composer under contract to MGM, Romberg was involved with numerous projects, some of which materialized, and others of which did not. *They Gave Him a Gun* (1937), a seventeen-minute short about the plight of veterans, included the uncredited "A Love Song of Long Ago," with lyrics by Gus Kahn. "A Love Song of Long Ago" is a quintessential slow waltz and appears as underscoring when Rose (Gladys George) learns that her lover, Fred (Franch A. Tone), has been killed in battle.[24] The waltz is used as a symbol of loss and remembrance, one of the style's typical functions in many of Romberg's early stage operettas.

Not every song Romberg wrote for Hollywood made it to the screen. He composed six songs for *Out of the Blue* (1938), a film that never was released.[25] Romberg also wrote "Where's the Girl?" for the comedy *Honolulu* (1939) and "No Time to Argue" for the Jeanette MacDonald feature *Broadway Serenade* (1939): both songs were cut.

Film Adaptations

Eleven film adaptations of Romberg's stage operettas appeared between 1923 and 1954: *Maytime* (1923, 1927, 1937), *The Student Prince* (1954), *The Desert Song* (1929, 1932, 1943, 1953), *The New Moon* (1930, 1940), and *Up in Central Park* (1948) all made it to the silver screen in either silent or sound versions. The amount of Romberg's music that was heard in the cinematic renditions ranged considerably—from one song in the 1937 *Maytime* to virtually the entire score in the 1929 *The Desert Song*. It is the film versions of the operettas rather than the original stage versions that are most familiar to audiences at the beginning of the twenty-first century—many of them are available on commercial video, and it is easier to watch a film than to find and attend a live production. Hence, much of Romberg's fame and reputation rests on the Hollywood interpretations of his most famous Broadway shows.

Many factors must be considered when discussing the transfer of stage shows to the screen. Perhaps the greatest challenge to filmmakers was trimming down what had been a full evening's entertainment into something that lasts less than two hours. Subplots and scenes often had to be cut, and, in some instances, it was simpler to jettison the original plot altogether and begin anew, with some, but rarely all, and occasionally very little, of the musical material. Additionally, with the studio star system, all the major songs went to the film's singing stars. The leads sang music on-screen that had been afforded to secondary characters on-stage—after all, it was the singing stars who were the box office draws. People came to see their heroes and heroines sing beautiful melodies; plots could be changed, but the music and its singers had to live on.

The Romberg adaptations followed the basic model of the original film operettas. Romberg realized that the film operetta was different from its stage cousin, writing that "Mr. Hammerstein and I believe that the present form of stage operetta is too artificial for the screen. The screen projects a realism that will not tolerate sudden halts in action for the purpose of introducing songs and incidental music. In our screen plays we . . . try to make our songs and music contribute to the story's development."[26] In the adapted film plots, romance and sentiment reigned supreme, and comedy was minimized. Therefore, the sweeping operetta numbers, especially the waltzes and the marches, became the film's focal points, and humorous songs were often cut. The unashamedly emotive and heroic songs, as interpreted by Hollywood's cadre of vocal stars, achieved increased fame through the wide distribution and popularity of the films. Likewise, so did the songs' composers, a group that included Romberg.

For the ease of organization, the film adaptations are discussed in the chronological order of their source material.

Maytime

Maytime appeared on-screen three times. In each version, the common feature is the inclusion of "Will You Remember." Romberg's quintessential waltz with Rida Johnson Young's nostalgic lyric was the operetta's greatest selling point, and likewise the salient feature when the stage work was transferred to the screen.

The first *Maytime* film was a 1923 silent feature that starred Harrison Ford (not to be confused with the screen actor who made his name in the last quarter of the twentieth century), Ethel Shannon, and Clara Bow, the "It" girl. Olga Printzlau prepared the screen adaptation, and Louis J. Gasnier was its director. Romberg's music was used to accompany the screen images in performance.[27] Sheet music for *Maytime* was issued with special covers that included a still of Ford and Shannon, cementing the relationship between the film and its source. The eighty-minute film is presumed lost.

The 1927 version of *Maytime* has the distinction of being the first sound film based on an operetta.[28] Lasting a mere eight minutes, the Vitaphone short starred John Charles Thomas and Vivienne Segal. The film's advertising slogan read: "John Charles Thomas, Outstanding American Baritone, and Vivienne Segal, Broadway Musical Comedy Star, Singing: Will You Remember, The Sweetheart Song from Maytime." Both stars had close associations with Romberg operettas: Thomas had appeared in *Maytime* on Broadway, while Segal was still reveling in her success from the previous year as Margot in *The Desert Song*. (Segal starred in *Viennese Nights* three years later.)

In the third screen incarnation of *Maytime*, the classic Jeanette MacDonald and Nelson Eddy version from 1937, most of the original stage music and plot were jettisoned, leaving only the signature tune "Will You Remember."[29] MacDonald plays an American opera singer, Marcia Mornay, who is studying in Paris, where she meets and falls in love with an American plebian singer, Paul Allison (Eddy), although she is engaged to her lecherous voice teacher, Nicolai Nazaroff (John Barrymore). Years later, Marcia and Paul end up as operatic singing partners in the Russian opera *Czaritza* (written for the film by Herbert Stothart and based on themes from Tchaikovsky's Fifth Symphony). After its gala premiere, Nazaroff, realizing that Marcia and her co-star are still in love, kills Paul. The entire story is told as a flashback, with Miss Morrison, the older Marcia Mornay, telling her saga to a young singer, Barbara. The film ends with a scene borrowed from *Viennese Nights*. As Miss Morrison falls asleep on a bench, a ghostly apparition of Paul appears and her younger self rises from her dying body. She joins her true love in the afterlife singing "Will You Remember." Cascades of falling petals add to the otherworldly quality of the sentimental finale.

Herbert Stothart, the film's music director, emphasized the difference in personality traits of the characters through their style of music: MacDonald's "highbrow" opera ("Nobles seigneurs, salut" and "Une dame noble et sage" from *Les Huguenots* and a montage of passages from *Il trovatore*, *La traviata*, *Tristan und Isolde*, and *Lucia di Lammermoor*, along with other well-known operas) and Eddy's "lowbrow" popular song (the Breton folk song "Plantons la vigne" and "Virginia Ham and Eggs" by Stothart, Bob Wright, and Chet Forrest). As Ronald Rodman asserts, the world of the operetta is their meeting ground, and "Will You Remember" becomes "the structural centerpiece of the film, an intersection of high and low, or opera and popular song, and, ultimately, of Paul and Marcia."[30]

The Student Prince

Somewhat surprisingly, *The Student Prince* was filmed only once. The 1954 MGM release starred Ann Blyth as Kathie, and Edmund Purdom's looks and speaking voice with Mario Lanza's singing voice as Karl Franz. Mario Lanza was slated to play the title role in the film; however, his excessive weight and poor mental condition kept him from being able to fulfill his contractual obligation.[31] A standoff between Lanza and MGM ensued, with the studio filing suit against the tenor and ultimately firing him. Following standard

Hollywood practice, Lanza had already prerecorded the film's soundtrack. Part of the settlement between MGM and Lanza allowed the studio to use his prerecorded singing voice.

A great deal of Romberg's music was cut, leaving only "Students Marching Song," "Kathie's Entrance," "Come, Boys, Let's All Be Gay, Boys," "Drinking Song," "Serenade," "Deep in My Heart, Dear," and "Golden Days." Three songs by Nicholas Brodsky and Paul Francis Webster, who were friends of Lanza, were added to the score at the singer's request: "Summertime in Heidelberg," "Beloved," and "I'll Walk with God."[32]

Sonja Levien and William Ludwig's screenplay followed the basic premise of Donnelly's libretto, but there were some substantive changes. In the film, Karl Franz has a stronger sense of entitlement because of his royal stature than he does in the stage play. He kisses Kathie soon after they meet and makes unwelcome romantic advances, believing he has the right to do so because of his birthright. She repels his actions, though the two eventually declare their mutual love. Karl Franz's relationship with his student colleagues is also changed for the film: he joins the Westphalians, who do not have titles, rather than the Saxons, who allow only nobility to join their ranks. When von Asterberg, leader of the Saxons, discovers Karl Franz's royal blood, he forces him to join his corps. Karl Franz, rather than join a group whose attitude he has grown to dislike, instead challenges their leader to a duel.

The power of the male chorus in the stage operetta was transferred to the screen. Seemingly hundreds of students sing the "Students Marching Song" through the streets of Heidelberg on their way to the inn. Other features for the large male chorus include "Drinking Song" and traditional student songs with new lyrics by Paul Francis Webster that were added to the score ("Yu-Hu-Day, Yu-Hy-Dee" "Crambambuli," "Beer Here [Bier Hier]," and "Round and Round and Round").[33] The presence of these numbers not only accentuates the dramatic importance of the male chorus in the film but also emphasizes the lack of a female one.

The dramatic placement and purpose of several musical numbers are also modified for the screen version. For example, Karl Franz sings "Serenade" as a solo to Kathie while the two are walking together at night. The camaraderie of the original setting is replaced by the intimacy of two young people in love. The male chorus is heard, but not seen, at the end of the middle and final sections of the number. In another example, "Golden Days" does not appear until late in the film, when Karl Franz sings it to his tutor, Professor Juttner (Engel's character in the stage operetta, whose name is returned to that of the original Meyer-Foerster play), as he is on his way to Nordhausen to marry Princess Johanna. While singing the song, Karl Franz remembers his days in Heidelberg. He commands that the train be stopped at Heidelberg so that he can keep the promise he made to Kathie to return. Nostalgia is still the central focus of the waltz; however, now it is exclusively Karl Franz's property rather than belonging jointly to Engel and Karl Franz. Significantly, both of these central songs in *The Student Prince* that Karl Franz shared with other singers on stage are now solo numbers on film. Mario Lanza's voice and his impassioned interpretations make them as powerful in the film as they were on stage, though in different dramatic contexts.

The omission of the secondary love stories, the sentimental one between the Princess and Tarnitz represented by the waltz "Just We Two" and the comic one between Gretchen and Lutz, certainly streamlines the overall plot, but also eliminates the dramatic and musical foils for Kathie and Karl Franz. Furthermore, the extended musical sequences, such as the act 1 finale, which were defining elements of the stage version, are eliminated in the film. The changes were certainly necessary in order to tell the story of Kathie and her Student Prince within 107 minutes (the length of the film) and also to accommodate a genre that was more concerned with individual songs than with unified musical scenes. These transformations in effect bring greater focus to the ill-fated romance between the singing leads.

Nostalgia and young love are certainly not forgotten, to be sure. This is readily apparent at the end of the film, which concludes not with a reprise of "Deep in My Heart, Dear" but rather with Karl Franz and his professor riding in a carriage to the strains of "Gaudeamus igitur," sung by the students. Juttner's translation of the Latin appears in on-screen script as the memorable final line of the film, "Let us rejoice when we are young." Attention is thus drawn away from the unhappy fate of Kathie and Karl Franz and a more optimistic message completes this tender fable of young love.

The Desert Song

Just as *Maytime* was a historic work in the history of musical film as the first short based on an operetta, so was *The Desert Song* a landmark opus as the first all-sound feature-length film adaptation of an operetta. A private screening of the film took place at the Warner Brothers Theatre in Hollywood on April 8, 1929, followed by a general release on May 11, 1929. The film starred John Boles in the dual role of Pierre/Red Shadow and Carlotta King as Margot. A young Myrna Loy played Azuri, the native girl who discovers the identity of the Red Shadow.

Harry Gates, director of the adaptation, remained extremely faithful to the original stage version. The closeness was so tight that it posed legal problems regarding production rights. Lillian Macloon, who claimed stage rights for *The Desert Song* west of and including Denver and Winnipeg, filed a suit against Warner Brothers, claiming that the film's release caused unfair competition for her stage productions.[34]

Music is constant throughout the film: every line of dialogue is underscored with musical material. This is a carryover from the mute film era, when live musical accompaniment provided continuous sound in the theater. Rex Dunn adapted Romberg's music for underscoring beneath the dialogue, basing his choices on the idea of having specific music associated with specific characters (leitmotifs) and thus endorsing standard Hollywood practice. For example, when the Riffs are conferring, "The Riff Song" plays in the background, and when Benny and Susan are on-screen, it is against an instrumental version of their signature duet, "It."

The film ably demonstrated the possibilities of synchronized recorded sound, and the variety of styles present in the original score made *The Desert Song* an excellent choice for an early screen treatment. Although recording technology was still in its early phases, the operatic quality of the title waltz, the robustness of the male chorus in "The Riff Song," the effervescence of "My Little Castagnet," and the lightheartedness of "It" clearly showed the variety of musical styles that could be accommodated on sound film.

This was the first of four film adaptations of *The Desert Song*, which ended up being Romberg's most often filmed operetta. The show offered, in addition to its captivating music, plenty of opportunities for cinematic desert spectacle, lavish costumes, and exotic Orientalist appeal. Producers and audiences alike were drawn to the story and especially to its alluring setting. Of the four versions, only the last one, from 1956, has been released on commercial home video.

The second screen version of *The Desert Song* was a Vitaphone short from 1932 entitled *The Red Shadow*. The nineteen-minute film starred Alexander Gray (who played Otto in *Viennese Nights*) and Bernice Clark. Like the 1929 version, all of the dialogue is underscored. The basic plot outline is present, albeit in a severely abridged form. Because of the short length, only four songs were included in the film: "The Desert Song," "The Riff Song," "One Alone," and "One Flower Grows Alone in Your Garden."

The second full-length film version of *The Desert Song* had its premiere in December 1943, during World War II. Like the original, contemporary military activities in Morocco provided the backdrop for the tale. In 1926, these were the Riff Wars; in 1943, it was the Nazi campaigns in North Africa. The heroes of the film are the Americans, making this a propaganda piece for its U.S.-based audience. Dennis Morgan and Irene Manning starred in the desert adventure. In publicity materials for the film, Morgan is wearing munitions sashes, an obvious military reference, while smiling broadly, proud of his wartime involvement.

Rather than Pierre, it is Paul Hudson (Morgan), an innocuous American pianist, who is El Khobar, the leader of the Riffs. Because of fears surrounding Communism, a hero named the "Red Shadow" was unthinkable, and his name had to be changed. (El Khobar, the hero's new name, is actually a city in Saudi Arabia.) The revised plot takes place in 1939, and the French Vichy government has enslaved the Riffs to build a railroad from the interior of Northern Africa to Dakar. El Khobar leads the Riffs in a revolt against their European oppressors. Paul, meanwhile, finds plenty of time to sing love songs to Margot (Manning), a French music hall singer, while, on the desert, the Moroccan Youseff schemes to sell the Riff-built railroad to the Nazis. El Khobar uncovers Youseff's plan, the democracy-loving Free French restore the rights of the Riffs, and Paul affirms his faith in France because, as he says, "they are a democracy." The ambiguous portrayal of the French caused a great deal of controversy, and led to the film not entering general release until 1944. This *Desert Song* ends differently than its predecessors: the romantic leads are not together, for Paul—as a democracy-loving American during World War II—joins the Riffs to secure freedom for all who are oppressed.

Six songs from the operetta were retained for the film, and six numbers were written specifically for the reworking. (See Table 9.1.) Thus, half of the musical numbers would be familiar to fans of *The Desert Song* and half would be new. The heroic "Riff Song" was kept, as were four of the operettas sentimental numbers. "French Military Marching Song" was present, though it was substantially altered. Among the new material were three songs by Dave Bonnesar that provided aural depictions of the Riffs. As far as

Table 9.1 Songs in the 1943 and 1953 film versions of *The Desert Song**

1943 Songs from the 1926 stage version	Newly composed songs
"The Riff Song"	"Male El Sham" (music and lyrics by Dave Bonnesar)
"One Flower Grows Alone in Your Garden"	"Asmar El Loon" (music and lyrics by Dave Bonnesar)
"Romance"	"Fifi's Song" (music by Romberg, lyrics by Jack Scholl)
"One Alone"	"Gay Parisienne" (music by Serge Walter, lyrics by Jack Scholl)
"The Desert Song"	"Howid Men Hina" (music and lyrics by Dave Bonnesar)
"French Military Marching Song"	"Long Live the Night" (music by Romberg, lyrics by Mario Silva and Jack Scholl)

1953 Songs from the 1926 stage version	Songs from the 1943 film
"The Riff Song"	"Gay Parisienne"
"Romance"	"Long Live the Night"
"The Desert Song"	
"One Flower Grows Alone in Your Garden"	
"One Alone"	

*Adapted from Ken Bloom, *Hollywood Song: The Complete Film & Musical Companion* (New York: Facts on File, 1995), vol. 1, 217–18.

the other songs are concerned, "Fifi's Song" and "Gay Parisienne" are in the style of French cabaret, while "Long Live the Night" is a 1940s croon-style ballad.

Because the lead characters are musicians, many of the songs in this version of *The Desert Song* are performed in a diegetic context (that is, where the music is heard by the characters). Margot sings at Benoit's Concert Palace, a commercial establishment for the French in Morocco. Among her selections are the new waltz "Gay Parisienne" and an "old" waltz, Romberg's "Romance." It is not just Margot's solo singing that is featured at Benoit's, but also songs intended to evoke the atmosphere of the Folies-Bergère, including "Fifi's Song." "French Military Marching Song" is moved here, transformed into a Folies-type showpiece for Margot and the female chorus. Paul, by contrast, plays piano at Fanfan's Café, a venue favored by locals, where he offers renditions of "One Alone," "The Desert Song," and the new

"Long Live the Night," to the delight of his Arab audience. Shades of the previous year's *Casablanca*, also set in Nazi-occupied French Morocco, are strongly present.

Romberg's attempts at Oriental sounds in the stage production are magnified in the 1943 film. The opening Riff motif, for example, appears as a secret code for the Riff bands; its North African origins are never directly stated but are strongly implied. El Khobar uses it early in the film to signal his troops, and Paul interjects the motif in a rendition of "One Alone" as a warning to the Riffs at Fanfan's Café.

In another endorsement of musical exoticism, Paul identifies the pentatonic melody of the second part of the verse of "The Desert Song" (sung to "My desert is waiting") as "an old Toric love song," emphasizing its Middle Eastern, and therefore non-European, origin. Margot, in her Eurocentric manner, calls it "weird music." Thus, the subtle plays at musical Orientalism in the stage version are made blatantly obvious for the film audience.

The film is an overt Hollywood attempt to demonstrate American superiority during World War II. Paul is American, not French. It is an American who will save the proverbial day. Furthermore, a frightening stereotype of Arabs as villains and inherently inferior to the French appears in the film—the different, but fundamentally benign Morocco of the original is replaced by a vilified view of the region and its peoples. Youssef, the villain, is an Arab. (In the original, there was no single villain: tyranny and oppression were the enemies.) Even El Khobar, the Riff's ardent supporter, calls the Arabs "savages about their freedom." In another scene, the Western bartender retorts, "It's a shame these Muhammadans don't drink."[35] Taken in this context, Margot's remark about Moroccan indigenous music being "weird" is not only ignorant but also self-aggrandizing. The fundamental aesthetic of the film magnifies the Colonial Gaze of the original.

What was omitted in favor of the film's political message was the romance of the principals. The comic elements were also curtailed, making the film much more of an adventure-drama than an operetta. The frequent diegetic treatment of the music added to the film's fundamental attempt at realism. The magic and mystique of the operetta were replaced with overt political messages and references to current affairs.

Aspects of the 1943 film were continued in the third full-length version, released in 1953 and again by Warner Brothers. Although the setting was returned to the 1920s French Morocco of the stage version, the character name of El Khobar was retained, along with several plot aspects, including a villain named Youssoff, who this time is a sheik. Gordon MacRae and Kathryn Grayson starred in the lavish Technicolor version.

Now, Paul Bonnard (a.k.a. El Khobar, leader of the Riffs) is an anthropology professor from the University of Paris, and Margot Birabeau is the daughter of the French governing general. Pierre's surname in the original has become that of Margot in the film. Margot, a coy student, has no desire to study under Professor Bonnard; she is much more interested in flirting with Captain Paul Fontaine. El Khobar takes her to his desert village, from where the evil Sheik Youssoff arranges for her to be kidnapped and sequestered in his palace. El Khobar (Paul) rescues Margot from Youssoff's clutches (another colonial rescue fantasy like Valentino's *The Sheik*), but Paul emerges with the news that El Khobar was killed in the attack. Margot mourns her rescuer's death, but when Paul sings "One Alone," she responds in song and realizes the dual identity of her lover.

In this version, inter-Arab conflict becomes central to the plot, something that did not exist in the operetta's libretto. The Riffs oppose the sheik, who is being supported by the French. As in the original stage play, and following the premises of figures such as Lawrence of Arabia, the Arabs are portrayed as peoples who cannot solve their own problems and therefore must be aided by Europeans.

The Moroccans are portrayed in the 1953 film as extremely inept and deceptive, and hence in need of French help in order to sort themselves out. In one scene, a group of Moroccans are even shown milking a male goat! Secret troops are billeted at the sheik's palace, a sign of deceit on their part. Central to the plot, the villainous Sheik Youssoff is behind a master plan to simultaneously starve villagers and overthrow French rule. El Khobar not only uncovers his plan and defeats him but also rescues the European heroine from the Arab's domain.

Many of the musical attributes of the 1943 version reappear in the 1953 film, with minor modifications. The 1953 version is in some ways a musical remake of the 1943 version, though not a dramatic one. The Riff motif from the 1943 version reappears with the same function as a signaling tune when the Riffs need to call for El Khobar to come to their aid. Several songs are given new dramatic or musical contexts. Margot now sings the interpolated "Gay Parisienne" as she enters the French compound, with the French soldiers providing musical support as the trademark male operetta chorus. Margot, not Paul, sings "Long Live the Night," which she describes as her "favorite song." Not all the music was retained, for Dave Bonnesar's Riff music and two cabaret numbers, "Fifi's Song" and "French Military Marching Song," were cut.

The "Eastern and Western Love" sequence from the original receives an entirely new treatment in the 1953 film. Margot sings "One Flower Grows Alone in Your Garden" as she wanders around a flower garden. She interprets the lyric as a woman wanting to collect as many men as possible, not being happy with only one. El Khobar responds with "One Alone"—he is the one and only man who can satisfy her. No longer does the sequence focus on differences between the East and the West; it now depicts disparities between the sexes when it comes to love. "One Alone" reappears at the end of the film as the final duet and musical realization of the love between Margot and Paul, just as in the original stage version.

Attitudes toward non-European music are also presented differently in the 1953 film when compared with the version from a decade earlier. Paul describes the pentatonic section of the verse to "The Desert Song" as a "Moorish folk chant." Margot calls it "beautiful" and Paul responds, "primitive and beautiful." The tune's origins are now more general, and Margot's description of it as "weird" is omitted, replaced by Paul's "primitive" descriptor. The timeliness of the desert and its underdevelopment (by European standards) are thus endorsed, rather than an attitude of mere difference.

The Desert Song is the only Romberg operetta to exist in a made-for-television version. NBC did a live broadcast of an eighty-eight-minute adaptation on May 7, 1955.[36] Nelson Eddy and Gale Sherwood sang the lead roles, and Metropolitan Opera star Salvatore Baccalone played Ali Ben Ali. William Friedberg, Neil Simon, and Will Glickman prepared the teleplay, which Max Liebman produced and directed. The plot, though abridged, basically follows the stage original, and Romberg's music is returned to its original dramatic contexts.

The New Moon

MGM filmed *The New Moon* twice, in 1930 and 1940. The two versions have a great deal in common, though their plots are radically different: both are called *New Moon*, without the definite article, both were filmed in black and white, and both starred pairs of famous singing actors—Lawrence Tibbett and Grace Moore in 1930, and Nelson Eddy and Jeanette MacDonald in 1940.

The 1930 film also appeared under the title *Parisian Belle*, a ploy by the studio to increase ticket sales to those who thought Paris might be a synonym for naughtiness, even though the film had nothing to do with Paris.[37] In casting the film, MGM officials signed two of the era's most prominent opera stars, Lawrence Tibbett and Grace Moore.

Lawrence Tibbett (1896–1960) rose to meteoric fame singing Ford in *Falstaff* at the Metropolitan Opera in 1925. Of first-class male opera stars, Tibbett was an obvious candidate for movie stardom, and signed with MGM in 1929. His first film, *The Rogue Song*, was a personal triumph. Tibbett sang all the musical numbers in the tale of a bandit chief in Imperial Russia who abducts a headstrong princess and falls in love with her. The film is now lost, but recordings of Tibbett's singing survive. His voice recorded well, and his screen presence was exuberant.[38]

Tibbett's success prompted MGM to sign another American opera star to its studio, Grace Moore (1898–1947). She garnered great praise for her portrayal of Mimi in *La bohème* at the Opera-Comique in Paris and later at the Metropolitan Opera in New York. Her first film was *A Lady's Morals* (1930), a pseudo-biography of Jenny Lind. The only part of the film that received praise was Moore's singing. Her greatest screen triumph was *One Night of Love* (1934), the tale of a singer who falls in love with her teacher and which features a truly stunning rendition of "Un bel di" from *Madama Butterfly*.

MGM paired its two opera stars in 1930 for its version of Romberg's *The New Moon*. The idea was to create a team of singers that would become household names—something the studio later realized with Jeanette MacDonald and Nelson Eddy. For whatever reason, this was the only film that featured Tibbett and Moore together. There was talk at one point of casting them in *Naughty Marietta*, but this plan never materialized.[39] Instead, the eventual 1935 film introduced the legendary screen couple of MacDonald and Eddy.

New Moon begins on board the ship of the same name on the Caspian Sea. Russian Lt. Michael Petroff sings a vulgar Gypsy song, "The Farmer's Daughter" (by Herbert Stothart and Clifford Grey) and fears that he has offended Princess Tanya Strogoff.[40] The princess asks him to translate, which he does in a toned-down fashion. She then defiantly sings it back to him in Gypsy, proving that she knew *exactly* what he was singing. On the last night aboard the ship, after Michael and Tanya confess their growing mutual attraction, Tanya is asked to sing. The two sing "Wanting You" for an adoring audience.

The ship arrives at Krasnov, where Tanya's engagement to the governor, Boris Brusiloff, is announced. Michael is devastated, and finds his way to the Caspian Tavern to the strains of "Lover Come Back to Me." Meanwhile, a ball is taking place, where Tanya is asked to sing "One Kiss." Michael sees the governor and Tanya, enters, and takes Tanya into a private room. The governor discovers them alone and punishes Michael by putting him in command of the dangerous Fort Darvaz.

When Michael arrives at Darvaz, the native Khirghizes have overtaken the fort. He regains control, but soon learns that fifteen hundred Turkemans are in the pass, with two thousand more on the way, ready to attack. The men — both Russians and Khirghizes — are despondent, and Michael summons their courage in "Stouthearted Men."

Boris and Tanya arrive at the fort, but Michael is not there, for he is leading the defense of the pass. The governor accuses Michael of desertion, and Tanya resolutely reminds him that Michael regained control of the fort and gave his life in battle. The governor subsequently awards Michael the honored crosses of St. Stanislas, St. Vladimir, and St. George.

Russian soldiers dance in the courtyard, and Tanya joins them as the music moves to a reprise of "Lover Come Back to Me." Michael responds from the distance as the troops return. The couple sings the duet version of the song as the troops enter the fort and the soldiers raise their hats to the reunited lovers.

The screen incarnation was miles and years away from the stage version, especially considering how closely Warner Brothers adhered to the original in their version of *The Desert Song* the previous year. MGM's *New Moon* took an almost opposite approach in allegiance to its source.[41] A plausible reason for the changes is economic — the film appeared at the beginning of the Depression, after all. Rather than creating new sets and costumes for eighteenth-century Louisiana, it would be less expensive to reuse sets and costumes from another film. The most logical choice for a new setting for *New Moon* was that of the previous year's *The Rogue Song* — Imperial Russia — especially since the two films shared the same star and fundamental plot.

Only four numbers from the stage version appear in the 1930 film: "Wanting You," "Lover, Come Back to Me," "One Kiss," and "Stouthearted Men." Other aspects of the original are also retained, often in slightly obscured guises. The tavern sequence remains, with "Lover, Come Back to Me" replacing "Softly, As in a Morning Sunrise" as the primary musical material. Likewise, the ball scene that surrounds "One Kiss" is kept, complete with the banishment of the male lead at its conclusion. "Stouthearted Men" fulfills the same dramatic part in both films: the hero rallies his allies (the male chorus) to fight tyranny. Part of the song was filmed at night, a feature that was immortalized by Nelson Eddy and his followers in the 1940 film. Local color is created not only through the inclusion of the gypsy song and Russian dance but also through the addition of a balalaika to the orchestration for "Lover, Come Back to Me."

Herbert Stothart and Clifford Grey wrote two new songs for the film, "Farmer's Daughter" and "What Is Your Price, Madame?" Both are comic songs that feature Tibbett. In choosing music for the film, director Jack Conway kept Romberg's sentimental-style songs and jettisoned the comic numbers such as "Gorgeous Alexander," replacing them with new material by Stothart and Grey. Romberg's nearly operatic music was thus emphasized in the film, and its performances by Tibbett and Moore, two of the era's outstanding singers, are glorious.

It is not the 1930 version of *New Moon* but rather the one from a decade later that is among the most famous operetta films ever made. The 1940 film was the sixth MacDonald-Eddy film, and many of the duo's established tropes (discussed above) appear in the film. Its swashbuckling romance and impassioned heroism made it an audience favorite on the eve of America's entry into World War II.[42]

Jacques Deval and Robert Arthur wrote the screenplay, which opens on board a ship. Passengers include Marianne de Beaumanoir, who is on her way from Paris to New Orleans to oversee her uncle's estate. Also on board are bondsmen, among whom is Charles Michon, Duc de Villiers, an enemy of the king who is escaping execution. Ribaud arrives at Marianne's plantation and exposes Charles's true identity. Charles, overhearing the conversation, organizes an escape and, with his fellow bondsmen, flees, seizes a ship, and sails away to the strains of "Stouthearted Men." Marianne leaves for Paris on the ship *New Moon*. Charles and a group of pirates overtake the vessel as a storm ensues. In order to survive, the crews of both ships unite. They subsequently land on an island and create a new life and a new society together. As a French ship approaches, Charles decides to give himself up for the good of the colony. Marianne finally confesses her love for him just as representatives of the new French Republic herald the news of their successful revolution and Charles's resultant freedom.

Several features from the original stage version are restored in the 1940

Lobby card for the 1940 film *New Moon*. Author's collection.

film. First and foremost are the settings: a plantation near New Orleans, on board a ship, and on an island, presumably the Isle of Pines. Second, the film ends like the stage production, with the news that France is a republic and with Marianne's declaration of her love for Charles (Robert in the original). Third, the surnames of the romantic leads are corruptions of those in the stage version: Misson becomes Michon and Beaunoir is elongated into Beaumanoir. These subtle changes are almost certainly due to copyright issues surrounding the film. Six musical numbers from the original appear in the film, though their placement is sometimes altered: "Lover, Come Back to Me," "Wanting You," "Softly, As in a Morning Sunrise," "Stouthearted Men," "One Kiss," and "Marianne." Another song, "Gorgeous Alexander," is given new lyrics and becomes Eddy's comic "Shoe-Shining Song," which in turn becomes the verse for "Softly, As in a Morning Sunrise." Neither "Gorgeous Alexander" nor "Softly, As in a Morning Sunrise" were in the 1930 film.

As in the 1930 version, Romberg's more sentimental numbers are retained, in addition to the rousing "Stouthearted Men." Stothart and Grey's two new songs for the 1930 film were not kept for the 1940 version; in fact, humorous songs did not appear at all in the new film, save for the Nelson Eddy feature, "Shoe-Shining Song." The score remained focused on Romberg's romantic and heroic numbers, and the plot endorsed these same two dimensions, especially the former.

Similar to the relationship between the 1943 and 1953 versions of *The Desert Song*, aspects of the 1930 *New Moon* film are retained in the 1940 remake. Both open on board a ship, where the romantic leads make their initial acquaintance, and both cinematic renditions of "Stouthearted Men" include dramatic marching scenes at night. Diegetic performances of a Romberg song exist in both versions: "Wanting You" in 1930 and "One Kiss" in 1940. In both instances, the female lead is asked to sing. In the 1930 film though, Tanya invites her suitor to join her. Both films include a duet reprise of "Lover Come Back to Me" near the end. The musical setting is similar: the singers are not in physical proximity to each other for the first part of the song, but are together by its conclusion.

Finally, conventions established for Jeanette MacDonald and Nelson Eddy's films appear in *New Moon*. Eddy is in uniform for the first half of the film, including the principal love duet, "Wanting You." The song is performed against a marsh, a watery backdrop, as are "Indian Love Call" in *Rose Marie* (1936) and "Señorita" in *Girl of the Golden West* (1938). The serenading minstrels who sing "Marianne" to the first lady of the island late in the film (as opposed to serenading the heroine in act 1 in the stage version) have their cinematic roots in the Italian street singers in *Naughty Marietta*. From *Girl of the Golden West* comes the idea of MacDonald's character singing a religious number: the Bach-Gounod "Ave Maria" in *Girl of the Golden West* and Handel's "Largo" in *New Moon*. The film was as much about its stars as its plot, and Romberg's music served both.

Up in Central Park

Deanna Durbin (b. 1921), one of Universal Studios' most talented singing stars of the 1940s, starred in her studio's film adaptation of *Up in Central Park*, released in 1948, just three years after the show opened in New York. The short time it took for the tale to make it to the screen attests to both its stage popularity and its modern musical sensibilities.

While the stage version's overall story line is present, many of its details and subplots were eliminated for the film. Durbin played Rosie Moore, an Irish immigrant recently arrived with her illiterate father, Timothy (Albert Sharpe). Boss Tweed (Vincent Price) appoints Mr. Moore superintendent of Central Park. Rosie, meanwhile, falls in love with *New York Times* reporter John Matthews (Dick Haymes), who is trying to expose Tweed's ring of corruption. By the end of the film, Timothy has learned to read and has seen Tweed's corruption. John's exposé of Tweed appears on the front page of the *Times*, and Rosie is with John, the man of her dreams.

Only three songs from the stage play made it to the screen: "Boss Tweed," "Carousel in the Park," and "When She Walks in the Room." "Boss Tweed," a march, is the film's opening chorus, and sets the scene for the forced support for Tweed and his Tammany Hall machine. "Carousel in the Park" becomes a romantic waltz duet for Rosie and John. It thus functions in a traditional musico-dramatic role for a Romberg operetta, unlike in the stage version, where it is an expression of Rosie's dream for Central Park. "When She Walks in the Room" is retained as John's soliloquy on his love for Rosie.

Romberg and Fields wrote an additional song for the film: "Oh, Say Can You See," sung by Rosie as the ship on which she is traveling approaches Ellis Island. In the patriotic number Rosie tells of the hopes and dreams she and her fellow immigrants have for their new lives in America. It thus follows the lead of "Where Else But Here" in *Let Freedom Ring*, complete with a reference to the "Star-Spangled Banner."

Conclusion

Romberg's work in Hollywood complemented that for Broadway. The composer's approach to film music was similar to that for the stage. Waltzes meant romance, or in some instances loss and nostalgia, while marches exerted a quest for social justice and freedom from oppression. Furthermore, Romberg alluded to his stage legacy in his original film operettas, especially in *Viennese Nights*, where the story is reminiscent of *Maytime*.

The film versions of Romberg's *Maytime* (1937), *The Student Prince* (1954), *The Desert Song* (1953), and *The New Moon* (1940) are the vehicles through which Romberg's music and legacy are best known. These films reached an extremely wide populace, and because of their commercial availability, are the primary means through which audiences in the twenty-first century experience Romberg's operettas. While all four films certainly capture the nostalgic and escapist nature of operetta, they also offer a distorted view of the complexities and possibilities of the genre. The role of music in establishing character is missing, since the film's stars sing all the music, and do so gloriously. The stage genre's comic elements, and the songs written in a musical comedy style, are similarly pushed to the background. Clever and memorable numbers such as "It" and "Gorgeous Alexander" are forgotten if one looks only at the film versions as a testament of Romberg's 1920s operetta heritage.

The film adaptations are fine examples of film operetta, the genre in which they truly belong and through which they should be interpreted. They extol the best attributes of the genre: sentimental tales, lavish visual spectacle, and—above all—glorious singing of extremely appealing music. They should not be viewed as substitutes for the stage originals, for these films are substantially different entities. The variety of music and musical characterizations associated with operetta is notably and necessarily curtailed in the screen versions, and perhaps it is because of these screen versions, wonderful in their own right, that 1920s American operetta is often thought of as a monodimensional art form filled with nostalgic sentiment.

There was, and still is, an audience for these unashamedly romantic films. The continued popularity and television broadcasts of operetta films, especially those featuring Jeanette MacDonald and Nelson Eddy, attests to this fact. Their innate charm, sentimentality, and fine music will undoubtedly ensure them lasting places in American popular culture.

CHAPTER 10

Building a Legacy

ROMBERG REALIZED THE IMPORTANCE OF AN AUDIENCE AND ITS tastes. He also knew that during the 1940s, his style of operetta was becoming outmoded. Although he proved that he could write a successful "modern" show with *Up in Central Park* (1945), his heart remained with the nostalgia-driven works of the teens and twenties. Romberg, ever the entrepreneur and romantic, began searching for the audience that he knew appreciated his old-fashioned melodies.[1] He accomplished this first through radio programs, and then through annual tours from 1943 through 1949 with an orchestra, chorus, and soloists, offering programs entitled "An Evening with Sigmund Romberg." These were immensely popular with audiences. He also recorded selections from his operettas with the Sigmund Romberg Orchestra. His self-promotion paid off, for he was certainly among America's most beloved musical personalities of the 1940s.

Factors beyond Romberg's own efforts also contributed to the creation of his legacy. The film versions of his operettas were extremely popular and brought his name and his music to millions. His work also appeared on *The Railroad Hour*, a radio program hosted by singer Gordon MacRae that featured abridged versions of musical theater works. Romberg's operettas were a regular feature of the long-running series. Furthermore, studio recordings of several Romberg operettas appeared in the middle part of the century. Thus, the modern media of film, radio, and sound recording were extremely significant in promoting Romberg and his music. They did a great deal to keep his classic melodies alive in the public consciousness.

Revivals constitute a major part of Romberg's legacy. His operettas have been staged since the time of their creation, not only in the United States but also in the United Kingdom, continental Europe, Australia, and New Zealand. Romberg's works have been extremely important in the exportation of the Broadway musical away from American shores.

Romberg's music has also found a home in jazz. Artists such as Louis Armstrong and John Coltrane, among many others, have recorded versions of Romberg's most famous tunes.

Popularity can be gauged, at least in part, through cultural allusions. Parody is a measure of common knowledge, for audiences will not understand the humor if they do not have at least some idea of the original. Romberg's music has been the subject of allusions and parody throughout the second half of the twentieth century, and these cultural references form a significant part of the composer's continuing legacy.

Radio Programs

Romberg hosted two radio programs on which his music was featured, *The Swift Hour* in the 1930s and *An Evening with Sigmund Romberg* in the 1940s. He also appeared several times as a guest on the *U.S. Steel Hour*. Romberg enjoyed the opportunity to speak to his airwave audience as well as to offer them performances of his music.

The Swift Hour was co-hosted by Romberg and retired Yale University English professor William Lyon Phelps (1865–1950). The hour-long program, sponsored by Swift and Company (of sausage fame), played for twenty-eight weeks on NBC in 1934 and 1935. As part of the program, Romberg conducted a studio orchestra that played his music, as well as that of other composers.[2] Many young singers who later went on to major careers in opera and the concert hall appeared on the show, including mezzo-soprano Risë Stevens, soprano Nadine Connor, and tenor James Melton.

Phelps, Romberg's co-host, was one of the most public personalities in academia. He was especially known for introducing works by contemporary authors into the curriculum at Yale.[3] As a radio celebrity, the retired academic became the most successful of the many literary scholars who promoted reading on the airwaves and on the lecture circuit. In 1939, columnist Lucius Beebe stated that Phelps did more to develop reverence for the written word than did any other living person. Certainly part of this was accomplished through *The Swift Hour*. One year after its inception, it drew more than sixteen percent of the radio audience, making Phelps and Romberg extremely influential in the creation of American taste during the 1930s.[4]

Phelps wrote of his experience with Romberg: "I enjoyed this experience as much as any I have had. Even now, after three years, I am constantly spoken to by strangers, who hear my voice on the train or on the golf course, and ask me if I am not, etc. Not only are these experiences agreeable because of the number of invisible friends one collects, but I have always intensely enjoyed the radio hour in the studio with my singing or playing or performing colleagues. It has always been like a happy family engaged in a fascinating game."[5]

Romberg likewise enjoyed the experience. He called Phelps "Professor" on the air, using the title as a term of endearment and respect. Both men adored murder mysteries and obviously took great pleasure in each other's company.[6] The program included the obligatory advertising for Swift and Company's pork sausages, reminding the listeners to keep their knives cold while cutting sausage.

Romberg returned to the airwaves in the 1940s, hosting the short-lived *An Evening with Sigmund Romberg*. The series, sponsored by Raleigh Cigarettes, began during the summer of 1945 and ran through the late autumn, except for a brief hiatus when Romberg was touring with his orchestra. The weekly half-hour program included ten minutes of talk and twenty minutes of music. It was briefly revived in the summer of 1947.

In the late 1940s Romberg made several guest appearances with the NBC Symphony Orchestra on WNBC's *U.S. Steel Hour*. The programs typically consisted of classical works along with selections or medleys from Romberg's operettas. Typical of Romberg's broadcasts was the one of July 17, 1949.[7] Singers Genevieve Rowe and Donald Johnson joined Romberg and the orchestra in a program that included selections from Otto Nicolai's *The Merry Wives of Windsor*, Johann Strauss's *Emperor Waltzes*, Georges Bizet's "Ouvre ton coeur," and Sergei Rachmaninoff's Prelude in C-Sharp Minor. Selections from *The Student Prince*, *The Desert Song*, and *The New Moon*, along with the song "Faithfully Yours" and a medley of other Romberg tunes, completed the hour-long broadcast. In this program, Romberg himself endorsed the trilogy of 1920s operettas that was the cornerstone of his reputation.

On Tour and in the Recording Studio

In addition to his various broadcasting activities, Romberg toured extensively throughout the United States with an orchestra, soloists, and sometimes a chorus. Billed as "An Evening with Sigmund Romberg," these concerts were immensely popular with audiences and critics. Romberg organized his first tour in early 1940 with a modest series of six shows in different cities. By 1944 the endeavor had grown to 277 performances in 128 cities. Between January 1943 and May 1949 the concerts grossed $2,420,000, making the enterprise an extremely lucrative one.[8] Audiences adored the unashamedly sentimental and nostalgic affairs. For each tour Romberg usually engaged an orchestra of forty-five or fifty players and a handful of vocal soloists. Don Walker, who had worked with Romberg as an orchestrator since 1935 (on *May Wine*), provided the musical arrangements.

A typical program included a light overture (by a composer such as Offenbach or Nicolai), opera excerpts, and popular classics in the first half, and musical theater numbers in the second. The concluding segment featured Romberg's music.

Curiously, Romberg arranged the orchestra sideways across the stage and conducted from the side. This created visual problems for the audience, since many of them could see Romberg only when he entered or exited the stage. As far as the sound was concerned, it caused a distracting echo.[9] Romberg apparently chose this arrangement so that he could watch the response of the audience. His conducting gestures could be histrionic and often humorous, but this just led to further goodwill between Romberg and his audience.

While on tour, Romberg was frequently asked which he preferred: conducting or composing. His reply was consistent: "I can't tell. One complements the other. Once music is created, it must be heard to survive."[10]

Romberg made several recordings with his orchestra for RCA Victor. Some releases featured Romberg's music only, while others included music by several other composers as well. Many of the soloists featured on his tours were also engaged for the recordings. Don Walker's orchestrations are rich and string-dominated, following standard practices of the 1940s. While the recordings are useful historical documents as to how Romberg interpreted his own music, the vocal styles are often closer to radio-style crooning than to the legitimate singing that characterized 1920s operetta. (Some of these historic recordings have been reissued on the Naxos label. See appendix C for

Advertisement for "An Evening with Sigmund Romberg." Author's collection.

bibliographical information and contents of CD re-issues of historic Romberg performances.)

The Railroad Hour and Studio Recordings

As discussed in the previous chapter, the film versions of Romberg's operettas are the means through which the works are best known. But film was not the only technology used to disseminate Romberg's music, for radio and studio recordings were also very important.

The most important radio series for Romberg's operettas was *The Rail-*

road Hour, sponsored by the Association of American Railroads. Gordon MacRae hosted and starred in the series that was broadcast weekly from 1948 to 1954.[11] Broadcasts began as forty-five-minute programs, and were truncated to thirty-minute ones within a year of the series' inception. Noted choral conductor Norman Luboff and arranger Carmen Dragon were involved with aspects of musical production. Romberg's operettas were frequent choices for the program. (See appendix B for a list of *Railroad Hour* programs that featured Romberg operettas.) *The Railroad Hour* brought Romberg's music to millions across the United States.

The proliferation of studio recordings of Romberg operettas during the mid-century attest to the popularity of the music and the public's desire to hear it. Many leading singers of the era went into the studios to record Romberg's best-known songs, all of which were given new orchestrations. (See the discography for a list of these recordings available on CD as of 2006.) For instance, Robert Rounseville and Dorothy Kirsten recorded *The Student Prince* for Columbia in 1952, and Jan Peerce and Roberta Peters followed suit in 1963. Gordon MacRae recorded all three of Romberg's major shows: *The Student Prince* (in which Karl Franz became a baritone), *The Desert Song* (film soundtrack), and *The New Moon* (with Dorothy Kirsten). *Treasury of Great Operettas*, the famous boxed set issued by *Reader's Digest* in the 1960s, includes four Romberg operettas, *The Desert Song, Blossom Time, The Student Prince,* and *The New Moon*. Anna Moffo sings the female lead in each, and Lehman Engel conducted an orchestra and chorus in grandiose arrangements by Henri René.[12]

Revivals

There is no substitute for live performance, and revivals of Romberg shows are a constituent, though problematic, part of the composer's legacy. Numerous issues arise when mounting revivals of operettas, including what to do with a libretto that includes contemporary references as the basis for much of its humor, and whether or not to alter lyrics, orchestrations, staging, and other aspects of the production. While these factors affect performances today, the temporal distance from the 1920s allows them to be staged as period pieces much more effectively than could be done in the 1940s and 1950s, when the operettas acquired their reputations as being outdated. "Outdated" in the 1940s and 1950s for musical theater was an unfavorable place to be; however, in the early twenty-first century, this attitude has changed. The quest for historicity evident in Tommy Krasker's reconstructions of Gershwin musicals, the complete *Show Boat* recording from 1988 conducted by John McGlinn, and new recordings of Broadway music from the 1920s and 1930s by singers such as Mandy Patinkin, Jerry Hadley, Dawn Upshaw, Audra McDonald, and Lesley Garrett shows a resurgence of interest in pre-Rodgers-and-Hammerstein musical theater.

During the 1930s and 1940s, New York revivals seemed far less popular with critics, at least in part because they were still so close in time to the original productions. The reception of two revivals of *The Desert Song* in Boston, the first in 1937 and the second in 1945, confirm this assertion. The Federal Theatre Music Project sponsored the production that opened on May 3, 1937, about which Elinor Hughes, writing for the *Boston Herald*, complained that the book was old-fashioned and that topical themes quickly recede. But regarding the musical score, she called it "still fresh, melodious and stirring despite multitudinous repetitions over the radio."[13] In 1945, a reviewer for the same paper wrote of the Oscar Hammerstein–produced revival: "[It] is faithful to the original operetta, which in many ways is a mistake. Theater audiences have grown up since 'The Desert Song' was first produced 19 years ago. The story . . . is decidedly ludicrous today. The humor, too, is of the burlesque variety, with an ineffectual little comedian being intimidated by statuesque blondes."[14]

Similarly, a revival of *The New Moon* at Carnegie Hall in August 1942 received mixed reviews. Many critics found the performance wanting and plagued by poor singing and inadequate rehearsals, but it was the book that was repeatedly condemned. Remarks such as "the book was a bore 14 years ago and age has definitely not improved it" and, after praise for the music, "but all this isn't enough to fit the antiquated libretto to the 1942 taste" were typical.[15]

In addition to East Coast productions, touring companies were immensely popular and plentiful, and local productions, both professional and amateur, abounded. These of course varied greatly in terms of quality, but they nonetheless proved the popularity of the works because performers and audiences kept them alive.

Quantity rather than quality characterized most of the tours of *Blossom Time* and *The Student Prince* that visited nearly every major American theatrical town annually until the 1940s.[16] Production standards were generally low, sets were tattered, and the singing, especially that of secondary characters and the chorus, was often inadequate. In a marketing ploy, J. J. Shubert often ran the tours for a week in New York so that he could advertise the productions as "Direct from Broadway!" The huge number of tours led to the quip that lost *Blossom Time* companies were still touring somewhere in the Midwest.

Romberg operettas were the initial productions at two significant musical venues in their respective cities: the Music Hall at Fair Park in Dallas, Texas, and Starlight Theatre in Kansas City, Missouri. On October 10, 1925, *The Student Prince* opened the Music Hall at Fair Park. Here was a work less than one year old that was chosen to open a new performance hall. When Starlight Theatre, an outdoor amphitheater in Kansas City's Swope Park, opened its doors for the first time on June 25, 1951, it was to the strains of *The Desert Song*. Romberg himself was on hand to conduct the overture; surely no one expected his untimely death five months later.[17]

The Civic Light Opera movement, which blossomed in the middle part of the twentieth century, also did a great deal to establish Romberg's legacy. The goal of these community-based groups was to stage operettas and light operatic fare in grand style. While professional stars were occasionally engaged for lead roles, most performers were local singers. Romberg's operettas, especially *The Student Prince, The Desert Song,* and *The New Moon,* were favorites with these companies.

By the 1970s, the patina of time had made the old-fashionedness of operetta something to be admired rather than ridiculed, though the latter activity certainly continued. The reviewer for the *Christian Science Monitor* wrote about a revival of *The Desert Song* in 1973, "It is equally full of melody and nonsense, which for viewers today add up to a kind of nostalgia for innocence lost." The passing of time had made the work a period piece. He continued, describing the lead female actress: "Chris Callan as Margot is all that a '20's musical heroine should be—pretty, forthright, and romantically adventurous—a glistening portrayal which she conveys with visual and aural fidelity."[18]

The 1973 Broadway revival of the same operetta at the Uris Theatre had some inherent conceptual problems, including a papier mâché campfire center stage and a six-member French army storming a ten-member Riff band. Despite these visual shortcomings in the production, the music received praise. Walter Kerr wrote about Romberg's tunes: "[T]hey are marvels of their kind, and if you doubt it for a moment then just try an extended second-act passage in which Michael Kermoyan, as the turbaned, white-bearded patriarch of the Riffs, begins to roll his strong bass-baritone upward over the faintly Mideast inflections of 'Let Love Go,' swelling and then dipping in a tidal course that is hypnotic. . . . By the time the eight or nine minutes has soared to its fast blackout, you do know what audiences of 1926 responded to in 1926."[19]

A *Desert Song* production by The Light Opera of Manhattan in November 1980 received good reviews in the *New York Times*. Raymond Ericson called the version "an absolute charmer" and referred to the seriousness of purpose in the revival, "with the result that one accepts the foolishness of the plot and the unsophistication of the lyrics with amused affection. The production has a period quality to match the material."[20] When one views the works as period pieces, they succeed and entertain.

Romberg operettas continue to grace stages nationwide, though not in full-fledged Broadway revivals, unlike many "Golden Age" classics such as *Guys and Dolls* (1992), *Show Boat* (1994), *Annie Get Your Gun* (1999), and several Rodgers and Hammerstein shows, including *Carousel* (1994) and *Oklahoma!* (2002). The New York City Opera, however, mounted productions of *The Student Prince*, *The Desert Song*, and *The New Moon* in the 1980s; their version of *The New Moon* with Richard White (one of the foremost Romberg singers of the late twentieth century), Leigh Munro, and Michael Cousins appeared on PBS's *Great Performances* in 1989. Paper Mill Playhouse in Millburn, New Jersey, mounted a production of *The New Moon* in 1983, followed by one of *The Desert Song* in 1984, and *The New Moon* made it to New York's City Center Encores! series in 2003 as part of the esteemed concert-musical series' tenth anniversary season. It is a combination of the types of singers required for operettas, their nonmodernist plots, and their age that have mitigated against their revival on Broadway. Encores!'s production turned these parameters to its advantage by casting opera baritone Rodney Gilfry as Robert Misson and by encasing the stage in a double row of gilt frames, one at the front and the other at the back, giving the stage the look of a museum *tableau vivant*.

Outside the metropolitan New York area, Romberg's works have found new lives on summer opera programs. Central City Opera in Colorado, Utah Festival Opera, Ohio Light Opera, and Musical Theatre Wichita (Kansas) are just a few of the companies that have included Romberg works on their performance calendars in the early twenty-first century.

Periodicity is the key to successful Romberg revivals. The genre's charm is now found in its totality rather than in just its music. The works themselves have become symbols of nostalgia; they are relics from the Roaring Twenties, a time long ago that has been re-created not as it was but as it should have been, full of glamour, panache, and the dual tines of modernism and nostalgia. In the 1920s, it was the operetta plots that reconstructed the past, pointing back to the nineteenth century; in the early twenty-first century, it is the works themselves that look backward to the time of their creation and reflect a time that lives only in memory.

John Hanson and British Revivals

Romberg operettas appeared regularly in Britain. Like many American musical theater works, they transferred to London within years of their original Broadway productions. When it came to revivals, actor John Hanson (1922–1998) did more for Romberg's popularity than did any other individual. He made it a point to cultivate the so-called lost audience, which he described as "middle-aged or elderly women, the 'Aunt Ednas' of the theatre."[21]

Hanson's most famous role was Red Shadow/Pierre, his identification with the part so close that he entitled his autobiography *Me and My Red Shadow*.[22] Hanson starred in productions of *The Desert Song* at the Opera House in Manchester in 1954 and 1957. His 1967 revival of *The Desert Song* played for 433 performances, one more than during the operetta's initial London run.

He also popularized *The Student Prince*, a show that did not fare well in its first British production in the 1920s. He first appeared in a touring production of *The Student Prince* that opened in Brighton in February 1959. The audience was large and enthusiastic, and Hanson's rendition of "Serenade," according to him, stopped the show.[23] The tour also played in Chiswick, Hanley, Sheffield, Liverpool, Glasgow, Dundee, and Southampton. It was the largest grossing show of the year for Moss Empires, the sponsors of the production. Hanson continued to appear in productions of the show throughout the 1960s and 1970s.

Romberg in Europe: Paris, Osijek, and Heidelberg

Romberg's works also enjoyed tremendous popularity in continental Europe. The French have been drawn to the exotic spectacle of several of his works, while in Osijek, Croatia, where Romberg was a student, the citizens pay homage to the composer with an annual festival. And with *The Student Prince* being set in Heidelberg, how could the famous university town not celebrate the operetta that made it a recognizable name to American tourists?

During the early 1930s, Parisian stages were filled with shows imported from Vienna, Berlin, Budapest, New York, and London. Romberg's works fit comfortably into this scenario. *The Desert Song* appeared in Paris as *Le Chant du désert* in 1929 and was even recorded twice in its French version.[24] *The New Moon* became *Robert le Pirate* (1930), but it was the Peruvian-set *Nina Rosa* (1932) with its far-flung exotic spectacle that was Romberg's biggest success in France.

People in Osijek honored their former resident through "Rombergove svečanosti" ("Romberg Evenings") during the 1990s. (Romberg lived there from 1897 to 1901.) The festival included screenings of film versions of Romberg operettas and performances of songs by Romberg. As part of the festival activities in 1995, on November 9, the anniversary of Romberg's death, the organizers mounted a plaque on the house where Romberg lived for two years. The inscription reads, in translation, "The unique spirit of Osijek, in accordance with the musical sounds of the world, inspired Sigmund Romberg for two years. Through this inspiration, Romberg rewarded the world with hundreds of eternal melodies."

Since *The Student Prince* is set in Heidelberg, it was inevitable that the operetta would be produced in the German city. Since 1974, the fiftieth anniversary of the premiere of *The Student Prince*, Romberg's operetta has been featured every year at the Heidelberger Schlossfestspiele (Heidelberg Castle Festival). It is performed in English for American tourists and has been immensely popular.[25]

A new Heidelberg production by Ingo Waszerka opened in 2001. The director adhered to the original concept, and chose not to modernize it. As she said in an interview, "The material can be transferred only by the spectators into today, mental and emotional. On the stage it plays in the past." Waszerka explained that this aspect was fundamental in the production's popularity with American audiences for whom Heidelberg Castle was the epitome of Old Europe, a part of history that did not exist in America. The operetta and its setting in the Castle brought a longing for romance to its foreign audience.[26]

Productions in Australia and New Zealand

Romberg operettas were popular fare in Australia and New Zealand soon after their premieres in New York.[27] J. C. Williamson, J. J. Shubert's counterpart in Australia, managed the productions. *Maytime*, performed by the Royal Comic Opera Company, played at various locales in Australia and New Zealand between 1919 and 1921, ending its run at Her Majesty's Theatre in Sydney. The Royal Comic Opera Company also introduced *The Student Prince* at His Majesty's Theatre in Melbourne on November 5, 1927, with James Liddy and Beppie de Vries in the lead roles. Like *Maytime*, *The Student Prince* toured Australia and New Zealand for several years.

The Desert Song was the most popular Romberg operetta in Australia. The work's Australian premiere took place at His Majesty's Theatre in Melbourne on September 15, 1928, with Lance Fairfax and Marie Bremner in the lead roles. As was typical, the production then toured both Australia and New Zealand. Such was the popularity of *The Desert Song* that a second company opened in Tasmania on March 30, 1929, the same day the "number 1" company opened in Sydney, its second port of call. Years later, Robert Halliday, star of the original New York production, traveled to Melbourne to reprise his role in an eight-performance revival that began on December 4, 1937, at His Majesty's Theatre.

The New Moon had its Australian debut at Her Majesty's Theatre in Sydney on January 4, 1930, with Lance Fairfax and Marie Bremner, stars of the original Australian production of *The Desert Song*, in the lead roles. Like its predecessors, *The New Moon* toured in Australia and New Zealand, but its total run lasted only twenty-two months, substantially less than those of its predecessors. Australians were drawn more to Morocco and Germany than to colonial Louisiana.

Jazz Standards

The New Moon's "Lover, Come Back to Me" and "Softly, As in a Morning Sunrise" have both become standards in the jazz repertory. Max Morath lists "Lover, Come Back to Me" in *The NPR Curious Listener's Guide to Popular Standards*, even though he made a disclaimer that operetta composers Romberg, Friml, and Herbert would not be included in the songwriter section. The importance of the tune overrode its origins. "Lover, Come Back to Me" has been used to showcase the talents of legendary jazz singers Mildred

Bailey, Billie Holiday, and Ella Fitzgerald. Louis Armstrong, Charlie Parker, Dizzy Gillespie, Lester Young, Earl Hines, Bud Powell, Art Tatum, Oscar Peterson, and the Dave Brubeck Quartet are among those to have recorded the classic tune. Bandleaders Harry James, Artie Shaw, and Luther Henderson each recorded it with their orchestras, and since 1970 renditions have appeared by artists as diverse as Rahsaan Roland Kirk, John Coltrane, Carl Fontana, Stéphane Grappelli, and the Concord All-Stars.[28]

"Softly, As in a Morning Sunrise" is another favorite of jazz performers and audiences. In his textbook *Jazz Arranging and Orchestration*, Leslie M. Sabina includes the tune as one of his arrangements for analysis, placing it firmly in the jazz canon. Among the many renditions are those by saxophonists John Coltrane, Sonny Rollins, Buddy Tate, and Stan Getz, as well as ones by the Modern Jazz Quartet, the Sonny Clark Trio, and the Toshiko Trio. The tune is the title of albums by the Eric Dolphy Quartet and the Junior Mance Trio. Vocal versions exist from singers ranging from crooner Tony Bennett and the McPartlands to Surinam-born Denise Jannah and Polish singer Marianna Wróblewska.[29]

Appropriations, Allusions, and Parodies

As with any popular songs, those by Romberg have occasionally been borrowed for uses outside of their original theatrical contexts. The rousing nature of his marches has led them to being appropriated for patriotic purposes during the Second World War, with new lyrics added to the familiar melodies. "Your Land and My Land" from *My Maryland* had a new set of lyrics appended to it for the "Patriotic Version" in 1941. Similarly, a "U.S. Navy Version" of "Stouthearted Men" appeared in 1943.

One of the most intriguing appropriations of "Stouthearted Men" is that by the Karlakór Reykjavíkur (Reykjavik Male Choir). "Hraustir menn," the song's title in Icelandic, is one of the chorus's most popular numbers and appears as the title for their 1999 compilation CD as well as the book celebrating the ensemble's fiftieth anniversary.[30] The song is extremely popular in Iceland, largely due to the Karlakór Reykjavíkur's performances featuring soloist Gudmundur Jónsson. Jakob Jóhannesson Smári's translated lyrics capture the spirit of Hammerstein's original.

Romberg's music has returned to Broadway and television in compilation programs focused on artists other than Romberg. To date, an all-Romberg revue has yet to make it to Broadway, although baritone Michael

McFarlane traveled with a program entitled *Romberg Remembered* on the Community Concert circuit in the 1980s. "Stouthearted Men" was a featured number in *Dancin'* (1978), directed and choreographed by Bob Fosse, and Peabo Bryson and Audra McDonald performed an operetta medley that included "Romance," "Lover, Come Back to Me," "One Kiss," and "The Desert Song" in the 1995 television special *Some Enchanted Evening: Celebrating Oscar Hammerstein II*.

Just as Romberg's revues from the 1910s looked to popular culture for inspiration, so too did Broadway figures after Romberg look to the operetta master for source material. *Seven Lively Arts* (1944), with a score by Cole Porter and a ballet by Igor Stravinsky, included a scene in which Bert Lahr, as a drunk Lord Nelson, sang "Drink," a parody of the "Drinking Song" from *The Student Prince*. Its lyric included the line, "Drink to Nelson Eddy before you faint / And here's to J. J. Shubert, our patron saint."[31] Likewise, Jerry Bock and Sheldon Harnick referred to the popularity of outdoor productions of Romberg operettas in their song "Summer Is" from *The Body Beautiful* (1958) in the couplet "Summer is Sigmund Romberg / In a music tent."

Rick Besoyan created a parody of *The Student Prince* in *The Student Gypsy, or the Prince of Liederkrantz* (September 30, 1963, 54th Street), a show that played for a mere sixteen performances. Besoyan's more famous parody of *Rose Marie*, *Little Mary Sunshine* (1959) was much more successful and still enjoys revivals. *The Student Gypsy* included songs with endearing titles such as "Singspielia," "The Grenadier's Marching Song," "Kiss Me," "Seventh Heaven Waltz," "The Gypsy Violin and I," "Gypsy of Love," and, of course, "The Drinking Song." Waltzes, marches, and Magyar themes, identifiable stereotypes of Ruritanian operetta, fill the score.

Stephen Banfield suggests Romberg influences in two songs from the film (and subsequent stage musical) *Beauty and the Beast* (1991; music by Alan Menken, lyrics by Howard Ashman). He identifies "The Mob Song" as a cinematic re-creation of Nelson Eddy's nocturnal march "Stouthearted Men" in the 1940 film of *The New Moon*, while "Gaston" pays tribute to "Drinking Song" from *The Student Prince*.[32]

References to Romberg and his style have also appeared in several television programs. One of the most telling is "The Operetta" episode of *I Love Lucy*, first broadcast on October 13, 1952, where Lucy and Ethel conspire to create the operetta *The Pleasant Peasant*.[33] When the need arises to create a production for the Wednesday Afternoon Fine Arts League, Lucy refers to herself and Ethel as "Ethel Romberg and Lucy Friml"—an overt homage to the major proponents of the genre.

A Romberg reference was featured in the CBS television series M*A*S*H in the episode "Oh, How We Danced," first broadcast on February 23, 1981. In the story line, the staff is looking for a harmonica for a patient when Corporal Klinger remarks, "He'll be playing 'Desert Song.'" The statement has several levels of meaning. First, Maxwell Q. Klinger is of Lebanese heritage and makes frequent references to the desert domain of his ancestors. Second, the backdrop of the television series is a semiarid landscape. Third, considering the popularity of *The Desert Song* in the 1950s, Americans serving in Korea at the time would have been familiar with the operetta. The desert domain common to the operetta, Klinger, and Korea coalesce in the reference.

Romberg allusions still appear in the early twenty-first century, more than a half century after the composer's death. One of the most entertaining is Mark Russell's "Fainthearted Wimps" (2002), a lampooning of the Democratic Party to the music of "Stouthearted Men" with a corruption of Hammerstein's lyrics.[34] Another example that brings a smile to one's face is Aquafina's television commercial from early 2005. The bottled-water company used the "Drinking Song" to promote drinking not beer but water. Revelers in a German beer garden swing their water glasses to Romberg's boisterous refrain.

EPILOGUE

Romberg's Influence on the American Musical Theater

As a central figure in the metamorphosis of operetta from a European-based genre to its American incarnation, Sigmund Romberg made contributions to the American musical theater that are indeed significant. He wrote music for some of the finest songs of the first half of the twentieth century, and his waltzes and marches, especially the ones for large male choruses, helped define American musical theater during the 1920s. Romberg codified two different formulas for a Broadway operetta. The first, developed with the Shuberts, is centered on nostalgia: *Maytime*, *Blossom Time*, and *The Student Prince* are the shows that established Romberg's place as a leading Broadway composer. A recurring waltz duet for the romantic leads, who are not together at the final curtain, was the centerpiece of the score. The second, developed with Oscar Hammerstein 2nd, focused on romance and heroism. In shows such as *The Desert Song* and *The New Moon*, glorious waltz duets are complemented by duple-meter love songs. Love and justice prevail in these canonic works, for the romantic leads are together at the end. Both paradigms have important legacies on Broadway.

Nostalgia, the Waltz, and Unhappy Endings

Nostalgia permeates Romberg's output, and is especially strong in his early operettas. In works such as *The Blue Paradise* and *Maytime*, Romberg portrayed nostalgia musically through a strong emphasis on the waltz. In the printed program for his 1947 Transcontinental Tour, Romberg included a list entitled "My Favorite Waltzes." The six numbers, with incipits in Romberg's own hand, are 1) "Deep in My Heart, Dear" from *The Student Prince*; 2) "One Kiss" from *The New Moon*; 3) "The Desert Song" from *The Desert Song*; 4) "Silver Moon" from *My Maryland*; 5) "Faithfully Yours"; and 6) "You Will Remember Vienna" from *Viennese Nights*. These were certainly among Romberg's favorite waltzes, but space limitations could likely have kept the list from being larger.

Equating the waltz with nostalgia began with the establishment of the waltz as an aural icon of Vienna. After the First World War, with the end of the Habsburg monarchy and the resulting cataclysmic changes for its capital, the waltz, the symbol of the city, began to embody a sense of memory for what had been lost. Maurice Ravel's *La valse* (1920), originally entitled *Wien*, was a musical depiction of the collapse of Vienna and its culture. Just as the city decayed from its core, the waltz's demise erupts from the low sounds of the orchestra: the string basses, the cellos, and the bassoons. Arnold Schoenberg's first twelve-tone piece was a waltz, the last movement of his Suite for Piano, op. 23 (1923). Here, the waltz (Vienna) is re-created in new terms—it is not the same as it was, nor should it be. Romberg's "You Will Remember Vienna" from *Viennese Nights* (1930), by contrast, calls for the city to be remembered as it was. Romberg and Hammerstein blissfully ignore any of the city's faults and remember only its beauty.

In American musical culture of the 1950s, the waltz was a strong reminder of the Viennese musical heritage. James Francis Cooke wrote an article for *Etude* in which he exalted the dance in over-romanticized imagery:

> One does not have to be in Vienna more than a few hours to comprehend the mysteries of the Viennese Waltz—those irresistible things of Lanner, Strauss, Lehár and a score of writers. Like the champagnes of Epinay, the Viennese waltz calls for special soil. It demands the sunlight and the moonlight of Viennese life. This sweet languor, mixed with the effervescent sparkle, is bottled at its best only on the hillsides of Grinzing and other Viennese environs. Just as marching marines shout the sprit of "Sousa," so does Grinzing sing "Strauss."
>
> Ah, waltzes of dear old Vienna—rhapsodies of Terpsichore! Who can resist your ingratiating caresses? Fresh as the flower-starred meadows of June, undulating as a sea of aspen leaves, warm as the suns of the Côte d'azur,

> sweet as the song of the thrush, intoxicating as the Alpine dawn . . . all done in the workshop of dreams, the only real land of immortality. You make the aged young and bring long life to youth. Hail to the waltzes of Vienna![1]

Cooke's subjective analysis of the core essence of the Viennese waltz continues the same romance and nostalgia that is present in Romberg's operetta waltzes.

It was not just memories of Vienna, but memories in general that began to be associated with the waltz. Hence, the dance was used as a means to depict nostalgia. Romberg employed it as a conduit for farewell and sadness as early as 1915: the waltz "Auf Wiedersehn" from *The Blue Paradise* suggests the nostalgia and memory that will emerge after farewells have been said (or sung). This sense of memory is further endorsed in "Mother" from *Her Soldier Boy* (1916) and "Will You Remember" from *Maytime* (1917). Multigenerational love stories such as those in *Maytime* and *Melody*, where the same actors portray their own descendents, are dramatic embodiments of the waltz's theatrical ability to grant immortality to its partakers—love survives through the generations because of the waltz.

The waltz as a conduit for memory and a metaphor for the inability to reclaim the past continued in the second half of the twentieth century. "Try to Remember" from *The Fantasticks* (1960, music by Harvey Schmidt, book and lyrics by Tom Jones) and "One More Kiss" from Stephen Sondheim's *Follies* (1971) are two examples of this treatment. In *Follies*, a score that emulates earlier styles in musical theater, the Viennese waltz "One More Kiss" is a nostalgic song about the inevitable fading away of everything and the passing of a time that cannot be recaptured. Furthermore, the entire score and concept of Sondheim's *A Little Night Music* (1973) continues this powerful symbolism attached to the waltz.

The waltz does not always look backward to what may be thought to have been a better time. In a more general sense, the waltz can portray an existence better than reality itself. This is particularly evident in the work of Rodgers and Hammerstein. Hammerstein's lyrics for "The Desert Song" or "One Kiss" paved the way for such wishful waltzes as "Out of My Dreams" *(Oklahoma!)* and "Hello, Young Lovers" *(The King and I).* "The Carousel in the Park," the principal waltz in *Up in Central Park*, also functions in this type of dramatic context, for Rosie sings it as a vision of the future. In each of these waltzes the lyrics point toward making the world a better place and encourage its inhabitants to find true happiness.

The early Romberg operettas also show the dramatic possibilities inherent in stories where love does not succeed. *Maytime, Blossom Time,* and *The Student Prince* all have bittersweet, if not unhappy, endings. Despite this, they were among the most popular shows of the era. Many Broadway musicals have followed this plan, including Rodgers and Hammerstein's *Carousel* (1945) and *South Pacific* (1949, for Joe and Liat). The work of Stephen Sondheim likewise is filled with tales of ill-fated love: *A Little Night Music* (1973), *Sunday in the Park with George* (1984), *Into the Woods* (1987), and *Passion* (1994) are four prominent examples.

The Duple-Meter Love Song, the Male Chorus, the Heroic March, and Happy Endings

Just as Romberg's Shubert-produced operettas have their legacy, so do those on which he worked with Oscar Hammerstein, principally *The Desert Song* and *The New Moon*. In these works, duple-meter love songs appear alongside the waltzes, and the male chorus, already present in *Blossom Time* and *The Student Prince*, takes on a new dramatic role singing heroic marches with socially relevant themes that draws its members together around a common cause. Furthermore, these shows are distinguished from their famous predecessors in the Romberg canon by having happy endings—love and justice are victorious.

Duple-meter love ballads are certainly plentiful in the history of the Broadway musical and could even be said to dominate it at mid-century. Consider, for example, Rodgers and Hammerstein's "If I Loved You" from *Carousel* and "Younger than Springtime" from *South Pacific*, or "If I Were a Bell" and "I've Never Been in Love Before" from Frank Loesser's *Guys and Dolls* (1950), among many others. Songs such as "One Alone" and "Lover, Come Back to Me" were important predecessors to these beloved songs.

But it is the heroic male chorus singing their thundering marches that truly are the distinguishing features of these shows. The male chorus continued in Rodgers and Hammerstein shows with boisterous songs such as "The Farmer and the Cowman" in *Oklahoma!*, "Blow High, Blow Low" in *Carousel*, and "There Ain't Nothin' Like a Dame" and "Bloody Mary" in *South Pacific* (1949). Frank Loesser used it for "Luck Be a Lady Tonight" and "Sit Down, You're Rockin' the Boat" in *Guys and Dolls*, and Leonard Bernstein followed suit in "Cool" and "Gee, Officer Krupke" from *West Side Story* (1957). *Guys and Dolls* even includes a direct reference to Romberg's male choruses when the police officer tells the gamblers, who are all innocently standing in a line, that they look like "the male chorus from *Blossom Time*," even though *Blossom Time* is not especially known for its male chorus.[2]

Foster Hirsch cites the influence of the Romberg male choral numbers in Kurt Weill and Alan Jay Lerner's *Love Life* (1948) in the number "Ho, Billy O!" which opens the second act. In the song, sixteen singers boast a litany of modern ailments that interfere with love.[3] The catalogue of woes binds the men together, fulfilling the same function as the male chorus numbers in Romberg shows.

Romberg was a firm believer in human rights, and the music he wrote for lyrics that endorsed these views, most notably "Stouthearted Men," holds an esteemed place in the pantheon of musical theater songs. Similar to other songs that call for overcoming social ills, including "The Internationale" and "We Shall Overcome," these musical theater numbers call for all to join in the quest for a better humanity. Romberg advocated human rights not through speeches and public endorsements but rather through writing powerful music. Romberg's "songs of social injustice" are examples of a dramatic song type that others in the English-language musical theater world emulated, including Rodgers and Hammerstein, Claude-Michel Schönberg, Stephen Sondheim, and John Kander. Rodgers and Hammerstein's poignant "You've Got to Be Carefully Taught" from *South Pacific* is one of the most famous examples of this type of song.

In the 1980s and 1990s, songs of social injustice infused many musical theater works.[4] The spirit of "Stouthearted Men" lives on in numbers such as "Do You Hear the People Sing?" from *Les Misérables* (Claude-Michel Schönberg, Alain Boublil, and Herbert Kretzmer, 1985) and "The Day After That" from *Kiss of the Spider Woman* (John Kander and Fred Ebb, 1992). A turnabout version appeared in Sondheim's *Assassins* (1991) in "Another National Anthem," a song sung by the have-nots of society, the victims of social injustice. These marches are all Romberg's progeny.

On the page opposite Romberg's list of his favorite waltzes in the 1947 tour program is a list of six of his favorite marches, again with incipits. The marches include: 1) "The Riff Song" from *The Desert Song*; 2) "Stouthearted Men" from *The New Moon*; 3) "Give Me a Roll on a Drum" from *Melody*; 4) "Students Marching Song" from *The Student Prince*; 5) "Your Land and My Land" from *My Maryland*; and 6) "Military Marching Song" from *The Desert Song*.[5]

Romberg playing the piano, Kansas City, Missouri, June 1951, months before his death in November. Used by permission of the University of Missouri–Kansas City Libraries, Special Collections Department.

A happy ending is a feature of *The Desert Song* and *The New Moon* (in addition to *Nina Rosa*, *May Wine*, and *Up in Central Park*, among others), but unfortunately Romberg's career did not end on such a high note. His last completed show, *My Romance*, was a failure and the posthumous *The Girl in Pink Tights* a curiosity. Fortunately, these shows did not tarnish Romberg's reputation as a composer of beautiful songs, as the MGM biopic *Deep in My Heart* so ably proves.

A journey through his career reveals the richness of his creative achievement. It is a fascinating trek. A forbidden love that is realized only two generations later in *Maytime*, a composer who dies of a broken heart at the end of *Blossom Time*, and the royal who cannot be with the commoner he loves in *The Student Prince*: these are the plots that inspired the immortal waltzes "Will You Remember," "Song of Love," and "Deep in My Heart, Dear." Likewise, the mystique of the desert and a masked hero captivated audiences in *The Desert Song*, with its title waltz, "Romance," and "One Alone." Then, the tale of two rival aristocrats who become the leaders of a democracy is at the heart of *The New Moon*. The operetta includes the famous songs "Wanting You," "Lover, Come Back to Me," and "Softly, As in a Morning Sunrise" in addition to the riveting march "Stouthearted Men." Not to be forgotten is the ballad-filled show of Romberg's final decade, *Up in Central Park*, with its stunning evocations of Americana and its central duet, "Close as Pages in a Book."

When Romberg died of a cerebral hemorrhage on November 9, 1951, at age 64, in his hotel room at the Ritz Towers in New York City, the world lost a great composer and humanitarian. Services were held on November 11 at the Frank E. Campbell Funeral Home in New York. Otto Harbach, then president of the American Society of Composers, Authors, and Publishers, delivered the eulogy, in which he referred to the composer as one of "the great triumvirate," which also included Jerome Kern and Victor Herbert. L. P. Cookingham, city manager of Kansas City, Missouri, in condolences he sent to Romberg's widow, wrote, "[T]he world has lost a great composer. He will live forever in the greatness of his music."[6] Cookingham was certainly correct in his assessment, for Romberg's "melodies immortal" have delighted audiences since 1914 and their luster continues to shine.

Appendix A: Work List

BROADWAY PRODUCTIONS

Romberg contributed musical material, either song(s) or the entire score, for the following Broadway musicals. For detailed information on the shows, including the length of their runs, collaborators, and musical numbers, see Richard C. Norton, *A Chronology of American Musical Theater*, 3 vols. (New York: Oxford University Press, 2002). For additional details on shows that involved Oscar Hammerstein 2nd as lyricist or librettist, see Stanley Green, ed., *Rodgers and Hammerstein Fact Book* (New York: Lynn Farnol Group, 1980). For song listings for films, see Ken Bloom, *Hollywood Song: The Complete Film & Musical Companion*, 3 vols. (New York: Facts on File, 1995.)

The Whirl of the World, January 10, 1914, Winter Garden, 161 performances
The Midnight Girl, February 23, 1914, 44th Street, 104 performances
The Passing Show of 1914, June 10, 1914, Winter Garden, 133 performances
Dancing Around, October 10, 1914, Winter Garden, 145 performances
Maid in America, February 18, 1915, Winter Garden, 108 performances
Hands Up, July 22, 1915, 44th Street, 52 performances
The Blue Paradise, August 5, 1915, Casino, 356 performances
A World of Pleasure, October 14, 1915, Winter Garden, 116 performances
Ruggles of Red Gap, December 25, 1915, Fulton, 33 performances
Robinson Crusoe, Jr., February 17, 1916, Winter Garden, 139 performances
The Passing Show of 1916, June 22, 1916, Winter Garden, 140 performances
The Girl from Brazil, August 30, 1916, 44th Street, 61 performances
The Show of Wonders, October 26, 1916, Winter Garden, 209 performances
Follow Me, November 29, 1916, Casino, 78 performances
Her Soldier Boy, December 6, 1916, Astor, 198 performances
The Passing Show of 1917, April 26, 1917, Winter Garden, 196 performances
My Lady's Glove, June 18, 1917, Lyric, 16 performances
Maytime, August 16, 1917, Shubert, 492 performances
Doing Our Bit, October 18, 1917, Winter Garden, 130 performances

Over the Top, December 1, 1917, 44th Street Roof, 78 performances
Sinbad, February 14, 1918, Winter Garden, 64 performances
The Passing Show of 1918, July 25, 1918, Winter Garden, 142 performances
The Melting of Molly, December 30, 1918, Broadhurst, 88 performances
Monte Cristo, Jr., February 12, 1919, Winter Garden, 254 performances
The Passing Show of 1919, October 23, 1919, Winter Garden, 280 performances
The Magic Melody, November 11, 1919, Shubert, 143 performances
Poor Little Ritz Girl, July 28, 1920, Central, 93 performances
Love Birds, March 15, 1921, Apollo, 103 performances
Blossom Time, September 29, 1921, Ambassador, 516 performances
Bombo, October 6, 1921, Jolson's, 218 performances
The Blushing Bride, February 6, 1922, Park, 144 performances
The Rose of Stamboul, March 7, 1922, Century, 111 performances
Springtime of Youth, October 26, 1922, Broadhurst, 68 performances
The Dancing Girl, January 24, 1923, Winter Garden, 142 performances
Caroline, January 31, 1923, Ambassador, 151 performances
The Passing Show of 1923, June 14, 1923, Winter Garden, 118 performances
Innocent Eyes, May 20, 1924, Winter Garden, 126 performances
The Passing Show of 1924, September 3, 1924, Winter Garden, 106 performances
Artists and Models of 1924, October 15, 1924, Astor, 258 performances
Annie Dear, November 4, 1924, Times Square, 103 performances
The Student Prince in Heidelberg, December 2, 1924, Jolson's, 608 performances
Louie the 14th, March 3, 1925, Cosmopolitan, 319 performances
Artists and Models, Paris Edition, June 24, 1925, Winter Garden, 416 performances
Princess Flavia, November 2, 1925, Century, 152 performances
Cherry Blossoms, March 28, 1927, 44th Street, 56 performances
My Maryland, September 12, 1927, Jolson's, 312 performances
My Princess, October 6, 1927, Shubert, 20 performances
The Love Call, October 24, 1927, Majestic, 88 performances
Rosalie, January 10, 1928, New Amsterdam, 335 performances
The New Moon, September 19, 1928, Imperial, 509 performances
Nina Rosa, September 20, 1930, Majestic, 137 performances
East Wind, October 27, 1931, Manhattan, 23 performances
Melody, February 14, 1933, Casino, 79 performances
May Wine, December 5, 1935, St. James, 213 performances
Forbidden Melody, November 2, 1936, New Amsterdam, 32 performances
Sunny River, December 4, 1941, St. James, 36 performances
Up in Central Park, January 27, 1945, New Century, 504 performances
My Romance, October 19, 1948, Shubert, 95 performances
The Girl in Pink Tights, March 5, 1954, Mark Hellinger, 115 performances

Films

Foolish Wives, 1922, Universal
Viennese Nights, 1930, Warner Brothers and Vitaphone
Children of Dreams, 1931, Warner Brothers
The Night Is Young, 1935, MGM

The Girl of the Golden West, 1938, MGM
Let Freedom Ring, 1939, MGM
Balalaika, 1939, MGM
They Gave Him a Gun, 1939, MGM

Nontheatrical Works (selected list)

American Humoresque (instrumental, solo piano)
"Baby's Asleep" (song)
"Broadcasting Signature" (instrumental)
Concerto for Clarinet and Orchestra (incomplete)
"Crescendo" (instrumental)
"Devil in Disguise" (song)
"Faithfully Yours" (solo piano, song)
Four Sketches for Two Violins, Cello, and Piano
"He Walks with Me" (song)
"I'll Save My Heart" (song)
"I'm in Love with You" (song)
Impromptu in E-flat (solo piano)
"A Leg of Mutton" ("Le Gigot") (solo piano)
"Like a Star in the Night" (song)
March of the Owls (solo piano, band)
"Mine" (song)
"Mist on the Mirror" (song)
"No Use Pretending" (song)
"Off the Shores of Somewhere" (song)
"Omar Khayyam" (solo piano)
"Le Poème" ("The Poem") (solo piano)
"Some Smoke" ("De la fumée") (solo piano)
Suite for Orchestra (partially orchestrated)
"Take Everything but Leave Me You" (song)
"There Is a Rainbow" (song)
"Valse Parfumée" (solo piano)
"Wherever You May Be" (song)
"Zing, Zing, Zoom, Zoom" (song)

Writings

"Can There Be Television Without Music?" *Variety* 177 (January 4, 1950): 99.
"How to Write a Song," *Etude* 68, no. 12 (December 1950): 15.
"A Peep into the Workshop of a Composer," *Theatre Magazine* 48, no. 6 (December 1928): 27, 72, 74.
"Screen Operetta," *Pacific Coast Musician*, May 30, 1930, 16.
"A Short History of American Operetta," in *Music and Dance in California*, ed. José Rodriguez, 88–103. Hollywood: Bureau of Musical Research, 1940.
"So You've Got a Song to Publish," *Notes* 1, no. 4 (September 1944): 7–13.

Appendix B:
Broadcasts of *The Railroad Hour* Featuring Operettas by Romberg

Operettas are listed in alphabetical order.

Broadcast date	Guests	Time	Program no.
Blossom Time			
Jan. 24, 1949	Kenny Baker, Patrice Munsel	44:30	17
Oct. 31, 1949	Kenny Baker, Lucille Norman	28:00	57
Jan. 7, 1952	Scott Douglas, Nadine Conner	26:30	171
The Blue Paradise			
Feb. 16, 1953	Nadine Conner	29:30	229
The Desert Song			
Dec. 27, 1948	Nadine Conner, Sterling Holloway		
	Francis X. Bushman	44:30	13
Dec. 12, 1949	Dorothy Sarnoff	30:00	63
Jan. 21, 1952	Mimi Benzell	29:30	173
East Wind			
Feb. 4, 1952	Mimi Benzell	25:50	175
Maytime			
Oct. 6, 1952	Dorothy Kirsten	30:00	210
Feb. 1, 1954	Nadine Conner	30:00	279
My Maryland			
May 26, 1952	Raymond Burr, Virginia Grey, Dorothy Kirsten, John Shay	30:00	191

My Romance
Jan. 5, 1953   E. Conner   30:00   223

The New Moon
Nov. 29, 1948   Nadine Conner, Rudy Valle   —   9
Oct. 10, 1949   Louise Massey   30:00   54
Jan. 29, 1951   Dorothy Kirsten   30:00   122
June 21, 1954   Lucille Norman   30:00   299

Rosalie
Dec. 17, 1951   Nadine Conner   30:00   168
June 7, 1954   Nadine Conner   30:00   297

The Student Prince
Oct. 26, 1948   Kenny Baker, Hans Conried,
                      Bobby Driscoll, Betty Lou Gerson,
                      Dorothy Kirsten   44:50   4
Nov. 28, 1949   Jane Powell   30:00   61
Jan. 15, 1951   Evelyn Case, John Frank,
                      Betty Lou Gerson, Lamont Johnson   30:00   120
Oct. 5, 1953   Mary Jane Croft, Lamont Johnson,
                      Dorothy Kirsten   30:00   262

Up in Central Park
Mar. 9, 1953   Mimi Benzell   30:00   232

Appendix C:
Selected Discography

This list consists only of compilations dedicated to Romberg and cast recordings of individual operettas issued on CD prior to 2006.

COMPILATIONS

Deep in My Heart, original motion picture soundtrack (1954), Sony AK 47703 (1991 CD reissue)
Overture ("Deep in My Heart, Dear"), Orchestra and chorus
"You Will Remember Vienna," Helen Traubel
"Leg of Mutton," José Ferrer and Helen Traubel
"Softly, as in a Morning Sunrise," Betty Wand and girls
"Softly, as in a Morning Sunrise," Helen Traubel
"Mr. and Mrs.," Rosemary Clooney and José Ferrer
"I Love to Go Swimmin' with Wimmen," Gene and Fred Kelly with girls
"Road to Paradise"/"Will You Remember (Sweetheart)," Vic Damone and Jane Powell
"Girls Goodbye," José Ferrer
"Fat Fat Fatima," José Ferrer
"Jazza-Dada-Doo," José Ferrer
"It," Ann Miller and chorus
"Serenade," William Olvis and chorus
"One Alone," Carol Richards
"Your Land and My Land," Howard Keel and chorus
"Auf Wiedersehn," Helen Traubel
"Lover, Come Back to Me," Tony Martin with Joan Weldon
"Stout-hearted Men," Helen Traubel
"When I Grow Too Old to Dream," José Ferrer and chorus

A Night with Sigmund Romberg (1959), Percy Faith and His Orchestra, Columbia COL-CD-6640/Sony A 31592 (2000 CD reissue)

"The Desert Song"
"Stout Hearted Men"
"Song of Love"
"Serenade"
"Lover, Come Back to Me"
"Golden Days"
"One Alone"
"The Riff Song"
"Will You Remember (Sweetheart)"
"Deep in My Heart, Dear"
"One Kiss"
"When I Grow Too Old to Dream"

An Evening with Sigmund Romberg (1978), Carmen Dragon, Hollywood Bowl Pops Orchestra, EMI Angel CDM-7 69053 2 (1987 CD reissue)
From *The Student Prince*
From *The Desert Song*
From *Up in Central Park*
From *The New Moon*

Sigmund Romberg: When I Grow Too Old to Dream (1985), Teresa Ringholz, Donald Hunsberger, The Eastman-Dryden Orchestra; Arabesque Z6540
The New Moon (selections)
Maytime (selections)
Doing Our Bit (fox-trot featuring "Sally" and "Fine Feathers")
[*The*] *Desert Song* (selections)
"When I Grow Too Old to Dream"
Her Soldier Boy (selections)

Sigmund Romberg—Great Hits
Historic recordings, Pearl PAST CD 9761 (1991)
"It" from *The Desert Song*
    Jack Hylton and his Orchestra
Maytime Waltz Medley
    Victor Orchestra, Nathaniel Shilkret
"Who Are We to Say?" from *The Girl of the Golden West*
    Nelson Eddy, orchestra, Leonard Joy
The *New Moon* Selection
    London Theatre Orchestra, Sigmund Romberg
"The Gaucho March" from *Nina Rosa*
    Helen Gilliland, Robert Chisholm, Gaiety Theatre Orchestra, Maurice Besley
"Waltz" from *The Desert Song*
    Sacha Jacobsen, violin, with piano
Viennese Nights Selection
    Debroy Somers and his Band
"Song of Love" from *Blossom Time*

    Harry Horlick and his Orchestra
My Maryland Selection
    Victor Light Opera Co., Nathaniel Shilkret
"In Old Granada" from *Bombo*
    The Savoy Havana Band
The Desert Song Selection
    Commodore Grand Orchestra, Joseph Muscant
"Farewell to Dreams" from *Maytime*
    Jeanette MacDonald, Nelson Eddy, orchestra, Nathaniel Shilkret
"Your Smiles, Your Tears" from *Nina Rosa*
    Harry Horlick and his Orchestra
"Marianne" from *The New Moon*
    Howett Worster, chorus, Drury Lane Theatre Orchestra, Herman Finck
"Softly, As in a Morning Sunrise" from *The New Moon*
    De Groot and his Orchestra
"My First Love, My Last Love" from *Nina Rosa*
    Helen Gilliland, Gaiety Theatre Orchestra, Maurice Besly
"I Bring a Love Song" from *Viennese Nights*
    Harry Bidgood and his Broadcasters
"When I Grow Too Old to Dream" from *The Night Is Young*
    Evelyn Laye, orchestra, Carroll Gibbons
The Student Prince Selection
    London Palladium Orchestra, Clifford Greenwood

The Ultimate Sigmund Romberg, vol. 1
Original cast recordings, GEM 0112 (2001)
Maytime
"Will You Remember?" John Charles Thomas (of original cast)
Blossom Time
"Song of Love" Hollis Davenny, Gertrude Lang (of 1928 New York cast)
"Song of Love" Everett Marshall (of 1938 New York cast)
The Student Prince
"Overture" His Majesty's Theatre Orchestra (of 1926 London production)
"Golden Days" Allan Prior, Herbert Waterous (of 1926 London cast)
"Students' Entrance" Raymond Marlowe, Paul Clemon, Olaf Olson, chorus (of 1926 London cast)
"Drinking Song" Raymond Marlowe, Paul Clemon, Olaf Olson, chorus (of 1926 London cast)
"Deep in My Heart" Harry Welchman, Rose Hignell (of 1926 English touring cast)
"Serenade" Allan Prior, Raymond Marlowe, Paul Clemon, Olaf Olson, chorus (of 1926 London cast)
"Just We Two" Lucyenne Herval, John Coast, chorus (of 1926 London cast)
"Memories" Alan Prior, chorus (of 1926 London cast)
"Serenade" Harry Welchman (of 1926 English touring cast)
"I'm Coming at Your Call/Come Boys" Elise Gergely, chorus (of 1927 Sydney, Australia cast)

SELECTED DISCOGRAPHY 305

"Vocal Medley" (1926 London company)
The Desert Song
"Let Love Go/One Flower Grows Alone in Your Garden" Herbert Browne (of 1928 Australian cast)
"The Desert Song" Sidney Burchall (of 1935 Australian cast)
"One Alone" Sidney Burchall (of 1935 Australian cast)
My Maryland
"Mother" Evelyn Herbert (of original cast)
"Silver Moon" Evelyn Herbert (of original cast)

The Ultimate Sigmund Romberg, vol. 2
Original cast recordings, Pearl GEM 0119 (2002)
The New Moon
"Softly, As in a Morning Sunrise" William O'Neal (of original cast)
"Stouthearted Men" William O'Neal (of original cast)
"Lover, Come Back to Me" Evelyn Herbert (of original cast)
"Wanting You" Evelyn Herbert (of original cast)
"One Kiss" Evelyn Herbert (of original cast)
"Stouthearted Men" Perry Askam, chorus (of 1930 Los Angeles cast)
"Lover, Come Back to Me" Perry Askam, chorus (of 1930 Los Angeles cast)
"Gorgeous Alexander" Dolores Farris, Gene Gerrard, chorus (of 1929 London cast)
"Wedding Chorus/Try Her Out at Dances" Dolores Farris, Gene Gerrard, chorus (of 1929 London cast)
"Softly, as in a Morning Sunrise" Sidney Burchall (of 1930 Melbourne, Australia cast)
"Lover, Come Back to Me" Sidney Burchall (of 1930 Melbourne, Australia cast)
Nina Rosa
"Nina Rosa" Geoffrey Gwyther, chorus (of 1931 London cast)
"My First Love, My Last Love" Helen Gilliland (of 1931 London cast)
"Adored One" Geoffrey Gwyther (of 1931 London cast)
"The Gaucho March" Helen Gilliland, Robert Chisholm (of 1931 London cast)
The New Moon (1930 film cast)
"Wanting You" Lawrence Tibbett
"Lover, Come Back to Me" Lawrence Tibbett
The Night Is Young (1935 film cast)
"The Night Is Young" Evelyn Laye
"When I Grow Too Old to Dream" Evelyn Laye
"The Night Is Young" Ramon Novarro
Maytime (1937 film cast)
"Farewell to Dreams" Jeanette MacDonald and Nelson Eddy
"Will You Remember?" Jeanette MacDonald and Nelson Eddy

Romberg Conducts Romberg, vol. 1
Sigmund Romberg and his Orchestra, Naxos 8.110866 (2003)
Blossom Time
"Blossom Time Waltzes" (recorded 1945)
"Tell Me Daisy"

"Song of Love"
Lawrence Brooks, Warren Galjour, Lois Hunt, Genevieve Rowe, recorded 1945–50
The Blue Paradise
"Auf Wiedersehen" Shirley Emmons, Warren Galjour, recorded 1950
Maytime
"Will You Remember" Lawrence Brooks, Genevieve Rowe, recorded 1945
The Student Prince
"Drinking Song"
"Deep in My Heart, Dear"
"Ballet Music"
"Golden Days"
"Serenade"
"Student Prince Waltzes"
Lawrence Brooks, Stuart Churchill, Shirley Emmons, Warren Galjour, Eric Mattson, Genevieve Rowe, RCA Victor Chorus, Robert Shaw Chorale, recorded 1945–51
Rosalie
"West Point Song" Warren Galjour, Richard Wright, Robert Shaw Chorale, recorded 1950
The Night Is Young
"When I Grow Too Old to Dream" Lillian Cornell, RCA Victor Chorus, recorded 1945
The Desert Song
"Riff Song"
"One Alone"
"Romance"
"French Military Marching Song"
"Desert Song Waltz"
"One Flower Grows Alone in Your Garden"
"Desert Song Medley"
Lawrence Brooks, Stuart Churchill, Lillian Cornell, William Diehl, Warren Galjour, Genevieve Rowe, RCA Victor Chorus, Robert Shaw Chorale, recorded 1945–50

Romberg Conducts Romberg, vol. 2
Sigmund Romberg and his Orchestra, Naxos 8.110886 (2003)
My Maryland
"Your Land and My Land"
"Silver Moon"
"Mother"
"Boys in Grey"
Lawrence Brooks, Lillian Cornell, Warren Galjour, RCA Victor Chorus, Robert Shaw Chorale, recorded 1945–46 and 1950
The New Moon
"Softly, as in a Morning Sunrise"
"Lover, Come Back to Me"
"Stout-hearted Men"
"Wanting You"

"One Kiss"
Eric Mattson, Lillian Cornell, Lawrence Brooks, Genevieve Rowe, RCA Victor Chorus, recorded 1945
Viennese Nights
"I Bring a Love Song"
"You Will Remember Vienna"
"Viennese Nights Waltzes" ("You Will Remember Vienna," "I Bring a Love Song," "Opening Waltz," "Prater Scene")
Jean Carlton, William Diehl, Shirlee Emmons (recorded 1946 and 1950)
May Wine
"Dance, My Darlings"
"Just Once Around the Clock"
"Something New Is in My Heart"
Shirlee Emmons, Jo Cameron, Lois Hunt, recorded 1950
Sunny River
"Lordy" Jo Cameron, Robert Shaw Chorale, recorded 1950
Up in Central Park
"Close as Pages in a Book"
"April Snow"
"The Big Back Yard"
Jean Carlton, Larry Douglas, Lois Hunt, William Diehl, Robert Shaw Chorale, recorded 1950

Individual Shows

Shows are listed in alphabetical order, then by the year of the original recording.

The Desert Song
Original London Cast (1927, Harry Welchman, Edith Day); Pearl GEMM CD 9100 (1994 CD reissue, with *The New Moon* and Robert Stolz's *The Blue Train*)

Kitty Carlisle, Wilbur Evans, Felix Knight, Jeffrey Alexander Chorus, orchestra directed by Isaac Van Grove (1944); Decca Broadway 440 018 730–2 (2002 CD reissue, with *The New Moon*)

Mario Lanza, orchestra conducted by Constantine Callinicos (1959); RCA Victor 60048–2-RG (1989 CD reissue)

Edmund Hockridge, June Bronhill, Bruce Forsyth, Inia Te Wiata, Rita Williams Singers, Michael Collins & His Orchestra (highlights, 1959); Classics for Pleasure 0946 3 35987 2 (2005 CD reissue, with songs from *The New Moon* and Friml's *The Firefly*)

Dorothy Kirsten, Gordon MacRae, Orchestra and Roger Wagner Chorale conducted by Van Alexander (1963); EMI Angel CDM-7 69052 2 (1987 CD reissue)

The Girl in Pink Tights
Original Broadway Cast (1954, with Jeanmaire, Charles Goldner); DRG 19019 (2002 CD reissue)

Maytime
2005 Ohio Light Opera Cast Recording (Robin De Leon, Joshua Kohl, Grant Knox, Danielle McCormick, Tyler Nelson, conducted by Steven Byess); Albany TROY 808/09, 2 CDs (2005)

The New Moon
Original London Cast (1929, Evelyn Laye, Howett Worster, Ben Williams); Pearl GEMM CD 9100 (1994 CD reissue, with *The Desert Song* and Robert Stolz's *The Blue Train*)

Thomas Hayward, Jane Wilson, Lee Sweetland, Victor Young and his Orchestra and Chorus (1953); Decca Broadway 440 018 730-2 (2002 CD reissue, with *The Desert Song*)

Andy Cole and Elizabeth Larner, Rita Williams Singers, Tony Osborne and His Orchestra (songs, 1957); Classics for Pleasure 0946 3 35987 2 0 (2005 CD reissue, with highlights from *The Student Prince* and songs from Friml's *The Firefly*)

Dorothy Kirsten, Gordon MacRae, Orchestra and Roger Wagner Chorale conducted by Van Alexander (1963); EMI Angel CDM-7 69052 2 (1987 CD reissue)

1998 Media Theatre Cast Recording (Kyle Gonyea, Maureen Francis, Brian S. Hunt, musical direction by Eric R. Lofstrom); Media Theatre IND 90152 (1998)

2003 City Center Encores! Cast Recording (Rodney Gilfry, Christiane Noll, Lauren Ward, Burke Moses, Peter Benson, Simon Jones, Danny Rutigliano, Alix Korey, and Brandon Jovanovich with the *Encores!* Orchestra, musical direction by Rob Fisher); Ghostlight Records 4403-2 (2004)

The Student Prince
Lauritz Melchior, with Jane Wilson, orchestra and male chorus under the direction of Victor Young (1950); Decca Broadway 440 018 732-2 (2002 CD reissue, with Lehár's *The Merry Widow*)

Dorothy Kirsten, Robert Rounseville, chorus and orchestra conducted by Lehman Engel (1952); DRG 19018 (2002 CD reissue)

John Hanson, with Jane Fyffe, the Peter Knight Orchestra and Chorus (1960); Castle Communications MAC CD 334 (1996 CD reissue, with Friml's *The Vagabond King*)

Mario Lanza, orchestra conducted by Constantine Callinicos (1954); RCA Victor 60048-2-RG (1989 CD reissue)

John Wakefield, Marion Grimaldi, Christopher Keyte, Barbara Elsy, Linden Singers, Sinfonia of London, John Hollingsworth (highlights, 1961); Classics for Pleasure 0946 3 35988 2 9 (2005 CD reissue, with songs from Herbert's *Naughty Marietta* and Straus's *The Chocolate Soldier*)

Dorothy Kirsten, Gordon MacRae, Orchestra and Roger Wagner Chorale conducted by Van Alexander (1962?); EMI Angel CDM-7 69052 2 (1987 CD reissue)

Erik Geisen, Celia Jeffreys, Dieter Hönig, Members of the Hamburg State Opera Chorus and Orchestra conducted by Stefan Gyártó (1979–80); Bayer Records BR 150 004 CD

Norman Bailey, Marilyn Hill Smith, Diana Montague, David Bendall, Ambrosian Chorus and Philharmonia Orchestra conducted by John Owen Edwards (1990); TER CDTER2 1172 (2 discs)

Up in Central Park
Original Broadway Cast (1945, Wilbur Evans, Eileen Farrell, Betty Bruce, and Celeste Holm) [Although billed as an Original Broadway Cast recording, neither Eileen Farrell nor Celeste Holm were in the original cast.]; Decca Broadway B0000554–02 (2003 CD reissue, with Morton Gould and Dorothy Fields's *Arms and the Girl*)

Notes

Prologue

1. Other musicals of the decade that played more than 500 performances include *Rose Marie* (1924, music by Rudolf Friml, book and lyrics by Otto Harbach and Oscar Hammerstein 2nd) at 581 performances, *Show Boat* (1927, music by Jerome Kern, book and lyrics by Oscar Hammerstein 2nd) at 575 performances, *Good News!* (music by Ray Henderson, book by Laurence Schwab and B. G. "Buddy" De Sylva, lyrics by De Sylva and Lew Brown) at 551 performances, *Ziegfeld Follies of 1922* at 541 performances, *Blackbirds of 1928* (music by Jimmy McHugh, lyrics by Dorothy Fields) at 518 performances, *Sunny* (music by Jerome Kern, book and lyrics by Otto Harbach and Oscar Hammerstein 2nd) at 517 performances, and *The Vagabond King* (1927, music by Rudolf Friml, lyrics by Brian Hooker, book by W. H. Post) at 511 performances.

2. "Need to Know." First broadcast on the Fox Television Network, February 7, 2006.

CHAPTER 1. Sigmund Romberg

1. Elliott Arnold, *Deep in My Heart: A Story Based on the Life of Sigmund Romberg* (New York: Duell, Sloan and Pearce, 1949).

2. "Sigmund Romberg, Last of Operetta Triumvirate, Dies Suddenly in N. Y. at 64," *Variety*, November 14, 1951. Other MGM biopic subjects included Jerome Kern (*Till the Clouds Roll By*, 1946) Richard Rodgers and Lorenz Hart (*Words and Music*, 1948), and Bert Kalmar and Harry Ruby (*Three Little Words*, 1950). For more on composer biopics, see John C. Tibbetts, *Composers in the Movies: Studies in Musical Biography* (New Haven and London: Yale University Press, 2005), especially chapter 3, "The New Tin Pan Alley: Hollywood Looks at Popular Songwriters."

3. Robert Tucker provided the music arrangements, and orchestrations were by Alexander Courage and Hugo Friedhofer.

4. This was the only film role for the Wagnerian soprano. Traubel received the *Look* magazine award for "best newcomer" of the year for her screen debut, some-

thing she herself found amusing, since she began her professional singing career in 1939 (Helen Traubel, *St. Louis Woman* [New York: Duell, Sloan and Pearce, 1959; rpt. Columbia: University of Missouri Press, 1999], 254).

5. Tibbetts, *Composers in the Movies*, 121. For more on the dynamics of this process as it was practiced in Hollywood, see Neal Gabler, *An Empire of Their Own: How the Jews Invented Hollywood* (New York: Crown, 1988), and Steven Alan Carr, *Hollywood and Anti-Semitism: A Cultural History Up to World War II* (Cambridge and New York: Cambridge University Press, 2001).

6. Lillian Romberg, telegram to Oscar Hammerstein 2nd, read during the radio program *A Tribute to Sigmund Romberg*, broadcast on October 23, 1954, NBC (recording of broadcast in Sigmund Romberg Duplication Project, reel 25, side B, Recorded Sound Division, Library of Congress). Two short articles that provide some insight into Romberg's hobbies are Gordon Allison, "Sigmund Romberg Here to Celebrate," *New York Herald Tribune*, March 12, 1950, and Martin Roe, "Romberg Means Romance," *Popular Songs* 2, no. 8 (December 1936): 10.

7. John W. Frick, *New York's First Theatrical Center: The Rialto at Union Square* (Ann Arbor: UMI Research Press, 1985), 136–38.

8. Peter Salwen, *Upper West Side Story: A History and Guide* (New York: Abbeville Press, 1989), 181.

9. Hugh Fordin, *Getting to Know Him: A Biography of Oscar Hammerstein II* (New York: Random House, 1977; rpt. New York: Ungar, 1986), 68.

10. Gerald Bordman, *American Operetta: From "H.M.S. Pinafore" to "Sweeney Todd"* (New York and Oxford: Oxford University Press, 1981), 123.

11. Fordin, *Getting to Know Him*, 68.

12. Sigmund Romberg, New York, typescript letter to Lt. Cdr. C. B. Cranford, Seattle, September 21, 1944, author's collection.

13. Fordin, *Getting to Know Him*, 169–70.

14. Hammerstein Collection, Library of Congress, *The King and I* file; quoted in William Hyland, *Richard Rodgers* (New Haven: Yale University Press, 1998), 203.

15. This account is based on two radio programs, "The Man I Married," featuring Jo Stafford, with endorsement by Lillian Romberg (recording of broadcast in Sigmund Romberg Duplication Project, reel 25, side A, selections 7–9, Recorded Sound Division, Library of Congress), and *A Tribute to Sigmund Romberg*, broadcast on October 23, 1954, NBC (recording of broadcast in Sigmund Romberg Duplication Project, reel 25, side B, Recorded Sound Division, Library of Congress).

16. "Sigmund Romberg Puts War to Music," *Click: The National Picture Monthly*, January 1943, 20–21.

17. The song does not appear in the playbill for the show printed in Richard C. Norton, *A Chronology of American Musical Theater*, vol. 2 (New York: Oxford University Press, 2002), 98–99, although there is a number titled "How to Make a Pretty Girl" that does not have a composer credit. For more on the first Gershwin-Romberg meeting, see Edward Jablonski, *Gershwin: A Biography* (New York: Doubleday, 1988), 20.

18. Alan Kendall, *George Gershwin* (London: Harrap, 1987), 42.

19. Stephen Citron, *Noel and Cole: The Sophisticates* (New York and Oxford: Oxford University Press, 1993), 37.

20. Citron, *Noel and Cole*, 58.

21. Melville B. Nimmer and Gavin McFarlane, "Copyright, Sec. V, 14: USA: Copyright Collecting Societies," in *The New Grove Dictionary of Music Online*, ed. Laura Macy (accessed September 13, 2002), http://www.grovemusic.com.

22. Arnold, *Deep in My Heart*, 338.

23. "Named to Direct Song Writers' Group," *New York Times*, September 1, 1931; "Romberg Heads Song Men," *New York Times*, March 11, 1932.

24. The company's debts, as reported in the *New York Times*, included $934.56 to costume supplier J. M. Gidding & Co. ("Business Records," *New York Times*, June 22, 1921), another $899.70 to the same company ("Business Records," *New York Times*, June 28, 1921), and $1,089 to G. B. Road ("Business Records," *New York Times*, June 13, 1922).

25. Jerome Kern also had a passion for collecting, although his library consisted of books and autographs, not scores. See Gerald Bordman, *Jerome Kern: His Life and Music* (New York and Oxford: Oxford University Press, 1980), 300–3.

26. "A Salute to Sigmund Romberg," *International Musician* 49 (November 1950): 15.

27. Bordman, *Jerome Kern*, 361.

28. "A Salute to Sigmund Romberg."

29. The catalog is among the uncataloged Sigmund Romberg materials in the Music Division, Library of Congress.

30. "Sigmund Romberg Quietly Completes a Score," *New York Times*, March 5, 1933.

31. Quoted in Derek Watson, *The Wordsworth Dictionary of Musical Quotations* (Ware, Hertfordshire: Wordsworth, 1994), 273.

32. Louis V. DeFoe, "Drama: Al Jolson Has a Red-Letter Night," *New York World*, October 7, 1921.

33. Stephen Citron, *The Wordsmiths: Oscar Hammerstein 2nd & Alan Jay Lerner* (New York and Oxford: Oxford University Press, 1995), 90.

34. Ethan Mordden, *Sing for Your Supper: The Broadway Musical in the 1930s* (New York: Palgrave Macmillan, 2005), 108.

35. "Rooneys in 'Love Birds,'" *New York Herald*, March 16, 1921; "Rooney Holds His Own as Star in Musical Play," *New York American*, March 16, 1921; and Alexander Woollcott, "The Play: Love Birds," *New York Times*, March 16, 1921.

36. "Rooney Holds His Own as Star in Musical Play."

37. Fordin, *Getting to Know Him*, 68.

38. Brooks Atkinson, "'May Wine,' A Musical Drama with Book and Tunes but No Chorus," *New York Times*, December 6, 1935.

39. "Most Prolific of Composers: Sigmund Romberg Can Write a Musical Comedy Score 'While You Wait,'" unidentified Boston newspaper, September 4, 1927, Romberg clipping file, Harvard Theatre Collection.

40. J. J. Shubert, New York, letter to J. Witmark, New York, August 9, 1922, Shubert Archive.

41. J. J. Shubert, New York, letter to J. Witmark, New York, April 17, 1923, Shubert Archive. The show in question is most likely a proposed adaptation of Carlo Lom-

bardo's Italian-language operetta *La Duchessa del Bal Tabarin* (1917), which never materialized.

42. "'My Golden Girl' at the Shubert," *Boston Globe*, September 6, 1927.

43. Sigmund Romberg, "A Peep into the Workshop of a Composer," *Theatre Magazine* 46, no. 6 (December 1928): 27.

44. The minor mode was also associated with Jewish identity among several Broadway composers, including Irving Berlin, during the 1920s. See Jeffrey Magee, "Irving Berlin's 'Blue Skies': Ethnic Affiliations and Musical Transformation," *Musical Quarterly* 84, no. 4 (Winter 2000): 537–80. Unlike Berlin, though, Romberg did not compose Jewish novelty songs.

45. Stephen Banfield, *Sensibility and English Song* (Cambridge and New York: Cambridge University Press, 1985, paperback edition 1988).

46. Bordman, *Jerome Kern*, 364.

47. Max Wilk, *Overture and Finale: Rodgers & Hammerstein and the Creation of Their Two Greatest Hits* (New York: Back Stage Books, 1999), 34.

48. Fordin, *Getting to Know Him*, 132.

49. *Naughty Marietta* was not the first American operetta to have an American setting. *The Mocking Bird* (1902) was set in Louisiana, like *Naughty Marietta*, and Julian Edwards's *When Johnny Comes Marching Home* took place during the American Civil War.

50. "Back to the Stage in Various Vigors Still Undiminished," unidentified newspaper, clipping file, *The Dream Girl*, Billy Rose Theatre Collection, New York Public Library.

51. Andrew Lamb, *150 Years of Popular Musical Theatre* (New Haven: Yale University Press, 2000), 92.

52. Stanley Green suggests that music publisher Edward Marks encouraged Romberg to write a turkey trot in the style of a French tune (Stanley Green, *The World of Musical Comedy*, 4th ed. [San Diego: A. S. Barnes, 1980; rpt. New York: Da Capo, 1984], 42).

53. The unpublished song is in the *Sketchbook, 1938–1939*, in the Music Division of the Library of Congress.

54. A restored version of *Foolish Wives*, with Romberg's score realized and performed by Rodney Sauer, is available on DVD (Kino K247, 2003).

CHAPTER 2. Finding a Voice

1. Zvonko Penović, "Od Belišća do New Yorka," *Vjesnik* (Zagreb, Croatia), November 11, 1995.

2. Ibid.

3. Recording on Romberg Duplication Project, reel 28, selections 2 and 3, Recorded Sound Division, Library of Congress. An important and telling aspect of the broadcast is that all the sung excerpts are in English. Although a program that presented an Italian opera aria sung in English in a German-speaking house might offend purists, it certainly did not bother Romberg or his fans.

4. Andrew Lamb, *150 Years of Popular Musical Theatre* (New Haven: Yale University Press, 2000), 42–43.

5. Ibid., 43.

6. The country's name is also a play on that of the actual Spanish Galician city and autonomous region of Pontevedra.

7. For detailed discussions of the creation of literary Ruritania, see Maria Todorova, *Imagining the Balkans* (New York and Oxford: Oxford University Press, 1977), and Vesna Goldsworthy's *Inventing Ruritania: The Imperialism of the Imagination* (New Haven: Yale University Press, 1998).

8. Goldsworthy, *Inventing Ruritania*, 64.

9. Todorova, *Imagining the Balkans*, 116.

10. John Drinkrow, *The Vintage Operetta Book* (Reading, U.K.: Osprey, 1972), 92.

11. Todorova, *Imagining the Balkans*, 119. For more on Orientalism and the Other in this context, see Edward W. Said, *Orientalism* (New York: Random House, 1978), and Susan McClary, *Carmen* (Cambridge: Cambridge University Press, 1992), especially chapter 3, "Images of Race, Class and Gender in Nineteenth-Century French Culture" (29–43).

12. "Most Prolific of Composers Sigmund Romberg Can Write a Musical Comedy Score 'While You Wait,'" unnamed Boston newspaper, September 4, 1927, "Sigmund Romberg" clipping file, Harvard Theatre Collection. Stanley Green gives a slightly different account, asserting that it was the music publisher Edward Marks who encouraged Romberg to write a turkey trot in the style of a French tune (Stanley Green, *The World of Musical Comedy*, 4th ed. [San Diego: A. S. Barnes, 1980; rpt. New York: Da Capo, 1984], 42).

13. The family's surname in the 1890s appeared in various ways, including Schubart, Shubard, and Szemanski. Shubert was the form used by the brothers when they arrived in New York City.

14. Marc Eliot, *Down 42nd Street* (New York: Warner Books, 2001), 74–75.

15. The Shubert Archive (Maryann Chach, Reagan Fletcher, Mark E. Swartz, and Sylvia Wang), *The Shuberts Present: 100 Years of American Theater* (New York: Harry N. Abrams, in association with the Shubert Organization, Inc., 2001), 299, 305.

16. Alan Jenkins, *The Twenties* (New York: Universe Books, 1974), 191.

17. John Seabrook, *Nobrow: The Culture of Marketing, The Marketing of Culture* (New York: Knopf, 2000; New York: Vintage Books, 2001), 26. For more on this phenomenon, see Lawrence W. Levine, *Highbrow/Lowbrow: The Emergence of Cultural Hierarchy in America* (Cambridge, MA: Harvard University Press, 1988).

18. Seabrook, *Nobrow*, 26. See also Bernard Rosenberg and Ernest Harburg, *The Broadway Musical: Collaboration in Commerce and Art* (New York and London: New York University Press, 1993).

19. Edward Jablonski, *Gershwin* (New York: Doubleday, 1987), 20.

20. Felicia Hardison Londré and Daniel J. Watermeier, *The History of North American Theater* (New York and London: Continuum, 2000), 290.

21. For more on New York Roof Gardens, see Stephen Burge Johnson, *The Roof Gardens of Broadway Theatres, 1883–1942* (Ann Arbor: UMI Research Press, 1985).

22. Londré and Watermeier, *History of North American Theater*, 290.

23. Shubert Archive, *The Shuberts Present*, 287.

24. "Jean Schwartz, Composer of 'Chinatown' with William Jerome, Dies on Coast at 78," *New York Times*, December 1, 1956.

25. "Harold Atteridge, Broadway Author," Obituary, *New York Times*, January 17, 1938.

26. Document at Shubert Archive, New York.

27. Roof theaters were popular in New York from the 1880s to the 1930s as venues for smaller revues and other more intimate types of entertainment. One reviewer remarked that *Over the Top* came about because the "Shuberts heard their patrons ask for a little Winter Garden, that there was too much in the Winter Garden spectacles to be enjoyed at one sitting, or that a little of the Winter Garden goes a long way" (Burns Mantle, "*Over the Top* a Second Edition Winter Garden," *New York Evening Mail*, 3 December 1917, quoted in Johnson, *The Roof Gardens*, 169).

28. The theater's name, Winter Garden, was an overt reference to the New York Roof Garden where Ziegfeld's *Follies* appeared (Johnson, *The Roof Gardens*, 132). In 1896, the Roof Garden, then the Olympia Roof Garden, was heated and renamed the "Winter Garden." The Shuberts alluded to Ziegfeld's performance space in christening their showcase revue palace. They were quick to take advantage of any publicity opportunity and would maximize name potential as a means to demonstrate their entrenchment and primacy in New York theater, just as they had done in appropriating Lederer's title for their long-running series. They also endorsed the theater's roof garden ambiance by leaving the beams exposed and painting the ceiling with images of the sky and landscapes (William Morrison, *Broadway Theatres: History and Architecture* [Mineola, New York: Dover, 1999], 69).

29. Shubert Archive, *The Shuberts Present*, 267–68. For *The Whirl of Society* (1912), the Shuberts installed a runway that extended the length of the auditorium. The runway was popular with Winter Garden audiences, who dubbed it "The Bridge of Thighs," a reference to Venice's Bridge of Sighs. The Shuberts' "Beauty Brigade of Bewitching Broadway Blondes and Brunettes" paraded along the runway to the delight of the patrons. However, the ramp eliminated twenty-one seats that could otherwise be sold to paying customers eight times a week, and was removed in 1922.

30. For more on ragtime, see Edward A. Berlin, *Ragtime: A Musical and Cultural History* (Berkeley and Los Angeles: University of California Press, 1980; rpt. Lincoln, NE: Universe, 2002); John Edward Hasse, ed., *Ragtime: Its History, Composers, and Music* (New York: Schirmer, 1985); and David A. Jasen and Trebor Jay Tichenor, *Rags and Ragtime: A Musical History* (New York: Seabury, 1978).

31. Charles Hamm, *Yesterdays: Popular Song in America* (New York and London: W. W. Norton, 1979), 321.

32. Charles Hamm, *Irving Berlin, Songs from the Melting Pot: The Formative Years, 1907–1914* (New York and Oxford: Oxford University Press, 1997), 100, 213–15.

33. Richard C. Norton, *A Chronology of American Musical Theater*, vol. 2 (New York: Oxford University Press, 2002), 128.

34. Lewis also described it as a branch of scholarship that focuses on Arab and Asian cultures and the relationships and perceptions between the Oriental and Occidental realms (Bernard Lewis, *Islam and the West* [New York and Oxford: Oxford University Press, 1993], 101–3).

35. "Way Down East" was dropped after the revue's opening (Norton, *Chronology*, vol. 2, 54).

36. "Shimmy à la Egyptian" was replaced for the subsequent tour by "(You Can't Get into Heaven Unless You Have a) Jazz Band" (Norton, *Chronology*, vol. 2, 192).

37. The Lithuanian-born singer's name underwent several transformations in its Americanization process. It was originally Asa Yoelson, followed by Al Yoelson, then Al Joelson, and finally Al Jolson.

38. Foster Hirsch, *The Boys from Syracuse: The Shuberts' Theatrical Empire* (Carbondale: Southern Illinois Press, 1998; rpt. New York: Cooper Square Press, 2000), 85.

39. Curiously, *Bombo* was the only show in which Jolson appeared in the theater that bore his name. Jolson's Theatre remained a Shubert property for years to come and was the house where Romberg's *The Student Prince* opened three years later.

40. Credits for the songs are as follows: "Rock-a-Bye Your Baby with a Dixie Melody" (music by Jean Schwartz, lyrics by Joe Young and Sam Lewis), "Swanee" (music by George Gershwin, lyrics by Irving Caesar), "My Mammy" (music by Walter Donaldson, lyrics by Sam Lewis and Joe Young), "Toot, Toot, Tootsie! (Goodbye)" (music and lyrics by Ernie Erdman, Dan Russo, and Gus Kahn), "April Showers" (music by Louis Silvers, lyrics by Buddy G. De Sylva), and "California, Here I Come" (music and lyrics by Al Jolson, Joseph Meyer, and Buddy G. De Sylva).

41. Hirsch, *The Boys from Syracuse*, 146.

42. Ibid.

43. *The Blushing Bride*'s book by Cyrus Wood was based, according to the playbill, on a libretto by Edward Clark and the play *The Third Party* by Brandon and Arthur as adapted by Mark Swan.

44. "A Regular Girl" was published with the title "Just a Regular Girl."

45. "Monte Cristo, Jr. Emulates Daddy," *New York Sun*, February 13, 1919.

46. "Rooneys in 'Love Birds' Make Musical Comedy Debut," *New York Herald*, March 16, 1921; "Love Birds," *New York Post*, March 16, 1921; "Rooney Holds His Own as Star in Musical Play," *New York American*, March 16, 1921.

47. "'The Dancing Girl' Has Premiere at Winter Garden," *New York American*, January 25, 1923.

48. Auber's *La muette di Portici* (*The Mute Girl of Portici*, 1828) is a precedent in the opera repertory where the title character is a dancing role.

49. *The Dancing Girl* was Tom Burke's Broadway debut. He also appeared on Broadway in revivals of *The Mikado* (1925) and *H.M.S. Pinafore* (1926), and in the short-lived musical *Lace Petticoat* (1927), with music by Emil Gerstenberger (Romberg's principal orchestrator for his operettas during the 1920s) and Carle Carlton.

50. The English version of *The Midnight Girl* was by Adolf Philipp and Edward A. Paulton. Jean Briquet and Philipp were the credited composers on the playbill, but Briquet was Philipp's pseudonym, which meant that Philipp was the show's sole composer.

51. For more on the dieting craze of the era and the history of beauty in the United States, see Lois W. Banner, *American Beauty* (New York: Knopf, 1983).

52. For a detailed account of *Poor Little Ritz Girl*, its genesis, and its innovations, see Armond Fields and L. Marc Fields, *From the Bowery to Broadway: Lew Fields and the Roots of American Popular Theater* (New York and Oxford: Oxford University Press, 1993), 385–95.

53. Heywood Brown, "Jokes at Last Have a Place in Musical Shows," *New York Tribune*, July 30, 1920.
54. Richard Rodgers, *Musical Stages: An Autobiography* (New York: Random House, 1975; rpt. New York: DaCapo, 1995 and 2002), 39.
55. Brown, "Jokes at Last."
56. Geoffrey Block, *Richard Rodgers* (New Haven and London: Yale University Press, 2003), 27.
57. C. P. S., "The Play: 'Poor Little Ritz Girl,'" *New York Post*, July 30, 1920.
58. Norton, *Chronology*, vol. 2, 222.
59. McElliott, "'First Nights' Finds Central Revue Tuneful," *New York Illustrated News*, July 30, 1920.
60. "The Theatre: 'Poor Little Ritz Girl,'" *New York Evening Sun*, July 30, 1920.
61. Meryle Secrest, *Somewhere for Me: A Biography of Richard Rodgers* (New York: Knopf, 2001), 45.

CHAPTER 3. Staging Nostalgia

1. See Katherine K. Preston, "American Musical Theatre Before the Twentieth Century," in *Cambridge Companion to the Musical*, ed. William A. Everett and Paul R. Laird (Cambridge: Cambridge University Press, 2002), 3–28. For scores of representative works, see Deane L. Root, ed., *Nineteenth-Century American Musical Theater* (New York: Garland, 1994–95), 16 vols.
2. "'Princess Flavia' Sets New High Standard," *New York Commercial*, Nov. 4, 1925.
3. Maria Todorova, *Imagining the Balkans* (New York and Oxford: Oxford University Press, 1977), 122.
4. Ibid.
5. *Oxford English Dictionary*, 2nd ed. (1987), 537.
6. Richard Teleky, *Hungarian Rhapsodies* (Seattle and London: University of Washington Press, 1997), 85.
7. Elliott Arnold, *Deep in My Heart: A Story Based on the Life of Sigmund Romberg* (New York: Duell, Sloan and Pearce, 1949), 294.
8. "Sigmund Romberg Puts War to Music," *Click: The National Picture Monthly*, January 1943, 20–21.
9. Sigmund Romberg, New York, letter to Lt. Cdr. C. B. Cranford, Seattle, September 21, 1944, author's collection.
10. See Stuart Feder, "Homesick in America: The Nostalgia of Antonin Dvořák and Charles Ives," in *Dvořák in America: 1892–1895*, ed. John Tibbetts (Portland, Oregon: Amadeus Press, 1993), 182–90; Leon Botstein, "Innovation and Nostalgia: Ives, Mahler, and the Origins of Modernism," in *Charles Ives and His World*, ed. J. Peter Burkholder (Princeton: Princeton University Press, 1996), 35–74; Raymond Knapp, "Suffering Children: Perspectives on Innocence and Vulnerability in Mahler's Fourth Symphony," *19th-Century Music* 22, no. 3 (spring 1999): 233–67; and Feder, "The Nostalgia of Charles Ives: An Essay in Affects and Music," in *Psychoanalytic Explorations in Music*, ed. Feder, Richard L. Karmel, and George H. Pollock (Madison, Connecticut: International Universities Press, 1990), 233–66.
11. Svetlana Boym, *The Future of Nostalgia* (New York: Basic Books, 2001), xvi.

12. Robert Davis and B. Scully, untitled newspaper clipping, *Boston Globe*, September 30, 1941, Sigmund Romberg clipping file, Harvard Theatre Collection.

13. Robert Davis and B. Scully, "'The Student Prince' Returns," *Christian Science Monitor*, February 3, 1942.

14. Richard Eyre and Nicholas Wright, *Changing Stages: A View of British and American Theatre in the Twentieth Century* (New York: Knopf, 2001), 137.

15. Foster Hirsch, *The Boys from Syracuse: The Shuberts' Theatrical Empire* (Carbondale: Southern Illinois Press, 1998; rpt. New York: Cooper Square Press, 2000), 19.

16. Kurt Gänzl, *The Musical: A Concise History* (Boston: Northeastern University Press, 1997), 99.

17. For a complete listing of the songs included in each production, see Richard C. Norton, *A Chronology of American Musical Theater*, vol. 2 (New York: Oxford University Press, 2002).

18. The show's pre-Broadway title, *A Brazilian Honeymoon*, also paid homage to an earlier show, *A Chinese Honeymoon* (1902), the first musical Sam S. Shubert produced on Broadway.

19. Gerald Bordman, *American Musical Theatre: A Chronicle*, 3d ed. (New York and Oxford: Oxford University Press, 2001), 365.

20. For more on Thomas, see Michael Maher, "Launching a Career: John Charles Thomas on Broadway," *Passing Show: Newsletter of the Shubert Archive* 24 (2004–5): 16–26.

21. Kálmán also wrote a song with the same title that was published as a selection from the operetta. Kálmán's song is much shorter than Romberg's, and while it is not known which song was performed on opening night, Richard C. Norton suggests that it was the one by Romberg (Norton, *Chronology*, vol. 2, 110). From the expansiveness of Romberg's song, it seems likely that Romberg's version of the number would have been the preferred choice.

22. "'Her Soldier Boy' at Shubert Theatre," *Christian Science Monitor*, October 24, 1916.

23. See Carol A. Hess, "John Philip Sousa's *El Capitan*: Political Appropriation and the Spanish-American War," *American Music* 16, no. 1 (spring 1998): 1–24.

24. "'My Lady's Glove' Comes from Vienna," *New York Times*, June 19, 1917.

25. Document at the Shubert Archive, New York, *Maytime* file.

26. According to documents at the Shubert Archive, on April 4, 1916, Young was engaged to adapt the book and write lyrics for a play called *The Star Gazer*. On September 14, 1917 (after *Maytime* opened), the Shuberts and Young made an agreement that the contract for *The Star Gazer* would apply to *Maytime* (Shubert Archive, *Maytime* file).

27. Bartsch, on August 9, 1917, less than a week before *Maytime* opened, wrote to the Shuberts, reminding them that, according to the signed agreement, "the book of the piece shall not be used without the score as written by Kollo & Bredschneider." He continued, "I must also insist, according to our contract, that you announce the names of Rudolf Schanzer and Rudolf Bernauer as the authors of the original from which Mrs. Young has made the American version" (letter from Hans Bartsch, International Play Agency, New York, to J. J. Shubert, August 9, 1917, Shubert Archive, *Maytime* file).

28. A similar treatment appeared in Arnold Bennett's English play *Milestones*, which played in New York in the 1912–13 season. Young adopted Bennett's idea of a play with each act set in a different time period for *Maytime*, but did not refer to any of its plot details (letter from J. J. Shubert, New York, to Hans Bartsch, August 15, 1917, Shubert Archive, *Maytime* file).

29. "Spanish Dance" is listed in the playbill, although music for it does not appear in the vocal score.

30. The song is called "Selling Gowns" in the playbill.

31. The song is called "Only One Girl for Me" in the playbill.

32. John Corbin, "'Maytime,' and After That, 'The Deluge,'" *New York Times*, August 26, 1917.

33. Stanley Green, *The World of Musical Comedy*, 4th ed. (San Diego: A. S. Barnes, 1980; rpt. New York: Da Capo, 1984), 44.

34. "Romance in 'Maytime' Still Holds Audience with Its Fascination," *Star* (Montreal), January 11, 1921.

35. Following previews at Stamford Theatre in Stamford, Connecticut, beginning on August 7, 1917, and at the Newport Opera House (Newport, Rhode Island) from August 10, *Maytime* opened in New York at the Shubert Theatre on August 16, 1917. It transferred to the 44th Street Theatre on February 18, 1918, then to the Broadhurst on April 1, and to the Lyric on August 5. Its final move was back to the Broadhurst on September 9, where it closed on October 19, 1918.

CHAPTER 4. Continued Success

1. Both Princes are Russian, but while Orlofsky is a pant role, Potemsky, a speaking part, is played by a man.

2. Alan Dale, "Magic Melody Staged at Shubert," *New York American*, November 11, 1919.

3. "Gorgeous Music Show Is 'The Magic Melody,'" *New York World*, November 12, 1919.

4. "'The Magic Melody' Is Unique Blend," *New York Sun*, November 12, 1919.

5. "The Magic Melody," *New York Globe*, November 12, 1919.

6. "Gorgeous Music Show," Is 'The Magic Melody,'" *New York World*, November 12, 1919.

7. "'The Magic Melody' is Unique Blend," *New York Sun*, November 12, 1919.

8. "Gorgeous Music Show," Is 'The Magic Melody,'" *New York World*, November 12, 1919.

9. *Das Dreimäderlhaus* was based on Rudolf H. Bartsch's novel *Schwammerl* (published serially in *Leipziger Illustrierte Zeitung* [*Leipzig Illustrated Journal*] in 1911 and in book form [Leipzig: Staackmann] the following year).

10. The Ambassador Theatre production that opened on September 29, 1921, closed on July 1, 1922, but reopened at the same house on August 7. It moved to Jolson's 59th Street Theatre, where it ran October 2–21. It then went to Philadelphia, where it opened on October 23 at the Lyric Theatre. A second company opened in New York at the Century Theatre, where it played from October 23, 1922, to January 27, 1923 (dates obtained at the Shubert Archive).

11. Foster Hirsch, *The Boys from Syracuse: The Shuberts' Theatrical Empire* (Carbondale: Southern Illinois Press, 1998; rpt. New York: Cooper Square Press, 2000), 144.

12. Alexander Woollcott, "Franz Schubert in a Play," *New York Times*, September 30, 1921.

13. Publicity announcement for *Blossom Time*, Shubert Archive.

14. Ibid.

15. Ibid.

16. "'Blossom Time' Is Charming with Its Schubert Melodies," *New York Herald*, September 30, 1921.

17. Item located in the press package for *Blossom Time* at the Shubert Archive, dated January 23, 1922.

18. This scene is based on a fable that Schubert wrote another "Ständchen," D. 889 ("Horch! Horch! Die Lerch"), in a beer garden (Richard Morris, "Of Mushrooms and Lilac Blossom," *The Schubertian: Journal of the Schubert Institute (UK)*; online version, http://myweb.tiscali.co.uk/franzschubert/articles/mlbplot.html, accessed August 27, 2005). In this scene, however, he writes the one from *Schwanengesang*. Such details are curious, but considering the overall lack of factual accuracy in the show, are ultimately of minor consequence.

19. Stanley Green, *Broadway Musicals Show by Show*, 5th ed., revised and updated by Kay Green (Milwaukee, Wisconsin: Hal Leonard, 1996), 38.

20. See John C. Tibbetts, *Composers in the Movies: Studies in Musical Biography* (New Haven and London: Yale University Press, 2005), for an examination of composer biopics.

CHAPTER 5. Young Love in Old Heidelberg

1. For more on the German-language musical theater in New York at this time, see John Koegel, "Adolf Philipp and Ethnic Musical Comedy in New York's Little Germany," *American Music* 24, no. 3 (Fall 2006): 267–319.

2. Joseph Horowitz, *Wagner Nights: An American History* (Berkeley and Los Angeles: University of California Press, 1994), 305. For more details on activities at the Metropolitan Opera, see the Metropolitan Opera's online database at www.metoperafamily.org/metopera/history/.

3. "'Alt Heidelberg' in the United States," *New York Times*, October 26, 1902.

4. Thomas Quinn Curtiss, *Von Stroheim* (New York: Farrar, Straus and Giroux, 1971), 52. A German film version of Meyer-Foerster's play, entitled *Alt Heidelberg*, was released in 1923 from Czerepy-Film. When the film played in the United States it was under the title *The Student Prince*, again capitalizing on the fame of the operetta.

5. J. J. Shubert, New York, letter to Gustave Schirmer, New York, February 28, 1919, Shubert Archive.

6. J. J. Shubert, Shubert Theatrical Company, New York, letter to Dorothy Donnelly, New York, August 1922 [no day given], Shubert Archive.

7. *Romance* was a play by Edward Sheldon that opened at the Maxine Elliott Theatre on February 10, 1913. Romberg's musical adaptation of the work, *My Romance* (1948), was the last operetta to be produced by the Shuberts.

8. J. J. Shubert, New York, letter to Dorothy Donnelly, New York, August 21, 1922, Shubert Archive.

9. Elliott Arnold suggests that Romberg was interested in *The Student Prince* in 1922 (Elliott Arnold, *Deep in My Heart: A Story Based on the Life of Sigmund Romberg* [New York: Duell, Sloan and Pearce, 1949], 502). According to dates on the holograph vocal score at the Library of Congress, Romberg completed "Farmer Jacob" on February 10, 1923, "Golden Days" on February 11, "Take Care" on February 12, "For You" on February 13, and "There's No Joy but Love" on February 18. Only the first two numbers made it to Broadway. A copy of Romberg's contract to write *The Student Prince* is at the Shubert Archive.

10. These selections were deposited for copyright at the Library of Congress on November 13, 1924.

11. David Ewen, *New Complete Book of the American Musical Theater* (New York: Holt, Rinehart and Winston, 1970), 513.

12. Sigmund Romberg, "A Peep into the Workshop of a Composer," *Theatre Magazine* 48, no. 6 (December 1928): 72.

13. J. J. Shubert, New York, letter to William Klein, New York, November 28, 1924, Shubert Archive.

14. William Klein, New York, letter to J. J. Shubert, New York, November 26, 1924, Shubert Archive.

15. J. J. Shubert, New York, letter to Adolph Hirsch, Berlin, November 12, 1924, Shubert Archive.

16. Although the full title *The Student Prince in Heidelberg* appears on sheet music selections with the final two words as a subtitle, both the long version and the abbreviated *The Student Prince* were used on publicity materials for the original production. Elliott Arnold tells of a rather heated meeting after the work's Atlantic City tryout where, among other things, the title was abridged (Arnold, *Deep in My Heart*, 323). The shorter title appeared in legal documents, held at the Shubert Archive, between the Shuberts and Romberg as early as May 6, 1925. Thus, both titles for the operetta, the longer *The Student Prince in Heidelberg* and the shorter *The Student Prince*, are bibliographically correct.

17. The production played at Jolson's Theatre until December 12, 1925, when it moved to the Ambassador Theatre, where it played from December 14, 1925, to January 30, 1926. On February 1, 1926, the production relocated to the old Century Theatre, where it remained until March 27, 1926. It returned to its original house, Jolson's Theatre, where it played from April 5 to May 22, 1926.

18. Franco P. Coli, "Ilse Marvenga: J. J. Shubert's Student Princess," *Passing Show* 9, nos. 1–2 (1985): 5–6.

19. George Jean Nathan, "The Theatre, VI," *American Mercury* 4 (February 1925): 248–49.

20. "'The Student Prince' Brings Out Cheers," *New York Times*, December 3, 1924. Although the article does not have a byline, it appears in the music section, which was written by Olin Downes. Stark Young wrote the section "The Play" that appeared on the page before *The Student Prince* review.

21. Lord Chamberlain's Plays Correspondence Files, *The Student Prince*, Manuscripts Department, British Library, LC Plays 1926/6676.

22. London Bureau of *New York Herald Tribune*, "U.S. Musical Comedy Invasion of London Receives a Setback," *New York Tribune*, February 27, 1926.

23. Ibid.

24. For more on this topic, see Cecilia Hopkins Porter, *The Rhine as Musical Metaphor: Cultural Identity in German Romantic Music* (Boston: Northeastern University Press, 1996). Many versions of "Die Wacht am Rhein" are included in the Library of Congress's "American Memory Project" Web site, available at www.loc.gov.

25. For a more extended discussion of the sequence, see William A. Everett, "Golden Days in Old Heidelberg: The First-Act Finale of Sigmund Romberg's *The Student Prince*," *American Music* 12, no. 3 (fall 1994): 255–82.

26. Ibid., 267.

27. Ibid., 269.

28. John Hanson, *Me and My Red Shadow* (London: W. H. Allen, 1980), 99.

29. Richard and Paulette Ziegfeld, *The Ziegfeld Touch: The Life and Times of Florenz Ziegfeld, Jr.* (New York: Abrams, 1993), 118–19. Percy Hammond, "'Annie Dear' Is Billie Burke in a Feathery Frolic, Plus Ballets and Tableaux, by F. Ziegfeld Jr.," *New York Herald-Tribune*, November 5, 1924.

30. For more on *Louie the 14th*, see Ethan Mordden, *Make Believe: The Broadway Musical in the 1920s* (New York and Oxford: Oxford University Press, 1997), 69–71.

31. Romberg was not the first to quote "Old Folks at Home" in his own music. The song also appears in Berlin's "Alexander's Ragtime Band" and Gershwin's "Swanee." Before that, Dvořák combined the tune with his own "Humoresque" in the 1890s.

32. Romberg was not the first to attempt a musical version of the defining Ruritanian tale; Richard Rodgers and Herbert Fields completed a version for the amateur stage the previous year. Nor was he the last. In 1963 Vernon Duke wrote the music for *Zenda* to a libretto by Everett Freeman. The musical starred Alfred Drake, and the proper name of the country was changed from Ruritania to Zenda. See Ethan Mordden, *Open a New Window: The Broadway Musical in the 1960s* (New York: Palgrave, 2001), 85–86.

33. "'Princess Flavia'—at the Century Theatre," *New York Wall Street News*, November 6, 1925.

34. Stephen Rathburn, "A Brilliant Premiere: 'Princess Flavia' Comes Up to Expectations at Century," *New York Sun*, November 3, 1925.

35. Robert Coleman, "'Princess Flavia,'" *New York Mirror*, November 7, 1925.

CHAPTER 6. Romance and Exoticism in North Africa

1. The operetta's tryout included performances at the Playhouse in Wilmington, Delaware, October 21–23, Poli's Theatre in Washington, D.C., October 25–30, Shubert Theatre in New Haven, November 1–6, and Shubert Theatre in Boston, November 8–27 (Stanley Green, ed., *Rodgers and Hammerstein Fact Book: A Record of Their Works Together and with Other Collaborators* [New York: Lynn Farnol Group, 1980], 328).

2. Charles Brackett, *The New Yorker*, December 11, 1926; quoted in Green, *Rodgers and Hammerstein Fact Book*, 332.

3. For more on London productions of Romberg operettas, see William A. Everett, "London Productions of Romberg Operettas During the 1920s: *The Student*

Prince, The Desert Song, and *The New Moon,*" *Sonneck Society Bulletin* 21, no. 1 (spring 1995): 4–6. For more on *Chu Chin Chow* and Orientalist musical theater of the time, see William A. Everett, "*Chu Chin Chow* and Orientalist Musical Theatre in Britain," in *Portrayal of the East: Music and the Oriental Imagination in the British Empire, 1780–1940,* ed. Bennett Zon and Martin Clayton, forthcoming.

4. Lord Chamberlain's Plays Correspondence Files, for *The Desert Song,* Manuscripts Department, British Library, LC Plays 1927/4.

5. For insight on Bizet's musical depiction of Carmen, see Susan McClary, *Carmen* (Cambridge: Cambridge University Press, 1992), 54–57.

6. E. Nelson Bridwell, *Superman from the Thirties to the Eighties* (New York: Crown Publishers, 1983), 10.

7. Michael North, *Reading 1922: A Return to the Scene of the Modern* (New York: Oxford University Press, 1999), 21.

8. Grauman's Egyptian, which sits at 6712 Hollywood Boulevard, does not enjoy the fame of its younger sister, Grauman's Chinese (1927), home of the famous forecourt with handprints and footprints of famous stars. Egyptian motifs engulf Grauman's Egyptian, both outside and inside. Cast heads of pharaohs on pylons flank the doors, while twin black plaster Anubises guard the lobby. Inside the 1,800-seat auditorium, lotus-capital columns, and hieroglyph-stenciled beams form the proscenium arch (David Naylor, *Great American Movie Theaters* [Washington, D.C.: Preservation Press, 1987], 209).

Other theaters to bear the name "Egyptian" rose in many cities. These included houses in Ogden, Utah (1924), Coos Bay, Oregon (1925), Bala-Cynwyd, Pennsylvania (1927), Boise, Idaho (1927), and DeKalb, Illinois (1929). Especially noteworthy were those in Coos Bay and DeKalb. Coos Bay's Egyptian, built within the shell of a parking garage, has a lobby dominated by a pair of eight-feet-tall seated golden pharaohs (Naylor, *Great American Movie Theaters,* 228–29). The DeKalb theater has a multicolored auditorium, complete with a painted curtain and columns designed to resemble papyrus. Golden pharaohs sit on either side of the proscenium (Naylor, *Great American Movie Theaters,* 136).

9. Stephen Burge Johnson, *The Roof Gardens of Broadway Theatres, 1883–1942* (Ann Arbor: UMI Research Press, 1985), 9, 13–16. The Casino Theatre was demolished in 1930. By that year, it was on the southern fringe of the northward-moving theater district. As a result of the Depression, many theaters, including the Casino, were demolished.

10. Ella Shohat, "Gender and Culture of Empire: Toward a Feminist Ethnography of the Cinema," in *Visions of the East: Orientalism in Film* (New Brunswick, New Jersey: Rutgers University Press, 1997), 32. For more on the topic, see Edward W. Said, *Orientalism* (New York: Random House, 1978).

11. Shohat, "Gender and Culture," 39.

12. Ibid., 41.

13. Ibid., 39.

14. Adele O. Brown, *What a Way to Go: Fabulous Funerals of the Famous and Infamous* (San Francisco: Chronicle Books, 2001), 165. For the tenth edition of *Earl Carroll Vanities,* Jack McGowan created a sketch entitled "Mourning Becomes Impossible" that addressed the madness surrounding Valentino's funeral. Harold Arlen and

Ted Koehler wrote the songs. For more on Valentino, see Emily W. Leider, *Dark Lover: The Life and Death of Rudolph Valentino* (New York: Farrar, Straus and Giroux, 2003).

15. Hugh Fordin, *Getting to Know Him: A Biography of Oscar Hammerstein II* (New York: Random House, 1977; rpt. New York: Ungar, 1986), 68.

16. Alan Jenkins, *The Twenties* (New York: Universe Books, 1974), 205.

17. Shohat, "Gender and Culture," 32, 47–48.

18. Quoted in Sue Rickard, "Movies in Disguise: Negotiating Censorship and Patriarchy Through the Dances of Fred Astaire and Ginger Rogers," in *Approaches to the American Musical*, ed. Robert Lawson-Peebles (Exeter: University of Exeter Press, 1996), 77.

19. "More Operetta: American Style, African Setting," *Boston Transcript*, November 9, 1926.

20. "Drury Lane: The Desert Song," unknown London newspaper, April 10, 1927, Clipping File for *The Desert Song*, Harvard Theatre Collection.

21. "More Operetta: American Style, African Setting."

22. "'Desert Song' at the Majestic: Melodious Operetta of Stirringly Romantic Appeal Welcomed Here Again," *Boston Globe*, January 24, 1928.

23. Steven C. Caton, "The Sheik: Instabilities of Race and Gender in Transatlantic Popular Culture of the Early 1920s," in *Noble Dreams, Wicked Pleasures: Orientalism in America, 1870–1930*, ed. Holly Edwards (Princeton: Princeton University Press in association with the Sterling and Francine Clark Art Institute, 2000), 100–1.

24. Lowell Thomas, *With Lawrence in Arabia* (Garden City, New York: Garden City, 1924), 4–5.

25. Caton, "The Sheik," 104.

26. Bell's books included *The Desert and the Sown* (1907), *The Thousand and One Churches* (1909, with Sir William Ramsey), and *Amurath to Amurath* (1911).

27. Sigmund Romberg, "A Peep into the Workshop of a Composer," *Theatre Magazine* 48, no. 6 (Dec. 1928): 27.

28. Romberg was certainly not the first composer to use tonality to create a sense of musical Other. During the eighteenth century, the minor mode carried with it associations of weakness, instability, or mutability, all of which contributed to a gendered reading of the mode as inherently female. See, for example, Timothy D. Taylor, "Peopling the Stage: Opera, Otherness, and New Musical Representations in the Eighteenth Century," *Cultural Critique* 36 (spring 1997): 55–88, esp. 64, 71–73; and Gretchen A. Wheelock, "*Schwarze Gredel* and the Engendered Minor Mode in Mozart's Operas," in *Musicology and Difference: Gender and Sexuality in Music Scholarship*, ed. Ruth A. Solie (Berkeley: University of California Press, 1993), 201–24.

29. *It* was made into a film in 1927 and starred Clara Bow, who subsequently became known as the "It" girl.

CHAPTER 7. Exploring New Possibilities

1. Foster Hirsch, *The Boys from Syracuse: The Shuberts' Theatrical Empire* (Carbondale: Southern Illinois Press, 1998; rpt. New York: Cooper Square Press, 2000), 158.

2. The complete performance history for *My Maryland* in Philadelphia during

the 1920s and 1930s is as follows: Original production—January 24–September 26, 1927, Lyric; September 27–October 29, 1927, Chestnut Street Opera House. Revivals—February 27–March 17, 1928, Lyric; October 22–27, 1928, Erlanger; February 21–March 28, 1931, Shubert; April 9–21, 1934, Forrest; and December 25, 1935–January 4, 1936, Forrest.

3. One positive aspect of the show closing after a very short run is that it freed Marsh to create the role of Gaylord Ravenal in *Show Boat* (John Franceschina, *Harry B. Smith: Dean of American Librettists* [New York and London: Routledge, 2003], 270).

4. "'Cherry Blossoms' Has Tunes and Color," *New York Times*, March 29, 1927. For more on Japanese elements in *Pacific Overtures*, see chapter 8, "*Pacific Overtures*," in Stephen Banfield, *Sondheim's Broadway Musicals* (Ann Arbor: University of Michigan Press, 1993), 249–80.

5. For more on *My Maryland*, see William A. Everett, "Barbara Frietchie and *My Maryland*: The Civil War Comes to Operetta," *Passing Show* 16, no. 2 (fall 1993): 2–8.

6. The show was called *My Golden Girl* during its pre-Broadway tryout. Albertina Rasch (1896–1967) was an Austrian-born dancer and choreographer whose "Albertina Rasch Dancers" appeared in many Broadway musicals of the 1920s and 1930s and Hollywood films of the 1930s. Her choreography integrated classical ballet technique with precision ensemble dancing.

7. The "blonde bombshell" Hope Hampton (1897–1982) was known primarily for her work in silent film. *My Princess* was her only Broadway credit.

8. "'My Golden Girl' at the Shubert," *Boston Globe*, September 6, 1927.

9. *The Love Call* played as *My Golden West* and *Bonita* during its pre-Broadway tryout.

10. "'Cherry Blossoms' Has Tunes and Color."

11. Elyn Feldman, "Musicals in the Shubert Archive, 1926–1930," *Passing Show* 3, no. 2 (summer 1979), 6.

12. According to Richard Crawford, these songs all had preexisting melodies to which new words were added. "Dixie" was a *Northern* blackface minstrel song, "The Bonnie Blue Flag" was sung to the traditional song "The Irish Jaunting Car," and "Maryland, My Maryland" used the tune of the familiar German Christmas carol "O Tannenbaum" (*The Civil War Songbook* [New York: Dover, 1977], vii).

13. Gerald Bordman, *American Musical Theatre: A Chronicle*, 3d ed. (New York: Oxford University Press, 2001), 481. The song also shares its title with a number from the previous year's *Rio Rita* (February 2, 1927, Ziegfeld; music by Harry Tierney, lyrics by Joseph McCarthy, book by Guy Thompson and Fred Thompson).

14. Richard C. Norton, *A Chronology of American Musical Theater*, vol. 2 (New York: Oxford University Press, 2002), 515.

15. The unnamed author of "Source of 'The Love Call'" (*New York Times*, November 13, 1927) claimed that the Mexican elements were added in order to provide Romberg with the opportunity to create Hispanic-style music, in addition to Indianist numbers, for the score. However, *Arizona* included the song "Adios Amor" ("Farewell, Love"), subtitled "A Mexican Love Song," with music by Joseph Dane and words by Augustus Thomas.

16. "'Cherry Blossom' Is 'Willow Tree' With Romberg Music," *New York Tribune*, March 29, 1927.

17. Colgate Baker, "*My Maryland*: Gloried American Opera, and Evelyn Herbert," *New York Review*, September 17, 1927.

18. Franceschina, *Harry B. Smith*, 272.

19. P. G. Wodehouse and Guy Bolton, *Bring on the Girls! The Improbable Story of Our Life in Musical Comedy, with Pictures to Prove It* (New York: Simon and Schuster, 1953; rpt. Pleasantville, New York: Akadine Press, 1997), 246.

20. Edward Jablonski, *Gershwin* (New York: Doubleday, 1987), 150. For an account of Queen Marie's sojourn in America, see Hannah Pakula, *The Last Romantic: A Biography of Queen Marie of Romania* (New York: Simon and Schuster, 1984), 342–55.

21. Tommy Krasker and Robert Kimball, *Catalog of the American Musical* (Washington, D.C.: National Institute for Opera and Musical Theater, 1988), 126.

22. For information on the source material for the recycled Gershwin songs and discarded numbers, see Edward Jablonski and Lawrence D. Stewart, *The Gershwin Years: George and Ira* (New York: Doubleday, 1958; rpt. New York: Da Capo Press, 1996), 127–28; Jablonski, *Gershwin*, 149–50; and Krasker and Kimball, *Catalog of the American Musical*, 122–29.

23. The song was published with different lyrics (credited to P. G. Wodehouse) as "Why Must We Always Be Dreaming?" in *Sigmund Romberg Song Album, Book II* (New York: Harms, 1942).

24. As it underwent revisions, the show played in Cleveland (August 27, 1928, Hanna) and Pittsburgh (September 10, 1928, Alvin) before arriving on Broadway.

25. A great deal of music written for the earlier versions was cut. This material survives in several places. Most important is the holograph vocal score for the Philadelphia version at the Library of Congress. Mrs. Lillian Romberg donated the score to the Library in 1959. The score, among the uncataloged Romberg materials in the Music Division, consists of individual musical numbers bound together in a hardcover volume. Some of the contents are in incorrect order. Items related to the Cleveland and Pittsburgh productions are at the Warner Brothers Warehouse in Secaucus, New Jersey. Although Harms (the publisher of *The New Moon*, later acquired by Warner Brothers) never published a score for the tryout version, they did issue sheet music selections for numbers ultimately cut from the show. Five selections from *The New Moon* were published on December 30, 1927, during the operetta's Philadelphia tryout: "'Neath a New Moon," "When I Close My Eyes!," "Marianne" (not the same song that was in the final version of the show), "Stouthearted Men" (with the first word not hyphenated), and "Try Her Out at Dances." The first three titles never appeared in stage productions of *The New Moon* after January 1928. Only the last two, "Stouthearted Men" and "Try Her Out at Dances," made it to Broadway. Harms published an additional nine numbers in September 1928. From the tryout version came three titles, all of which were cut before the New York opening: "Liar," "I'm Just a Sentimental Fool," and "One Kiss Is Waiting for One Man." Appearing at the same time were six songs that were in the Broadway version: "Softly, As in a Morning Sunrise," "Wanting You," "The Girl on the Prow," "Lover, Come Back to Me," "One Kiss," and "Marianne."

26. Rob Fisher, "Keeping Score," City Center Encores!: *The New Moon*, www.citycenter.org/encores/newmoonkeepingscore.cfm (accessed August 27, 2005).

27. The German version of the name of Croatian-born composer-conductor Ivan Zajc is Ivan Zayts.

28. "Pirate Utopias," *Do or Die* 8 (1999), online version, http://www.eco-action.org/dod/no8/pirate.html, note 42 (accessed December 18, 2002).

29. Other names for the island included La Evangelista (The Evangelist) — the name given to it by its discoverer, Christopher Columbus, in 1494, Isla de Cotorras (Isle of Parrots), and Isla de Tesoros (Treasure Island).

30. Arthur Pollock, "Grace and Charm and Sprightliness in 'The New Moon' at the Imperial Theater," *Brooklyn Daily Eagle*, September 20, 1928.

31. Concerning gender and formal aspects of music, including meter, see Susan McClary, "Narrative Agendas in 'Absolute' Music: Identity and Difference in Brahms's Third Symphony," in *Musicology and Difference: Gender and Sexuality in Music Scholarship*, ed. Ruth A. Solie (Berkeley: University of California Press, 1993), 326–44, and elsewhere in her writings. This notion of gender and meter is not necessarily idiomatic of the American musical theater, or even of Romberg's own overall output. For example, in *Show Boat*, Gaylord Ravenal introduces the waltz portion of "Make Believe," and he and Nola are on equal musical footing in "You Are Love." In *South Pacific*, Emile de Becque sings "This Nearly Was Mine" as an evocative solo number. In Romberg's own work, the male and female leads sing the primary love duets in the shows he wrote with the Shuberts, as well as in *The Desert Song*; furthermore, the man often introduces the refrain in these numbers. This conflation of gender and meter, therefore, is limited to *The New Moon*.

32. Chiori Santiago, "Tango—One Heart Plus Four Legs," *Smithsonian Magazine* 24, no. 8 (November 1993): 156–57.

CHAPTER 8. Emulating the Past

1. Unidentified press clipping, *Brooklyn Daily Eagle*, September 23, 1928, Show file for *The New Moon*, New York Public Library.

2. Lee Davis, *Scandals and Follies: The Rise and Fall of the Great Broadway Revue* (New York: Limelight, 2000), 271.

3. Orry-Kelly began his work as an actor before turning to design. He is best known for his work in motion pictures (The Shubert Archive [Maryann Chach, Reagan Fletcher, Mark E. Swartz, and Sylvia Wang], *The Shuberts Present: 100 Years of American Theater* [New York: Harry N. Abrams, in association with the Shubert Organization, Inc., 2001], 132).

4. The two shows also shared an orchestrator, for Hans Spialek, one of the team who worked on *The New Moon*, scored *Nina Rosa*. Additionally, both shows had exceptionally long tryout periods. Whereas that of *The New Moon* was due to rewrites, *Nina Rosa*'s had to do with finding the right leading lady. Five different actresses played the title role within thirty weeks ("'Nina Rosa' on a Junket," *New York Times*, September 28, 1930). Its tryout began in Detroit on October 20, 1929, and it was eleven months later to the day when it finally opened at the Majestic Theatre.

5. Irving Caesar and Otto Harbach wrote the lyrics for "My First Love, My Last Love." The song was replaced by the lyrical 6/8 ballad "Adored One" in London.

6. Foster Hirsch, *The Boys from Syracuse: The Shuberts' Theatrical Empire* (Carbondale: Southern Illinois Press, 1998; rpt. New York: Cooper Square Press, 2000), 158.

7. In this regard, it supports the thesis of Edward V. Said's *Orientalism*.
8. Gerald Bordman, *American Musical Theatre: A Chronicle*, 3d ed. (New York: Oxford University Press, 2001), 523.
9. "Producers to Offer 'East Wind' to Cast," *New York Times*, November 13, 1931; "'East Wind' May End Today," *New York Times*, November 14, 1931.
10. Robert Russell Bennett, *The Broadway Sound: The Autobiography and Selected Essays of Robert Russell Bennett*, ed. George J. Ferencz (Rochester: University of Rochester Press, 1999), 148. Also, according to Ferencz, in Hans Spialek, "A Passing Note," unpublished memoirs, ca. 1956, Alice Gruber, Andover, New Jersey, 166.
11. Bordman, *American Musical Theatre: A Chronicle*, 533.
12 Danièle Piston, "Opera in Paris During the Roaring Twenties," trans. E. Thomas Glasow, *Opera Quarterly* 13, no. 2 (winter 1997): 59; Benoît Duteurtre, *L'Opérette en France* (Paris: Seuil, 1997), 113; and Andrew Lamb, *150 Years of Popular Musical Theatre* (New Haven: Yale University Press, 2000), 217.
13. Elliott Arnold, *Deep in My Heart: A Story Based on the Life of Sigmund Romberg* (New York: Duell, Sloan and Pearce, 1949), 393.
14. Bordman, *American Musical Theatre: A Chronicle*, 548.
15. Walter Woolf, who previously appeared in *Melody*, went to Hollywood, and added a new surname, King, upon his return to New York.
16. Robert Garland, "'May Wine' Appears at St. James Theater," *New York World-Telegram*, December 6, 1935; Robert Coleman, "Schwab Has 'Twists' that Sparkle," *New York Daily Mirror*, December 6, 1935.
17. Percy Hammond, "The Theaters: 'May Wine,'" *New York Herald Tribune*, December 6, 1935.
18. Ibid.
19. Stephen Citron, *The Wordsmiths: Oscar Hammerstein 2nd & Alan Jay Lerner* (New York and Oxford: Oxford University Press, 1995), 115. Although the verse begins with the words "No regrets," this is a different song than the one sung by Billie Holiday.
20. Coleman, "Schwab Has 'Twists' that Sparkle."
21. The legendary Robert Russell Bennett also contributed orchestrations to the show.
22. Reported in *New York Times*, November 27, 1936, clipping file, *Forbidden Melody*, Billy Rose Theatre Collection, New York Public Library.
23. Reported in *New York American*, May 21, 1936, clipping file, *Forbidden Melody*.
24. Reported in *New York Times*, September 8, 1936, clipping file, *Forbidden Melody*. The plot received a wholesale restructuring. The working title for the operetta was *The Lady in the Window*, and it is under this title that Harbach's book evolved into its final version (Otto Harbach Collection, Series II, Box 13, folder 7. Billy Rose Theatre Collection, New York Public Library). It was not only the show's concept but also its title that underwent a metamorphosis. A script entitled *Lavender Lady* in the Otto Harbach collection at the New York Public Library of the Performing Arts appears to be an earlier version of the operetta, at least as far as the musical numbers are concerned (Otto Harbach Collection, Series II, Box 13A, folder 1).
25. John Mason Brown, "'Forbidden Melody' Staged at the New Amsterdam," *New York Evening Post*, November 3, 1936.
26. Brooks Atkinson, "Forbidden Melody," *New York Times*, November 3, 1936.

27. Burns Mantle, "Stale Story Relieved but Little by Romberg Tunes of Another Decade," *New York Daily News*, November 3, 1926.

28. Arthur Pollock, "The Theater: 'Forbidden Melody,' Something in the Viennese Manner by Harbach and Romberg, Opens at the New Amsterdam," *Brooklyn Daily Eagle*, November 3, 1936.

29. Romberg indicated the gypsy band on a separate score from the pit orchestra in his holograph vocal score (Sigmund Romberg, *Lady in the Window* [working title for *Forbidden Melody*], holograph vocal score, Music Division, Library of Congress, ML96.R745 case).

30. Carl Brisson's son was the producer Frederick Brisson, who was married to Rosalind Russell.

31. For more on this topic, see Raymond Knapp, *The American Musical and the Formation of National Identity* (Princeton: Princeton University Press, 2005), especially chapter 5, "Whose (Who's) America?" and chapter 6, "American Mythologies."

32. *Sunny River* was originally entitled *New Orleans* and received its first tryout performance during the summer of 1941 at the St. Louis Municipal Opera. Romberg recorded "Lordy" from *Sunny River* with Jo Cameron, mezzo-soprano, the Robert Shaw Chorale, and the Sigmund Romberg Orchestra on October 26, 1950 (re-released on the CD *Romberg Conducts Romberg*, vol. 2. Naxos 8.110886). The number was cut before the New York opening (Stanley Green, ed. *Rodgers and Hammerstein Fact Book: A Record of Their Works Together and with Other Collaborators* [New York: Lynn Farnol Group, 1980], 493). It is in the style of an African American spiritual, and as such, suggests the American south, the show's setting.

33. Deborah Grace Winer, *On the Sunny Side of the Street: The Life and Lyrics of Dorothy Fields* (New York: Schirmer Books, 1997), 134.

34. Ibid., 135–38.

35. Ibid., 135.

36. Ethan Mordden, *Beautiful Mornin': The Broadway Musical in the 1940s* (New York and Oxford: Oxford University Press, 1999), 105.

37. Lyman W. Atwater painted the scene used in the lithograph.

38. Mordden, *Beautiful Mornin'*, 106.

39. Romberg was at least the fourth composer approached by the Shuberts to write *My Romance*, and the second to write a complete score for the show. The Shuberts asked Cole Porter in 1946 and Walter Jurmann in 1947 (Richard J. Madden [Cole Porter's agent], New York, letter to J. J. Shubert, New York, September 27, 1946, Shubert Archive; and signed contract between Walter Jurmann and the Shuberts, March 1947, Shubert Archive). Dennis Agay wrote a complete score that received poor reviews in tryouts. Philip Redowski then wrote some additional numbers. J. J. got rid of Agay and Redowski's score and contracted Romberg to write a new one. The show's title, coincidentally, is the same as that of the classic Rodgers and Hart song introduced in *Jumbo* (1935), though there does not appear to be a connection between the song and the operetta.

40. Anne Jeffreys, telephone interview with Fred Hirsch, December 1, 1993; quoted in Hirsch, *The Boys from Syracuse*, 204.

41. Ethan Mordden, *Coming Up Roses: The Broadway Musical in the 1950s* (New York and Oxford: Oxford University Press, 1998), 94–95.

42. For more on *The Black Crook* and the mythology surrounding it, see Knapp, *The American Musical and the Formation of National Identity*, 20–29.

CHAPTER 9. Romberg in Hollywood

1. Grace Moore sang excerpts from *Madama Butterfly* in *One Night of Love* (1934), while Nelson Eddy led "Silent Night" in *Balalaika* (1939).

2. Lawrence Tibbett, "A Talk on the 'Talkies,'" reprinted in *Lawrence Tibbett, Singing Actor*, ed. Andrew Farkas (Portland, Oregon: Amadeus Press, 1989), 102.

3. Sigmund Romberg, "Screen Operetta," *Pacific Coast Musician*, May 3, 1930, 16.

4. For a list of songs used in films, drawn primarily from cue sheets, see Ken Bloom, *Hollywood Song: The Complete Film & Musical Companion*, 3 vols. (New York: Facts on File, 1995).

5. Stephen Citron, *The Wordsmiths: Oscar Hammerstein 2nd & Alan Jay Lerner* (New York and Oxford: Oxford University Press, 1995), 88. Hugh Fordin, *Getting to Know Him: A Biography of Oscar Hammerstein II* (New York: Random House, 1977; rpt. New York: Ungar, 1986), 108.

6. Citron, *Wordsmiths*, 88–89.

7. Sigmund Romberg and Oscar Hammerstein, *Viennese Nights: A Vitaphone Operetta* ([New York]: Harms, 1930).

8. Although all copies of the film are apparently lost, musical materials are extant at the Library of Congress and the University of California, Berkeley Music Library. The creative process of *Children of Dreams* was atypical in that it took place over vast distances. When writing *Children of Dreams*, Hammerstein was with his wife, Dorothy, and their baby Susan on a two-month trip to Australia to visit Dorothy's family, from where he wired story ideas to Romberg, who then created the musical score around the concepts (Citron, *Wordsmiths*, 90).

9. Stanley Green, ed., *Rodgers and Hammerstein Fact Book: A Record of Their Works Together and with Other Collaborators* (New York: Lynn Farnol Group, 1980), 420.

10. Fordin, *Getting to Know Him*, 107.

11. Citron, *Wordsmiths*, 113.

12. Fordin, *Getting to Know Him*, 132.

13. Citron, *Wordsmiths*, 113.

14. Ibid., 114.

15. Harold Arlen and E. Y. "Yip" Harburg wrote the songs for the film, while Stothart composed—or co-composed—the instrumental music heard throughout the film as underscoring for dialogue or in the many parts of the film where there is no dialogue and only music. See Aljean Harmetz, *The Making of "The Wizard of Oz"* (New York: Delta, 1977), 89–93.

16. Ronald Rodman, "Tonal Design and the Aesthetic of Pastiche in Herbert Stothart's *Maytime*," in *Music and Cinema*, ed. James Buhler, Caryl Flinn, and David Neumeyer (Hanover, New Hampshire: Wesleyan University Press, 2000), 187–206.

17. Daniel C. Gerould, "The Americanization of Melodrama," editor's introduction to *American Melodrama: "The Poor of New York," "Uncle Tom's Cabin," "Under*

the Gaslight," and "The Girl of the Golden West" (New York: Performing Arts Journal Publications, 1983), 23, 25.

18. The films that followed *The Girl of the Golden West* were *Sweethearts* (1938), *New Moon* (1940), *Bitter Sweet* (1940), and *I Married an Angel* (1942). MacDonald and Eddy sang music by Victor Herbert in *Naughty Marietta* and *Sweethearts*, Rudolf Friml in *Rose Marie*, Noël Coward in *Bitter Sweet*, and Richard Rodgers and Lorenz Hart in *I Married an Angel*.

19. Frank S. Nugent, "The Screen: A World or Two on the Capitol's 'Girl of the Golden West,' 'Fools for Scandal' and 'Tip-Off Girls,'" *New York Times*, March 25, 1938.

20. John Koegel, "The Film Operettas of Sigmund Romberg," M.M. thesis, California State University, Los Angeles, 1984, 68.

21. Latin numbers continued to appear in musical films of the early 1940s such as *Down Argentine Way* (1940), *That Night in Rio* (1941), *Moon over Miami* (1941), and *Springtime in the Rockies* (1942). For more on the topic, see Walter Aaron Clark, "Doing the Samba on Sunset Boulevard: Carmen Miranda and the Hollywoodization of Latin American Music," in *From Tejano to Tango: Latin American Popular Music*, ed. Walter Aaron Clark (New York and London: Routledge, 2002), 252–76.

22. Jennifer R. Jenkins, "'Say It with Firecrackers': Defining the 'War Musical' of the 1940s," *American Music* 19, no. 3 (fall 2001): 316.

23. The other two songs were "Beneath the Winter Snows" and "In a Heart as Brave as Your Own" (from the "First Opera Sequence" and based on Tchaikovsky) (Philip Castanza, *The Complete Films of Jeanette MacDonald and Nelson Eddy* [New York: Citadel, 1978, 1990], 160).

24. In the film, Fred in fact is not killed, but returns from the war. Rose, thinking he is dead, marries Jimmy (Spencer Tracy). Fred, knowing only how to shoot a gun, becomes a member of a gang, goes to prison, and escapes. The film therefore is a propaganda piece about the problem of veterans whose only skill is shooting.

25. Songs for *Out of the Blue* include "Chopsticks Number," "Dream Boat," "The World Is Ours Tonight," "I Can't Make Up My Mind," "No Time to Argue," and "Medley of Old Favorites," all with lyrics by Gus Kahn. Copies of the songs are in the volume "Numbers Written for MGM" in the Sigmund Romberg collection at the University of California, Berkeley Music Library (call number M1527.2/R654/M6/case x). "Where's the Girl?" is in the same volume.

26. Romberg, "Screen Operetta."

27. Ken Wlaschin, *Opera on Screen: A Guide to 100 Years of Films and Videos Featuring Operas, Opera Singers and Operettas* (Los Angeles: Beachwood Press, 1997), 341 (reprinted as *Encyclopedia of Opera on Screen: A Guide to More Than 100 Years of Opera Films, Videos, and DVDs* [New Haven: Yale University Press, 2004], 437).

28. Ibid.

29. An earlier version of the film went into production in summer 1936 for which Romberg wrote additional music, including the march "When Love Comes a Marching Along" (reused in *The Girl of the Golden West* as "Soldiers of Fortune") and the duet "Farewell to Dreams" (of which MacDonald and Eddy made a studio recording). The film was aborted and recast after the death of its producer, Irving Thalberg. See Edward Baron Turk, *Hollywood Diva: A Biography of Jeanette MacDonald* (Berkeley, Los Angeles, and London: University of California Press, 1998), 196–97.

30. Rodman, "Tonal Design," 197–98.

31. Constantine Callinicos with Ray Robinson, *The Mario Lanza Story* (New York: Coward-McCann, 1960), 158–59, 161; Roland L. Bessette, *Mario Lanza: Tenor in Exile* (Portland, Oregon: Amadeus Press, 1999), 140, 142, 145.

32. Raymond Strait and Terry Robinson: *Lanza: His Tragic Life* (Englewood Cliffs, New Jersey: Prentice-Hall, 1980), 100.

33. Bloom, *Hollywood Song*, vol. 2, 916.

34. Documents in the Warner Bros. Archives at the Cinema-Television Library, University of Southern California, Los Angeles.

35. Jack G. Shaheen, *Reel Bad Arabs: How Hollywood Vilifies a People* (New York and Northampton: Olive Branch Press, 2001), 168.

36. See "Memories of *The Desert Song*: An Interview, June 1999, with Earl William," *The Desert Song* Web site, http://www.dandugan.com/maytime/dsrtsong.htm (accessed September 10, 2001).

37. Hertzel Weinstat and Bert Wechsler, *Dear Rogue: A Biography of the American Baritone Lawrence Tibbett* (Portland, Oregon: Amadeus Press, 1996), 105.

38. The only commercially available film featuring Tibbett is *House of Strangers*, a film noir from 1949 in which the actor had a brief cameo.

39. Richard Barrios, *A Song in the Dark: The Birth of the Musical Film* (New York and Oxford: Oxford University Press, 1995), 307.

40. Stothart also wrote "What Is Your Price Madame," another song for Tibbett, for the film.

41. The various changes to the scenario are documented in continuity scripts in the Archives of Performing Arts at the Cinema-Television Library, USC. The earlier treatments are close to the original operetta, with the leads called Robert and Marianne and the overall setting 1780s New Orleans. In a draft from May 10, 1930, the shipboard opening sequence is first mentioned, along with Robert, as the hero is still called, singing a "gay, light-hearted *mocking song*." The change of locale from Louisiana to Russia first appears in a version dated June 30 and dictated by Florence Ryerson, perhaps best known for her work on the screenplay of *The Wizard of Oz*. In a script from July 3, the leads are called Michael and Tanya for the first time. In this script, the opening scene, still on board a ship, included the gypsy song sequence.

42. Another swashbuckling maritime romance, *The Sea Hawk*, starring Errol Flynn and Olivia de Havilland, also appeared to tremendous audience acclaim in 1940, the same year as *New Moon*.

CHAPTER 10. Building a Legacy

1. Gordon Allison, "Sigmund Romberg Here to Celebrate," *New York Herald Tribune*, March 12, 1950.

2. Romberg wrote six songs specifically for the radio program. Edward Heyman was the lyricist, and Harms published the individual numbers with a specially designed cover that included the phrase "Written Especially for the Swift Radio Program." Titles included "Devil in Disguise," "Two Hearts Are We," "Mist on the Mirror," "Go South Young Man," "The Keeper of the Ivory Keys," and "Last Waltz with You." All of these songs were in the sentimental vein of Romberg's operettas from the late 1920s and

1930s. In addition to the newly composed songs, Harms republished "My Mimosa," from *My Princess,* with the Swift Radio Program cover.

3. Phelps was composer Charles Ives's favorite English professor at Yale during the 1890s.

4. William McBrien, *Cole Porter* (New York: Random House, 1998), 34–35.

5. William Lyon Phelps, *Autobiography with Letters* (New York and London: Oxford University Press, 1939), 940.

6. Swift Radio Program, October 27, 1934, Sigmund Romberg Recording Project, Division of Recorded Sound, Library of Congress, reel 25, selection 6.

7. Sigmund Romberg Recording Project, Division of Recorded Sound, Library of Congress, reel 2, side A.

8. "Romberg's 'Middle-Brow' Music Paying Off Big," *Variety* 175, no. 4 (July 6, 1949): 42. The musical materials used on the tours are now in the New York Public Library for the Performing Arts at Lincoln Center.

9. Rudolf Elie, Jr., "Romberg Concert," *Boston Herald,* September 20, 1943. Allison, "Sigmund Romberg Here to Celebrate."

10. Allison, "Sigmund Romberg Here to Celebrate."

11. *The Railroad Hour* was first broadcast on ABC on October 4, 1948, in forty-five-minute segments. On April 25, 1949, the length was reduced to thirty minutes. The last ABC broadcast took place on September 26, 1949, when the program transferred to NBC. It ran on NBC from October 3, 1949, to June 21, 1954.

12. *Treasury of Great Operettas,* Reader's Digest RD 40-P. 9 LPs.

13. Elinor Hughes, "The Theater: The Desert Song," *Boston Herald,* May 4, 1937.

14. D.W.S., "The Desert Song," *Boston Herald,* December 26, 1945.

15. George Freedly, "'The New Moon' Revived at Carnegie; Teddy Hart, Wilbur Evans Get Laughs," *Morning Telegraph New York,* August 29, 1942. Mark Schubart, "'The New Moon' Is a Fine Old Gal," *P.M. New York,* August 19, 1942.

16. Gerald Bordman, *American Operetta: From "H.M.S. Pinafore" to "Sweeney Todd"* (New York and Oxford: Oxford University Press, 1981), 147. Ethan Mordden, *Make Believe: The Broadway Musical in the 1920s* (New York: Oxford University Press, 1997), 41. Brooks McNamara, *The Shuberts of Broadway* (New York: Oxford University Press, 1990), 122.

17. Kathleen Hegarty Thorne, *The Story of Starlight Theatre* (Eugene, Oregon: Generation Organization, 1993), 103.

18. "Desert Song Opens Broadway's New Season," *Christian Science Monitor,* September 8, 1973.

19. Walter Kerr, "1973 Wrongs 'Desert Song,'" *New York Times,* September 16, 1973. See also Mel Gussow, "The Desert Song," *New York Times,* September 6, 1973.

20. Raymond Ericson, "Operetta: 'Desert Song' by Light Opera Troupe," *New York Times,* November 2, 1980.

21. Michael Moynihan, "How the Aunt Ednas Confound the Critics," *Sun Times* (London), June 2, 1968.

22. John Hanson, *Me and My Red Shadow* (London: W. H. Allen, 1980).

23. Ibid., 99.

24. Kurt Gänzl, *The Blackwell Guide to Musical Theatre on Record* (Oxford and Cambridge, Massachusetts: Blackwell Reference, 1990), 168.

25. The production was recorded in 1979 with the Hamburg State Opera Chorus and Orchestra, and with American tenor Erik Geisen in the title role.

26. "Die Poesie aufspüren," *Stadt Heidelberg Stattblatt Online* 32 (August 8, 2001).

27. Information on performances in Australia and New Zealand comes from the J. C. Williamson Card File and other materials at the Performing Arts Museum in Melbourne.

28. Max Morath, *The NPR Curious Listener's Guide to Popular Standards* (New York: Grand Central Press, Perigee, 2002), 54. A selected list of jazz versions of "Lover, Come Back to Me" includes: *Mildred Bailey: Her Greatest Performances, 1929–1946* (Columbia JC3L-22), *A Recital by Billie Holiday* (Verve MG V 8027), *Concert at Carnegie* (Billie Holiday version, Atlantis ATSD2), *Lover Come Back to Me — Billie Holiday* (Drive CD 3509), *Ella Fitzgerald* (LaserLight CD 15 705 [recorded ca. 1939–41]), *Ella Fitzgerald at Newport* (Verve MG V 8234 [recorded in 1957]), *The Essential Louis Armstrong* (Vanguard VSD 91/92), *Birth of the Bebop — Charlie Parker* (Stash Records ST-260), *Diz — Dizzy Gillespie* (Quintessence QJ-25071), *Dizziest — Dizzy Gillespie* (Bluebird RCA Victor 5785-1-RB), *The Aladdin Sessions — Lester Young* (Blue Note BN-LA456-H2), *Live at the Village Vanguard — Earl Hines* (Columbia CJ 44197), *Bud Powell Broadcast Performances*, vol. 1, 1953 (ESP-Disk ESP-BUD-1), *Birdland 1956, New York City — Bud Powell* (Musidisc JA5167), *The One and Only — Art Tatum* (Book-of-the-Month Records 51–5400), *Tenderly — Oscar Peterson* (Verve MG V 2046), *Dave Brubeck and Jay & Kai at Newport* (Columbia CL 932), *Harry James and His Orchestra*, vol. 6, 1947–49 (Hindsight Records HSR-150), *The Complete Artie Shaw*, vol. 1, 1938–39 (Bluebird RCA AX2-5517), *Clap Hands — Luther Henderson and His Orchestra* (Columbia CL 1340), *A Meeting of the Times — Rahsaan Roland Kirk & Al Hibbler* (Atlantic SD 1630), *Black Pearls — John Coltrane* (Prestige P-24037), *Oleo — Carl Fontana* (Pausa 7025), *Violinspiration — Stéphane Grappelli & the Diz Disley Trio* (Pausa 7098), and *Fujitsu-Concord Jazz Festival in Japan '87*, vol. 3, take 8 (Concord Jazz CJ-347).

29. Leslie M. Sabina, *Jazz Arranging and Orchestration* (New York: Schirmer Books, 2002). A selected list of jazz versions of "Softly" includes: *The Best of John Coltrane: His Greatest Years* (Impulse! AS-9200–2), *A Night at the Village Vanguard — Sonny Rollins* (Blue Note BST-81581), *The Great Buddy Tate* (Concord Jazz CJ-163), *People Time — Stan Getz, Kenny Barron* (Verve CD P2-10823), *Concorde — with the Modern Jazz Quartet* (Prestige PRLP 7005), *The Last Concert — The Modern Jazz Quartet* (Atlantic SD 2-909), *Sonny Clark Trio* (Blue Note BLP 1579), *The Toshiko Trio* (Storyville STLP 912), *Eric Dolphy Quartet: Softly, as in a Morning Sunrise* (Nathasha Imports NI-4001), *Junior Mance Trio: Softly as in a Morning Sunrise* (Enja/Weber 8080), *Tony Bennett, The McPartlands, and Friends Make Magnificent Music* (Improv IMP-7123), *Denise Jannah: The Madness of Our Love* (Blue Note CD 7243 5 22642 2 3), and *Sound of Mariana Wróblewska*, Polish Jazz, vol. 31 (Muza Polske Nagrania SXL 0847).

30. Karlakór Reykjavíkur (Reykjavik Male Choir), *Hraustir menn* (Stouthearted Men). Íslenskir tónar IT005 (1999); Þorgrímur Gestsson, *Hraustir menn: saga Karlakóror Reykjavíkur* (Stouthearted Men: The Story of the Reykjavik Male Choir) (Reykjavik: Karlakór Reykjavíkur, 2001).

31. Lee Davis, *Scandals and Follies: The Rise and Fall of the Great Broadway Revue* (New York: Limelight Editions, 2000), 356.

32. Stephen Banfield, "Popular Song and Popular Music on Stage and Film," in *The Cambridge History of American Music*, ed. David Nicholls (Cambridge: Cambridge University Press, 1998), 333.

33. Lucille Ball later starred in the Broadway musical *Wildcat* (December 16, 1960, Alvin), the show that introduced "Hey, Look Me Over."

34. This was part of his PBS *Comedy Special*, broadcast on December 11, 2002.

Epilogue

1. James Francis Cooke, "Vienna, Capital of the Kingdom of Music," *Etude*, January 1953, 8.

2. Abe Burrows wrote the book for *Guys and Dolls*. Jo Swerling was also credited due to contractual obligations after Loesser and his associates rejected Swerling's libretto.

3. Foster Hirsch, *Kurt Weill on Stage: From Berlin to Broadway* (New York: Knopf, 2002), 285–86.

4. See William A. Everett, "Songs of Social Injustice in Musicals from the 1980s and 1990s," in *Looking Back, Looking Ahead: Popular Music Studies 20 Years Later*, ed. Kimi Kärki, Rebecca Leydon, and Henri Terho (Turku, Finland: ISAPM-Norden, 2002), 521–24.

5. Two songs have slightly altered titles: "Stouthearted Men" appears as "Stout Hearted Men" and "Students Marching Song" is "Students March Song."

6. "Final Tribute Paid to Romberg by 600," *New York Times*, November 12, 1951. L. P. Cookingham, Kansas City, Missouri, telegram to Mrs. Sigmund Romberg, November 10, 1951. Cookingham Papers, Special Collections, Miller Nichols Library, University of Missouri-Kansas City.

Selected Bibliography

Principal Primary Source Collections

British Library
Free Library of Philadelphia
Harvard Theatre Collection
Library of Congress
Museum of the City of New York
New York Public Library for the Performing Arts, Lincoln Center
Shubert Archive, New York
Theatre Museum (London)
University of California, Berkeley Music Library
University of California, Los Angeles Film and Television Archive
University of California, Los Angeles Music Library Special Collections
University of Southern California Cinema-Television Library

Musical Theater and Theater History

Banfield, Stephen. "Popular Song and Popular Music on Stage and Film." In *The Cambridge History of American Music*, ed. David Nicholls, 309–44. Cambridge: Cambridge University Press, 1998.
Block, Geoffrey. *Enchanted Evenings: The Broadway Musical from "Show Boat" to Sondheim.* New York and Oxford: Oxford University Press, 1997.
Bordman, Gerald. *American Musical Comedy: From "Adonis" to "Dreamgirls."* New York and Oxford: Oxford University Press, 1982.
———. *American Musical Revue: From "The Passing Show" to "Sugar Babies."* New York and Oxford: Oxford University Press, 1985.
———. *American Musical Theatre: A Chronicle.* 3rd ed. New York and Oxford: Oxford University Press, 2001.
———. *American Operetta: From "H.M.S. Pinafore" to "Sweeney Todd."* New York and Oxford: Oxford University Press, 1981.

Citron, Stephen. *The Wordsmiths: Oscar Hammerstein 2nd & Alan Jay Lerner.* New York and Oxford: Oxford University Press, 1995.
Colerick, George. *From "The Italian Girl" to "Cabaret."* London: Juventus, 1998.
Coli, Franco P. "Ilse Marvenga: J. J. Shubert's Student Princess." *Passing Show* 9, nos. 1–2 (1985): 5–6.
Davis, Lee. *Scandals and Follies: The Rise and Fall of the Great Broadway Revue.* New York: Limelight, 2000.
DeMille, Agnes. *America Dances.* New York: Macmillan, 1980.
Drinkrow, John. *The Vintage Operetta Book.* Reading, U.K.: Osprey, 1972.
Everett, William A. *The Musical: A Research and Information Guide.* New York and London: Routledge, 2004.
Everett, William A., and Paul R. Laird, eds. *The Cambridge Companion to the Musical.* Cambridge and New York: Cambridge University Press, 2002.
Eyre, Richard, and Nicholas Wright. *Changing Stages: A View of British and American Theatre in the Twentieth Century.* New York: Knopf, 2001.
Fordin, Hugh. *Getting to Know Him: A Biography of Oscar Hammerstein II.* New York: Random House, 1977; New York: Ungar, 1986.
Frick, John W. *New York's First Theatrical Center: The Rialto at Union Square.* Ann Arbor: UMI Research Press, 1985.
Gänzl, Kurt. *Musicals.* London: Carlton, 1995, 2001.
———. *The Musical: A Concise History.* Boston: Northeastern University Press, 1997.
Green, Stanley. *The World of Musical Comedy.* 4th ed., revised and expanded. San Diego: A. S. Barnes, 1980; reprint ed. New York: Da Capo, 1984.
Green, Stanley, ed. *Rodgers and Hammerstein Fact Book: A Record of Their Works Together and with Other Collaborators.* New York: Lynn Farnol Group, 1980.
Hirsch, Foster. *The Boys from Syracuse: The Shuberts' Theatrical Empire.* Carbondale: Southern Illinois Press, 1998; reprint ed., New York: Cooper Square Press, 2000.
Johnson, Stephen Burge. *The Roof Gardens of Broadway Theatres, 1883–1942.* Ann Arbor: UMI Research Press, 1985.
Kirle, Bruce. *Unfinished Show Business: Broadway Musicals as Works-in-Progress.* Carbondale: Southern Illinois University Press, 2005.
Knapp, Raymond. *The American Musical and the Formation of National Identity.* Princeton: Princeton University Press, 2005.
———. *The American Musical and the Performance of Personal Identity.* Princeton: Princeton University Press, 2006.
Lamb, Andrew. *150 Years of Popular Musical Theatre.* New Haven: Yale University Press, 2000.
Lawson-Peebles, Robert, ed. *Approaches to the American Musical.* Exeter: University of Exeter Press, 1996.
Londré, Felicia Hardison, and Daniel J. Watermeier. *The History of North American Theater: The United States, Canada, and Mexico, From Pre-Columbian Times to the Present.* New York and London: Continuum, 2000.
McNamara, Brooks. *The Shuberts of Broadway.* New York: Oxford University Press, 1990.
Mordden, Ethan. *Beautiful Mornin': The Broadway Musical in the 1940s.* New York and Oxford: Oxford University Press, 1999.

SELECTED BIBLIOGRAPHY 339

———. *Coming Up Roses: The Broadway Musical in the 1950s.* New York and Oxford: Oxford University Press, 1998.
———. *Make Believe: The Broadway Musical in the 1920s.* New York and Oxford: Oxford University Press, 1997.
———. *Sing for Your Supper: The Broadway Musical in the 1930s.* New York: Palgrave Macmillan, 2005.
Morrison, William. *Broadway Theatres: History and Architecture.* Mineola, New York: Dover, 1999.
Norton, Richard C. *A Chronology of American Musical Theater.* 3 vols. New York: Oxford University Press, 2002.
Shubert Archive (Maryann Chach, Reagan Fletcher, Mark E. Swartz, and Sylvia Wang). *The Shuberts Present 100 Years of American Theater.* New York: Abrams, in association with the Shubert Organization, Inc., 2001.
Traubner, Richard. *Operetta: A Theatrical History.* Garden City: Doubleday & Company, 1983; rev. ed. New York and London: Routledge, 2004.
Würz, Anton. *Reclams Operettenführer.* Stuttgart: Philipp Reclam, 1982.

Musical Film and Film History

Barrios, Richard. *A Song in the Dark: The Birth of the Musical Film.* New York: Oxford University Press, 1995.
Castanza, Philip. *The Complete Films of Jeanette MacDonald and Nelson Eddy.* New York: Citadel, 1978, 1990.
Hischak, Thomas S. *Through the Screen Door: What Happened to the Broadway Musical When It Went to Hollywood.* Lanham (Maryland), Toronto, and Oxford: Scarecrow, 2004.
Lulay, Gail. *Nelson Eddy: America's Favorite Baritone.* San Jose: Authors Choice Press, 2000.
Rodman, Ronald. "Tonal Design and the Aesthetic of Pastiche in Herbert Stothart's *Maytime.*" In *Music and Cinema,* ed. James Buhler, Caryl Flinn, and David Neumeyer, 187–206. Hanover, New Hampshire: Wesleyan University Press, 2000.
Tibbetts, John C. *Composers in the Movies: Studies in Musical Biography.* New Haven and London: Yale University Press, 2005.
Turk, Edward Baron. *Hollywood Diva: A Biography of Jeanette MacDonald.* Berkeley: University of California Press, 1998.

Romberg

Allison, Gordon. "Sigmund Romberg Here to Celebrate." *New York Herald Tribune,* March 12, 1950.
Arnold, Elliott. *Deep in My Heart: A Story Based on the Life of Sigmund Romberg.* New York: Duell, Sloan and Pearce, 1949.
Braggiotti, Mary. "Romberg: A Study in Successful 'Corn' Cultivation." *New York Post,* June 18, 1943, 43.
"Catalogue of the Romberg Opera Collection." Typescript. Music Library, University of California, Berkeley.

Crawford, Richard. "Romberg, Sigmund." *Dictionary of American Biography*, supplement 5: 1951–55. Ed. John A. Garratz. New York: Charles Scribners, 1955, 584–86.
Duckles, Vincent. "Detailed Description and Appraisal of the Romberg Collection." Typescript [photocopy], January 19, 1953. Music Library, University of California, Berkeley.
Everett, William A. "*Barbara Frietchie* and *My Maryland*: The Civil War Comes to Operetta." *Passing Show* 16, no. 2 (fall 1993): 2–8.
———. "Formulating American Operetta in 1924: Friml's *Rose-Marie* and Romberg's *The Student Prince*." *American Music Research Center Journal* 11 (2001): 15–33.
———. "Golden Days in Old Heidelberg: The First-Act Finale of Romberg's *The Student Prince*." *American Music* 12, no. 3 (fall 1994): 255–82.
———. "London Productions of Romberg Operettas During the 1920s: *The Student Prince*, *The Desert Song*, and *The New Moon*." *Sonneck Society Bulletin* 21, no. 1 (spring 1995): 4–6.
———. "Romance, Nostalgia and Nevermore: American and British Operetta in the 1920s." In *The Cambridge Companion to the Musical*, 46–52. Cambridge and New York: Cambridge University Press, 2002.
———. "Sigmund Romberg and the American Operetta of the 1920s." *Arti musices* 26, no. 1 (1995): 49–64.
———. "Sigmund Romberg's Operettas *Blossom Time*, *The Student Prince*, *My Maryland*, and *My Princess*." Ph.D. dissertation (musicology), University of Kansas, 1991.
Koegel, John. "The Film Operettas of Sigmund Romberg." M.M. thesis, California State University, Los Angeles, 1984.
Lester, Edwin. "A Reminiscence of Romberg." *Curtain Call* (program magazine of the San Francisco Civic Light Opera) 2, no. 4 (1966): 15–16.
Roe, Martin. "Romberg Means Romance." *Popular Songs* 2, no. 8 (December 1936): 10.
S.S.S. "A Salute to Sigmund Romberg." *International Musician* 49 (November 1950): 14–15.
No author given. "The Story of Sigmund Romberg." *Music Journal* 12 (September 1954): 38–42.
———. "Romberg, Sigmund." *Current Biography 1945*. Ed. Anna Rothe. New York: A. W. Wilson, 1945, 510–12.

Cultural History and Related Studies

Bernstein, Matthew, and Gaylyn Studlar, eds. *Visions of the East: Orientalism in Film*. New Brunswick, New Jersey: Rutgers University Press, 1997.
Boym, Svetlana. *The Future of Nostalgia*. New York: Basic Books, 2001.
Edwards, Holly. *Noble Dreams Wicked Pleasures: Orientalism in America, 1870–1930*. Princeton: Princeton University Press in association with the Sterling and Francine Clark Art Institute, 2000.
Eliot, Marc. *Down 42nd Street: Sex, Money, Culture, and Politics at the Crossroads of the World*. New York: Warner Books, 2001.
George, Rosemary Marangoly. *The Politics of Home: Postcolonial Relocations and Twentieth-Century Fiction*. Berkeley: University of California Press, 1996. Paperback ed., 1999.

Goldsworthy, Vesna. *Inventing Ruritania: The Imperialism of the Imagination.* New Haven: Yale University Press, 1998.
Jenkins, Alan. *The Twenties.* New York: Universe Books, 1974.
Levine, Lawrence W. *Highbrow/Lowbrow: The Emergence of Cultural Hierarchy in America.* Cambridge: Harvard University Press, 1988.
Naylor, David. *Great American Movie Theaters.* Washington, D.C.: The Preservation Press, 1987.
North, Michael. *Reading 1922: A Return to the Scene of the Modern.* New York: Oxford University Press, 1999.
Said, Edward W. *Orientalism.* New York: Random House, 1978. Paperback ed., New York: Vintage Books, 1979.
Seabrook, John. *Nobrow: The Culture of Marketing, The Marketing of Culture.* New York: Knopf, 2000; New York: Vintage Books, 2001.
Todorova, Maria. *Imagining the Balkans.* New York: Oxford University Press, 1997.

Index

Abarbanell, Lina, 110
Abd-El-Kim, 168
accusations of musical thievery, 23–27
adaptations: film operettas, 4–5, 246, 257–274; musical adaptations, 26–27, 115–120, 187–188; operettas, 83–92, 187–188, 257
"After the Ball," 58
"Ah, Sweet Mystery of Life," 31
"Alexander's Ragtime Band," 54–55
"All Alone," 131
"All Alone in a City of Girls," 90
allusions to Romberg's music, 288–289
"All Year Round," 31
"Along the Winding Road," 231–232
"A Love Song of Long Ago," 256
Alt-Heidelberg (1901), 124–128
Americana, 230–244
"American Humoresque," 34
American operettas: characteristics, 77–83; duple-meter compositions, 86–88, 101, 107, 186; lost love story lines, 85–86; musical style, 101, 105–107; sense of place, 198–199; waltzes, 85–86, 90, 105–107, 123, 186–190
"American Punch, The," 19
American Society of Composers and Publishers, 15
American Society of Composers, Authors, and Publishers (ASCAP), 20
"America's Popular Song," 57

America's Singing Sweethearts. *See* Eddy, Nelson; MacDonald, Jeanette
Annie Dear (1924), 150
appropriated music, 287–288
"April Showers," 62
"April Snow," 235, 236
Arabian culture. *See Desert Song, The* (1926); Orientalism
"Are You Love?," 218
Arnold, Elliott, 6, 11, 13–14, 80
Artists and Models productions, 17, 48, 50
Asaf, George, 91
Astaire, Adele, 18, 19, 53, 131
Astaire, Fred, 18, 19, 53, 54, 131
Atkinson, Brooks, 27, 228
Atteridge, Harold B.: collaboration with Romberg, 16, 29; lost love story lines, 58; as lyricist, 18; musical comedies, 62, 65–66; portrayal in *Deep in My Heart* (1954), 10; ragtime-style music, 56
"Auf Wiedersehn," 77, 84–86, 86, 87, 94
Australian productions, 286
authors' rights, 20
Avedon, Doe, 8, 9
Ayres, Agnes, 164
"Azuri's Dance," 173

Babes in Toyland (1903), 30
"Baby's Asleep," 34–35
"Bachelor Girl and Boy," 88

"Bagdad," 64
Balalaika (1939), 256
Balkans. See Ruritania
ballads. See *Up in Central Park* (1945)
ballet. See *Girl in Pink Tights, The* (1954)
"Ballet of the Flowers, The," 192
Barratt, Augustus, 71
Barron, Fred [Ted], 74
Barrymore, John, 259
Bartsch, Hans, 93
"Battle Hymn," 187–188
Baxter, June, 110
"Bedouin Girl," 59, 60
Belasco, David, 82–83, 182, 251–254
Bell, Gertrude, 168
"Beloved," 260
Benrimo, J. H., 182
Bent, Marion, 68
Berg, Clara, 38
Berlin, Irving, 20, 48, 54, 57–58
Bernauer, Rudolf, 93
Berté, Heinrich, 110, 115
Bettelstudent, Der/The Beggar Student (1882), 41, 42
Beverly Hills studio, 23
"Big Back Yard, The," 233, 240
biopics, 122. See also *Blossom Time* (1921); *Deep in My Heart* (1954)
Black Crook, The (1866), 242–243
Blossom Time (1921): characteristics, 3, 108–109, 111–112; and Howard Marsh, 130; lyricists, 11; musical adaptations, 26–27, 115–120; nomenclature, 79; performance runs, 1, 110–111; plot motifs, 113–114; reviews, 112–113; revivals, 281–282; road tours, 110–111
Blue Paradise, The (1915), 19, 66–67, 77, 79, 84–86, 92
Blushing Bride, The (1922), 65–66, 70
Boccaccio (1879), 42
Boggio, Luigi, 38
Bolton, Guy, 19, 190
"Bombay Bombashay, The," 74
Bombo (1921), 10, 16, 62–63, 70
"Bonnie Blue Flag, The," 188
Borodin, Alexander, 67
"Boss Tweed," 240, 273
Boucicault, Aubrey, 125

Bowers, Frederick V., 93
Bredschneider, Willy, 93
Brice, Fanny, 47, 131
British revivals, 284
"Broad Highway, The," 31
Broadway legacy, 1–3
Broadway musicals, 210–211, 293, 297–298
Broadway Serenade (1939), 257
Bronson-Howard, George, 50
Brooke, J. Clifford, 105
Brooks, Laurence, 241
Brown, Heywood, 72, 73
"Brown October Ale," 137
Bryan, Al, 72
Burke, Tom, 68–69
Bustanoby's Restaurant, 45

Caesar, Irving, 15, 18, 20, 212, 219
"California, Here I Come," 62
Campbell, George, 72, 73
Cantor, Eddie, 49
"Cardinal's Guard Are We, The," 243
Carey, A. J., 68
Carol II (King of Romania), 227, 230
Carousel (1945), 156, 237
"Carousel in the Park, The," 237, 273
Carpenter, Edward Childs, 219
Carroll, Earl, 48
Carroll, Harry, 45
Casino Theatre, 162, 221, 324n9
Castle, Vernon and Irene, 55
Castle walk, 55
Chanson d'amour/Song of Love (1921), 110
Chappelle, Frederick, 91
Cherry Blossoms (1927): and Howard Marsh, 130; musical compositions, 29; musical program, 189; performance runs, 182; plot motifs, 182–183; recurring waltz duets, 186, 187
childhood, 38
"Children of Dreams," 249
Children of Dreams (1931), 23, 246, 248–249
"Chinatown," 49
Chitty Chitty Bang Bang (1968), 79
Christie, Agatha, 79
cinema, 211, 245–257
Civil War songs, 187–188
classical music references, 57

Clements, Dolly, 74–75
"Close as Pages in a Book," 235, 236–237, 237
Clutsam, G. H., 110
Collaborations, as portrayed in *Deep in My Heart* (1954), 11
Colonial Gaze, 162–163, 167–168
"Come Back, Sweet Dreams," 88
"Come, Boys, Let's All Be Gay, Boys," 129, 140–141, 142, 260
Como, Perry, 35
composers' rights, 20
compositional process, 22, 22–29, 37, 53–61
contemporary operetta composers, 30–34
Cook, Olga, 113, 115
Corbin, John, 101
Coward, Noël, 211
Cranford, C. B., 15, 81
Crawford, Clifton, 89, 90
Creel, George, 52
Croatia, 37–39, 285
cross-dressing themes, 42
Cunningham, Michael, 74–75
"Currier and Ives," 238
"Currier and Ives Ballet," 238
Cuvillier, Charles, 110
czardas, 41, 92, 153
Czárdásfürstin (1915), 33
Czardas Princess, The (1915), 33

"Dainty Wisp of Thistledown," 201
Dale, Alan, 112
"Dance My Darling," 225
dance styles: in American operettas, 86–87; changing tastes, 54–55; *The Desert Song* (1926), 166–167, 173–176; *East Wind* (1931), 217; musical comedies, 66; revues, 58; *Up in Central Park* (1945), 238
Dancing Around (1914), 52, 62, 70
Dancing Girl, The (1923), 18, 19, 65–66, 68–69
"Dancing Will Keep You Young," 100
"Darling," 71
"Daughter of the Regiment—, The," 92
Davies, Maria Thompson, 70
Dean, Julia, 107
"Dear Girls, Goodbye," 190
"Dear Heart My Heart Sweetheart," 74

death of Romberg, 296
Deep in My Heart (1954): historical accuracy, 6–11, 69–70, 178; musical comedy selections, 69; musical program, 12–13; musical styles, 28, 69–70; setting, 39
Deep in My Heart: A Story Based on the Life of Sigmund Romberg (1949), 6, 11, 13–14, 80
"Deep in My Heart, Dear," 152; extended musical scenes, 144; Lillian's theme song, 17; musical style, 137, 139–140; *The Student Prince* (1924), 3, 128, 134; *The Student Prince* (1954), 260
De Koven, Reginald, 77, 137
Delorme, Hugues, 110
Demarest, Frances, 87, 88
"Desert Song, The," 174, 175, 179–180, 263–264
Desert Song, The (1926): characteristics, 3–4, 155–157; film adaptations, 261–267; lyricists, 11, 30, 155–157; motifs, 42; musical program, 27, 29, 160, 169–180; nomenclature, 79; Orientalism, 155, 158, 161–169, 216; performance runs, 1, 157–158; performer debuts, 19; plot motifs, 158–161, 163; popularity, 158; reviews, 157–158, 166; revivals, 281–285; similarities to other productions, 196–197
Desert Song, The (1929), 261–262
Desert Song, The (1932), 262–263
Desert Song, The (1943), 263–265
Desert Song, The (1953), 246, 265–267, 273
Desert Song, The (1955), 267
Deslys, Gaby, 10–11
De Sylva, B. G. "Buddy," xii, 10, 16, 157, 311
discography, 302–309
disguise and impersonation, 42–43, 154, 160–161, 167–168, 185
"Dixie," 188
"Doing My Bit," 58–59
Doing Our Bit (1917), 52, 58
Dolly, Rosie, 49
Donna Juanita (1880), 42
Donnelly, Dorothy: *Blossom Time* (1921), 119; collaboration with Romberg, 11, 27, 29, 109–110, 156–157; *My Maryland* (1927), 183–184; *My Princess* (1927), 185; portrayal in *Deep in My Heart* (1954), 11;

Donnelly, Dorothy (continued)
  The Student Prince (1924), 126–127, 132, 136, 149
Donnelly, Henry, 109
Donnelly, Sarah Williams, 109
Donnelly, Thomas Lester, 109
"Door of My Dreams," 33
"Down by the Nile," 107
Dramatists' Guild, 20
"Dream Girl," 31
Dream Girl, The (1924), 31, 49
"Dreams from Out of the Past," 58, 59
Dreimäderlhaus, Das/The House of the Three Maidens (1916), 110
"Drinking Song," 129, 134, 136–137, 138, 146, 260
duality themes, 7–8
Duchess of Chicago, The (1928), 33
Duchess of Dantzic, The (1905), 78
Dudley, Bide, 74
duets: *Blossom Time* (1921), 120–121; *The Blue Paradise* (1915), 85; *Children of Dreams* (1931), 249; *The Desert Song* (1926), 178–179; *The Girl from Brazil* (1916), 88; *Her Soldier Boy* (1916), 90–91; *The Melting of Molly* (1918), 71; musical comedies, 71; *New Moon* (1940), 272; *The Night is Young* (1935), 250; operettas, 182; *Princess Flavia* (1925), 152; recurring waltz duets, 186–187, 222; *The Student Prince* (1924), 135–137, 139–140, 149; *Sunny River* (1941), 231; *Viennese Nights* (1930), 248. *See also* love duets; waltzes
Duke of Duluth, The (1903), 78
Dumas, Alexandre, 65
duple-meter songs: in American operettas, 86–88, 101, 107, 186; *Blossom Time* (1921), 117; *Children of Dreams* (1931), 249; *The Desert Song* (1926), 178–180; dramatic role, 293; duets, 3, 88, 90–91; *East Wind* (1931), 218; *Forbidden Melody* (1936), 229; *The Girl from Brazil* (1916), 88; *Her Soldier Boy* (1916), 90–91; love duets, 206; *May Wine* (1935), 225; musical comedies, 70; *The New Moon* (1928), 201, 206; *Nina Rosa* (1930), 214–215; *Princess Flavia* (1925), 152; ragtime-style music, 70; recur-
ring themes, 36; *Viennese Nights* (1930), 248
Durbin, Deanna, 238, 272–273
Dvořák, Antonín, 32, 81

early career, 1–2, 14, 38–39
"Eastern and Western Love," 156, 163, 171, 267
East Wind (1931), 29, 157, 215–219
Eberhardt, Isabelle, 168
Eddy, Nelson, 271; *The Desert Song* (1955), 267; *The Girl of the Golden West* (1938), 246, 250–254; *Let Freedom Ring* (1939), 42, 255–256; *Maytime* (1937), 259; *New Moon* (1940), 270; *Rosalie* (1937), 193; and Victor Herbert, 30
"Edelweiss," 150
Egyptian history and culture, 161–162
Ellinger, Desiree, 183
Emerson, John, 125
Englefeld, Violet, 57
"Entrance of Azuri," 175
"Erlkönig, Die," 35
Errol, Leon, 150
"Esmerelda," 19
ethnic musical identifiers, 59, 99–100, 106–107
European heritage, 37–40
European revivals, 284–285
"Evening with Sigmund Romberg, An," 275, 278, 279
Evening with Sigmund Romberg, An, 276, 277
"Every Lover Must Meet His Fate," 31
"Evolution of Ragtime (Evolution of a Rag)," 66
exoticism: *Cherry Blossoms* (1927), 187; *The Desert Song* (1943), 262–265; *The Desert Song* (1953), 266; *East Wind* (1931), 215–219; Indianist identifiers, 188–189; as motif, 42–44, 59, 67–68; in musical comedies, 75–76; musical style, 29; *Nina Rosa* (1930), 212–215; sense of place, 211, 212–219. *See also* ethnic musical identifiers; Orientalism
"Eyes That Love," 186
Eysler, Edmund, 77

Faith, Percy, 35
"Faithfully Yours," 35
Fall, Leo, 30, 122
familiar/exotic dualities, 8. *See also* exoticism; Orientalism
"Farewell to Youth," 134, 140
"Farmer Jacob," 143–144
"Farmer's Daughter, The," 268, 270
"Fascinating Rhythm," 131
"Fat-Fat-Fatima," 67, 69–70
Fatinitza (1876), 42
female chorus, 149, 176, 208, 264
Ferrer, José, 6, 9, 9–10
fictional geography, 43–45
Fields, Dorothy, 29, 232, 236
Fields, Herbert, 73, 232
Fields, Lew, 19, 72–73
Fields, W. C., 47
"Fiesta," 189
"Fifi's Song," 264
film biopics, 6–11
films: adaptations, 4–5, 246, 257–274; film operettas, 4, 23, 189, 245–255, 274; influence on musical theater, 211; Romberg's compositions for, 255–257, 298–299
Firefly, The (1911), 32, 156, 198
"Fireman's Bride, The," 239–240
"Flag That Flies Above Us, The," 140, 143
Fledermaus, Die/The Bat (1876), 41, 42
Flora Bella (1916), 110
Flotte Bursche/Navy Lads (1863), 41
Fokine, Mikhail, 192
Follies, 48
"Follow the Sun to the South," 186, 187, 190
Follow Thru (1929), 157
"Foolish Little Maiden, I," 92
Foolish Wives (1922), 35–36
Forbidden Melody (1936), 226–230
"For the Sake of Humanity," 58
42nd Street (1933), 211
"For You," 139
Fox, Harry, 55
foxtrot: *The Blushing Bride* (1922), 66; musical comedies, 150; *My Princess* (1927), 190; *Nina Rosa* (1930), 214; popularity, 55; *The Student Prince* (1924), 144
Franz Schubert Memorial Committee, 113

"French Military Marching Song," 160, 169, 176, 263, 264
Friml, Rudolf, 32–33, 156, 188, 199
Fritchie, Barbara Hauer, 183–185
"Fruitpickers Song, The," 249

Galli-Curci, Amelita, 57
"Galli-Curci Rag, The," 57
Gardel, Carlos, 207
"Garlands Bright," 143
"Gaucho March," 214–215
"Gaudeamus igitur," 129, 141, 143, 146, 261
"Gay Parisienne," 264, 266
George White's *Scandals*, 48
Gerber, Alex, 19, 73, 107
German music and culture, 124–132, 136. *See also* World War I
Gershwin, George: collaborations, 181, 191–193; *The Dancing Girl* (1923), 68; Dramatists' Guild, 20; *Lady, Be Good!* (1924), 131; mentorship by Romberg, 18; as pianist, 22–23; *Rosalie* (1928), 191–193
Gershwin, Ira, 20, 131, 192
Gerstenberger, Emil, 149, 187, 192, 194
"Gianina," 106
"Gigolo," 190
Girl from Brazil, The (1916), 87–90
Girl from Utah, The (1914), 89
Girl in Pink Tights, The (1954), 241–243
Girl of the Golden West, The (1938), 4, 246, 250–255
"Girl on the Prow, The," 201
Gish, Dorothy, 125
"Give Me a Roll on a Drum," 220–221
Glyn, Elinor, 130, 177–178
"Go Away, Girls," 100–101
Goetz, E. Ray, 19, 65, 66
"Going to the Devil," 243
"Golden Days," 134, 135–136, 136, 140, 260
"Golden Pheasant, The," 58
Goldsworthy, John H., 88
Goodman, Alfred, 68, 194
Good News! (1927), 157
"Gorgeous Alexander," 197, 207, 207–208, 271
Graetz, Paul, 110
"Grandioso," 203

Grass Widow, The (1917), 130
Grauman's Egyptian Theater, 161–162, 324n8
Gray, Alexander, 247, 262
Greenwich Village Follies productions, 48, 50, 130
Grey, Clifford, 150, 268, 270
gypsy music, 228
"Gypsy Song," 98–99

Halliday, Robert, 157, 165, 194, 286
Hamilton, Cosmo, 110
Hamm, Charles, 55
Hammerstein, Arthur, 32, 198
Hammerstein, Oscar, 2nd: collaboration with Rodgers, 11, 156–157; collaboration with Romberg, 3, 15–16, 23, 29–30, 246–250, 293; *The Desert Song* (1926), 155–157; Dramatists' Guild, 20; *East Wind* (1931), 216; as lyricist, 29–30, 194; *May Wine* (1935), 223; *The New Moon* (1928), 194; *The Night is Young* (1935), 249–250; operettas, 211; portrayal in *Deep in My Heart* (1954), 11; *Sunny River* (1941), 231–232; *Viennese Nights* (1930), 246–247
Hampton, Hope, 185, 326n7
Hands Up (1915), 19, 65, 66
Hanson, John, 148–149, 284
Harbach, Otto, 29, 155–156, 198, 211, 212, 226–228
Harris, Charles K., 58
Harris, Lillian, 10, 16–17
Hart, Lorenz, 18, 19, 72–73
Hassell, George, 88–89
"Hear the Gypsies Playing," 228
Heidelberg (1901), 124–125
"Heidelberg Stein Song," 137, 143
"Hello, Central, Give Me No Man's Land," 49
Hello, Lola (1926), 110
Herbert, Evelyn, 151, 153, 184, 184, 194, 219, 221
Herbert, Victor, 14, 30–32, 49, 198
Her Soldier Boy (1916), 89–92
Herzogin von Chicago, Die (1928), 33
"He's Coming Home," 90
Heuberger, Victor, 39
"He Walks with Me," 34

Heyman, Eddie, 34–35, 255
High Jinks (1913), 32
Hirsch, Arthur, 128
Hirsch, Foster, 111
Hirsch, Louis Achille, 45, 130
"History," 90
Hitchy-Koo of 1922, 19
hobbies, 14
Hollywood: film adaptations, 4–5, 257–274; Romberg's compositions, 246–257
"Homeland," 150–151
Honolulu (1939), 256
Howard, Eugene, 57
Howard, Willie, 49, 57
"How Long Has This Been Going On?," 192
Huffman, J. C., 105, 108
"Huguette's Waltz," 33
human rights advocacy, 294
Hungarian nationality, 8–9, 14, 37
"Hussar March," 192

"I am the Pasha," 107
"I Built a Dream One Day," 224
"I Dare Not Love You," 152, 153
"I'd Be a Fool," 217–218
"I'll Bring a Love Song," 247–248
"I'll Walk with God," 260
"I Love to Go Swimmin' with Wimmin,'" 67–68, 69–70
"I'm Coming at Your Call," 137
impersonation. *See* disguise and impersonation
Indianist identifiers, 188–189
"Indian Love Call," 33, 188
Indigo und die vierzig Räuber/Indigo and the Forty Thieves (1871), 41, 42
influence on musical theater: Romberg's compositions, 288, 290; World War I, 77–80, 93, 100, 107–108, 124–127; World War II, 81, 229–232
In Heidelberg (1924), 127
"In Love with Romance," 241
"Interrupted Trio," 203
"In the Land of Yesterday," 74
invented geographic areas, 43–45
Irene (1919), 102
"I Saw Your Eyes," 218

"It," 177–178, 179, 262
"Italian Street Song," 31
"It Doesn't Cost You Anything to Dream," 235–236
"It's a Wonderful World," 217
"(I've) A Little Bit o' Scotch (in Me)," 59
"I Want a Kiss," 156
"I Want to Go Home," 31

Jackson, Stewart, 88
Jazzadoo, 69–70
"Jazz All Your Troubles Away," 71
Jazz Singer, The (1927), 61, 211, 245
jazz standards, 286–287
Jeanmaire, René "Zizi," 242
Jeans, Ronald, 47
Jeffreys, Anne, 241
Jerome, William, 49
Jewish roots, 9
Jolson, Al, 10, 16–17, 18, 49, 54, 61–64
Jones, Stephen, 110
"Jump, Jim Crow," 99
"Just Hello," 228
"Just We Two," 134, 140, 143

Kahn, Gus, 250–251, 253, 256
Kálmán, Emmerich, 33–34
"Kathie's Entrance," 260
Katinka (1915), 32
Kaufman, George S., 112
"Keep Repeating It," 92
Kelly, Fred, 69
Kelly, Gene, 6, 69
"Ker-Choo," 190
Kernell, William, 110
Kern, Jerome: collaborations, 156; Dramatists' Guild, 20; and Elizabeth Marbury, 19; musical comedies, 49, 89; music-word relationships, 29; operettas, 211; as pianist, 22–23; and Romberg, 15. See also *Show Boat* (1927)
"King Can Do No Wrong, The," 192–193
"Kingdom of Dreams," 192
"Kiss Waltz, The," 90
Kollo, Walter, 93, 122
Kummer, Clare, 150
Kummer, Frederick Arnold, 105–106

"Ladies from Hades," 243
Lady, Be Good! (1924), 131
Lady Fair. See Desert Song, The (1926)
Lady in Ermine, The/Die Frau im Hermelin (1922), 122
"Lady in the Window, The," 228
Lamb, Arthur J., 93
Lanza, Mario, 259–261
Lauder, Howell, 64
Lawrence, Thomas Edward (Lawrence of Arabia), 167–168
"Leading Lady," 64
Lean, Cecil, 84
Lederer, George W., 48
legacy, 275–289
"Leg of Mutton"/"Le gigot," 34, 45
Lehár, Franz, 39, 43–44, 78
Lehmann, Maurice, 221
Leichte Kavallerie/Light Cavalry (1866), 42
Leitzback, Adeline, 72
Let Freedom Ring (1939), 42, 255
"Let Love Go," 171
"Let Us Sing a Song," 140
Lewis, Bernard, 59
"Liberty Number," 58
librettists. *See* Donnelly, Dorothy
Lilac Time (1922), 110
Lindbergh, Charles, 191–192
"Little Church Around the Corner, The," 107
"Little Peach," 150
"Long Live the Night," 264–265, 266
"Lost in Loveliness," 243–244
lost love story lines: in American operettas, 85–86; *Blossom Time* (1921), 121–122; Broadway musicals, 293; Romberg's waltzes, 58, 63–64; *The Student Prince* (1924), 128; *The Student Prince* (1954), 261; *They Gave Him a Gun* (1937), 256
Louie the 14th (1925), 150–151, 154
"Love Birds," 25
Love Birds (1921), 20, 24, 65–68, 70
Love Call, The (1927): musical program, 190; nomenclature, 79; performance runs, 182; plot motifs, 185–186, 188–189; recurring waltz duets, 186
love duets: *Blossom Time* (1921), 120–121; *The Blue Paradise* (1915), 85; *The Desert*

love duets (continued)
Song (1926), 173–174, 178–179, 204, 206; duple-meter compositions, 206; *East Wind* (1931), 218; *Forbidden Melody* (1936), 228–229; *The Girl from Brazil* (1916), 88; *Her Soldier Boy* (1916), 90–91; *The Melting of Molly* (1918), 71; *My Romance* (1948), 241; *The New Moon* (1928), 195, 204; *New Moon* (1940), 272; *Nina Rosa* (1930), 214–215; *Princess Flavia* (1925), 152; *Rosalie* (1928), 192; *Up in Central Park* (1945), 235–237; *Viennese Nights* (1930), 248; waltzes, 204. *See also* duets; waltzes
"Love Is the Funniest Thing," 243
"Love Me Tonight," 33
"Lover, Come Back to Me," 205; jazz standards, 286–287; *The New Moon* (1928), 3, 196, 197, 203–204; *New Moon* (1930), 269–270; *New Moon* (1940), 271–272
"Love's Intense in Tents," 73
low brow/high brow dualities: *The Girl in Pink Tights* (1954), 243; *Maytime* (1937), 259; revues, 57; Romberg's attitude, 8
Lubitsch, Ernst, 125
Lüchow's Restaurant, 14–15
Luders, Gustav, 78, 137
Lustige Witwe, Die (1905), 43–44
Lydy, Beth, 88, 89
lyricists: collaborations, 11, 109, 192; musical comedies, 65; music-word relationships, 29–30; operettas, 70, 93, 155–156; revues, 49. *See also* Atteridge, Harold B.; Caesar, Irving; Donnelly, Dorothy; Hammerstein, Oscar, 2nd; Smith, Harry B.; Young, Rida Johnson

Macdonald, Ballard, 65
MacDonald, Jeanette, 271; *Broadway Serenade* (1939), 257; *The Girl of the Golden West* (1938), 246, 250–254; *Maytime* (1937), 259; *New Moon* (1940), 270; and Victor Herbert, 30
Macgowan, Kenneth, 112
MacRae, Gordon, 266, 275, 280
Magic Melody, The (1919), 20, 31, 104–108. *See also Maytime* (1917)
Maid in America (1915), 52, 56–57, 58

major mode, 28–29, 169
"Making of a Girl, The," 18
malapropisms, 15
male chorus: *Balalaika* (1939), 256; *Blossom Time* (1921), 127; *The Desert Song* (1926), 158, 169; dramatic role, 293–294; *Let Freedom Ring* (1939), 255–256; *Louie the 14th* (1925), 150–151; *My Maryland* (1927), 187; *The New Moon* (1928), 195; *Nina Rosa* (1930), 214; *Princess Flavia* (1925), 151–153; *Rosalie* (1928), 192; *The Student Prince* (1924), 129, 141, 143, 144, 146–147, 149; *The Student Prince* (1954), 260
Mandel, Frank, 155, 157, 194, 216, 223
Mansfield, Richard, 125
"Marche Militaire," 222
marches: appropriated music, 287–288; *Balalaika* (1939), 256; *Children of Dreams* (1931), 249; *The Desert Song* (1926), 180; dramatic role, 293–294; *The Girl in Pink Tights* (1954), 243; *The Girl of the Golden West* (1938), 253; *Let Freedom Ring* (1939), 255–256; *Maytime* (1917), 100–101; *Melody* (1933), 220–221; military themes, 58–59; *My Lady's Glove* (1917), 92; *My Maryland* (1927), 187–188; *The New Moon* (1928), 201, 203; *Nina Rosa* (1930), 214; *Rosalie* (1928), 192; *Rose de France* (1933), 222; *The Student Prince* (1924), 140–141; *The Student Prince* (1954), 260; *Up in Central Park* (1945), 240; *Up in Central Park* (1948), 273; Viennese operettas, 41
"Marche Triomphale," 222
"March of the Turkish Guard," 222
Margetson, Arthur, 68
"Mariache," 254–255
"Marianne," 271
Marie, Queen of Romania, 191
Marriage of Figaro, The/Le nozze di Figaro, 197
marriages, 9–10, 17
"Marseilles," 66
Marsh, Howard, 113, 115, 129, 130, 183
Marvenga, Ilse, 129–130, 132, 143
"Maryland, My Maryland," 188
"Mary, Queen of Scots," 72
May Blossoms (1885), 82

INDEX

Maynard, Dorothy, 88
Maytime (1917), 93–103; Australian and New Zealand productions, 286; characteristics, 3; film adaptations, 246, 258–259; importance, 102–103, 230; lyricists, 11; motifs, 42; musical style, 71, 98–101; nomenclature, 79; performance runs, 1, 101–102; plot motifs, 94–101; reviews, 101–102. *See also Magic Melody, The* (1919)
Maytime (1923), 258
Maytime (1927), 258
Maytime (1937), 246, 259, 273
May Wine (1935), 27, 157, 223–226
mazurkas, 41, 99
McCarthy, Joseph, 102
melodic similarities, 23–27
Melody (1933), 219–221
Melting of Molly, The (1918), 70–71
Mercer, Ruby, 227, 229
Merry Widow, The (1907), 78
Metro-Goldwin-Mayer (MGM), 6–7, 249, 254–261, 267–270
Mexican themes, 189
Meyer-Foerster, William, 124
Meyer, George, 72
Midnight Girl, The (1914), 69, 70
"Military Stamp," 90
military themes, 42, 52–53, 58–59
Miller, Marilyn, 190–193
Millöcker, Karl, 41
minor mode, 28–29, 169
Modern Eve, A (1915), 49
modern musical style, 73
Monte Cristo, Jr. (1919), 65, 66–67
Montgomery, James, 102
"Moonlight and Violins," 229
Moore, Grace, 131, 267–268, 270
morality themes, 56–57
"Mother," 90, 190
Motzan, Otto, 49
Mouse That Roared, The (1959), 80
movies, 211, 245–257
"Mr. and Mrs.," 66, 69–70
musical comedies: and Al Jolson, 61–64; changing tastes, 210–211; characteristics, 61; framing stories, 62–64; *The Girl in Pink Tights* (1954), 243; *The Magic Melody* (1919), 107; *My Princess* (1927), 185; narrative plots, 65–66; *Nina Rosa* (1930), 214–215; operetta-style compositions, 70–76, 88–89; ragtime-style music, 70–71, 74; revue-style compositions, 64–70; romantic musical comedies, 196; Romberg's compositions, 62–76, 150. *See also* revues
musical films, 211, 245–249
musical form. *See* marches; tangos; Tin Pan Alley musical style; waltzes
as musical score collector, 21–22
musical style: *Children of Dreams* (1931), 249; film operettas, 246–255; *The Girl in Pink Tights* (1954), 243; *Maytime* (1917), 71, 98–101; musical comedies, 69–70; operettas, 85, 88–90; Orientalism, 169; revues, 53–61; Romberg's compositions, 22–29; *Up in Central Park* (1945), 233–238
musical theater. *See* operettas; revues; Shubert Brothers
"Musical Trip Through Old Vienna, A," 39–40
Music Box Revues, 48, 131
as musician, 295
Music in the Air (1932), 156, 211
music library, 21–22
music-word relationships, 29–30, 54
"My Cleopatra Girl," 59
"My First Love Letter," 150
"My First Love, My Last Love," 215
"My Heart Is Calling," 123
My Lady's Glove (1917), 91–92
"My Mammy," 62
My Maryland (1927), 11; military themes, 42; musical program, 189; nomenclature, 79; performance runs, 182; plot motifs, 183–185; recurring waltz duets, 186, 187
"My Mimosa," 187
"My Own Willow Tree," 186, 187
My Princess (1927), 11; musical program, 27, 28, 190; nomenclature, 79; performance runs, 182; plot motifs, 185; recurring waltz duets, 186–187
My Romance (1948), 230, 240–241
"My Señorita," 88
"My Sleeping Beauty," 249
"My Springtime Thou Art," 114, 116–119, 117, 118

Nathan, George Jean, 130
Naughty Marietta (1910), 30–31, 93, 198
nautical themed operettas, 197
"Never For You," 204
"Never Had an Education," 221
New Moon, The (1928): characteristics, 3, 43, 208–209; film adaptations, 246, 267–272; historical accuracy, 198–199; lyricists, 11, 157; musical program, 193–194, 199–209, 327n25; nomenclature, 79; and Oscar Hammerstein II, 156, 194; performance runs, 1, 193; reviews, 201; revivals, 281–283, 285; setting, 31, 194–198; sheet music cover, 200; similarities to other compositions, 24; similarities to other productions, 196–197
New Moon, The (1930), 267–270
New Moon, The (1940), 246, 270, 273
New Zealand productions, 286
Night Is Young, The (1935), 11, 246, 249–250
"Nightlife," 190
Nina Rosa (1930), 79, 212–215, 285
Nobody Home (1915), 49
"No, No, Nanette!," 26
No, No, Nanette! (1924), 24, 157
non-theatrical compositions, 34–36, 299
nostalgia: Americana, 230–244; musical comedies, 150–151; *My Romance* (1948), 241; operettas, 80–86, 113, 131, 229; Romberg's waltzes, 92, 290–292; *The Student Prince* (1924), 128, 134–135, 149; *The Student Prince* (1954), 261; *Viennese Nights* (1930), 248. *See also* American operettas
"No Time to Argue," 257
"No Use Pretending," 228
Novarro, Ramon, 125, 250
novelty revues, 50
nudity, 50

Offenbach, Jacques, 41
"Officers of the 25th," 92
"Oh, Allah," 59
"Oh! Doctor, Doctor," 71
"Oh Gee! Oh Joy!," 192
"Oh, Promise Me," 78
"Oh, Say Can You See," 273
"Oh, You John," 69

Oklahoma!, 156, 230, 238
Old Heidelberg (1901), 124–126
Old Heidelberg (film version), 125
Old World/New World dualities, 7–8
"Omar Khayyam," 59
"On a Modern Wedding Day," 57
"Once Around the Clock," 225
"Once upon a Time," 31, 105–107
"One Alone," 173; *The Desert Song* (1926), 163; *The Desert Song* (1943), 263–265; *The Desert Song* (1953), 267; dramatic role, 171, 178–180; portrayal in *Deep in My Heart* (1954), 167
"One Flower Grows Alone in Your Garden," 163, 171, 263, 267
O'Neil, William J., 73
"One Kiss," 24, 26, 199, 201, 269–270, 271
one-step dance, 86–87
"One Step into Love," 86–87
"Only for You," 58
"Only One," 153
"Only One Love Ever Fills the Heart," 114, 116, 119
"(On) The Levee Along Broadway," 66
"On the Lonely Lagoon," 69
On the Town (1944), 238
operatic styles, 57–58
operettas: adaptations, 83–92, 122–123, 187–188, 257; American settings, 230–244; changing tastes, 210–211, 230; characteristics, 2–4, 40–44, 77–81; contemporary composers, 30–34; European settings, 219–230; film operettas, 4, 23, 189, 245–255, 274; historical background, 77–78; and musical comedies, 70–76, 88–89; musical style, 85, 88–90; nostalgia, 80–86, 92, 113, 128, 131, 229; recurring waltz duets, 186–187, 222; revivals, 2, 275–276, 280–285; Romberg's approach, 77–92, 104–123, 181–209, 211–244; similarities to other productions, 151–154, 188. *See also* American operettas; nostalgia
Orientalism: *The Desert Song* (1926), 155, 158, 161–169, 216; *The Desert Song* (1943), 262–265; *The Desert Song* (1953), 266; *East Wind* (1931), 215–219; Egyptian history and culture, 161–162; *The Magic*

INDEX 353

Melody (1919), 107; musical style, 59–61, 64, 67–68, 165–167, 169; plot motifs, 162–163, 167; sexuality, 162–166
Orry-Kelly, 213
Osijek, Croatia, 38–39, 285
Out of the Blue (1938), 257
Over the Top (1917), 19, 52–53, 58

Pagans (1921), 20
Parisian Belle (1930). See *New Moon, The* (1930)
parodies, 5, 276, 288
Passing Show productions, 18, 19, 48, 50, 51, 53, 57–59
patriotic themes, 52–53, 58–59, 255–256, 263–265, 273
"Payador," 214
"Peace, Peace to My Lonely Heart," 114, 116
Peacock, Bertram, 113, 115
"Peep into the Workshop of a Composer, A," 28, 169
pentatonicism, 4, 174, 188, 265, 267
performance runs, 297–298
performance styles, 54, 58
personality, 14–15, 17–18, 36
"Phantom Waltz, The," 74–75
Phelps, William Lyon, 276–277
Philipp, Adolf, 69
piano compositions, 34, 45
Piano Sonata, D. 568 (Schubert), 119
"Pictorial Overture," 232
Pitkin, Robert G., 87
Pixley, Frank, 78
Plaza Hotel, 15, 17
"Poem, The"/"Le poème," 34, 45
Poem Symphonic, 247, 248
polkas, 41
Poor Little Ritz Girl (1920), 19, 70, 71–76
Poppy (1923), 110
popularity, 275–280
popular music styles, 54–61
Porter, Cole, 18, 19, 68, 193
Powell, Eleanor, 193
Powell, Felix, 91
"Pretty Girl Is Like a Melody, A," 48
"Pretty Ming Toy," 75–76
Previn, Charles, 108

"Prince Charming," 187
Prince of Pilsen, The (1903), 78, 137, 143
Princess Flavia (1925), 79, 151–154
Prior, Allan, 132
as producer, 20–21
Purcell, Charles, 96; *The Magic Melody* (1919), 107; *Maytime* (1917), 101; *The Melting of Molly* (1918), 71; musical style, 66–67; *My Lady's Glove* (1917), 91–92; *Poor Little Ritz Girl* (1920), 72, 74

Radin, Oscar, 108
radio programs, 275, 276–277, 279–280
"Rag-Lad of Bagdad, The," 64
"Ragtime Arabian Nights," 55–56, 59–60, 60
"Ragtime Pinafore, The," 55
ragtime-style music, 34, 45, 54–61, 66, 70–71, 74
Railroad Hour, The, 275, 279–280, 300–301
"Ranger's Song, The," 188
Rasch, Albertina, 185, 326n6
reality versus fantasy, 176–178, 186, 203–204, 229–230
recordings, 278–279
Red Mill, The (1906), 30
Red Shadow, The (1932). See *Desert Song, The* (1932)
"Regular Girl, A," 66
remembrance motif, 94–98, 256, 290–292
revivals, 2, 275–276, 280–284
revues: characteristics, 47–48; musical styles, 53–61, 69–70; patriotic themes, 52–53; Romberg's compositions, 53–61, 287–288; Shubert Brothers, 49–53. See also musical comedies
Rhine River, 136
Rhodes, Harrison, 182
Ridge, Frank, 89
Ried, Wallace, 125
"Riff Song, The," 169, 172, 262–263
"Right Brazilian Girl, The," 88
Rio Rita (1927), 212–213
Rivera, Diego, 213
"Road to Paradise, The," 97
Robin Hood (1891), 77–78, 137
Robinson Crusoe, Jr. (1916), 62–64

"Rock-a-bye Your Baby with a Dixie Melody," 49, 62
Rodgers, Richard: collaboration with Hammerstein, 11, 156–157, 226, 233, 292, 294; Dramatists' Guild, 20; and Lorenz Hart, 19, 72–73; mentorship by Romberg, 18; *Poor Little Ritz Girl* (1920), 72–73
Rogers, Will, 47
"Romance," 27, 160, 169, 176, 177, 264
romantic musical comedies, 196
Romberg, Eugenia, 10
Rommyisms, 15
Rooney, Pat, 68
Rosalie (1928), 18–19, 181, 190–193
"Rose de France," 222–223
Rose de France (1933), 221–223
Rose Marie (1924), 32–33, 156, 188
Rosenberg, Adam, 38
Rosenberg, Clara, 38
Rosenberg, Hugo, 38
Rosenberg, Siegmund, 14
Rose of Stamboul, The/Die Rose von Stambul (1922), 122
Ross, Adrian, 110
"Rosy Posy," 66
Rowland, Adele, 89, 90–91
Ruritania, 43–45, 77–80, 151, 190–191, 226–228
"Rustle of Spring," 24, 25, 67

"Sabre Song," 160, 177
Said, Edward W., 162
Saint-Saëns, Camille, 67
Scandals, 48
Schanzer, Rudolf, 93, 122
Schubert, Franz, 26–27, 109–110, 113–122
Schubert Memorial Committee, 113
Schulz, Franz, 249
Schwab, Laurence, 157, 194
Schwartz, Jean, 49, 57, 65
Schwartzwald, Milton, 110
"Secret in Your Life, The," 215
Secret of Chimneys, The (Christie, 1927), 79
Segal, Vivienne, 165; *The Blue Paradise* (1915), 19, 84; *The Desert Song* (1926), 157; *Maytime* (1927), 258; mentorship by Romberg, 18; *My Lady's Glove* (1917), 92; *Viennese Nights* (1930), 247

self-promotion efforts, 275–280
Sellars, Peter, 80
"Señorita," 253–254
sense of place: in American operettas, 198–199; *The Desert Song* (1926), 180; exoticism, 211, 212–219; musical depictions, 182, 186–189, 209, 211, 249, 255; Orientalism, 61, 63; *The Student Prince* (1924), 135
"Serenade": *Blossom Time* (1921), 114, 116; *The Student Prince* (1924), 3, 129, 144, 146–148, 148; *The Student Prince* (1954), 260
"Serenade of Love," 214
sexuality: *The Desert Song* (1926), 155, 158, 178; 1920s views, 177–178; Orientalism, 162–166, 217; ragtime-style music, 56, 71; *Up in Central Park* (1945), 240
Shearer, Norma, 125
"Sheik of Araby, The," 164–165
Sheik, The (1921), 67, 164–165
"Shimmy à la Egyptian," 59
"Shoe-Shining Song," 271–272
Show Boat (1927), 3, 71, 130, 156, 231
Show of Wonders, The (1917), 49
Shubert Brothers, 10, 37, 45–46; and Al Jolson, 61–64; *Alt-Heidelberg* (1901), 124–128; *Blossom Time* (1921), 108–113, 122; and David Belasco, 82–83; *Maytime* (1917), 93, 102; operettas, 77–83, 104, 122–127, 181–186, 212–215, 240–241; revues, 49–53
Shubert, J. J.: *Alt-Heidelberg* (1901), 126–128; collaboration with Romberg, 3, 45–46; and David Belasco, 82; *The Love Call* (1927), 185; *Maytime* (1917), 93; *My Romance* (1948), 241; portrayal in *Deep in My Heart* (1954), 10; on Romberg's musical style, 28; touring productions, 281–282
Shubert, John, 215
Shubert, Lee, 10, 45, 76, 82, 185
Shubert, Sam, 45, 82, 185
Shubert Theatrical Corporation, 46
Shuster, Joe, 161
Siegel, Jerry, 161
Sigmund Romberg Orchestra, 275
"Silver Moon," 186

Sinbad (1918), 18, 62–63
Sinding, Christian, 24, 67
"(Sing Sing) Tango Tea," 66
"Sister Susie's Started Syncopation," 56–57
"Slavery," 90
"Smile, Smile, Smile," 91
Smith, Edgar, 65
Smith, Harry B., 77, 89, 164, 182–183, 185
Smith, Wallace, 223
social injustice themes, 294
"Softly, As in a Morning Sunrise," 3, 195, 206–207, 271, 287
"Soldiers of Fortune," 253
"Soldiers of the Czar," 256
"Somebody Ought to Be Told," 225
"Some Smoke"/"De la fumée," 34, 45
"Something New Is in My Heart," 224–225
"Something Old, Something New," 190
"Song of Love," 113, 116, 119–121
"Song of the Mounties," 33
Song Writers' Protective Association (SPA), 20
Son of the Sheik (1926), 166
sound films, 211, 245–257
South American–themed operettas, 212–214
"Spanish Dance," 99
Spialek, Hans, 192, 194, 218
Springtime of Youth/Sterne, die wieder leuchtet (1922), 122
Steinway, William R., 80
Stillman, Henry B., 73
"Stolen Kisses," 88
Stothart, Herbert, 250–251, 259, 268, 270
"Stouthearted Men," 3, 195, 196, 201, 269–272, 287–288
Straus, Oscar, 30, 44
Strauss, Johann, II, 41, 42
Street, G. S., 131, 158
"Student Life," 144
Student Prince, The (1924): Australian and New Zealand productions, 286; characteristics, 3, 41–43, 149; extended musical scenes, 144, 146; film adaptations, 246, 259–261; historical background, 124–128; importance, 149; love duet, 17; lyricists, 11; musical program, 132–149; nomenclature, 79; nostalgia, 81–82; parodies, 288; performance runs, 1, 128, 131–132; plot motifs, 128–129; reviews, 130–131; revivals, 281–285; similarities to other productions, 151–154
Student Prince, The (1954), 246, 259–261, 273
student-related themes, 41–43. See also *Student Prince, The* (1924)
"Students Marching Song," 260
"Students Marching Song" ("To the Inn We're Marching"), 129, 140
studio, 23
Studio Party, 39
studio recordings, 279, 280
"Summertime in Heidelberg," 260
Sunny River (1941), 230–232
Superman, 161
"Swanee," 18, 62
Swasey, William Albert, 53
"Sweetheart, Sweetheart." See "Will You Remember" (Sweetheart, Sweetheart)
"Sweethearts," 31
Sweethearts (1913), 30, 31
Swift Hour, The, 276–277
"Symphonic Pantomime," 232
Symphony No. 8 (Schubert), 120–122
syncopated music. See ragtime-style music

Tag im Paradies, Ein/A Day in Paradise (1913), 77
"talkies," 211
tangos, 206–207, 214–215; musical comedies, 66; *My Princess* (1927), 190; *The New Moon* (1928), 195; *Rose de France* (1933), 222
Tanner, James T., 89
Tauber, Richard, 110
Taylor, Deems, 39
"Tea for Two," 157
"Tell Me Daisy," 114, 121
Terry, Ethelind, 212–213
"That American Boy of Mine," 18
"That Naughty Show from Gay Paree," 243
"That Rare Romance," 249
Théâtre du Châtelet, 215, 221–222
as theatrical advocate, 18–21
theatrical realism, 82–83, 92
Theatrical Syndicate, 46
They Gave Him a Gun (1937), 256

Thomas, John Charles, 89, 102, 258
Thomas, Lowell, 167
Thomson, Carolyn, 102
"Thousand and One Arabian Nights, A," 64
"Three Little Maids," 114
Three Musketeers, The (1928), 32
Tibbett, Lawrence, 245, 267–268, 270
Tierney, Harry, 30, 58, 102
Tin Pan Alley musical style: *The Desert Song* (1926), 169, 171; *The Girl from Brazil* (1916), 88; *Her Soldier Boy* (1916), 90; *My Lady's Glove* (1917), 92; revues, 48, 57–58; Romberg's compositions, 45
"'Tis Love," 190
Tobias, Charles, 34, 35
Todd, Mike, 232–233
"Toot, Toot, Tootsie! (Goodbye)," 62
"Totem Tom Tom," 33, 188
touring productions, 275, 278–279
"Tramp, Tramp, Tramp," 31
Traubel, Helen, 7, 9, 11
"Trauerwalzer," 117
Trentini, Emma, 31, 32, 198
Trini, 68
"Try Her Out at Dancing," 197, 207–208
"Twentieth Century Rag, The," 55
"Two Little Love Birds," 67

unhappy endings, 293. *See also* lost love story lines
"Up from the Gutter," 237–238, 239
Up in Central Park (1945): film adaptations, 272–273; musical program, 230; musical style, 233–238; performance runs, 2, 232; playbill, 239; setting, 238–240
Up in Central Park (1948), 238, 272–273
Urban, Joseph, 192, 219
U.S. Steel Hour, 276, 277

Vagabond King, The (1925), 32–33
Valentino, Rudolph, 163–166, *164*
Vanities, 48
Viennese Nights (1930): characteristics, 247–248; lyricists, 11, 30; nostalgia, 81, 291; performer debuts, 19; Romberg's music for, 246
Viennese operettas, 40–44
vocal characterizations, 54, 117, 119, 160

Volksmuseum, 80
Von Stroheim, Erich, 35, 125, 223
Von Suppé, Franz, 41, 42

Wagner, Nathaniel, 184
Wagner, Richard, 124
Walker, Don, 225, 226, 242–244, 278
Wallace, Edgar, 91
waltzes: in American operettas, 85–86, 90, 105–107, 123, 178–179, 186–190; *Blossom Time* (1921), 113, 117, 119–122; *The Blue Paradise* (1915), 85; *Children of Dreams* (1931), 249; *The Desert Song* (1926), 178–179; *The Desert Song* (1943), 264; dramatic role, 3, 290–293; *East Wind* (1931), 218; *Forbidden Melody* (1936), 228–229; *The Girl in Pink Tights* (1954), 243–244; *The Girl of the Golden West* (1938), 253–254; *Her Soldier Boy* (1916), 90–91; *Maytime* (1917), 94, 98–101; *May Wine* (1935), 224–225; *Melody* (1933), 220; *The Melting of Molly* (1918), 71; musical adaptations, 187–188; in musical comedies, 63–64, 74–75; *My Romance* (1948), 241; *The New Moon* (1928), 194–195, 201, 203–204; *The Night is Young* (1935), 250; *Nina Rosa* (1930), 214–215; non-theatrical compositions, 35–36; nostalgia, 290–292; operettas, 182; recurring waltz duets, 186–187, 222; in revues, 58; *Rosalie* (1928), 192; *The Student Prince* (1924), 128, 132–140, 143, 149; *The Student Prince* (1954), 260–261; *Sunny River* (1941), 231; *They Gave Him a Gun* (1937), 256; *Up in Central Park* (1945), 237, 239–240; *Up in Central Park* (1948), 273; and Vienna, 290–292; *Viennese Nights* (1930), 248; in Viennese operettas, 40–41, 44. *See also* duets; love duets
Walzertraum, Ein/A Waltz Dream (1907), 44
"Wanting You," 195, 204, 206, 268, 271–272
Warner Brothers, 261–262, 265
wartime references, 58–59, 89–92, 229, 255–256
Watch Your Step (1914), 57–58
"Way Down East," 59, 60
Welisch, Ernst, 122
"We're All in the Same Boat," 243

"We're Going to Take the Germ Out of Germany," 93
"We're Off to Paris," 134, 140
Weston, Ruth, 227, 229
"West Point March," 192
"What Is Your Price, Madame?," 270
Wheeler, Francis, 164
"When Hearts Are Young," 123
"When I Found You," 74
"When I Grow Too Old to Dream," 30, 250
"When She Walks in the Room," 235–236, 273
"When the Spring Wakens Everything," 134, 140
"When You Are Young," 218
"When You're in Mexico," 189
"When You're Starring in the Movies," 64
"Where Else But Here," 42, 255–256
"Where's the Girl?," 257
Whirl of Society (1912), 62
Whirl of the World, The, 32, 37, 45, 52, 55–56, 59–60
White, George, 48, 219
Whittier, John Greenleaf, 183–184
"Who Are We to Say," 254
"Why Did We Marry Soldiers," 176
Wie einst im Mai/As Once in May (1913), 93
"Wien, Wien," 86
Willemetz, Albert, 221–222
"Willow Tree, The," 59
Willson, Meredith, 34
"Will You Remember" (Sweetheart, Sweetheart), 3, 94–99, 95, 101, 258–259
Wilner, Max, 20, 104
Wilner-Romberg Productions, 20–21, 104
"Wind in the Trees, The," 253
Winter Garden Theatre, 53, 62–65, 68, 316n28
witticisms, 15
Wodehouse, P. G., 19, 190, 192

"Won't You Marry Me?," 185
Wood, Cyrus, 65, 70, 99
Wood, Peggy, 96, 101
Woodward, Matthew C., 58
Woolf, Edgar Allen, 65, 249
Woolf, Walter, 219, 224
Woollcott, Alexander, 112
word-music relationships, 29–30, 54
World of Pleasure, A (1915), 52
World War I: influence on films, 256; influence on musical theater, 77–80, 93, 100, 107–108, 124–127
World War II: influence on films, 255, 263–265; influence on musical theater, 81, 229–232
writers' rights, 20
writings, 299

"You Are the Song," 220
"You Leave My Girl Alone," 190
Youmans, Vincent, 24, 157
"You May Drink to My Wedding Day," 190
Young, Rida Johnson: collaboration with Atteridge, 49; collaboration with Romberg, 29, 31; *Her Soldier Boy* (1916), 91; *Maytime* (1917), 93, 95–96; *Maytime* (1923), 258; *Naughty Marietta* (1910), 198; portrayal in *Deep in My Heart* (1954), 10, 11
"You Remember Me," 71
"Your Land and My Land," 187
"Your Smiles, Your Tears," 215
"You Will Remember Vienna," 248

Ziegfeld, Florenz, 19, 48, 150, 190–192
Ziegfeld's *Follies*, 48
Zigeunerbaron, Die/The Gypsy Baron (1885), 42
"Zing Zing, Zoom Zoom," 35

Credits

MUSICAL EXAMPLES

"No, No, Nanette"
Words by Otto Harbach
Music by Vincent Youmans
© 1924 (Renewed) WB Music Corp. and Bill/Bob Publishing Co.
All Rights Reserved. Used by Permission.

"Auf Wiedersehn"
By Sigmund Romberg and Herbert Reynolds
Copyright © 1915 (Renewed) by G. Schirmer, Inc. (ASCAP)
International Copyright Secured. All Rights Reserved.
Reprinted by Permission.

"Golden Days," "Come Boys, Let's All Be Gay, Boys," "Serenade," "Deep in My Heart Dear"
Words by Dorothy Donnelly
Music by Sigmund Romberg
© 1924 (Renewed) Warner Bros. Inc.
All Rights Reserved. Used by Permission.

"Drinking Song"
Words by Dorothy Donnelly
Music by Sigmund Romberg
© 1925 (Renewed) Warner Bros. Inc.
All Rights Reserved. Used by Permission.

"I Dare Not Love You"
Words by Harry B. Smith

Music by Sigmund Romberg
© 1925 (Renewed) Warner Bros. Inc.
All Rights Reserved. Used by Permission.

"The Riff Song," "One Alone," "The Desert Song," "If," "Romance"
from *The Desert Song*
Lyrics by Otto Harbach and Oscar Hammerstein II
Music by Sigmund Romberg
Copyright © 1926 by Bambalina Music Publishing Co., Warner Bros. Inc. and Bill/Bob Publishing Co. in the United States
Copyright Renewed
All Rights on behalf of Bambalina Music Publishing Co. Administered by Williamson Music
All Rights on behalf of Bill/Bob Publishing Co. Administered by The Songwriters Guild of America
International Copyright Secured. All Rights Reserved

"Entrance of Azuri"
Music by Sigmund Romberg
© 1926 (Renewed) Warner Bros. Inc.
All Rights Reserved. Used by Permission.

"One Kiss," "Lover, Come Back to Me," "Wanting You"
from *The New Moon*
Words by Oscar Hammerstein II
Music by Sigmund Romberg
Copyright © 1928 by Bambalina Music Publishing Co. and Warner Bros. Inc. in the United States
Copyright Renewed
All Rights on behalf of Bambalina Music Publishing Co. Administered by Williamson Music
International Copyright Secured. All Rights Reserved

"Gorgeous Alexander"
from *The Student Prince*
Words by Oscar Hammerstein II
Music by Sigmund Romberg
Copyright © 1927 by Bambalina Music Publishing Co. (administered in U.S.A. by Williamson Music) and Warner Bros. Inc.
International Copyright Secured. All Rights Reserved

"Close as Pages in a Book"
from *Up in Central Park*
Words by Dorothy Fields
Music by Sigmund Romberg

CREDITS

Copyright © 1945 Aldi Music and Williamson Music
Copyright Renewed
Print Rights for Aldi Music in the U.S. Controlled and Administered by Happy Aspen Music LLC c/o Shapiro, Bernstein & Co., Inc.
International Copyright Secured. All Rights Reserved
Used by Permission

Unpublished Prose

Excerpts from J. J. Shubert Correspondence
Used by permission of The Shubert Archive.

Excerpts from Lord Chamberlain's Collection (*The Student Prince* 1929/6676 and *The Desert Song* 1927/4)
By permission of The British Library.

Excerpt from L. P. Cookingham correspondence (telegram to Mrs. Sigmund Romberg, 10 November 1951)
Used by permission of the University of Missouri-Kansas City Libraries, Special Collections Department.

Images

Sigmund Romberg at the Great American Restaurant, Kansas City, Missouri, May 3, 1950
Used by permission of the University of Missouri-Kansas City Libraries, Special Collections Department.

Romberg composing at the organ with his music library in the background
Licensed by Corbis.
All Rights Reserved. Used by Permission.

Advertisement for *Passing Show of 1914*
Courtesy of the Shubert Archive.
All Rights Reserved. Used by Permission.

Peggy Wood (as Ottilie) and Charles Purcell (as Dick) in the original production of *Maytime*
Courtesy of the Shubert Archive.
All Rights Reserved. Used by Permission.

Bertram Peacock (as Franz Schubert), Olga Cook (as Mitzi), and Howard Marsh (as Baron Franz Schober) in the original production of *Blossom Time*
Courtesy of the Shubert Archive.
All Rights Reserved. Used by Permission.

Ilse Marvenga (as Kathie) and the male chorus in the original production of *The Student Prince*
Courtesy of the Shubert Archive.
All Rights Reserved. Used by Permission.

Rudolf Valentino and Agnes Ayres in *The Sheik*
Licensed by Getty Images.
All Rights Reserved. Used by Permission.

Pearl Regay (as Azuri), Edmond Elton (as General Birabeau), Vivienne Segal (as Margot Bonvalet), and Robert Halliday (as the Red Shadow) in the original production of *The Desert Song*
Licensed by Brown Bros.
All Rights Reserved. Used by Permission.

Evelyn Herbert (as Barbara Fritchie) and Nathaniel Wagner (as Capt. Trumbull) in the original production of *My Maryland*
Courtesy of the Shubert Archive.
All Rights Reserved. Used by Permission.

Sheet music cover for *The New Moon*
© 1928 (Renewed) Warner Bros. Inc. Rights for the Extended Renewal Term in the United States Controlled by Warner Bros. Inc. and Bambalina Music.
All Rights Reserved. Used by Permission.

Romberg playing the piano, Kansas City, Missouri, June 1951, months before his death in November
Used by permission of the University of Missouri-Kansas City Libraries, Special Collections Department.